W9-BZP-444

LONGSTREET HIGHROAD GUIDE
──── TO THE ────
CHESAPEAKE BAY

BY DEANE WINEGAR

FOREWORD BY THE CHESAPEAKE BAY FOUNDATION

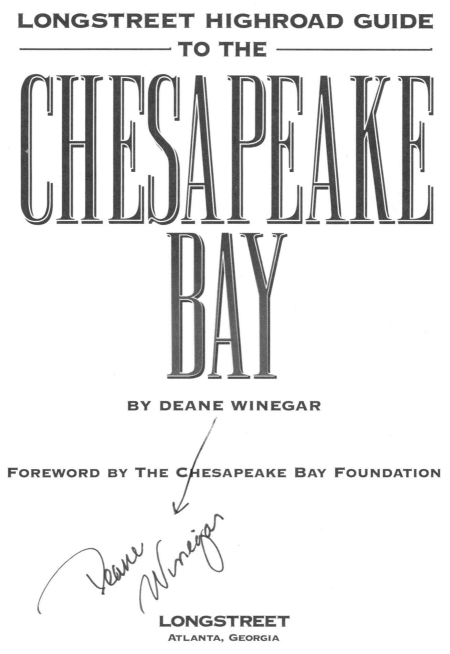

LONGSTREET
ATLANTA, GEORGIA

Published by
LONGSTREET PRESS, INC.
2140 Newmarket Parkway
Suite 122
Marietta, Georgia 30067

Great efforts have been made to make the information in this book as accurate as possible. However, over time, trails are rerouted and signs and landmarks may change. If you find a change has occurred to a trail in the book, please let us know so we can correct future editions.
A word of caution: Outdoor recreation by its nature is potentially hazardous. All participants in such activities must assume all responsibility for their own actions and safety. The scope of this book does not cover all potential hazards and risks involved in outdoor recreation activities.

Printed by RR Donnelley & Sons, Harrisonburg, VA

1st printing 2000

Library of Congress Catalog Number 99-068569

ISBN: 1-56352-544-5

Book editing, design, and cartography
by Lenz Design & Communications, Inc., Decatur, Georgia

Cover illustration by J. Douglas Woodward, *Picturesque America*, 1872

Cover design by Richard J. Lenz, Decatur, Georgia

Illustrations by Danny Woodard, Loganville, Georgia

Photographs by Deane Winegar

It is chilly, mid-March, long before dawn.
No breeze ripples the slatey calm of the bay. Only the wild, lost hallooing of swans
preparing to migrate north and the occasional sassing of a mallard break the silence.
For the next half an hour by fast boat, you'll see little but the black of the bay,
edged here and there by even blacker lines of salt marsh.
First light is seeping westward, tinting just the crests of our wake mauve and silver,
and showing the outlines of a low-lying island.
Just short of bumping a wall of needlerush marsh,
we find a hidden tidal gut and follow it deep into the island.

Tom Horton, *The Water's Way: Life Along the Chesapeake*

Contents

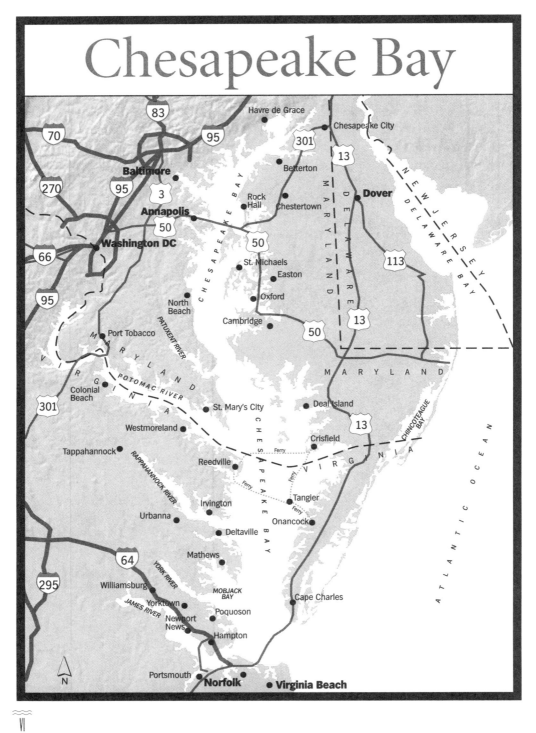

Chesapeake Bay

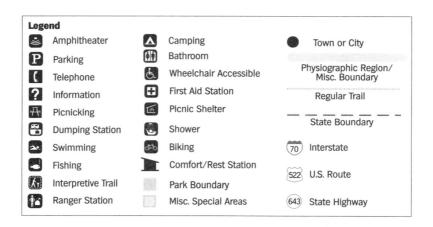

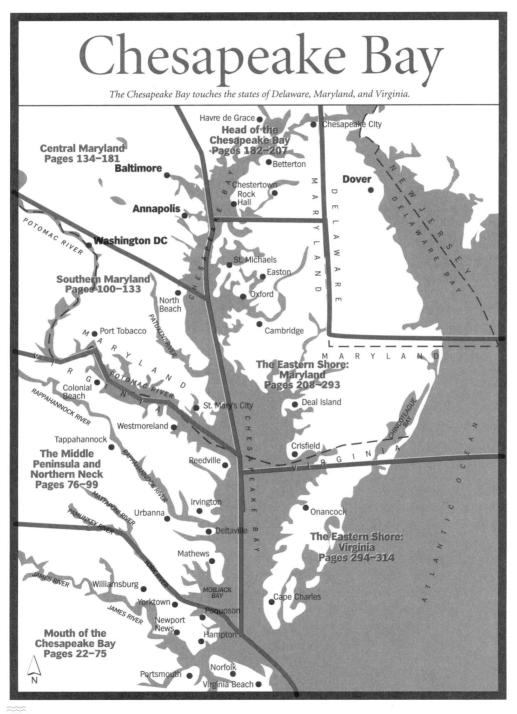

Chesapeake Bay

The Chesapeake Bay touches the states of Delaware, Maryland, and Virginia.

Havre de Grace

Chesapeake City

Head of the Chesapeake Bay Pages 182–207

Central Maryland Pages 134–181

Betterton

Dover

Baltimore

Chestertown
Rock
Hall

Annapolis

Washington DC

St. Michaels

Easton

Southern Maryland Pages 100–133

Oxford

North Beach

Cambridge

Port Tobacco

The Eastern Shore: Maryland Pages 208–293

POTOMAC RIVER

PATUXENT RIVER

M A R Y L A N D

D E L A W A R E

N E W   J E R S E Y

DELAWARE BAY

M A R Y L A N D

C H E S A P E A K E   B A Y

V I R G I N I A

Colonial Beach

RAPPAHANNOCK RIVER

POTOMAC RIVER

St. Mary's City

Deal Island

Westmoreland

Tappahannock

The Middle Peninsula and Northern Neck Pages 76–99

Crisfield

Reedville

RAPPAHANNOCK RIVER

MATTAPONI RIVER

PAMUNKEY RIVER

Irvington

Urbanna

Onancock

Deltaville

The Eastern Shore: Virginia Pages 294–314

Mathews

JAMES RIVER

Williamsburg

YORK RIVER

MOBJACK BAY

Cape Charles

Yorktown

JAMES RIVER

Poquoson

Newport News

Hampton

Mouth of the Chesapeake Bay Pages 22–75

Norfolk

Portsmouth

Virginia Beach

CHINCOTEAGUE BAY

V I R G I N I A

C H E S A P E A K E   B A Y

A T L A N T I C   O C E A N

N

How to Use Your Longstreet Highroad Guide

The *Longstreet Highroad Guide to the Chesapeake Bay* offers detailed information about the best places around the Chesapeake Bay in Virginia and Maryland to pursue your favorite outdoor activities. The book also includes restaurant, lodging, and night life information. These attractions are known to change, so it is wise to call ahead before making a long drive to visit an establishment listed here.

While the book is focused on outdoor pursuits and sites that relate to the Chesapeake Bay or its history, there is also extensive coverage of the many things to see and do in port cities such as Virginia Beach, Norfolk, Hampton, and Newport News in Virginia, and Annapolis, Baltimore, and Ocean City in Maryland. The book covers not only sites on the shores of the Chesapeake Bay, but also many sites that are on bay tributaries—sites such as Williamsburg, Virginia, and Patapsco Valley State Park in Maryland, and sites on the nearby Atlantic coast, such as Assateague Island National Seashore, Chincoteague Island National Wildlife Refuge, and the Virginia Coast Reserve.

The maps in the book are keyed by figure number and referenced in the text. They should help both casual and seasoned coastal travelers get oriented. DeLorme's Virginia Atlas and Gazetteer and DeLorme's Maryland/Delaware Atlas and Gazetteer, available in bookstores and department stores, are excellent companions to this guide. While some trails have remained unchanged for decades, others may be rerouted or closed. Many trails or sites are closed seasonally to protect nesting shorebirds.

A word of caution: The open waters of the bay and Atlantic Ocean can be dangerous. The wind and weather can change quickly and unexpectedly. Tides can come in and steal a boat or go out and leave a boater stranded until the next high tide. Sea kayakers, canoeists, and other boaters should check conditions and tides before starting out, carry proper flotation devices, and leave word of their whereabouts and estimated time of return with family or friends. Most local newspapers include the area's high and low tides. Marinas and tackle shops sell fishing licenses and provide tide charts and fishing regulations. Licensing requirements and fishing seasons and regulations vary from state to state and even from tributary to bay to ocean. Also, for information on freshwater fishing you can call the Virginia Department of Game and Inland Fisheries at (804) 367-1000 and for saltwater information, the Virginia Marine Resources Commission at (757) 247-2200. Use common sense when exploring the Chesapeake Bay environs to make sure all your memories are happy ones.

The Chesapeake Bay, as wild and beautiful as it is, has many sensitive natural areas whose ecological survival hangs in the balance. Visitors who resist the temptation to pick wildflowers, who put trash in proper containers, and who make every effort to avoid disturbing wildlife or natural habitat will help to ensure that these areas can be left open for all to enjoy.

Foreword

Since its founding more than 30 years ago, the Chesapeake Bay Foundation (CBF) has been identified by its motto, "Save the Bay." If you live or travel in the bay region, chances are good that you will see those three words often, on CBF's logo, publications, and more than a few car bumpers.

But "Save the Bay" must be more than a catchy slogan. It must actually be done—by restoring forests, wetlands, and underwater grasses, by increasing the numbers of oysters, crabs, and fish, by stopping pollution. Those are daunting challenges. The bay is a complex tapestry of life, and for too many years threads have been pulled from it. Today's bay has only a fraction of its historic levels of oysters, about 10 percent of its underwater grasses, 40 percent of its wetlands, and 50 percent of its woods. Oysters, grasses, wetlands, and forests are the bay's natural filters, its only resources to cleanse and sustain it. When they become diminished, we are left with poor water quality—and a tapestry that continues to unravel.

CBF works very hard to restore this tapestry that is the bay. We educate school children, we lobby governments, we file lawsuits, we grow trees and oysters, we engage, persuade, and energize. But we learned many years ago that CBF cannot create a healthy Chesapeake Bay alone. To truly save the bay, everyone who lives in the bay's 64,000-square-mile watershed must care.

And we have learned something else: To know the bay is to love the bay. That simple truth has driven our successful education program for years and has produced a

GREAT WHITE EGRET
(Casmerodius albus)

generation of people now in the workplace who look back on the days they spent on the deck of a skipjack, walking through marshes, or paddling through creeks as part of a CBF field trip and, because of that experience, possess a lifelong awareness, appreciation, and personal sense of stewardship for the bay.

That personal stewardship is needed today more than ever, for while much progress has been made to restore the bay, the job is far from done. We must not allow apathy to dull our resolve. And we must remember that the bay we know today and are trying so hard to save is but a glimmer of the wondrously clear, fecund, and resilient estuary that our parents and grandparents knew even as recently as 40 and 50 years ago. We must not settle for what the bay has become but strive for what the bay can be again.

So take this guide and go experience the Chesapeake Bay for yourself. Travel the back roads, explore the creeks, catch a crab, hook a striped bass, smell the marshes, and squint as the sunlight dances on the waves. Get to know the bay. For once you know the bay, you will love it. And that is how we all will Save the Bay.

—Charles C. Epes, Chesapeake Bay Foundation

BROWN PELICAN
(Pelecanus occidentalis)

Preface

The *Chesapeake*. For those of us with a touch of wanderlust, the words are magic. Say them and conjure up the smell of salt air, the image of a skipjack at full sail, or the crescendo of sound as wild geese rise from a marsh.

Say the words and become restless for adventure. Whether you want to watch wildlife, hike, bike, boat, bird, or just prowl rural fishing villages by automobile, the Chesapeake Bay is an explorer's dream.

The book in your hands was designed for the explorer in each of us. There's a longing for a fresh wind that sets sail in the mind when we've spent too many hours indoors. This book won't stop the longing, but it can give it direction.

Beginning at the mouth of the bay, where three wooden ships from England dropped anchor in 1607, this guidebook turns the Chesapeake Bay into a self-guided trail of discovery. Starting with Virginia Beach, the text follows the bay clockwise and describes the Hampton Roads area, the Williamsburg area, Virginia's Middle Peninsula, and Northern Neck. Southern Maryland, then Central Maryland and the cities of Annapolis and Baltimore are next. The Susquehanna River valley at the head of the bay is followed by Maryland's Eastern Shore and finally, the narrow peninsula that holds the Eastern Shore of Virginia.

Using the guidebook, you can explore parks, preserves, refuges, scenic drives, villages, counties, and cities in whatever part of the bay you happen to go. Perhaps you're near Blackwater National Wildlife Refuge and you want to know if that's a good place to photograph wintering wildfowl. Just flip to that section...yes, it's the perfect place. If you're in a state park and you want to know the best place to see fossils of marine life—and just how those fossils came to be imbedded on a high cliff—that information is here, too.

Maybe there've been times you've returned from a trip and found you missed a waterman's museum or a lighthouse that was right next to the marina where you chartered a moonlight cruise. Or maybe you were once camping at Martinak State Park and only later discovered that the campground was the former site of a Choptank Indian settlement. In the book, nearby sites are listed before and after the one you're visiting, so they're easy to find. So, the next time one of you is fishing out of Reedville, Virginia, the rest of the family can come along and go on the ferry ride to see the remote island of Tangier.

Far more than just a where-to-go and how-to-get-there book, this Highroad Guide is packed with all those secrets that help make a trip memorable. Here are tips on how to go clamming or crabbing, where you can find wild ponies, and what those little critters are that burrow in the sand right where the waves break on the beach. In short, the book is loaded with natural and cultural history—the extras that bring a place to life.

If you want the number of a charter fishing captain, it's here. If the youngsters want to experience an IMAX theater or want to know when the surfing competition is held at Virginia Beach, that's here too. Phone numbers to call for restaurant, camping, or lodging reservations are listed with each area. Special events are in an appendix by date, so if you're traveling in June, you can check the June listings to see if any of the events are close by. Whenever there's a person who will answer a phone and give you more information, that number is listed.

In fact, where was this book all those years I've poked about on the bay? I figured I couldn't go wrong writing a guidebook that is exactly what I'd want to take with me. I've written it to be truly useful, and not just something to gather dust on a shelf.

If you're a newcomer to the Chesapeake, then just close your eyes, open to any page and put your finger on a site. There. That's a great place to start. Even if you're a bay lover with many years of knocking about the bay under your belt, you've no doubt been amazed, as I have, that there's no end to the places to visit. The only limits are time and our own curiosity. If we're going to find all the hidden gems in one lifetime, it's high time we got started exploring.

Of course, some of the best finds are those we make on our own. The Chesapeake lends itself to that kind of freestyle rambling. Around every bend are boat docks that lead out into the bay, their far ends lost in the morning mist. Who has ever counted them? Weathered gray with the salt mist, each dock or pier seems to acquire its own family of ducks and a decomposing boat sprouting from marsh grasses.

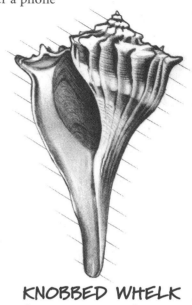

KNOBBED WHELK
(Busycon carica)

Many Maryland and Virginia back roads are just as rewarding as those with the official Scenic Highway designation. Quiet villages with a marina, docks stacked high with crab pots, a general store and a white chapel under old maple trees—these await discovery by those of us who love to prowl the back roads. Along narrow streets at places like Lewisetta, Virginia, with barely enough room for two cars to pass, are the once-grand homes and their ghosts of sea captains who grew wealthy from the Bay's bounty. This guidebook will enhance such travels with descriptions of the counties, the Indian tribes that fished the shores, and the willet and rail that inhabit the salt marsh.

Sitting at a computer day after day, describing the menus of my favorite seafood restaurants, is a kind of exquisite torture. Telling of boardwalks that lead over marshes where the yellow-billed cuckoo calls has left that tantalizing taste of salt air on my tongue. Even that ugly ol' blue crab is starting to look pretty.

I feel a trip to the bay coming on. Want to come along?

—Deane Winegar

Acknowledgments

I once saw on a friend's desk a plaque that read "It's amazing what can be accomplished when it doesn't matter who gets the credit." How true. In the case of this guidebook, one person's name goes on the cover. But the information in this book is available because there are hundreds of others who have put in their "dirt time" without ever expecting to receive thanks. There were representatives from parks and refuges and county and city visitor centers, biologists, naturalists, and countless other experts who helped. I am always grateful for the tireless and the curious who have researched the natural and cultural history of the Chesapeake Bay.

Thanks to the folks at Longstreet Press, especially Steve Gracie and Marge McDonald, for assigning the writing of the Chesapeake Bay guidebook to me. They also had the wisdom to put Lenz Design in charge of editing both the mountain and coastal *Highroad Guide* series. I've definitely become spoiled by editors who not only have incredible expertise on the subject matter, but also who are great to work with and turn out really handsome, usable, well-mapped books.

Editor Richard Lenz, as always, was an inspiration. The latest mission impossible was that somehow, Richard zipped off and wrote the highly enjoyable *Highroad Guide to the Georgia Coast and Okefenokee* without missing a beat, and was back at work editing my copy almost before I realized he'd been gone. You Georgians who haven't explored your coast, guidebook in hand, are in for a treat.

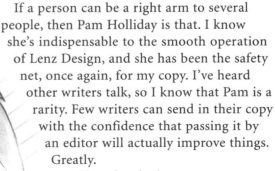

If a person can be a right arm to several people, then Pam Holliday is that. I know she's indispensable to the smooth operation of Lenz Design, and she has been the safety net, once again, for my copy. I've heard other writers talk, so I know that Pam is a rarity. Few writers can send in their copy with the confidence that passing it by an editor will actually improve things. Greatly.

Also, there's the encouragement from her friendly voice on the other end of the line when the hours before a computer screen get long and lonely.

ANHINGA
(Anhinga anhinga)

I wish the illustrator, Danny Woodard, were around to hear the oohs and ahs of people who enjoy the sprinkling of beautiful line drawings that make the book so much fun to browse.

Chuck Epes and John Page Williams of the Chesapeake Bay Foundation—both extraordinarily gifted men who apply their considerable talents to the difficult work of saving the bay—gave generously of their time in helping me understand the complexities of the problems facing the bay.

My heartfelt appreciation also goes to the following people, spread around the bay at parks, preserves, refuges, museums, and various county and city offices:

Anne Mannix, Cindy Yingling, Amy Bender, Catherine Harris, Renee L. Barrett, Jim Wychgram, Linda Hinds, Herman Schiekhe, Ruthie Buckler, Shirley Whittington, Sandy Maruchi-Turner, Diane Molner, Jean Cox, Jo Anne Fairchild, Barbara Siegart, Mary Calloway, Cindy Forester, Julie M. Horner, Terry Nyquist, Nell Baldacchino, Mark Haddon, Ginny Vroblesky, Terri Brower, Bobbi Pippin, R. Leader, Glenn Carowan, Arthur Shepherd, Bill Martin, Gary Schenck, Jennifer Cline, and Marty Kaehny.

Kudos to Edward Delaney, John Ohler, Dave Davis, Elllie Altman, Russ Hill, Nancy L. Howard, Suzanne Taylor, Jim Kenyon, Treve Morris, Lorraine Smith, Lisa Challenger, Denny Price, Scott Flickinger, Lynn Badger, Denise McNamara, Doug Samson, Sam Martinette, Hester Waterfield, Bobby Phillips, Suzanne Pearson, Debbie Algard, Anne Kernana, Tina Bianca, Fred Hazelwood, Ken Samples, Rob Riordan, and K. Michael Lathroum.

Also, hats off to Kelly Larkin, Debbie Perry, Susanne Bates, April Havens, Lynne Pines, Rick Smith, Lorrie Wolse, Offut Johnson, Mary Ann Cantwell, Gary Adelhardt, Sam Bennett, Joe Ward, John Schroer, Larry G. Points, Gary Waugh, Jim Meisner, Phil West, Neal Barber, Richard Ayers, Cameron Blandford, Susan Tipton, Kay Alferio, Carol Hanson, Dave Johnson, Jerry Williams, Chris Smith, Debbie Padgett, Danette McAdoo, Troy Snead, Holly Wood, and J. Rosalie Piper.

Finally, I want to thank my family-in-waiting and especially my husband and traveling companion, Garvey. His encouragement was unwavering, even at those times the project seemed bigger than I was. I have the good fortune of being married to a man whose ear is finely attuned to the written word. Most of all, he has been forever patient. When the finish line seemed to evade me like the view through a camera lens being turned to wide angle, he would just smile the smile of one who has been there.

Who would've ever thought I'd have the chance to dedicate a book to the best writer in the family? Honey, this one's for you.

—Deane Winegar

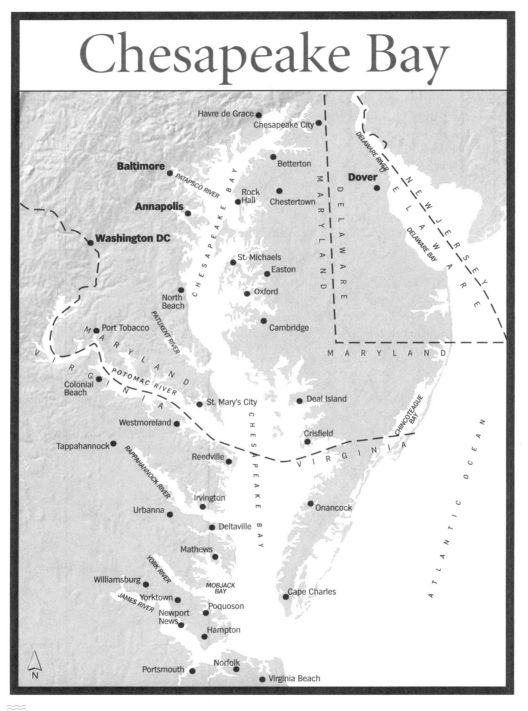

Chesapeake Bay

Havre de Grace
Chesapeake City
Betterton
Baltimore
PATAPSCO RIVER
Dover
DELAWARE RIVER
Rock Hall
Chestertown
NEW JERSEY
Annapolis
CHESAPEAKE BAY
MARYLAND
DELAWARE
DELAWARE BAY
Washington DC
St. Michaels
Easton
North Beach
Oxford
Cambridge
MARYLAND
Port Tobacco
PATUXENT RIVER
MARYLAND
VIRGINIA
POTOMAC RIVER
Colonial Beach
St. Mary's City
Deal Island
Westmoreland
CHESAPEAKE BAY
Crisfield
CHINCOTEAGUE BAY
Tappahannock
VIRGINIA
RAPPAHANNOCK RIVER
Reedville
Irvington
Urbanna
Onancock
ATLANTIC OCEAN
Deltaville
Mathews
YORK RIVER
Williamsburg
MOBJACK BAY
Yorktown
JAMES RIVER
Cape Charles
Newport News
Poquoson
Hampton
N
Portsmouth
Norfolk
Virginia Beach

The Natural History of the Chesapeake Bay

Compared to the billion-old mountains of the Blue Ridge in western Virginia, the Chesapeake Bay is just a pup. As recently as 10,000 years ago, the Susquehanna River flowed through the area between Havre de Grace, MD, and Virginia Beach, VA, that is now covered by the Chesapeake Bay. But by that time, the waters of the rising Atlantic Ocean were knocking at the door of the bay about to be born.

The stage began to be set for the creation of this large estuary with the close of the Pleistocene Epoch, starting some 20,000 years ago. The land at that time was inhabited by large, now-extinct mammals such as the wooly mammoth, the mastodon, and peccary. Mammoths (Mammuthus) were hairy-skinned and had long upward-curving tusks. Mastodons (Mastodontidae) were larger even than mammoths and elephants. The peccary (Tayassuidae) was a piglike creature with sharp tusks.

[*Above:* A wood duck enjoys the waters of Chesapeake Bay]

Geologic Time Scale

Era	System & Period	Series & Epoch	Some Distinctive Features	Years Before Present
CENOZOIC	**Quaternary**	Recent	Modern man.	11,000
		Pleistocene	Early man; northern glaciation.	1/2 to 2 million
	Tertiary	Pliocene	Large carnivores.	13 $\pm$ 1 million
		Miocene	First abundant grazing mammals.	25 $\pm$ 1 million
		Oligocene	Large running mammals.	36 $\pm$ 2 million
		Eocene	Many modern types of mammals.	58 $\pm$ 2 million
		Paleocene	First placental mammals.	63 $\pm$ 2 million
MESOZOIC	**Cretaceous**		First flowering plants; climax of dinosaurs and ammonites, followed by Cretaceous-Tertiary extinction.	135 $\pm$ 5 million
	Jurassic		First birds, first mammals dinosaurs and ammonites abundant.	181 $\pm$ 5 million
	Triassic		First dinosaurs. Abundant cycads and conifers.	230 $\pm$ 10 million
PALEOZOIC	**Permian**		Extinction of most kinds of marine animals, including trilobites. Southern glaciation.	280 $\pm$ 10 million
	Carboniferous	Pennsylvanian	Great coal forests, conifers. First reptiles.	310 $\pm$ 10 million
		Mississippian	Sharks and amphibians abundant. Large and numerous scale trees and seed ferns.	345 $\pm$ 10 million
	Devonian		First amphibians; ammonites; fishes abundant.	405 $\pm$ 10 million
	Silurian		First terrestrial plants and animals.	425 $\pm$ 10 million
	Ordovician		First fishes; invertebrates dominant.	500 $\pm$ 10 million
	Cambrian		First abundant record of marine life; trilobites dominant.	600 $\pm$ 50 million
	Precambrian		Fossils extremely rare, consisting of primitive aquatic plants. Evidence of glaciation. Oldest dated algae, over 2,600 million years; oldest dated meteorites 4,500 million years.	

Fossils indicate that Ice Age people roamed the forests, hunting these enormous creatures with spears. By about 10,000 years ago, most of the large mammals were extinct, and even camels and horses were extirpated from the North American continent. Were they overhunted, like the buffalo and wolf were in more recent times? Did a change in climate do them in? Scientists still speculate about the cause.

As the last glaciers retreated between 18,000 and 12,000 years ago, the Susquehanna River transported the melting waters from the north in an ever-deepening chasm, just as it had done at the end of previous glacial periods. Glaciers had extended as far south as what is now northern Pennsylvania. So much water was locked up in the ice cap that the seas were some 325 feet below their current level.

The melting waters caused the seas to rise on the East Coast, gradually backing up into the Susquehanna River Valley at a rate of 50 feet a year, flooding over the banks, finally claiming about a third of the ancient Susquehanna for the new bay. Woods bison, elk, and wolves retreated as the waters spread. Archeologists have also uncovered evidence of human habitation during the time the bay was forming by a semi-nomadic people of the Paleoindian Period, which lasted from 11,000 to 7,500 BC. These people gradually put down roots, creating permanent villages during the Woodland Period (1000 BC to 1600 AD).

This process of bay creation did not occur overnight. In fact, the sea only reached its northernmost limit at Havre de Grace, MD, about 3,000 years ago. The pattern is a typical one for bays on the Atlantic Seaboard as glaciers come and go over the millennia. The Susquehanna has weathered such treatment before and will continue to do so from all indications, say geologists.

The bay that formed as the rising seawaters drowned the river valley came to be known as *Chesepiooc*, or "great shellfish bay," by the Algonquin Indians who were living along its shoreline when the first European settlers arrived.

Great Shellfish Bay

The *Chesepiooc*, or Chesapeake Bay, covers 2,500 square miles and is North America's largest estuary.

Let's try to get a feeling for the size. Some figures and comparisons might help.

The bay proper, disregarding the tributary rivers, lies entirely within the states of Maryland and Virginia. It varies from 4 miles wide at Annapolis, MD, where it is spanned by the Bay Bridge, to 30 miles wide at Smith Point, VA. It is 195 miles in length, from the mouth of the Susquehanna River at the head of the bay in Maryland to the southern end at Hampton Roads in Virginia.

If you decided to prowl every cove and inlet, tracing the shoreline around the bay, you would travel an estimated 4,000 miles before you would come full circle. If you add the tributary rivers to the journey, the mileage would double. Just traveling around the bay itself, you would cover more ground than would someone following the western coastline from Canada to Mexico. Even a trip from Maine to California would be only three-quarters the distance of the Chesapeake Bay shoreline. A mere 2 percent of that shoreline is in the public domain.

Rain that falls over a 64,000-square-mile area, supplying water to some 15 million people in portions of six states ends up in the Chesapeake Bay. These states included in the Chesapeake Bay watershed are Virginia, West Virginia, Maryland, Delaware, Pennsylvania, and New York, as well as the District of Columbia. Follow the bay to its headwaters, and you'll wind up at Otsego Lake in Cooperstown, New York, where the Susquehanna River begins. Put fertilizer on your yard in Elmira, New York, or Scranton, Pennsylvania, and it will end up eventually in the Chesapeake Bay.

For all its size, the bay is shallow, averaging just 22 feet deep. Some holes and channels are deeper, with the deepest place measured at 174 feet just south of Kent Island, MD. The shallowness is important, because it allows sunlight to reach plant life and helps the estuary stay warm.

What is an Estuary?

Put simply, an estuary is nothing more than a partially enclosed area where the fresh water of rivers mixes with tidal salt water.

The definition may be accurate, but much is left unsaid. Estuaries perform vital functions, and their systems are interrelated. Get one system out of balance and others are affected, like tipping over the first domino in a row. Because of the enormity of the Chesapeake Bay, the importance of keeping its systems in good working order are greatly magnified.

Salinity of an estuary like the Chesapeake is influenced by several factors. Typically, the farther away from the sea you go, the fresher the water becomes. The northern part of the Chesapeake Bay, although tidal, is much less salty than the lower part of the bay.

Seasonal changes also cause salinity variations. During spring rains, the influx of fresh water causes a decline in salinity. In late summer and fall or during a drought, when the influx of fresh water is low, overall salinity may increase dramatically, and blue crabs and some saltwater fish may travel all the way to the fall lines of some tributaries.

Approximately twice a day, shorelines experience two high tides and two low tides. At low tide, mud flats that may have had several feet of water covering them at high tide are exposed to the air and sun.

Over the eons, aquatic life has evolved in harmony with these fluctuations. In fact, the different gradients of salinity from the ocean to the fall lines provide conditions suitable to a much greater variety of life than would be possible without the variations. An estimated 2,700 species of plants and animals, including 200 species of fish, live in the estuary. Some of these organisms live wholly or mostly in one part of the estuary or one level of salinity, while others travel from one area to the other. Various terms are used to describe the groups of organisms that have adapted to various salinity levels.

Euryhaline species, for example, are those with the most tolerance for changes in salinity, such as spot and Atlantic croaker. Anadromous is the term for saltwater species of fish such as striped bass, shad, river herring, and sturgeon that come upriver to spawn in fresh water.

FALL LINES

The mouth of the estuary is where the bay meets the Atlantic Ocean between Cape Charles and Cape Henry in Virginia. The head of the estuary is at the mouth of the Susquehanna at Havre de Grace, Maryland, and at the fall line of each tributary river. The fall line marks the end of the Piedmont Plateau, so named because the water often goes over falls on the Piedmont escarpment before it reaches sea level, where the Coastal Plain begins. The Piedmont physiographic region is composed of metamorphic rock that is more erosion resistant than the softer, sedimentary rock of the Coastal Plain.

Some rivers, such as the Mattaponi, on Virginia's western bay, have fall lines that are hardly discernible as the waters subtly go from nearly flat land to sea level. Others, however, are memorable.

A series of rapids on the James River fall line in the heart of Richmond, Virginia, is well known to whitewater kayakers and canoeists. A white-knuckle ride down the Great Falls of the Potomac above Washington, DC, runs through a 9-mile fall zone ending at the true fall line near Roosevelt Island at Washington. (Over the years, the falls have continually eroded away the edge of the Piedmont escarpment at Washington, so that the first 20-foot vertical drop now begins 9 miles upstream from its original edge at Roosevelt Island—a phenomenon called headward erosion.) Tackling the series of falls, boils, chutes, and twists down this section of the Potomac should only be undertaken by experts who have carefully scouted the river—and made out their wills. Some parts of the falls should not be attempted by anyone. There have been many deaths from swimmers or boaters swept into the falls by accident.

The escarpment that creates the fall lines of rivers also creates obstacles to shipping, influencing the way early Europeans settled the land. Cities such as Richmond (on the James River), Fredericksburg (on the Rappahannock), Washington (on the Potomac), and Baltimore (on the Patapsco) grew up at the fall lines of rivers where ships would unload goods and supplies.

Also, dams were built at many fall lines to supply power to the cities. It took years to realize the damming of the rivers had consequences that weren't all good. Anadromous fish—saltwater fish that make annual spring runs upriver to spawn in fresh water—began to disappear. No longer could you walk into the river and scoop up shad, herring, sturgeon, and striped bass in buckets and nets. Lacking a net, Capt. John Smith even wrote of catching fish in a frying pan.

Natural Communities of Chesapeake Bay

What follows is a discussion of the intricate workings of the Chesapeake Bay itself, from plant and animal communities at the high tide mark to the deepest waters. Of course, the Chesapeake Bay is strongly influenced by land or stream disturbances that occur anywhere within the watershed. This influence extends not only up the tributary streams and rivers and to the forested uplands that surround the bay, but also to the tiniest rivulet in the mountains of the six-state area of the Chesapeake Bay watershed.

Wherever a homeowner sprays his garden for pests or a farmer allows his cattle into a stream within the entire watershed, pesticide from the spray and the excess nutrients from cattle dung will eventually find their way into the vulnerable Chesapeake Bay. So important is wise stewardship that some states have adopted laws requiring certain permits for any work done in streams or rivers, or for the building of bridges and culverts, even hundreds of miles from the bay. Environmentalists complain that the permits are mostly a formality. What is lacking, they say, is a plan with limits to the permits based on the total effect of disturbances to the watershed.

PLANKTON

Scoop up a glass of water from the Chesapeake Bay. Doesn't matter where—from the deep waters to the shallows to the water that filters through the beach sand and the marshes—and put a drop of it under a microscope. What may have looked like a completely clear glass of water turns out to be anything but.

The water is filled with a veritable soup of free-floating plants and animals collectively called plankton. Plankton is further subdivided into the aquatic plant community, called phytoplankton—literally "green-celled wanderers"—and zooplankton, or animal plankton. Phytoplankton, like plants the world over, harness sunlight to carry on photosynthesis, and produce tremendous amounts of oxygen. Examples of phytoplankton include single-celled organisms such as algae, dinoflagellates, and diatoms. Large collections of blue-green algae can actually turn the water green in tidal freshwater or slightly brackish marshes. Diatoms, which are one-celled plants often found in clusters, are composed of silica—the same glassy mineral found in quartz and opal. Diatoms form the basis of the food chain.

Zooplankton includes copepods, waterfleas, and larvae of larger creatures such as snails, oysters, crabs, barnacles, and striped bass. The phytoplankton are eaten by the zooplankton, which, in turn, are eaten by larger animals in the food chain.

The importance of phytoplankton to the health of the estuary—indeed, to the world—cannot be overrated. Phytoplankton are the true lungs of the earth, producing 80 percent of the world's oxygen. Approximately 75 percent of the organic material on earth is produced by phytoplankton. If the phytoplankton should crash, the entire chain of life would crumble as if a child were to pull the lower piece from a stack of building blocks.

TIDAL MARSH

Tidal marshes are wetlands in the tidal zone characterized by grass-like vegetation. Marshes form a vital transition area between shallow water and uplands. Depending on their location, water in tidal marshes can be fresh, salty, or brackish, with daily, seasonal, and annual variations. The saltiness of a marsh greatly affects the type of life the marsh supports. Generally speaking, the fresher the marsh, the greater the variety of organisms that live there. Salt water poses problems for plants and animals that require adaptations for survival.

Complex ecosystems have evolved to thrive in the tidal fluctuations of marshes in the Chesapeake Bay watershed. Incoming tides bring nutrients needed by marsh plants for optimal growth. Larvae that depend on the marsh for sustenance are also brought in by waves and currents. Outgoing tides flush the marsh of decaying organic matter called detritus, carrying it to other environments where it serves as food for microorganisms and minute aquatic invertebrates. Species higher on the food chain such as aquatic insects, fish, birds, and mammals feed on the microorganisms, in turn.

In addition, marshes provide shelter and food for a wide variety of birds, mammals, reptiles, amphibians, fish, and shellfish. Many North American bird species use wetlands, according to the Chesapeake Bay Foundation. More than two-thirds of Atlantic and Gulf Coast fish and shellfish that are significant commercially rely on wetlands for at least part of their lives, say biologists at the National Marine Fisheries Service. These include striped bass, menhaden, bluefish, flounder, spot, blue crabs, oysters, and clams.

Before humans gained an understanding of their importance, wetlands were viewed as an obstacle to development and transportation. Farming the soggy ground was a challenge, although some people figured ways to do it. The marshes and swamps also challenged the ingenuity of developers and road builders. Consequently, thousands of acres were lost to ditching and draining or to filling operations. Now, in the light of research and media coverage, marshes are seen for the critical part they play as filters for pollutants, buffers that protect the shoreline and soil from waves and wind, and as nesting grounds, nurseries, food providers, and hiding places for fish, birds, crustaceans, and other life forms.

Tidal wetlands can be divided into freshwater, brackish, and saltwater habitats.

TIDAL FRESHWATER MARSH

Any angler who has sought out lily pads to find bass or pike, then silently cursed the plants for snagging his hook, has come face to face with some of the vegetation that is key to the health of tidal freshwater marshes. These marshes occur at the head of the Chesapeake Bay and along the upper reaches of the tidal portions of tributary rivers.

Besides the yellow pond lily or spatterdock (*Nuphar luteum*), plants associated with tidal freshwater marshes include broad-leaved plants called emergents extending above the water surface such as arrow arum (*Pedtandra virginica*) and pickerelweed (*Pontederia cordata*). Growing closer to water's edge are narrow-leaved cattails (*Typha augustifolia*), marsh hibiscus (*Hibiscus moscheutos*), American three-square (*Scirpus pungens*), and various rushes and sedges. Large expanses of wild rice (*Zizanis aquatica*) grow in the mud of the shallows.

Insects such as dragonflies, damselflies, honeybees, and butterflies flying above a freshwater marsh allude to the rich variety of life sustained here. Of course, there are also the ubiquitous biting flies, midges, and mosquitoes to contend with. A closer inspection reveals grasshoppers, crickets, and a variety of bugs—all of which attract insect-eaters such as swallows, flycatchers, and even spiders. The freshwater marsh is also home to reptiles and amphibians not found in the salt marsh such as the green frog (*Rana clamitans melanota*), the Eastern painted turtle (*Chrysemys picta picta*), and the Eastern ribbon snake (*Thamnophis sauritus sauritus*). Great blue herons, great egrets, a variety of marsh ducks, rails, sandpipers, and songbirds find protection and food in the marshes.

Beneath the surface are crustaceans such as the transparent freshwater grass shrimp (*Palaemonetes paludosus*), and mollusks such as the common river snail (*Goniobasis virginica*). Buried in the mud are even more critters, including freshwater mussels (*Anodonta*).

Freshwater habitats are discussed in the sections on Head of the Chesapeake Bay (*see* page 183), Elk Neck State Park (*see* page 197), Idylwild Wildlife Management Area (*see* page 239), and Tuckahoe State Park (*see* page 233).

BRACKISH MARSH

The farther down river from the fall line of tributary rivers and the closer to the mouth of the bay you go, the more brackish the tidal marshes are along the shoreline. Freshwater and saltwater plant species may mix here or dominant species may take over. One notable example is the nearly total domination in some area by that kudzu of tidal marshes, reed grass (*Phragmites australis*). Reed grass or phragmites can tolerate a wide range of salinity and grows prolifically in brackish marshes, especially where the soil has been disturbed, often crowding out more beneficial species. Olney three-square (*Scirpus americanus*) is a common plant in brackish marshes, along with big cordgrass (*Spartina cynosuroides*) and narrow-leaved cattail.

Brackish marshes are further described in the sections on Ragged Island Wildlife

SALT MARSH HAY
(*Spartina patens*)
Perrennial marsh grass that grows from rhizomes. Recognized by its tousled appearance.

Management Area (*see* page 54), Talbot County (*see* page 240), Eastern Neck National Wildlife Refuge (*see* page 219), Kings Creek Preserve (*see* page 245), Blackwater National Wildlife Refuge (*see* page 258), Robinson Neck/Frank M. Ewing Preserve (*see* page 264), and Smith Island (*see* page 289).

SALT MARSH

As the salinity of the lower bay exceeds 25 grams of dissolved salts per thousand grams of water (25 parts per thousand or 25 ppt) and approaches that of pure seawater (35 ppt), salt marshes predominate. Along most of Virginia's bay shoreline, at the bay mouth, and on the backside of the islands of the Virginia Coast Reserve on the Eastern Shore, smooth cordgrass (*Spartina alterniflora*), also called saltmarsh cordgrass, spreads along the lower edges of higher marshes or in pure stands as far as the high can see.

A tall form of the smooth cordgrass grows to 10 feet high in areas regularly and deeply flooded by incoming tides. Where the water is somewhat less salty, other species such as black needlerush (*Juncus roemerianus*) and saltmarsh bulrush (*Scirpus robustus*) are able to compete with the cordgrass for space. A short form of the cordgrass grows in higher areas near the high-tide line, along with salt hay cordgrass, spikegrass, saltmarsh aster, and glasswort. At the level of spring tides and storm tides (a level seldom flooded), just below the uplands, switchgrass and high-tide bush grow.

Despite the harshness of the environment, salt marshes are among the most productive ecosystems on earth. They serve as hiding places and food factories for many fish, crustaceans, and mollusks. Marsh crabs, marsh fiddler crabs, and the Atlantic ribbed mussel are at home here. Periwinkles and saltmarsh snails ascend and descend the stalks of cordgrass with the tides, feeding on detritus. The saltmarsh snail (*Melampus lineatus*) is strictly an air breather, and must time its climb to stay above the incoming tide.

Salt marshes are more productive than farmland. In general, East Coast wetlands can produce 5 to 10 tons of organic matter per acre annually compared to 0.3 to 5 tons for agricultural fields, according to the Virginia Institute of Marine Science.

Young blue crabs as well as 14 species of fish have been shown to be more abundant in salt marsh wetlands than in areas without vegetation. Mummichogs (minnows), fiddler crabs, snails, and other species live out their entire lives in these wetlands. Wetlands serve as nurseries for the young of spot, menhaden, mullet, and many other coastal fish. In fact, 30 percent of a menhaden's diet comes from marsh detritus, while 70 percent is derived from plankton. Shorebirds such as Forster's terns, clapper rails, willets, and laughing gulls make their nests in coastal salt marshes.

Very few reptiles and amphibians can tolerate the conditions of a salt marsh. Most birds that feed in the marshes, such as the great blue heron (*Ardea herodius*), glossy ibis (*Plegadis falcinellus*), and great egret (*Casmerodius albus*) are not full-time residents. Exceptions are the clapper rail (*Rallus longirostris*) and willet (*Catoptrophorus semipalmatus*).

Salt marsh habitats are discussed in the sections on the Horsehead Wetlands Center (*see* page 229), Chincoteague National Wildlife Refuge (*see* page 303), Mockhorn Island Wildlife Management Area (*see* page 305), Virginia Coast Reserve (*see* page 307), and Eastern Shore of Virginia and Fisherman Island National Wildlife Refuges (*see* page 310).

INTERTIDAL ZONE

The area of land around the edges of the bay that is exposed at low tide and covered at high tide is called the intertidal zone. This area forms a transition zone between uplands and shallow water. Depending on such factors as the salinity of the water and whether the bottom is composed of sand, mud, or a combination of these, the intertidal zone can host a variety of plant and animal communities. Where the zone is composed mostly of sand, beaches occur. On flat land composed of mud, an entirely different realm exists called mud flats.

BEACH

Beaches occupy a unique niche where they occur around the edges of the bay. To have the kind of wide, sandy beach that vacationers look for, certain conditions must be present, such as wave action, a gently sloping shoreline, and currents sufficient to gather up sand and deposit it on the shore. These conditions are more prevalent in the lower bay. In the upper bay, beaches are generally flatter and made up of a combination of sand and mud deposited in river deltas.

The fiddler crab (*see* sidebar, page xx) digs its burrows in the sand of the upper beach at or above the high tide mark. A creature that is a survivor from prehistoric times, the Atlantic horseshoe crab (*Limulus polyphemus*), comes ashore to deposit its egg cases in the sand. Empty egg cases of whelks and skates are commonly found on beaches in the lower bay and along the Atlantic coastline.

Many of the life forms supported on the intertidal beach between the high and low tide mark in the Chesapeake Bay are not readily apparent. However, the flocks of tiny peeps and sandpipers that run back and forth with the edge of the waves, stopping to probe here and there, is evidence that there is life beneath the sands. Oystercatchers, gulls, and even grackles are attracted to beaches for bits of marine life washed ashore or tiny crustaceans such as sand diggers and beach fleas that burrow into the sand.

Children often learn how to scoop up handfuls of hard-shelled mole crabs (*Emerita talpoida*), which burrow immediately back into the sand when deposited back on the beach. Although abundant along beaches on the Atlantic, mole crabs are pretty much restricted in the bay to the beaches near the mouth of the bay. They move higher and lower on the beach with the tides, always staying within the zone of breaking waves.

Also hidden within the sands is a microscopic community of copepods, protozoa, and other minute organisms moving upward between the grains of sand to greet each rising tide. Copepods are members of the zooplankton that float freely at the whim of currents. These tiny, uncelebrated crustaceans are the most abundant animals in the Chesapeake Bay, making up as much as 95 percent of the biomass.

MUD FLAT

If the land is flat enough, low tide may expose wide expanses of mud flats made up of silt, clay, and organic material. The flats may look deceptively like a wasteland of ooze where no plant or animal could survive. A closer look reveals the truth. Just beneath the surface is a variety of burrowing worms, snails, and clams. If you can view it just before the receding tide uncovers it, you may also see soft-bodied worms and other critters before they retreat to the mud. After the tide withdraws, fiddler crabs and snails appear. In fact, these flats are teeming with life and are a good place to take inquisitive children. Just like snow that varies in consistency, so do mud flats. Some will support your weight, but in others you may sink into the ooze a few inches.

A small chimney of mud reveals the home of the nocturnal burrowing crayfish (*Cambarus diogenes*). Various breathing holes in the ooze may give away the burrows of the common clamworm, the soft-shelled clam, or the common jackknife clam. Less obvious are mud shrimp and snapping shrimp, which rarely leave their some-times-deep burrows.

Opportunistic gulls, terns, and shorebirds such as the American oystercatcher (*Haematopus palliatus*), semipalmated plover (*Charadrius semipalmatus*), and dunlin (*Calidris alpina*) may also appear at low tide. Gulls and terns scavenge on the surface, while shorebirds have beaks adapted for probing into the mud.

SHALLOW WATER AND SUBMERGED AQUATIC VEGETATION (SAV)

People swimming or playing in the bay or ocean at beach areas may have come to realize that what one day may seem an empty body of shallow water will another day be full of schools of fish bumping the legs, crabs underfoot, or even worse, stinging jellyfish or stinging nettles. Shallow waters of a few feet deep harbor a fluid mix of marine life, including organisms buried in the bottom, migrating fish and the predators that follow them, and a whole microscopic community of microscopic plankton that float with the currents.

Burrowing worms, clams, snails and other benthic organisms inhabit the bottom. Life forms vary according to depth, salinity, substrate composition, and vegetation, if there is any. Sunlight can usually penetrate to the bottom in shallow waters, so aquatic grasses may take hold, creating an entirely new habitat for marine biologists to study.

Grass beds in the bay's shallow waters are known as submerged aquatic vegetation or SAV. The Chesapeake Bay has more than a dozen native species, including wild celery (*Vallisneria americana*), common waterweed (*Elodea canadensis*) and redhead grass (*Potamogeton perfoliatus*). Species vary according to salinity, among other factors. The wild celery is a freshwater species, while wigeon grass (*Ruppia maritima*) tolerates very brackish water and eelgrass (*Zostera marina*) can live in pure seawater.

SAV, perhaps more than any other plant community, is vital to the bay's health, producing much-needed oxygen underwater just as trees do above ground. They also provide hiding places and food for marine life, as well as for migrating, wintering, and nesting waterfowl. The grass beds act as a filter, absorbing nutrients such as nitrogen and phosphorous, and their thick stands trap sediments that might otherwise settle on oyster beds.

Just as wild turkey or deer inhabit above ground forests, SAV beds harbor aquatic animals such as minnows and blue crabs. In saltier areas, barnacles and scallop larvae attach themselves to the leaves and stems of eelgrass. In fresher water in the bay tributaries, anglers know to cast to underwater grass beds for bluegill and large-mouth bass. Tiny zooplankton that feed on the grasses are themselves food for larger organisms.

Sedimentation and a decline in water quality have taken a heavy toll on the Chesapeake's grass beds over the last several decades. Nutrients from car exhausts and power plant emissions can be carried for miles in air currents to settle in the bay. Governments have made good strides in curbing this point-source pollution—pollution that comes from an obvious source such as a smokestack or underground pipe. Finger pointing is easy when the pollution is so visible. Harder to get a handle on are the nonpoint sources such as fertilized farms and lawns, animal and human waste, and construction sites. Pollution from these sources runs off into streams or seeps into groundwater, often traveling many miles from the point of origin to reach the bay.

In smaller amounts, nutrients are a good thing. A healthy estuary is remarkably resilient and can even deal with excessive nutrients up to a point. Uncontrolled nutrient loading, however, causes algae bloom that clouds the water and blocks out sunlight necessary for the growth of SAV.

Only 11 percent of the bay's historic underwater grasses remain. The loss of vegetation is one more factor in the decline or disappearance of many species that depend on the bay. An estimated 80,000 migratory redhead ducks, for instance, once visited the bay annually to feed on seeds, roots, and tubers in the grass beds. Only a few thousand redheads now stop each year.

An overall increase in grasses has encouraged biologists over the past few years, but it's too early to tell if the trend will be long term. A reduction in nutrients is considered to be the primary reason for the resurgence in grasses. It is tempting to point to restrictions that have been put on industry and other point-source polluters as a factor in the nutrient reduction. However, the present increase in aquatic grasses has occurred during years of drought. Because the streams and rivers have been so low, they transported a much lighter load of nutrients. These nutrients build in the soils of the watershed, only to be flushed out in years of heavy rains.

For unknown reasons, the recent resurgence of underwater grasses did not benefit Tangier Sound on Maryland's lower Eastern Shore. Grass beds there, which have played an important historic role in the health of the ecosystem, continue a serious decline. More than 60 percent of the sound's underwater grasses have disappeared in just seven years.

OYSTER BAR

The reason humans have survived as a species, or so it has been postulated, is because they taste bad. Oysters, on the other hand, have been decimated *because* of their flavor.

The delectable oyster (*Crassostrea virginica*)—so abundant at the time European settlers arrived—has been largely wiped out. Much like the forests of North America that stretched as far as the eye could see when Lewis and Clark crossed the continent, oysters were once so abundant in the Chesapeake Bay they were imagined to be as eternal as the seas themselves. Reefs of oysters stacked upon oysters were so massive they were navigational hazards and appeared on maps.

These reefs, with live oysters living upon the heaped up empty shells of dead oysters, built into huge masses over thousands of years and were quite remarkable in their complexity. Examination of an oyster shell reveals the many bumps and ridges that greatly increase the surface area where other sessile creatures such as sea squirts, mussels, barnacles, anemones, and a variety of bryozoans can attach. These, in turn, provide food, hiding places, and nurseries for a variety of worms, crustaceans, fish, and the like.

Just as the American forests turned out to be finite after all when logging and mining operations of the nineteenth and early twentieth centuries left nothing but denuded, eroding hillsides, so too did oyster reefs turn out to have limitations. The world's insatiable taste for the Virginia oyster invited non-restricted harvesting. Sediment-filled runoff from development within the bay watershed and pollution have taken their toll. Dredging the bottom to create deeper water for navigation has destroyed oyster bars or covered them with sediment.

In recent years, the oyster's weakened immune system proved insufficient to battle two ravaging diseases caused by microscopic parasites known as MSX (*Haplosporidium nelsoni*) and Dermo (*Perkinsus marinus*), which are not harmful to humans. Although pathologists in the past five years have gained a much greater knowledge about the mechanisms the parasites employ in overcoming the oysters' defenses, no progress has been made toward curbing their devastating effects on the oyster population.

Loss of habitat, sedimentation, dredging, disease, oxygen-robbing nutrients, and over-harvesting have reduced this important bivalve to less than one percent of its historic numbers. The living oyster opens its shell, drawing water filled with plankton and detritus along its gills to the mouth. Scientists say that at their peak, the oyster population of the Chesapeake could filter the entire volume of water in the bay in 3 to 6 days. Whether or not that is true, it is certain that the bay lost not only its economic mainstay, but also a significant filter for its waters when the oyster reefs were wiped out.

Although the once-expansive reefs are gone, oyster communities still exist in the bay where the bottom is firm enough and where siltation is not a problem. The location of these communities fluctuates with freezing waters, heavy freshwater runoff, and sedimentation, which oysters cannot tolerate. In the Chesapeake Bay, most oyster bars and clusters are located in the transition zone between tidal wetlands and open waters. Researchers with the Virginia Marine Resources Commission are also involved in promising experimental projects to build artificial reefs of oyster shells, which will enable oysters to establish colonies that are above the siltation and low oxygen in the bottom substrate. The new reefs are turning out to be fish attractants as well, a benefit that is getting the attention of the bay's anglers.

THE BLUE CRAB

The blue crab is synonymous, in many minds, with the Chesapeake Bay. Travel brochures, menu covers, marina signs, and magazine articles on the bay are

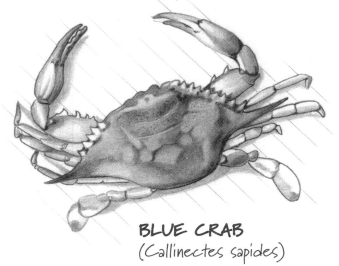

BLUE CRAB
(Callinectes sapides)

often adorned with a picture of this colorful, pugnacious crustacean.

The scientific name for blue crabs—*Callinectes sapides*—was popularized with the Pulitzer-prize-winning book, *Beautiful Swimmers*, by William Warner. The crab's scientific name is derived from Latin and Greek. The genus—*Calli* (beautiful) and *nectes* (swimmer)—does translate to beautiful swimmer. Add the species name, *sapidus* (savory), and you have a savory, beautiful swimmer.

Like so much of life in the estuary, the life cycle of the crab is truly amazing. Mature male crabs spend their lives in the estuary. Most females migrate to the mouth of the bay in fall where they crowd together and spend the winter in semi-hibernation buried in the mud. Some females don't make the journey until the following spring, when they have to run the crab-pot gauntlet, as one scientist put it, to make it to their spawning grounds.

In spring, the females release some 2 million microscopic larvae called

Crab Terminology

Apron: The shell's abdominal covering. The shape of the apron is one way to determine the sex of a crab. The male has a t-shaped apron. Immature females have a triangular apron sealed to the body. Mature females have a broadly rounded apron, which is not sealed to bottom portion of the shell. Another method of determining sex is claw color; males have blue claws and females have red-tipped claws.

Buckrams: Crabs in the stage following papershell, when the shell is harder but still pliable.

Doublers: A mating pair of crabs, when the male carries the female beneath him. During this period, which can last two days or more, the male protects the female during her vulnerable soft-shell stage. She does not leave him until her shell has hardened and she can protect herself.

Hardshells: Crabs with hard shells.

Jimmies: Male crabs.

Keepers: Crabs that measure 5 inches from tip to tip of the longest spikes is big enough to keep.

Papershells: Crabs with new shells that have begun to stiffen.

Peelers: Crabs that are just about to shed their hard shells. Peelers are easy to eat because the meat does not have to be picked from the shell. A pink dot shows up on the crab's back fin about a week before the molt.

She-crabs: Immature females.

Softshells: Crabs that have shed their hard shells, leaving them with thin, soft shells. Each time a crab molts, it takes about four days for the new shell to harden. During this stage, the crab is vulnerable to predators, including humans, who can eat the whole crab without the time-consuming task of picking the meat from the shell. The soft-shell season begins with the first full moon in May and continues through early fall.

Sooks: Adult females.

Sponge crabs: Female crabs with egg masses on their abdomens. Sponge crabs may not be kept.

zoea (pronounced zoe-EE-uh) into the salty water. The larvae are carried into the ocean where they undergo many changes, molting and discarding their shells as they grow larger. They metamorphose to a form called a megalops, when they resemble tiny lobsters. After about two months of life at sea, they migrate back into the bay, continuing to molt, and become what is called a first crab, or immature crab.

Immature females undergo 18 or more molts before they are mature and ready to mate, which usually occurs during their second summer. The sperm they carry can live up to a year, fertilizing all the eggs the female will produce during that time. The egg mass, contained beneath the apron on the shell, has about 1.5 to 2 million eggs. As the eggs hatch, larvae are released over a period of two or three weeks. After two spawns, which take place from May to September, the female dies.

Males also continually molt, shedding their old shells as they grow larger. Unlike the female, which stops growing after mating, males continue to grow larger, molting and mating into the third summer.

The blue crab has filled the void in the commercial market left with the demise of the once-dominant American oyster. Picking the meat from hard-shell crabs is a time-consuming task, so that "crab pickings," as they are called, have turned into social events. Friends gather around tables covered with brown paper or newspaper and spend an afternoon or evening feasting on plates of stacked-up crabs turned orange from steaming or boiling. Crabs have become so popular with diners that pressure is mounting to catch more and more of them by various methods, including crab pots, trotlines, and dredging the bottom.

Scientists are closely studying crab biology and trying to come up with better ways of monitoring the health of the population in the Chesapeake Bay. Many other species can be monitored by tagging, but a molting crustacean is a hard thing to tag. Annual surveys in the early-to-mid 1990s showed alarming declines, but various monitoring techniques turned up conflicting evidence, leaving scientists unsure about the true numbers. By all indications, the large grass beds that still remain in the lower bay seem to be critical to the survival of young crabs.

DEEP WATER

Along most of the shoreline of the Chesapeake, water depths do not exceed 10 feet. Between the subtidal shallows and the channels of the tributary rivers, the water is about 30 feet deep. Tributary rivers have gouged out channels of 60 foot depths or more, while the ancestral riverbed carved by the Susquehanna down the belly of the Chesapeake Bay is more than 100 feet deep for much of its length.

As the bay waters drop below 10 feet, less sunlight can penetrate to the bottom, and grasses disappear. Detritus from tidal wetlands and underwater grass beds is carried into deeper waters by the currents. Phytoplankton, those microscopic plants at the mercy of the currents, is the only plant life that exists in these deeper realms. Animal life that swims or floats with the currents includes jellyfish and the larvae and eggs of various fishes and invertebrates.

Swimming in the water column at various depths are the bay anchovy and the Atlantic silverside—the two most abundant baitfish in the Chesapeake—along with many larger fish. Charter boat captains spend lifetimes learning the habits and patterns of both migratory and resident fish in the Chesapeake Bay. In addition to feisty bluefish and striped bass, anglers seasonally catch flounder, gray trout, croaker, spot, red and black drum, tautog, and cobia. Even the habits and seasons of baitfish are important, because where there are minnows, menhaden, mullet, anchovies, shad, and herring, there also will be gamefish.

Deeper waters are a collection point for sedimentation, which creates a hostile environment for bottom-dwelling (benthic) invertebrates that are able to live in shallower water. Lower amounts of oxygen, especially during summer months, add to the inhospitable environment. However, certain fish such as flounder and croaker are well adapted to life as bottom dwellers. Flounder, also called flatfish or doormats, undergo a metamorphosis after they are hatched, with one eye rotating around to the same side as the other eye, and the swimming orientation changing to a horizontal position instead of a vertical position. The fish can lie on the bottom and cover itself with silt to hide and wait to ambush its prey.

The State of the Bay

▓ THE CHESAPEAKE BAY FOUNDATION

Sooner or later, anyone who spends any time in Virginia or Maryland will spot a "Save the Bay" bumper sticker. The slogan has been popularized by the 83,000-member Chesapeake Bay Foundation, headquartered in Annapolis, Maryland.

The Foundation releases annual reports called State of the Bay, much like the President of the United States describes the State of the Union each year. The union's health is considerably better than that of the bay. Based on a rating of 1 to 100, with 100 referring to the state of the estuary that Capt. John Smith described in his explorations during the early 1600s, the current health of the bay is rated at 28, up 5 points from the 1983 all-time-low of 23. Stated another way, the bay now operates at roughly a quarter of its historic potential, according to the CBF, with dramatically fewer fish, crabs, oysters, waterfowl, underwater grasses, wetlands, and trees than in past generations. If the bay were a hospital patient, doctors would have stabilized the vital signs, but the patient would still be in intensive care.

The foundation has spelled out specific goals to be achieved by the year 2010 and the actions necessary to achieve the goals. Categories for improvement—the same ones analyzed in rating the bay—include nitrogen and phosphorous amounts, dissolved oxygen, water clarity, toxics, wetlands, forest buffers, underwater grasses, resource lands, blue crabs, striped bass, oysters, and shad.

One of the CBF's objectives is to work to close the legal loophole that has allowed ongoing ditching and draining of wetlands, erasing restoration gains. The foundation is also encouraging enforcement of legislation and new laws that would protect and restore streamside buffers. Regulatory and monitoring systems on toxic chemicals are insufficient, as are erosion and sediment-control programs. Partnerships among state and federal resource agencies, private conservation groups, and citizens remain the best hope for accomplishing many of the foundation's objectives. The CBF has challenged the partners of the Chesapeake Bay Program to adopt the goals and the action plans.

THE CHESAPEAKE BAY PROGRAM

Following scientific research in the late 1970s indicating serious nutrient over-loads, dwindling aquatic grasses, and toxic pollution, a partnership was formed called the Chesapeake Bay Program. Members include the states of Maryland, Pennsylvania, and Virginia; the District of Columbia; the Chesapeake Bay Commission, a tri-state legislative body; the Environmental Protection Agency, representing the federal government; and advisory groups. With the signing of the Chesapeake Bay Agree-ment in 1983, the partners agreed on a goal of reducing the nutrients nitrogen and phosphorous entering the bay by 40 percent by the year 2000.

The goal was not met by 2000, largely because of a loophole in a law that was designed to curb the drainage of wetlands. However, a ban on phosphate detergents in the late 1980s did result in a marked reduction in the amount of phosphorous entering the bay. The government partnership is also attempting to remove old dams and other barriers to fish migration, protect the bay's eroding islands, restore wet-lands, and create aquatic reefs.

THE ENVIRONMENTAL PROTECTION AGENCY

The Environmental Protection Agency put the Chesapeake Bay on its "dirty waters list" in 1998 (Maryland portion) and 1999 (Virginia portion). The EPA says the bay and some of its tributaries are significantly low in dissolved oxygen, apparently because of excess nutrients that cause algae bloom, robbing the water of its oxygen. Until now, reduction of nutrients in much of the watershed has been left largely to voluntary efforts. The EPA listing puts teeth into environmentalists' efforts to clean up the bay by requiring localities to foot the bill for better sewage treatment plants. However, no time line for devising a clean-up plan has been put in place.

SO WHERE DO WE STAND?

Actually, there's a smidgen of good news mixed in with the bad. The good news is that the gradual decline in the overall health of the bay has been halted and, in some ways, actual gains have been made. There is less pollution, water quality is better, striped bass have made a remarkable comeback following a ban on fishing, and numbers of eagles and osprey are on the rise as a result of a ban on the pesticide, DDT. A ban on the use of detergents containing phosphorous has contributed to a decline in phosphorus loads delivered to the bay from all of its tributaries by 6 million pounds a year. Nitrogen loads have been reduced by 32 million pounds a year, but more needs to be done.

The bad news is that the bay's health is still rated as poor. Also looming on the horizon are mounting pressures from the steadily increasing human population around the bay, urban growth in the watershed, and the continued loss of wetlands, forests, and open space that buffer and renew the bay's waters. As one scientist put it, you can put all the pollution-control devices you want on the automobile, but if you drive more cars for more hours, you've still got a pollution problem.

URBAN SPRAWL

Growth is not necessarily a bad thing, but people in the Chesapeake Bay watershed may need to make hard choices about continuing to allow unrestricted growth that may well destroy the estuary. At present, homes and businesses are haphazardly spreading across the landscape.

The estimated 2 to 3 million people who will be added to the watershed in the next few years will also bring more cars, more houses, more blacktop, and more sewage treatment plants, replacing the green spaces that are filters and sponges for the bay with hard surfaces, and adding to the industrial discharges and air pollution. Although some improvement has been made in the bay's health through voluntary and regulatory actions, the fundamental message from environmentalists is that people must change the way they do things or risk losing the Chesapeake Bay.

Scientists say that sprawl produces from five to seven times the sediment and phosphorus as a forest and nearly twice as much sediment and nitrogen as compact development. Also, as lifestyles change, each person uses four to five times more land than he or she did just 40 years ago. More than 90,000 acres—150 square

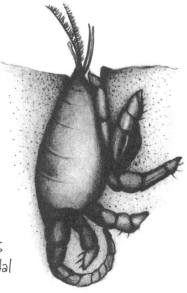

MOLE CRAB
(Emerita talpoida)
These small burrowing
crabs are filter feeders
that live in the intertidal
area of the beach.

miles—of open land are consumed annually by growth in the bay watershed.

Even when legislators are convinced of the importance of cleaning up the bay, the laws passed often are not enforced or loopholes are found. The Chesapeake Bay Preservation Act was passed in 1988, requiring that communities adopt local ordinance restricting certain kinds of development activities along the Chesapeake Bay shoreline. On paper, it looked good. But the law turned out to be riddled with loopholes, including a clause that allowed planned development to be grandfathered in with the law.

Concerned citizens who care about their watershed can encourage their city, county, and state officials to develop master plans to guide land use and provide for more compact growth. Organizations like the Chesapeake Bay Foundation have ideas to assist communities and information that can help allay fears that such land use plans might curb their freedoms or that their tax bases might be destroyed if they fail to attract more industry.

LOSS OF HABITAT

Loss of habitat is one of the major obstacles to restoring the bay's health. Maryland has lost approximately 73 percent of its original wetlands, Virginia has lost more than 42 percent, and Pennsylvania has lost 56 percent. The trend has slowed in recent years, but losses continue to be significant. Less than 60 percent of the original forests of the watershed remains today. Underwater grasses once covered most of the bay floor. After being reduced to just 11 percent of their historic levels, they have begun to make a comeback in recent years.

OVERHARVESTING

In 1999, a marine science professor at the Virginia Institute of Marine Science documented a 71-percent decline in the number of breeding-age female crabs in the bay in just 10 years. An official with the Virginia Marine Resources Commission fears the crab population may be on the brink of a collapse. Virginia and Maryland are considering the professor's proposal to create a corridor where no crabbing would be allowed between the crab spawning area at the mouth of the bay and the crab nursery area in selected shallow waters of the middle bay and upper bay. However, pressure from watermen desperate for income creates a dilemma. License agencies must decide whether or not to issue more "hardship licenses" that have already resulted in thousands of additional crab pots in the bay.

NUTRIENTS

Cattle that stand belly deep in farm ponds and hogs that make muddy paths on stream banks are bad news for the Chesapeake Bay. Animal waste and stream bank erosion add to the nutrient load and sedimentation. Virginia is now paying farmers to fence their livestock away from streams and rivers. Another law directed at agriculture is a restriction on fertilizing crops with chicken manure in amounts too great for the crops to absorb. However, no restrictions are in place for golf courses, private homeowners, and many other sources of nutrient runoff.

▓ HOPE FOR THE FUTURE

Recovery prospects are not hopeless. As scientists gain an understanding of the complex workings of the estuary, they are better able to recommend solutions to reverse the loss of wetlands and forestlands, revive oyster beds, encourage the growth of bay grasses, and curb urban sprawl and pollution. Given the high human density in the Chesapeake Bay watershed, the rating of 100 is a thing of the past. But in a half-century, if determined measures are taken by the six states that share the watershed, researchers say that a rating of 70 is a reasonable expectation.

It may be helpful to remind ourselves that the bay's decline is a recent crisis. The Chesapeake we are trying to return to is still in the memory of those who fished its water for striped bass or dug their toes in its muck for clams just 40 or 50 years ago. Humans, of all species, would benefit greatly from its restoration. Why pay high dollars for more and larger filtration systems, for example, to do what a vibrant estuary will do for free?

Great Blue Heron (Ardea herodius)

Given the assaults on the bay from pollution, rising sea levels, loss of habitat to development, and other sources, focusing on the bay's wonders is not always easy. As important as it is to understand what measures should be taken to restore the bay's health, it is also important to enjoy the ecosystem for what it is.

Birds migrating along the Atlantic Flyway still feed and rest in the salt marshes, sandpipers still probe the mud flats, and great blue herons find secluded woodlands for their rookeries. Rod-bending red and black drum still tax the endurance of surf anglers, and children still scream in delight when they net their first blue crab. The tides still ebb and flow, renewing entire ecosystems with each change.

For all its problems, the Chesapeake Bay is still a marvelous place.

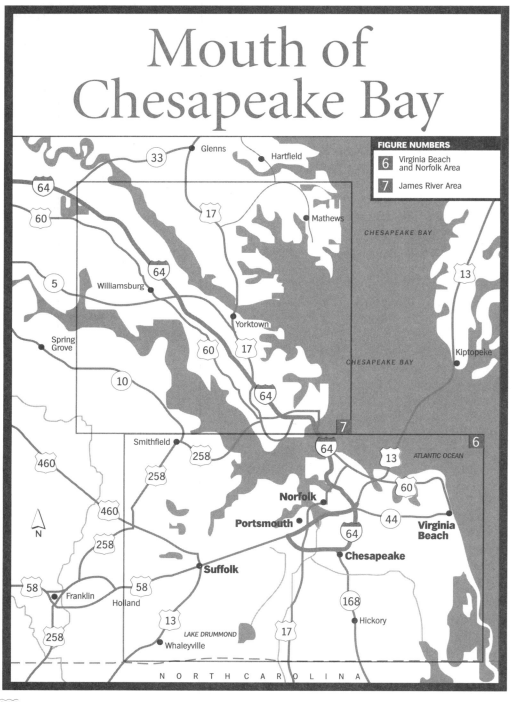

Mouth of Chesapeake Bay

FIGURE NUMBERS

6 Virginia Beach and Norfolk Area

7 James River Area

Mouth of the Chesapeake Bay

Before the first colonists sailed their wooden ships into the mouth of the Chesapeake Bay, some 18,000 Nansemond, Algonquin, and Chesapeake Indians inhabited the wooded coastal plains. They lived on oysters and fish from the rich waters of the estuary, in addition to game from the forests and crops from the rich soil. Remnants of oyster middens, grinding stones, and arrowheads around the bay shores provide evidence of the Indian culture.

On April 26, 1607, Admiral Christopher Newport and a landing party from the English ships, *Discovery*, *Godspeed*, and *Susan Constant*, climbed the high sand dunes at Cape Henry. After the many long days at sea, the fragrant blossoms of springtime must have seemed like heaven.

Capt. George Percy, one of 28 colonists who came ashore, recorded his first impression of the New World: "There wee landed and (found) faire meddowes and

[*Above:* Old Cape Henry Lighthouse]

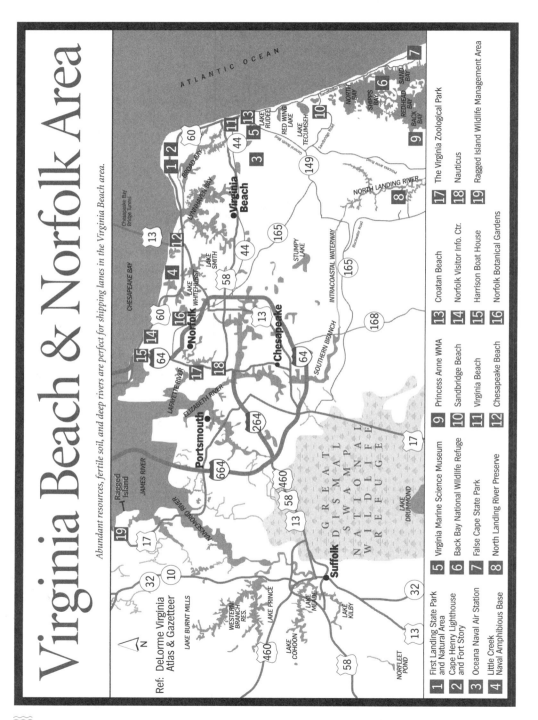

Virginia Beach & Norfolk Area

Abundant resources, fertile soil, and deep rivers are perfect for shipping lanes in the Virginia Beach area.

Ref: DeLorme Virginia Atlas & Gazetteer

1 First Landing State Park and Natural Area
2 Cape Henry Lighthouse and Fort Story
3 Oceana Naval Air Station
4 Little Creek Naval Amphibious Base
5 Virginia Marine Science Museum
6 Back Bay National Wildlife Refuge
7 False Cape State Park
8 North Landing River Preserve
9 Princess Anne WMA
10 Sandbridge Beach
11 Virginia Beach
12 Chesapeake Beach
13 Croatan Beach
14 Norfolk Visitor Info. Ctr.
15 Harrison Boat House
16 Norfolk Botanical Gardens
17 The Virginia Zoological Park
18 Nauticus
19 Ragged Island Wildlife Management Area

goodly tall Trees; with such Fresh-waters running through the woods, as I was almost ravished at the first sight thereof." Capt. John Smith was aboard but was not part of the landing party because of a mutinous indiscretion that had landed him in the ship's jail.

The colonists later returned to the site and erected a wooden cross to mark this first landing, naming Cape Henry after much-loved Henry, Prince of Wales, who was then 13 years old. They claimed the land for England and conducted the Church of England's first religious ceremony in America.

The cape where the colonists came aground was at the mouth of a broad bay. They called the bay Chesapeake— the same name used by local Indian tribes, a word thought to mean "great shellfish bay." The desolate dunes they climbed are now occupied by Fort Story, a U.S. Army base (*see* page 32), and First Landing State Park.

Newport decided to travel farther inland to find a more protected site for the first colony and to build a capital city. On May 13, 1607, the ships landed on a small island in the James River. Named Jamestown after King James of England, the island became the first permanent English colony in the New World. The capital was later moved inland to Williamsburg.

Virginia Beach

[Fig. 6] Early colonists were slow to realize the value of the abundant resources, fertile soil, and deep rivers that were perfect for shipping lanes in the Virginia Beach area. One of the earliest residents was Adam Thoroughgood, a member of the House of Burgesses. In 1635, the popular Englishman built what is believed to be the oldest surviving brick home in America. Today, visitors may stroll the herb and flower gardens and examine the cottage-style architecture of the **Adam Thoroughgood House** at 1636 Parrish Road (757-431-4002) in Virginia Beach.

With over 400,000 people, the City of Virginia Beach has the largest population of any Virginia city and it covers 310 square miles of land. The city extends some 27 miles from the mouth of the Chesapeake Bay south to the North Carolina line. The city boundary reaches inland about 12 miles to the easternmost portion of I-64. In addition to the 27 miles of oceanfront beaches, there are also beaches that border the Chesapeake Bay from Cape Henry 12 miles west to Norfolk.

That's big, as Virginia cities go. Some of what lies within those boundaries is just what you'd expect in a coastal resort city—wide, sandy beaches, high-rise hotels, nightclubs, restaurants, shopping malls, t-shirt and surf shops, mini-golf, a water park, museums, convention centers, concert halls, and historical sites. These attractions account for many of the city's 2.7 million visitors annually. Surprisingly, however, the city also contains two state parks, two major fishing centers, three saltwater fishing piers, a national wildlife refuge, a state wildlife management area, a natural area preserve, and a wildlife preserve. Much of the area where these sites are located was part of the former Princess Anne County, which merged with the city of Virginia Beach in 1963.

The northern portion of Virginia Beach, which borders Norfolk on its western side, fronts the Chesapeake Bay to the north, and meets the Atlantic Ocean to the east, is highly developed. Between I-64 and the oceanfront are busy VA 44 (Virginia Beach-Norfolk Expressway) and parallel US 58 (Virginia Beach Boulevard), carrying conventioneers, sight seers, and beach-goers with surfboards strapped to car tops. Located in this part of Virginia Beach are First Landing State Park and the two fishing centers at Lynnhaven Inlet and Rudee Inlet—places humming with activity from spring through fall.

Look for the **Virginia Beach Information Center** (800-VA-BEACH) at 2100 Parks Avenue at the first traffic light as you come into the resort area on VA 44/264. The center, which sits in the middle of the divided highway, is open from 9 to 8 daily from June 15 to the day after Labor Day and 9 to 5 daily the rest of the year.

The resort area of Virginia Beach is located along Atlantic and Pacific avenues, parallel streets one block apart extending from Cape Henry at the mouth of the Chesapeake Bay 6 miles south along the oceanfront to Rudee Inlet. For most of its length, Pacific Avenue and US 60 are one and the same.

The 3-mile walk along the famous **Virginia Beach Boardwalk** with its parallel bike trail is beautiful any time of year. The ocean scenery is enhanced by the board-walk's teak benches, old-fashioned lampposts, and colorful flags. Bikes may be rented at several locations along the boardwalk.

The Virginia Beach Boardwalk Art Show (757-425-0000), founded in 1955, takes place each June between 17th Street and 31st Street on a 14-block section of the boardwalk. The show is free and open to the public from 10 to 6 daily. The event— one of the premier art shows in the United States—draws some 300,000 visitors annually to view the carefully selected work of world-class sculptors, painters, photographers, and craftsmen.

In August, the East Coast Surfing Championship (800-861-SURF or Web site www.ecscl.com) also draws thousands to Virginia Beach to cheer on more than 100 of the world's top professionals and 400 amateurs who compete for some $70,000 in prize money. The festivities also include a golf tournament, volleyball tournament, 5K run along the oceanfront boardwalk, swimsuit competition, multi-hull regatta, outrigger canoe race, and outdoor concerts on the 4th Street stage.

The **Old Coast Guard Station** (757-422-1587) is on the Virginia Beach Boardwalk at 24th Street and Atlantic Avenue. Formerly called the Life-Saving Museum of Virginia, the museum honors the brave people who have risked their lives to save victims of shipwrecks. The wooden structure, built in 1903, was the former U.S. Life-Saving/Coast Guard Station.

The huge variety of birds that inhabit the shores and marshes of the Virginia

Beach/Back Bay area are the focus of the **Atlantic Wildfowl Heritage Museum** (757-437-8432) at 113 Atlantic Avenue. Operated by the Back Bay Wildfowl Guild, the museum has five galleries of wildfowl artwork and carved decoys. The museum is on the oceanfront, housed in the **Dewitt Cottage**, which was built in 1895 by the first mayor of Virginia Beach, B. P. Holland.

The **Norwegian Lady Statue** at 25th Street and Atlantic Avenue, was a gift from Norwegians commemorating the wreck of the *Dictator*. The **Association for Research and Enlightenment** (757-428-3588) at 67th Street and Atlantic Avenue houses the library and conference center of the famous psychic, Edgar Cayce.

Entertainment is available from April through October at the $18 million, 20,000-seat **GTE Virginia Beach Amphitheater** (757-368-3000), which attracts the biggest names in rock, country, rhythm and blues, classical, and other forms of music. Past entertainers include Jimmy Buffet, James Taylor, and Bruce Hornsby. The **Virginia Beach Pavilion Convention Center** (757-437-7600) at 1000 19th Street hosts theatrical and musical performances, as well as annual waterfowl festivals, gun shows, and other events. The center, with its white arched roofs, is located at the eastern end of VA 44, about 1 mile west of the oceanfront. Another source of hit musicals and drama is the **Little Theater of Virginia Beach** at 24th Street and Barberton Drive (757-428-9233). Performers at **Harrison Opera House** (757-623-1223) produce classics and original works.

Nightclubs offer a wide variety of music, including everything from reggae and Top 40 to jazz, country, and alternative. The **Thoroughgood Inn Comedy Club** (757-460-8398), located in Bayside Shopping Center, is a full-service restaurant featuring nationally known comedians. **Maxi's Rendezvous** at 313 Laskin Road (757-437-8828) is a swing and big-band club offering live music. Other popular spots for night life include **Chicho's** at 2112 Atlantic Avenue (757-422-6011), an old favorite; **Croc's Mighty Nice Grill** at 19th Street and Cypress Avenue (757-428-5444), a restaurant and gathering room with a Caribbean theme that was voted Best at the Beach; and **Peabody's** at 21st Street and Pacific Avenue (757-422-6212), a large dance club with pool tables, foosball, and a stage that attracts national recording artists.

At **Ocean Breeze Amusement Park** at 848 General Booth Boulevard (757-422-4444), youngsters and adults alike can cool off in a water park or enjoy the 36-hole mini-golf, batting cage, and Go Kart rides. Dive centers provide equipment and guided trips to exploring shipwrecks off Virginia Beach (*see* Outfitters, Guides, and Suppliers Appendix, page 315). Local surf shops also provide gear and surfboards for enjoying the waves.

In addition to limousine services, buses, and taxis, oceanfront visitors will find local trolleys (757-428-3388) a convenient way to get around the resort area in late spring and summer. The service runs from 19th Street south to General Booth Boulevard on Pacific Avenue, from 2nd Street to 42nd Street on Atlantic Avenue, and from the oceanfront to Lynnhaven Mall via the VA 44 Expressway.

Whale Watching

A growing attraction off the coast of Virginia is whale watching, mostly done in January and February on comfortable headboats, which charge by the passenger, or head. The whales spotted are usually humpbacks (*Megaptera novaeangliae*), which migrate slowly north, feeding on schools of mackerel and herring as they go. Whales, though they resemble fish, are warm-blooded and need thick layers of fat, or blubber, to protect them from frigid waters. And although their flippers may look like the pectoral fins of fish, they have all the bones found in the forelimbs or arms of land mammals.

The humpback can grow as long as a tractor-trailer and can live 70 or 80 years. This is an energetic whale, known for its spectacular leaps, its loud tail slapping, and its curious approach to boats. Humpback males sing a complex song that intrigues scientists and novices alike.

The new **Entertainment Express** also runs a trolley circuit of the major night spots and hotels until 2:30 a.m. The **North Seashore Park Trolley** operates between 19th Street and 68th Street year-round. Trolleys are also available for rent.

The southern part of Virginia Beach, on the other hand, contains horse farms, fields of soybeans and strawberries, and residential areas, as well as marshes, bays, inlets, creeks, coves, islands, sand dunes, and part of the Intracoastal Waterway (*see* page 47). In and around the waters of Back Bay in this part of the city are quiet places to walk, bike, canoe, or kayak—places such as Back Bay National Wildlife Refuge, False Cape State Park, Princess Anne Wildlife Management Refuge, and North River Landing Preserve.

Seven miles south of the resort strip at the junction of Princess Anne Road and Indian River Road is Pungo, site of a popular Strawberry Festival on Memorial Day weekend. Festivities include nearly 100 artists and craftsmen, food and alcohol-free refreshments, 4-H exhibits, a petting zoo, pony rides, pig races, and a simulated medieval encampment. Visitors may pick their own strawberries in nearby fields or buy fresh ones already picked. Since the event began in 1983, it has grown to attract an estimated 150,000 strawberry lovers.

Hidden away along the waterfront east of Pungo is Sandbridge. Here, rental cottages line the oceanfront along Sandbridge Beach, where the high-rise hotels of the resort area of Virginia Beach shimmer in the haze several miles to the north like a half-forgotten dream. While sunbathers pour onto Virginia Beach early on a June morning, the 5-mile stretch of Sandbridge Beach might have little more than a couple of beachcombers, a man throwing a stick in the ocean for his dog, and a surf fisherman or two.

The rental homes along Sandbridge are protected from the ever-encroaching ocean only by man-made dunes, bulwarks, and replenished beaches, which give way sooner or later when assaulted by northeasters or hurricanes. The unceasing wave action spawned by Hurricane Dennis dealt a particularly devastating blow. The storm arrived off North Carolina's Outer Banks in late August of 1999 and stayed like an unwelcome guest for a couple of interminable weeks. A drive down Sandfiddler Road will reveal the telltale foundations of the latest collapsed structures along the beach, where the ocean now laps at empty pilings and swirls around concrete blocks sprouting broken steel reinforcement—the supports that once held expensive homes. Even beachcombers who wish to walk any distance must come at low tide, because the once-wide beach is so narrow at some places that the ocean slaps against the seawalls.

For more information: Virginia Beach Information Center, 2100 Parks Avenue, Suite 500, Virginia Beach, VA 23451. Phone (800) VA-BEACH or (757) 437-4700. Web site www.vbfun.com. Buses: Tidewater Regional Transit (TRT), phone (757) 640-6300. Trolleys, phone (757) 428-3388.

FISHING AND CRUISING AT THE MOUTH OF THE CHESAPEAKE BAY

Charter boats, cruise boats, headboats, well-equipped marinas, and several boat ramps are available at two major inlets in Virginia Beach. Rudee Inlet is just south of the oceanfront resort strip. Call the **Virginia Beach Fishing Center** (800-725-0509) at 200 Winston Salem Avenue or **Fisherman's Wharf Charters** (757-428-2111) at 524 Winston Salem Avenue for information. Lynnhaven Inlet is north of the resort strip and just inside the mouth of the Chesapeake Bay. Two of several full-service marinas here are **Lynnhaven Seafood Marina** (757-481-4545) at 3311 Shore Drive and **Bubba's Marina** (757-481-3513) at 3323 Shore Drive.

Excursions include fishing for sea bass and tautog over sunken wrecks in the Atlantic Ocean or casting to the rock islands of the Chesapeake Bay Bridge-Tunnel to bottom fish for flounder, spot, croaker, and gray trout. Swarming seagulls in the bay and ocean indicate where baitfish are jumping at the surface to escape slashing schools of rockfish and bluefish—popular seasonal targets of fishermen armed with shad lures and bucktails. Charter boats also make the 40-mile-trip offshore to the clear blue waters of the Gulf Stream. In addition to tasty bluefin and yellowfin tuna and dolphin (mahi mahi), these waters contain giant blue and white marlin, known among sport fishermen for their exciting leaps and rod-bending tests of endurance and patience. There are also whale-watching and dolphin-watching trips.

Saltwater fishing piers offer anglers an excellent means to get closer to the spot, trout, croaker, flounder, blue crabs, and even occasional runs of such exciting fish as cobia and red drum that seasonally swim the waters just offshore. **Lynnhaven Fishing Pier** (757-481-7071) is just east of Lynnhaven Inlet on the bayside. Oceanfront piers include the **Virginia Beach Fishing Pier** (757-428-2333) in the resort area at 15th Street and Atlantic Avenue and **Little Island Park Fishing Pier** (757-426-7200) on the southern end of Sandbridge. In August 1999, a Virginia Beach 12-year-old proved how good pier fishing can be when a monster fish attacked the menhaden bait he had cast from the Sandbridge pier. On the other end of his line was a 52-pound, 2-ounce king mackerel that turned out to be a new state record.

The annual Virginia Saltwater Fishing Tournament, run by the Virginia Marine Resources Commission, awards citations for fish that meet or exceed a designated weight or length. Sharks, black and red drum, and billfish should be measured from nose to tail and released. Species that qualify for release citations may change from year to year. Other eligible species should be brought to an official weigh station located at certain tackle shops and marinas, where registration forms are available. Anglers are recognized annually for catching the largest fish of each species in the ongoing saltwater tournament. Also, Virginia Beach hosts the annual World Striped Bass Championship (800-446-8036) that runs from early October to the end of the year, with large cash prizes for the biggest striped bass. A saltwater fishing license, available from tackle shops and marinas, is required for the Chesapeake Bay and tributary rivers. Temporary freshwater licenses are available at city halls and at some sporting stores.

For more information: Saltwater: Virginia Marine Resources Commission, PO Box 756, Newport News, VA 23607-0756. Phone (757) 247-2200. Freshwater: Virginia Department of Game and Inland Fisheries, PO Box 11104, Richmond, VA 23230-1104. Phone (804) 367-1000.

FIRST LANDING STATE PARK AND NATURAL AREA

[Fig. 6(1)] First Landing State Park—called Seashore State Park until 1999—was one of the state's six original parks constructed in the 1930s by the Civilian Conservation Corps. The park's name was changed in 1999 to honor the first landing of settlers near the park on April 26, 1607.

With its location at the mouth of the Chesapeake Bay and just north of the extremely popular Virginia Beach oceanfront, First Landing State Park receives 1 million visitors annually—more than any other state park in Virginia. Adding to its appeal are its shady campground and the 1.25 miles of beachfront park property.

A total of 19 miles of hiking trails lace the park's natural area, which consists of cypress swamps, maritime forests, pine/beech forests, sand dunes, salt marsh, beach, and bay. The natural area has earned a spot on the National Register of Natural Landmarks because it contains the northernmost mix of subtropical and temperate habitats on the East Coast.

The 6-mile Cape Henry Trail, the only trail designated for biking, passes through baldcypress swamps, over an old dune area, and across a wooden bridge and salt marsh. Osprey nests can be seen from the benches on the bridge.

EASTERN CHICKEN TURTLE
(Deirochelyls reticularia reticularia)

First Landing's Chesapeake Bay Center features a wet lab, educational displays and an eco-tourism center. Park cabins are rented on a weekly basis. Pets are allowed in cabins for an additional charge.

Directions: From I-64, Exit 282 (US 13) in Norfolk, go east about 4.5 miles on US 13. Turn right onto US 60 and drive about 6.5 miles to the park entrance, on the right.

Activities: Hiking, camping, biking, boating, picnicking, saltwater fishing.

Facilities: 19 miles of hiking trails, 6-mile bike trail, bicycle rental, boat ramp, campground, camp store, cabins, picnic area, Chesapeake Bay Center, visitor center, bathhouses, restroom.

Dates: The park is open from 8 to dusk, year-round. Call for seasonal dates for the campground, camp store, visitor center, and bicycle rental.

Fees: There is a small parking fee and fees for camping, rental bicycles, and cabins.

Closest town: The park is located in northern Virginia Beach.

For more information: First Landing State Park, 2500 Shore Drive, Virginia Beach, VA 23451. Phone (757) 412-2300 or (804) 786-1712.

BALD CYPRESS NATURE TRAIL

The self-guided nature trail leads over boardwalks and sandy paths through a dimly lit baldcypress swamp draped with Spanish moss. The moss is a southern species, near the northern extent of its range here. The dark water of the swamp is stained with tannin from the breakdown of woody plants and leaves. Tannin helps water stay fresh, a quality that made it valuable to early explorers as drinking water on ships.

Chicken Turtle

The Eastern chicken turtle (*Deirochelyls reticularia reticularia*)—one of Virginia's endangered species—is found nowhere else in the state except at First Landing State Park. Even in the park, where there may be 10 or fewer individuals, the turtle is extremely rare. The chicken turtle takes its name from its long neck, which, when extended, is nearly as long as the brown-and-olive carapace. Hikers occasionally spot the turtles basking on a log in the park's freshwater swamp ponds.

Along the trail, look for wading birds such as green herons, snowy egrets, and great blue herons as they stalk fish, crayfish, and frogs at the swamp's edge. Frog species identified here include the tiny but noisy spring peeper (*Hyla crucifer*), the green frog (*Rana clamitans*), and the bullfrog (*Rana catesbiana*). The eyes of many frogs protrude above their heads, allowing them to watch for insects with nothing but their eyes and nostrils above water. Or frogs may sit motionless on a lily pad for long periods of time, striking with amazing swiftness when an insect wanders within range.

Trail. 1.5-mile, self-guided, easy loop from the visitor center through a cypress swamp. The trail may be cut in half by making a right turn on the intersecting road at the halfway point and returning to the visitor center. The park has an excellent brochure that interprets sites along the trail.

CAPE HENRY LIGHTHOUSES/FORT STORY

[Fig. 6(2)] Two lighthouses stand close enough together on the grounds of Fort Story to be photographed in the same picture. The old Cape Henry Lighthouse, funded by the first U.S. Congress and built in 1791, is the oldest government-built lighthouse in America. It was also the first of 61 lighthouses built to protect sailors from the Chesapeake Bay's treacherous shoals and points. The beautiful red brick structure is octagonal, its tower rising 75 feet into the air from a sand dune at the mouth of the Chesapeake in northern Virginia Beach. Lovingly maintained by the Association for the Preservation of Virginia Antiquities, the old Cape Henry Lighthouse is now a National Historic Landmark and is open to the public.

When cracks appeared in the walls in 1872, a new cast iron tower with masonry walls was built 347 feet southeast of the old one. The new tower stands 165 feet high and has a pattern of black and white rectangles. Equipped with a first-order Fresnel lens, the new light became operational in 1881 and has since been electrified. Despite the state-of-the-art LORAN, satellites, and radar operated by the U.S. Army on the same site, the flashing red and white beacon of the Cape Henry lighthouse is still the mariner's best friend on a foggy night.

Also at Fort Story is a 0.25-acre site with the granite **First Landing Cross**, a granite **Battle Off the Capes Monument**, and a statue of Admiral Comte deGrasse, commander of a French Navy fleet in the Revolutionary War. The cross is a replica of the wooden cross erected by English colonists when they first came ashore near this spot in 1607. The monument commemorates the cannon battle off Cape Henry and Cape Charles as the French Navy successfully kept the British Navy from relieving General Charles Cornwallis at Yorktown, helping to bring about Cornwallis' surrender at Yorktown. This site is an extension of the **Colonial National Historical Park** at Jamestown and Yorktown. A walkway leads to an overlook on the dunes, where there is a view of the mouth of the Chesapeake Bay. There are no other facilities.

A public beach, which is open to the public from Friday through Monday, fronts the Atlantic Ocean. Have your

New Cape Henry Lighthouse

driver's license and car registration handy in case you're asked for it when you receive your pass at the entrance. Otherwise, there are no restrictions to people who would like to enter this small fort.

Fort Story is a training facility for the U.S. Army's 11th Transportation Battalion and a testing site for new transportation equipment. The miles of sandy beaches at Cape Henry provide perfect condtions for what is called logistics-over-the-shore (LOTS) training.

Directions: The lighthouses are located at Fort Story, a military reservation on Cape Henry, at the northern end of Atlantic Avenue in Virginia Beach.

Activities: Visiting historical site, swimming.

Facilities: Historical monuments, short walkway, swimming beach.

Dates: The Old Cape Henry Lighthouse is open from 10 to 5 daily, from mid-Mar. to Oct. The new lighthouse may be viewed from the outside only. The beach is open to the public during daylight hours from Friday through Monday and is lifeguarded during summer months.

Fees: There is a charge to enter the lighthouse, but no fee for entering Fort Story or for using the beach.

Closest town: Fort Story is in northern Virginia Beach.

For more information: Historic Cape Henry, phone (757) 460-1688. Fort Story, Shore Drive, Virginia Beach, VA 23310 Phone (804) 4227101, ext. 230.

OCEANA NAVAL AIR STATION

[Fig. 6(3)] The U.S. Navy houses its most sophisticated aircraft at the Oceana Naval Air Station, including the F-18 Hornets and F-14 Tomcat fighter planes. From observation points on the perimeter roads, you can watch jets of the 22 aviation squadrons take off and land every few minutes. You may also drive on the base by showing a driver's license and car registration. Several Navy airplanes are on display at the Aviation Historical Park just inside the main gate. Tours of the air station are also available during the summer.

Directions: The air station is located just south of VA 44, about 2 miles west of the Virginia Beach resort strip. The station is bordered to the east by Oceana Boulevard and to the west by London Bridge Road. Aircraft observation parking areas are located on both of these roads. The Aviation Historical Park is just inside the main gate off Oceana Boulevard.

Activities: Observing airplane takeoffs and landings, visiting aviation historical park.

Facilities: Pull-offs for observation, aviation historical park, restrooms.

Dates: The gates are open from 5:30 a.m. to 9 p.m. daily, year-round.

Fees: None.

Closest town: The air station is located in Virginia Beach.

For more information: Aviation Historical Park, Princess Anne Road, Oceana Naval Air Station, Virginia Beach, VA 23460-5120. Phone (757) 433-3131.

LITTLE CREEK NAVAL AMPHIBIOUS BASE

[Fig. 6(4)] The U.S. Navy SEALS train at this amphibious base. Like other military bases in the area, Little Creek opened its grounds to the public in 1995. On weekends, one or more ships may be boarded and during the Christmas holiday season, ships are decorated with lights.

Directions: The base is located on US 60 (Shore Drive), just west of the Chesapeake Bay Bridge-Tunnel (US 13) in Virginia Beach.

Dates: The gates are open daily, year-round. One or more ships are open for touring from 1 to 4 p.m. on Saturdays and Sundays, year-round.

Fees: None.

Closest town: The base is in western Virginia Beach.

For more information: Little Creek Naval Amphibious Base, 2600 Tarawa Court, Norfolk, VA 23521-3229. Phone (757) 462-7923.

VIRGINIA MARINE SCIENCE MUSEUM

[Fig. 6(5)] It would be hard to imagine a more perfect family entertainment spot than the Virginia Marine Science Museum. Both adults and children lean over the touch tanks to stroke the backs of stingrays or examine a starfish or a hermit crab in its shell.

Teenagers, their faces reflecting the blue water and gold light of the 300,000-gallon Norfolk Canyon Aquarium, are mesmerized by the sight of sharks, barracuda, and crevalle jack at eye level. Giant loggerhead sea turtles (*Caretta caretta*), an endangered species, look prehistoric in the 70,000-gallon sea turtle aquarium.

What better way to learn the traditional art of oyster tonging than to try it with authentic oyster tongers? Visitors can also get into a simulated diving bell and experience what it's like to descend to the ocean depths. Some 300 such activities invite a hands-on approach to learning.

Words such as amazing or unbelievable or incredible are insufficient to describe the six-story-high IMAX theater. Special 3D glasses give a realistic third dimension to the two-dimensional images on the screen. Members of the audience reach into the empty air in front of them in an attempt to touch the kelp forests and schools of fishes that appear to be around them.

Between the pavilions of the museum, a nature trail winds through a salt marsh where a lesser yellowlegs (*Totanus flavipes*) preens its feathers and the heads of turtles poke above the briny waters.

A 40-foot-high observation tower gives a more expansive view of the marsh and the Atlantic Ocean to the east. The trail connects the first building with another, the Owls Creek Marsh Pavilion. At this pavilion, river otters with boundless energy play in a habitat where the underwater world is a part of the show.

Visitors can sign up for boat trips to watch whales and dolphins, too. Whale watching is best during the months of January and February.

Eastern Glass Lizard

The Eastern glass lizard (*Ophisaurus ventralis*) is at the northern part of its range at Back Bay. This legless lizard, which can grow to 42 inches, resembles a snake but is quite harmless. Its back is grayish-brown, with dark stripes along the sides. Most adults become greenish. The snake is at home in the park's maritime live-oak woodlands. Live oaks, like the glass lizard, are common farther south, but are rare in Virginia.

Directions: From the southern end of Pacific Avenue (the westernmost of two parallel streets along the resort waterfront), go south on General Booth Boulevard, crossing Rudee Inlet, about 1 mile to the entrance, on the right.

Activities: Museum tour, IMAX 3D theater, marsh walk.

Facilities: Museum with aquariums, IMAX 3D theater, Osprey Cafe, two gift shops, walking trail with boardwalk.

Dates: Open 9 to 5 daily, year-round, with extended evening hours in summer.

Fees: There is an entrance fee and a fee for the IMAX theater.

Closest town: The museum is located in Virginia Beach, about 2 miles south of the resort area.

For more information: Virginia Marine Science Museum, 717 General Booth Boulevard, Virginia Beach, VA 23451. Phone (757) 425-FISH. E-mail va-marine-science-museum@va-beach.com. Web site www.va-beach.com/va-marine-science-museum.

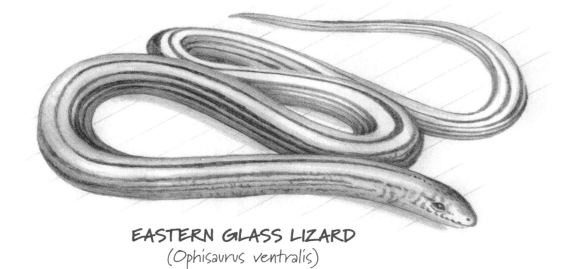

EASTERN GLASS LIZARD
(Ophisaurus ventralis)

■ BACK BAY NATIONAL WILDLIFE REFUGE/ FALSE CAPE STATE PARK

[Fig. 6(6), Fig. 6(7)] Bay Back National Wildlife Refuge, tucked away in Virginia's southeastern corner, is like a friend that grows on you. Each visit turns up some new facet of Back Bay's personality. The 4,608-acre refuge is located south of Sandbridge on a narrow peninsula that fronts the Atlantic Ocean to the east and Back Bay to the west. False Cape State Park lies on the southern end of the refuge.

Even the 1-mile entrance road between the pay booth and the visitor center can be fascinating. In spring, young red foxes play on the dunes in plain sight of bikers and motorists. Catbirds (*Dumetella carolinensis*), red-winged blackbirds (*Agelaius phoeniceus*), and yellow-breasted chats (*Icteria virens*) call from the shrubby thickets of wax myrtle, bayberry, and persimmon. Turtles sun themselves on logs and white-tailed deer stand like statues in the distance.

From the parking area at the visitor center, you can take a network of boardwalks and sandy paths along Back Bay and through dense forests. If it's spring, there are sure to be osprey nests on platforms out in the bay. Also watch for otters surfacing and diving. Wild horses are sometimes grazing the fields around the visitor center. The air may be full of swooping purple martins, which make good use of the many apartment-style birdhouses in front of the center.

A pond near the parking lot is full of lily pads where green frogs and painted turtles live. You may see a preening greater yellowlegs (*Tringa melanoleuca*) or a yellow-billed cuckoo (*Coccyzus americanus*) as you round a bend on the boardwalk trail. The prints of raccoons and many smaller critters are evidence of nocturnal goings-on in the muck of Back Bay. The Seaside Dune Trail leads to an entirely different habitat on the oceanfront, where you can watch ghost crabs (*Ocypode quadrata*), Caspian terns (*Hydroprogne caspia*), and semipalmated sandpipers (*Ereunetes pusillus*) foraging on the beach.

Some 20,000 snow geese (*Chen caerulescens*) and a tremendous variety of migratory ducks hang out in the refuge during the annual fall migration and during winter months. Occasionally, a lucky visitor even gets to see an endangered species using the refuge, such as a loggerhead sea turtle (*Caretta caretta*), piping plover (*Charadrius melodus*), peregrine falcon (*Falco peregrinus*), or bald eagle (*Haliaeetus leucocephalus*).

The marshland is ideal for snakes such as brown and northern water snakes, black rat snakes, and Eastern hognose snakes. The southeastern corner of Virginia is the only place where the poisonous cottonmouth moccasin is found in the state. Although it is a common sight, it poses no threat to humans if it is left undisturbed.

From the refuge, visitors can hike, bike, or take the tram 3 miles south to False Cape State Park. Those who wish to camp at False Cape can leave their vehicles at Little Island Park at the southern end of Sandbridge, just north of the Back Bay entrance. Camping is primitive. Pets are prohibited in the refuge but may be brought by boat to the park.

False Cape got its name from its resemblance to Cape Henry, which is located at the mouth of the Chesapeake Bay to the north. In the 1800s, many ships went aground as captains were lured into shallow water. The 4,321-acre park has nearly 6 miles of pristine beachfront. Five hiking and biking trails totaling 7.5 miles lead from beaches and dunes into maritime forests of oak and pine, then through swamps and marshes to Back Bay. The Barbour Hill Nature Trail is a 2.4-mile self-guided path that explores a variety of False Cape habitats, including loblolly pine forest, scrublands, and wetlands. An observation tower provides an expansive view of the area.

WAX MYRTLE
(Myrica cerifera)

Directions: From I-64, Exit 286, in western Virginia Beach, go east on Indian River Road (VA 407). Go about 12 miles (following Indian River Road signs through two turns at Elbow Road) to the traffic light at Pungo. Go straight through the light and go another 1 mile. Turn left on New Bridge Road and go a little over 1 mile to a T intersection. Turn right on Sandbridge Road and go about 3 miles. Turn right on Sandpiper Road (one block before a T intersection at the oceanfront) and drive a little over 4 miles to the refuge entrance. The park begins about 3 miles south of the refuge parking lot and is accessible by bike, tram, foot, or boat.

Activities: Refuge: hiking, biking, beachcombing, surf fishing, freshwater fishing, tram ride to state park, boating (only small hand-carried boats may be launched), seasonal hunting and trapping by permit. Park: primitive camping, hiking, biking, beachcombing, boating, tram ride from refuge.

Facilities: Refuge: visitor center, restrooms, boardwalks and nature trails, biking and hiking trails, handicap-accessible fishing dock, open-air tram. Park: boat dock, hiking and biking trails, primitive campground (no water), visitor contact station, pit toilet, two observation towers.

Dates: The park and refuge are open daily, year-round. Parts of the refuge are closed seasonally to protect breeding bird colonies. The tram runs Tuesday and Thursday through Sunday, spring through fall (reservations are required; 48-hour notice is required to arrange access for the disabled.)

Fees: There is a refuge entrance fee, which also applies to anyone continuing on to the park (except boaters), and a fee for the tram.

Closest town: Sandbridge is 4 miles north of the refuge.

For more information: Back Bay National Wildlife Refuge, PO Box 6286, Virginia Beach, VA 23456. Phone (757) 721-2412. False Cape State Park, 4001 Sandpiper Road, Virginia Beach, VA 23456. Phone (757) 426-7128. For tram reservations, phone (757) 498-BIRD.

▨ NORTH LANDING RIVER PRESERVE

[Fig. 6(8)] With an amazing patchwork of public and private lands, the Virginia Chapter of The Nature Conservancy and the Virginia Department of Conservation and Recreation have arranged for protection of 6,200 acres of wetlands along the North Landing River in the southwestern corner of the state. The North Landing River is home to four rare animal species, 35 rare plant species, and four natural communities rare in Virginia, including white-cedar swamp, canebrakes, freshwater to brackish tidal marshes, and pocosins. The preserve also lies in the path of the Atlantic Flyway, providing an important link of rest stops for migrating waterfowl.

In North Landing River and the nearby Great Dismal Swamp are some of the last holdouts in Virginia for bog-like forested or shrubby wetlands called pocosins. Pocosins, when burned on a regular basis, support a natural community of unusual plant species including sphagnum moss (*Sphagnum*), Atlantic white cedar (*Chamaecyparis thyoides*), fetterbush (*Lyonia lucida*), and Virginia chain fern (*Woodwardia virginica*). Ditching has destroyed most pocosins in the state.

Although protection of habitat is of prime consideration here, public interests have not been forgotten. A 10-foot-high observation deck has been erected at the mouth of Pocaty Creek, rewarding canoeists with a sweeping view of the marshlands. A 1,000-foot boardwalk in the southern part of the preserve leads through forested swamp and open marsh. Interpretive signs help visitors understand this freshwater wind-tide marsh. Winds from the north push the river out into Currituck Sound, resulting in mud flats, while south winds push the water back into the creeks and guts along the river. A wide variety of plants and animals that are uniquely suited to the complex ecosystem have evolved over time.

Flatwater canoeists and kayakers can explore the preserve several ways. The put-in for the Pocaty Creek Canoe Trail is at a bridge on Blackwater Road. The trail consists of a 2-mile paddle (one way) to the creek's confluence with the North Landing River and back. At the far end is the observation deck.

A 0.5-mile carry over a wide footpath and boardwalk through wetland forest is necessary to access the Altons Creek Canoe Trail. The trail follows Altons Creek about 2.5 miles to its mouth on the North Landing River. Canoeists can also put in at Blackwater Creek, a North Landing River tributary that bisects Blackwater Road just south of the juncture with Pungo Ferry Road. Brochures with maps of the Pocaty Creek and Altons Creek canoe trails in the preserve are available from Department of Conservation and Recreation or from The Nature Conservancy.

ATLANTIC WHITE CEDAR
(*Chamaecyparis thyoides*)

Directions: From I-64 in Virginia Beach, take Exit 286B. Go about 8 miles east on Indian River Road (VA 407). Be sure to follow Indian River Road through a zigzag at Elbow Road. Turn right onto North Landing Road and go 2.2 miles. Turn left onto Fentress Airfield Road and make another immediate left onto Blackwater Road. Several accesses to the preserve lie along this road. At about 3.5 miles, you'll cross Pocaty Creek where the Pocaty Creek Canoe Trail begins. After 5 miles along Blackwater Road, look for a parking lot on the right, just past Old Carolina Road, where you can hike 0.5 mile to Altons Creek for the Altons Creek Canoe Trail. At about 8 miles, just past the junction with Pungo Ferry Road, you'll cross Blackwater Creek, where there's another canoe put-in. At 9.3 miles, a few hundred yards past the Blackwater Fire Station, look for the preserve entrance (location of the boardwalk), on the left.

Atlantic White Cedar

The Atlantic white cedar (*Chamaecyparis thyoides*) of southeastern Virginia pocosins is a medium-sized conifer with lightweight wood used in shipbuilding and house shingles. The wood is resonant and was once used to make organ pipes. Many people are more familiar with the horticultural varieties of white cedar known as arborvitae, valued for their beauty, resistance to diseases and pests, and aromatic quality.

Activities: Canoeing, walking boardwalk.

Facilities: Canoe launch, observation tower, boardwalk.

Dates: The preserve is open from dawn to dusk, year-round.

Fees: None.

Closest town: Pungo is about 13 miles north of the boardwalk.

For more information: The Virginia Department of Conservation and Recreation, Natural Heritage Program, 203 Governor Street, Richmond, VA 23219. Phone (804) 786-7951. The Nature Conservancy, Virginia Chapter, 1233A Cedars Court, Charlottesville, VA 22903-4800. Phone (804) 295-6106.

PRINCESS ANNE WILDLIFE MANAGEMENT AREA

[Fig. 6(9)] Three tracts of land totaling 1,546 acres on Back Bay in southern Virginia Beach make up the Princess Anne Wildlife Management Area. Two of the tracts—Whitehurst and Trojan—are on the western shore of the bay. The Pocahontas Tract is composed of several marshy islands just north of the North Carolina line.

Biologists manipulate water levels of several impoundments on the Whitehurst tract to provide ideal growing conditions for plants that attract waterfowl. Nesting platforms and boxes as well as planted fields further enhance the waterfowl habitat.

Several stationary and floating blinds for hunters here and at False Cape State Park (*see* page 36) on the eastern side of Back Bay are carefully controlled by lottery and seasonal passes, which are available from the area headquarters at the Trojan Tract. A boat ramp is also located at the headquarters. White perch are the primary fish in the brackish water of Back Bay, while largemouth bass and bluegill live in the feeder creeks. There is also good fishing for channel catfish during the spring spawn.

Directions: From Pungo in southern Virginia Beach, go about 9 miles south on VA 615. About 1.8 miles south of Creeds, turn left on VA 699 (Back Bay Landing Road) and go about 1.5 miles to the boat ramp and headquarters.

Activities: Fishing, waterfowl hunting (by permit), boating.

Facilities: Boat ramp, hunting blinds.

Dates: The area is open from dawn to dusk daily, year-round.

Fees: None.

Closest town: The area is in southern Virginia Beach, about 10 miles south of the community of Pungo.

For more information: Princess Anne Wildlife Management Area, Virginia Department of Game and Inland Fisheries, Region I Office, 5806 Mooretown Road, Williamsburg, VA 23118. Phone (757) 253-7072.

BEACHES IN VIRGINIA BEACH

[Fig. 6(11)] Lifeguards are on duty from 9:30 a.m. to 6 p.m. daily from mid-May to mid-September at the Virginia Beach resort strip, which stretches from 1st Street to 38th Street. Rental chairs, rafts, and umbrellas are available at the lifeguard stands at each block. Parking is available under the Rudee Inlet Bridge at 4th Street, as well as at 9th Street and Pacific Avenue, at 18th and 19th streets and Pacific Avenue, and at 25th Street and Pacific Avenue. Public restrooms are at 2nd, 17th, 24th, and 30th streets.

Surfers, who are prohibited from using Virginia Beach from 10 a.m. to 6 p.m., are allowed to surf at **Croatan Beach** [Fig. 6(13)] all day. This beach is located just south of the resort area and Rudee Inlet. Go south on Atlantic Avenue, which becomes General Booth Boulevard. Continue about 0.5 mile and turn left onto Croatan Road to access the beach. Lifeguards are on duty at the northern end of the beach, which is also the area where surfers are allowed.

Sandbridge Beach [Fig. 6(10)] is a 5-mile stretch of lightly used oceanfront at Sandbridge, south of the resort area. (From the southern end of the resort area, take General Booth Boulevard to Princess Anne Road to Sandbridge Road and follow the signs.) Public parking, restrooms, and lifeguarded sections of beach are available at both ends of Sandfiddler Road, including a beach at **Little Island Park** between the southern end of Sandbridge and Back Bay National Wildlife Refuge. Signs along Sandfiddler Road identify public access points for the beaches, but parking can be hard to come by away from the lifeguarded beach areas. Little Island Park has a fishing pier, snack bar, shaded picnic areas, and a playground. A bait and tackle shop is across the street. The wildlife refuge (*see* page 36) and False Cape State Park (*see* page 36) south of the refuge also have beaches.

North Virginia Beach is an unguarded stretch of the Atlantic between 40th Street and 80th Street in Virginia Beach. There are no public facilities or lifeguards and parking may be hard to find.

A variety of beaches await visitors to the mouth of Chesapeake Bay region.

The **Fort Story Beach**, which is open to the public from Friday through Monday, is located at the northern end of the resort area inside Fort Story (*see* page 32). The wide, fairly remote beach has free parking and a portable toilet. Lifeguards are on duty during summer months.

The beaches of the Chesapeake Bay, with their gentle waves and smaller crowds, are an excellent place to introduce young children to the ocean or to launch kayaks and sailboats. First Landing State Park (*see* page 30) has a beach on the bay off Shore Drive (US 60), just west of Fort Story. There is also a ranger station and restroom here. **Chesapeake Beach** [Fig. 6(12)] is located on the bay side of Shore Drive between the Chesapeake Bay Bridge-Tunnel (US 13) and Fort Story. One of the best places to access it is just west of the Lesner Bridge, where Shore Drive crosses Lynnhaven Inlet. Park on the side streets and walk across the dune. **Chick's Beach Sailing Center** (757-460-2238) at 3716 Shore Drive is on the northwest side of the Lesner Bridge.

RESTAURANTS IN VIRGINIA BEACH

Fresh oysters, crabs, shrimp, striped bass, flounder, spot, and trout are highlights at Virginia Beach restaurants. Here are a few suggestions of popular places to eat:

ALEXANDER'S ON THE BAY. 4536 Ocean View Avenue, Virginia Beach. The menu at this upscale restaurant features Cape Henry rockfish, seafood Madagascar, blackened tuna, and Cajun scallops Provencal. Views are of the Chesapeake Bay and bridge-tunnel. *Moderate to expensive. Phone (757) 464-4999.*

CROC'S MIGHTY NICE GRILL. 19th Street and Cypress Avenue, Virginia Beach. On the menu are seafood, pastas, sandwiches, and other items in keeping with the Caribbean theme such as red baby back ribs, bayou pasta, and catfish cutter. Kids' meals. *Moderate to expensive. Phone (757) 428-5444.*

THE HAPPY CRAB RESTAURANT AND OYSTER SHUCKING BAR. 550 Laskin Road, Virginia Beach. Seafood items include crabs, scallops, oysters, clams, and shrimp. Located on Little Neck Creek. Reservations are recommended. Casual. *Moderate to expensive. Phone (757) 437-9200.*

HOT TUNA. 2817 Shore Drive, Virginia Beach. This restaurant specializes in fresh yellowfin tuna, black Angus beef, and pasta dishes. Local entertainment. Recommended by *Southern Living Magazine* and voted first place by the local Choice Awards. *Moderate. Phone (757) 481-2888.*

II GIARDINO RISTORANTE. 910 Atlantic Avenue, Virginia Beach. Upscale, beautifully decorated Italian restaurant in the resort area, known for its variety, service, and sumptuous dessert cart. Open-air cafe. Piano bar. *Moderate. Phone (757) 422-6464.*

RUDEE'S RESTAURANT & RAW BAR. 227 Mediterranean Avenue, Virginia Beach. Housed in a replica of a Coast Guard station, this casual restaurant overlooks busy Rudee Inlet on the southern end of the resort area. Open year-round. *Moderate. Phone (757) 425-1777.*

LODGING IN VIRGINIA BEACH

There's no easier place to find lodging than Virginia Beach, with its 11,000 hotel rooms, as well as rental cottages, bed and breakfast inns, and campgrounds. On Sandbridge Beach, Siebert Realty (800-231-3037) and Sandbridge Realty (800-933-4800) manage most of the rental cottages. Two services handle reservations for Virginia Beach motels and hotels: City of Virginia Beach Reservations (800-VA BEACH), and Virginia Beach Central Reservations (800-ROOMS VB).

BLUE MARLIN MOTEL. 2211 Pacific Avenue, Virginia Beach. Located in the resort area. Outdoor pool, bicycles. Children free. *Inexpensive to moderate. Phone (800) 643-3230.*

CAPTAINS QUARTERS RESORT HOTEL. 304 28th Street, Virginia Beach. Located in the resort area. Outdoor pool, hot tub/Jacuzzi, bicycles. *Expensive. Phone (800) 333-6020.*

COLONIAL INN. 29th Street and Atlantic Avenue, Virginia Beach. Located in the resort area. Pool, hot tub/Jacuzzi/kiddie pool, oceanfront rooms with balconies available. Children free. *Moderate. Phone (800) 344-3342.*

DAYS INN OCEANFRONT. 32nd Street and Atlantic Avenue, Virginia Beach. Located in the resort area. Indoor pool, hot tub/Jacuzzi, game room. Oceanfront rooms with balconies are available. Children free. *Expensive. Phone (800) 292-3297.*

ECONO LODGE AT BAY BEACH. 2968 Shore Drive, Virginia Beach. Located on the Chesapeake Bay. Outdoor pool, tennis. Children free. *Moderate. Phone (800) 553-2666.*

OCEAN HOLIDAY HOTEL. 25th Street and Atlantic Avenue, Virginia Beach. Located in resort area. In-room Jacuzzi. *Expensive. Phone (800) 345-7263.*

RAMADA PLAZA RESORT. 57th Street and Atlantic Avenue, Virginia Beach. Oceanfront. Outdoor and indoor pool, hot tub/Jacuzzi, bicycles, exercise room, pub. *Expensive. Phone (800) 365-3032.*

CAMPGROUNDS IN VIRGINIA BEACH

In addition to campgrounds at First Landing State Park and False Cape State Park, several private campgrounds are located in Virginia Beach.

HOLIDAY TRAV-L-PARK. 1075 General Booth Boulevard, Virginia Beach. 700 sites, hookups, 14 cabins, pool, restrooms/showers, camp store, playground. *Phone (800) 548-0223.*

NORTH BAY SHORE CAMPGROUND. 3257 Colchester Road, Virginia Beach. 165 sites, 4 cabins, hookups, pool, restrooms/showers, camp store, boat ramp, playground. *Phone (757) 426-7911.*

OUTDOOR RESORTS VIRGINIA BEACH RV RESORT. 3655 South Sandpiper Road, Virginia Beach. 250 sites, hookups, pool, restrooms/showers, boat ramp, tennis court. *Phone (800) 333-7515.*

VIRGINIA BEACH KOA CAMPGROUND. 1240 General Booth Boulevard, Virginia Beach. 497 sites, hookups, 13 cabins, pool, restrooms/showers, camp store, playground. *Phone (800) 562-4150.*

Hampton Roads Area

Hampton Roads is the name for the waters where the James River, the Nansemond River, and the Elizabeth River meet the Chesapeake Bay. Oil tankers and container ships, as well as vessels from around the world importing goods such as cocoa beans and rubber, visit the busy ports at Norfolk, Portsmouth, and Newport News. Long trains bearing coal from the mountains of western Virginia and West Virginia rumble to Hampton Roads, where the black gold is put on ships for export.

In addition to being one of the world's foremost deep-water harbors and trading centers, Hampton Roads has been a strategic location for war maneuvers from the Revolutionary War to present times. The proximity of the excellent harbor to the Atlantic has helped Hampton Roads acquire bases of every branch of the military, as well as the world's largest concentration of naval operations. Private shipbuilders, who hire thousands of workers, help keep the local economy strong. Many area museums are dedicated to preserving the marine, shipbuilding, and naval history.

Engineers have designed nine underwater tunnels to allow ships to pass over auto traffic, making Hampton Roads second only to Japan as the world leader in underwater tunnels.

In the Hampton Roads area are the cities of Norfolk, Portsmouth, Suffolk, and Chesapeake to the south and Hampton and Newport News to the north. Suffolk, with 430 square miles, is Virginia's largest city in landmass. Peanut farms occupy much of the land, and give Suffolk its nickname, Peanut Capital of the World. The aroma of peanuts roasting in large processing plants is one of the side benefits of visiting Suffolk.

Anglers, boaters, canoeists, and wildlife observers can find plenty of recreational opportunities in Suffolk and Chesapeake. Several tributaries of the Nansemond River in Suffolk have been dammed to form water supplies and fishing lakes, including **Western Branch Reservoir**, **Lake Prince**, **Lake Cohoon**, **Lake Meade**, and **Lake Kilby**. The Virginia Department of Game and Inland Fisheries (804-539-62160) manages them for largemouth bass, striped bass, crappie, chain pickerel, bluegill, redear sunfish, white perch, and yellow perch. The Intracoastal Waterway (*see* page 47) flows through Chesapeake. Also, a portion of the beautiful North Landing River Natural Area Preserve (*see* page 38), including a canoe trail and observation tower on Pocaty Creek, are in Chesapeake. **Northwest River Park** (757-421-3145) on the Northwest River in southern Chesapeake offers camping and a boat launch on the Northwest River.

Suffolk, Chesapeake, and the State of North Carolina share the **Great Dismal Swamp National Wildlife Refuge** (757-986-3705). The refuge [Fig. 6] is comprised of nearly 107,000 acres of forested wetlands with 3,000-acre Lake Drummond at the heart of the swamp. Black bear, bobcat, white-tailed deer, red and gray foxes, raccoon, and mink make use of the swamp, as do some 200 species of birds and 58 species of turtles, lizards, salamanders, frogs, and toads.

Visitors to the Great Dismal may hike or bike the unpaved roads or follow the Boardwalk Trail on Washington Ditch Road about 1 mile through the swamp. Fishing and boating are allowed all year on Lake Drummond. A public boat ramp is located on the north side of the Feeder Ditch, which connects Lake Drummond with the Dismal Swamp Canal and US 17 on the east side of the refuge. The refuge headquarters is located on the western side of the swamp, south of Suffolk. Heading south from Suffolk's downtown area on US 13, bear left on VA 32, go south for 4.5 miles, and follow signs.

Stargazers will want to take in the **Chesapeake Planetarium** (757-547-0153) at 300 Cedar Road, next to the city hall. The planetarium, which is operated by the Chesapeake School District, attracts some 40,000 visitors annually. Reservations are recommended for the hour-long show at 8 p.m. on Thursdays.

For more information: Virginia Waterfront (regional tourism information for area from Williamsburg to Virginia Beach), c/o City of Norfolk, 232 East Main Street, Norfolk, VA 23510. Phone (800) FUN-IN-VA. Hampton Roads Chamber of Commerce, 1001 West Washington Street, Suffolk, VA 23434, phone (757) 539-2111, and 400 Volvo Parkway, Chesapeake, VA 23320, phone (757) 547-2118. Also, see sections on Norfolk, Hampton, and Newport News for other information.

Norfolk Area

As travelers on I-64 emerge from the tunnel to the bridge of the Hampton Roads Bridge-Tunnel on their way to Norfolk and Virginia Beach, huge tankers and Navy ships come into view in the waters of Hampton Roads. To the south are giant destroyers, submarines, and aircraft carriers at the **Norfolk Naval Station** (757-444-7955), the world's largest Navy base, which offers guided tours on a daily basis. The base is located at the western end of I-564 and the northern end of VA 337 (Hampton Boulevard).

Where the bridge-tunnel joins the mainland at Norfolk, US 60 and I-64 diverge. US 60 becomes Ocean View Avenue, tracing Norfolk's northern border as it passes through **Ocean View** along the Chesapeake Bay. Ocean View has 7 miles of wide beaches fronting on the gently lapping waters of the Chesapeake Bay. Hotels, motels, efficiencies, rental cottages, and seafood restaurants line the waterfront. Though Ocean View is not as plush as the resort area of Virginia Beach and not as modernized as Norfolk's downtown, many families prefer the less-populated beach and smaller waves for boating, swimming, and windsurfing. Restrooms are placed at intervals along the beach.

On Sunday evenings in the summer, families bring their children for the free Big Bands on the Bay concerts at **Ocean View Park**. The soothing surf and the fading play of light on the bay water enhance the band music and other performances at the park gazebo. The 6.5-acre park has a beach with a boardwalk and restrooms. Lifeguards are on duty during summer months.

I-64 heads generally south through Norfolk, with connections to the downtown area, as well as to other Norfolk attractions and to Virginia Beach. In recent years, Norfolk's downtown harbor area at the mouth of the Elizabeth River has undergone a renaissance. Gleaming theaters and museums, giant shopping and entertainment facilities, and high-rise hotels have replaced deteriorating warehouses and weed-choked vacant lots. The $52-million National Maritime Center called Nauticus (*see* page xx) represents the grand style in which this 300-year-old port city has embraced the future while celebrating its maritime history.

Many visitors come to shop, dine on the waterfront, or enjoy night life or special events at **The Waterside** (757-627-3300) at 333 Waterside Drive. The reflections of the lights on the Elizabeth River are mesmerizing as tugboats, sailboats, cruise boats, and Navy ships pass by. Hours are 10 to 9 Monday through Saturday and 12 to 6 on Sunday. Most restaurants and nightclubs are open until 2 a.m. except on Sundays. The Waterside operates its own visitor information center (757-622-3602) Tuesdays through Saturdays. The office, located on the first floor, is stocked with maps and brochures on the Norfolk area. An entertaining film highlights Norfolk's history.

Several exciting boat cruises depart daily from The Waterside from late spring to fall. These include tall ship cruises aboard the **American Rover** (757-627-SAIL), trips on the Mississippi-style paddle wheeler, **Carrie B** (757-393-4735), and dining and dancing excursions on the **Spirit of Norfolk** (757-627-7771).

Also, the **Elizabeth River Ferry** (757-640-6300) takes pedestrians year-round from The Waterside in Norfolk across the Elizabeth River to Portsmouth. The ferry docks at North Landing in the **Portsmouth Olde Town Historic District**, which contains in a single square mile one of Virginia's largest collections of antique homes. Architectural styles include Colonial, Federal, Greek Revival, Georgian, and Victorian. A walking tour of the district, which takes about an hour, encompasses 300 years of American history. Sites include the **Lightship Museum**, the **Arts Center**, the **Children's Museum**, and the **Virginia Sports Hall of Fame and Museum**.

HarborLink (757-722-9400), a fast ferry passenger service between Norfolk and Hampton, docks at Waterside Drive next to Nauticus (for more information, *see* page 58). The **Naval Shipyard Museum** (757-393-8591) at 2 High Street in Portsmouth offers the chance to learn what goes on at the nearby U.S. Naval Shipyard. The shipyard is the oldest in the country and one of the largest employers in the area. For a brochure on the Portsmouth walking tour, call (757) 393-5111 or (800) PORTS-VA.

From Memorial Day to Labor Day, **Norfolk Trolley Tours** (757-540-6300) provides a one-hour narrated round trip from The Waterside to many of Norfolk's most celebrated sites. You can stop at the places that interest you and catch a later trolley back. Included on the route are such attractions as the **Norfolk Naval Base** (757-444-7955), the world-renowned Tiffany glass collection at the **Chrysler Museum of Art** (757-664-6200), the museum and theater of the **Douglas MacArthur Memorial** (757-441-2965), **St. Paul's Episcopal Church** (757-627-4353) where a Revolutionary War cannonball is lodged in the wall, and **Historic Ghent** where you can stroll old streets lined with interesting boutiques, cafes, and formal gardens.

In 1999, the $300-million **MacArthur Center** (757-627-6000) opened just a few blocks from the waterfront in downtown Norfolk. A 70-foot-high atrium is the centerpiece, surrounded by Nordstrom, Dillard's, and 150 other stores, restaurants, and cafes with outdoor tables. An 18-screen theater complex offers a tremendous variety of movies. Brochures are available at the center for nearby sites and for walking tours of Norfolk's **Historic District,** beginning at the center.

Enjoy AAA baseball at **Norfolk Tides' Harbor Park** (757-622-2222), which is within walking distance of the downtown covered garage in the 200 block of East Main Street. The Norfolk Tides are an AAA affiliate of the New York Mets. Summer in downtown Norfolk also brings musical performances and special events to **Town Point Park**, which is located on the Elizabeth River next to The Waterside. Major events include Harborfest, Art Explosure, and First Night Norfolk. Call Norfolk Festevents at (757) 441-2345 for more information.

Norfolk is rich with the performing arts. Broadway shows are produced at **Chrysler Hall** (757-664-6464). The nationally acclaimed **Virginia Opera** stages five productions annually at the **Harrison Opera House** (757-623-1223). Also, the **Virginia Symphony** (757-623-2310) performs more than 140 concerts a year in the Tidewater area. The 31-day Virginia Waterfront International Arts Festival, held at waterfront locations in the Norfolk area annually from early April into May, features both local and touring symphony orchestras, ballet groups, opera companies, jazz musicians, world-class instrumentalists and vocalists, and more.

Norfolk is a participant in the **Civil War Trails** program linking more than 200 Civil War sites in Virginia. Sites in Norfolk, designated by Civil War Trails signs, include **Fort Norfolk**, the **Historic Freemason District**, and the **Civil War Memorial** commemorating black Union troops. You can begin the tour wherever you see a sign. Brochures are available at information centers.

Mile Zero of the Atlantic Intracoastal Waterway is in Norfolk, marked by a flashing red buoy. The waterway, which stretches 1,095 miles from Norfolk to Miami, Florida, was created during the Roosevelt years to move goods up and down the Atlantic Seaboard. In recent years, however, the waterway has become important to recreational boaters as a scenic, protected route for cruising the coastline. "The Ditch," as it is whimsically called, follows inland sounds and rivers in what is the most extensive system of inland waterways in the country. The U.S. Army Corps of Engineers maintains it.

The Virginia portion of the Intracoastal Waterway follows the Elizabeth River inland and southward between Portsmouth and Chesapeake, then turns sharply eastward in a straight canal that connects with the North Landing River. It follows the North Landing River southward through The Nature Conservancy's North Landing River Preserve (*see* page 38) into North Carolina.

Directions: Norfolk Visitor Information Centers (800-368-3097) operated by the Norfolk Convention and Visitors Bureau are at three locations. The first (757-441-1852) is in the Ocean View area just off Exit 273 of I-64, which is the second exit after coming to Norfolk on the Hampton Roads Bridge Tunnel. (Tip: The Monkey Bottom Walkway at the center, which leads out over Chesapeake Bay wetlands, provides a nice break from driving.) A second center is located on the downtown waterfront at Nauticus, the National Maritime Center (757-664-1009), at 1 Waterside Drive. A third location (757-664-6620), also downtown, is at 232 East Main Street under the Main Street Parking Garage.

The **Portsmouth Convention and Visitors Bureau** (757-393-5327 or 800-PORTS-VA) has its main office at 505 Crawford Street in Portsmouth. The bureau also operates the Visitor Information Center (757-393-5111) at North Landing, 6 Crawford Parkway, where the ferry from Norfolk docks.

The **Waterside Information Center** (757-622-3602) is on the first floor of The Waterside at 333 East Main Street.

Dates: Norfolk Visitor Information Centers are open at Ocean View from 9 to 5 daily, year-round; at Nauticus from 10 to 7 daily from Memorial Day through Labor Day and from 10 to 5 daily except Mondays during the rest of the year; and at 232 East Main Street from 8:30 to 5 Monday through Friday, year-round. The Waterside Information Center is open from 10 to 6 Tuesday through Saturday from mid-Apr. through fall and from 10 to 2 during winter. The Portsmouth Visitor Information Center at North Landing is open daily, year-round, except for Christmas and New Year's Day.

For more information: Norfolk Visitor Information Centers, 1 Waterside Drive, Norfolk, VA 23510. Phone (800) 368-3097. Web site www.norfolk.va.us/tourism. Virginia Waterfront International Arts Festival, 232 East Main Street, Norfolk, VA 23514. Phone (757) 664-6492. Web site www.virginiaartsfest.com. Portsmouth Visitor Information Center, 6 Crawford Parkway (North Landing), Portsmouth, VA 23704. Phone (757) 393-5111. Portsmouth Convention and Visitors Bureau, 505 Crawford Street, Portsmouth, VA 23704. Phone (757) 393-5327 or (800) PORTS-VA. Web site www.ci.portsmouth.va.us. E-mail portscvb@ci.portsmouth.va.us.

FISHING AND BOATING IN THE NORFOLK AREA.

Pier fishing, tackle, and charter fishing boats are available at **Harrison Boat House and Pier** (757-587-9630) at 414 West Ocean View Avenue and at **Willoughby Bay Marina** (757-588-2663) at 1651 Bayville Street. Both facilities are near the eastern end of the Hampton Roads Bridge-Tunnel. For information on public boat ramps, contact the City of Norfolk's Facility Maintenance Department at (757) 625-2000.

NORFOLK BOTANICAL GARDEN

[Fig. 6(16)] Next to the busy Norfolk International Airport is a tranquil oasis that contains some of the largest collections of azaleas, camellias, roses, and rhododendrons on the eastern seaboard. The Norfolk Botanical Garden has 12 miles of quiet pathways that wind from one sun-dappled visual smorgasbord of trees, shrubs, and flowers to another.

At the park entrance is Lake Whitehurst, where wintering waterfowl and spring nesting ducks and geese make it hard for motorists on the causeway to keep their eyes on the road. Just inside the park gates, though, you can pull over into the picnic area on the left and get out the camera to photograph long-legged wading birds or maybe ducklings or goslings that are already learning to beg for breadcrumbs. The sprawling lake, which nearly encircles the botanical garden, also has a fishing pier. Don't forget your fishing license.

The next treat is Baker Hall Visitor Center, with nearly 12,000 feet of sunlit space beneath a magnificent atrium. Here, visitors can learn about the garden, buy tickets for tram and boat rides, and check out the gift shop.

Norfolk Botanical Garden: What is Blooming When?

January: Sasanqua camellias, witch hazel.
February: Wintersweet, nandina, pyracantha.
March: Camellias, daffodils, pieris japonica, magnolias.
April: Tulips, azaleas, dogwoods.
May: Rhododendrons, roses, azaleas.
June: Oleander, hydrangea, day lilies, roses.
July: Crape myrtle, annuals, hibiscus.
August-September: Annuals, roses, crape myrtle.
October-December: Roses, camellias, wintersweet.

The 155 acres of the garden are lovely in any season. A young couple in spring, after passing through the flowering arboretum, breathes air sweetened by a quarter-million roses at the peak of bloom in the Bicentennial Rose Garden.

Aerobic walkers in summer inhale the heady aroma from the Fragrance Garden. An office worker needing a break on a crisp fall day can wander by the tranquil Japanese Garden, pause to watch migrating butterflies in the English Border Garden, and climb the steps for the panoramic view from the Hill of Nations Observation Tower.

Even in winter, when new life waits beneath the soil for spring, there is color in the climate-controlled Tropical Pavilion, where rain forest vegetation and colorful plants from the equatorial regions of the world flourish. Outside the pavilion, evergreens, camellias, witch hazel, and other hardy plants defy the elements.

From spring through summer, tour boats glide beneath stone archways and past quiet pools with multicolored, watery reflections of hydrangea, day lilies, and cascading roses. Trackless trains offer another way to tour the gardens from spring into fall.

The garden has become well known for the International Azalea Festival each spring, which puts a visual end to winter with a vivid display of color. For the two weekends preceding Halloween, the Vietnam veterans host a Haunted Forest (advance tickets required). Also, each evening between Thanksgiving and New Year's Day, you can drive through the garden for the stunning Garden of Lights display.

Workshops for adults and children are held on a tremendous variety of subjects, such as medicinal plants, native plants, water gardening, attracting butterflies, tough plants for tough sites, perennial favorites, and spring pruning.

Directions: From I-64 in Norfolk, take Exit 279 north onto Norview Avenue. Go about 1 mile and turn left on Azalea Garden Road. Go about 0.5 mile and turn right at the garden entrance.

Activities: Walking, picnicking, tram rides, boat tours, fishing.

Facilities: Paved walking paths, observation tower, tour boats and trams, cafe, gift shop, visitor center, restrooms.

Dates: Open daily, 9 to 7 from Apr. 15 to Oct. 15 and 9 to 5 from Oct. 16 to Apr. 14. Tram tours, 10 to 4, mid-Mar. through Oct. Boat tours, 10 to 4, Apr. through Sept.

Fees: There are fees for admission, tram and boat rides, the Haunted Forest event, and the holiday lighting tour.

Closest town: The garden is in Norfolk.

For more information: Norfolk Botanical Garden, 6700 Azalea Garden Road, Norfolk, VA 23518. Phone (757) 441-5830.

THE VIRGINIA ZOOLOGICAL PARK

[Fig. 6(17)] Children especially love the 53-acre zoo situated on the Lafayette River in Norfolk. On the grounds are some 350 animals, ranging from such common species as white-tailed deer (*Odocioleus virgianus*) and red-tailed hawks (*Buteo jamaicensis*) to endangered species such as Siberian tigers (*Panthera tigris altaica*) and white rhinos (*Ceratotherium simum simum*).

The exhibits of primates, including spider monkeys (*Ateles geoffroyi*) and gibbons (*Hylobates lar*) always draw a crowd. But the two-toed sloth (*Choloepus didactylus*), which appears to move through the trees in slow motion, and Bennett's wallaby (*Macropus rufogriseus*), a southeastern Australia cousin of the kangaroo, also fascinate both children and adults.

One of the zoo's newest additions, part of an expansion and modernization, is a 10-acre African Okavango river delta exhibit with a Xaxaba Village. When the plan is completed, zoo animals will live in enlarged spaces with habitats more closely resembling their homes in the wild.

Directions: From I-64, Exit 276, go south on US 460 (Granby Street) about 3 miles to the park, on the left.

Activities: Walking zoo paths and (outside the zoo grounds) picnicking and playing on the playground.

Facilities: Concession stand, gift shop, restrooms, and (outside the zoo in Lafayette Park) picnic facilities and playground.

Dates: Open 10 to 5 daily, year-round, except major holidays.

Fees: There is an admission fee.

Closest town: The zoo is in Norfolk.

For more information: The Virginia Zoological Park, 3500 Granby Street, Norfolk, VA 23504. Phone (757) 441-2706.

NAUTICUS, THE NATIONAL MARITIME CENTER

[Fig. 6(18)] The 120,000-square-foot Nauticus, the National Maritime Center, is in an impressive building that rises from Norfolk's downtown waterfront looking like a giant ship. Outside the structure is a 600-foot deep-water pier where U.S. Navy, foreign, and commercial vessels dock and allow visitors to tour on weekends. Working boats such as the Norfolk skipjack and the Huntington tugboat are exhibited. Inside is a host of computer and video interactive projects on subjects including navigation, a sonar sub hunt, time travel, and reef diving.

A multimedia naval battle is an attraction in the Aegis Theater, while the Academy-Award-nominated *The Living Sea* shows on a wide screen in the Nauticus Theater. At the touch tanks, children and adults can dip an arm into the water to stroke live sharks, starfish, and horseshoe crabs.

The Hampton Roads Naval Museum is part of Nauticus. The museum tour explains the naval history of Hampton Roads, beginning with the Battle off the Capes in 1781, progressing through the Civil War battle of the ironclads, then the Battle of the Atlantic in World War II, and culminating in exhibits about today's U.S. Navy.

Directions: From I-64 in Norfolk, take Exit 284 to west I-264 to the Waterside Drive Exit.

Facilities: More than 150 hands-on activities, virtual adventures, naval museum, lunch galley, gift shop, restrooms.

Dates: Open from 10 to 5 daily, Memorial Day through Labor Day. Open 10 to 5 Tuesday through Saturday and 12 to 5 Sunday the remainder of year except Thanksgiving, Christmas, and New Year's Day.

Fees: There is an admission fee.

Closest town: Nauticus is located on the downtown waterfront in Norfolk.

For more information: Nauticus, The National Maritime Center, 1 Waterside Drive, Norfolk, VA 23510. Phone (800) 664-1080 or (757) 664-1000. Web site www.nauticus.org. Hampton Roads Naval Museum, 1 Waterside Drive, Norfolk, VA 23510. Phone (757) 444-8971 or (757) 445-1867.

RESTAURANTS IN THE NORFOLK AREA

Norfolk restaurant cuisine is influenced not only by the proximity to the Chesapeake Bay and Atlantic Ocean, but also by the many servicemen stationed here, as well as by patronage by visitors from abroad. Here is a list of some of Norfolk's many fine restaurants.

FISHERMAN'S WHARF. 1571 Bayville Street, Norfolk. Watch boats bringing the catch of the day into the Hampton Roads Harbor while you sample the huge seafood buffet. Serves lunch Tuesday through Saturday and dinner nightly. *Moderate to expensive. Phone (757) 480-3113.*

FREEMASON ABBEY. 209 West Freemason Street, Norfolk. Fresh lobster, pasta, fish, other seafood, and prime rib are on the menu at this unusual restaurant in a

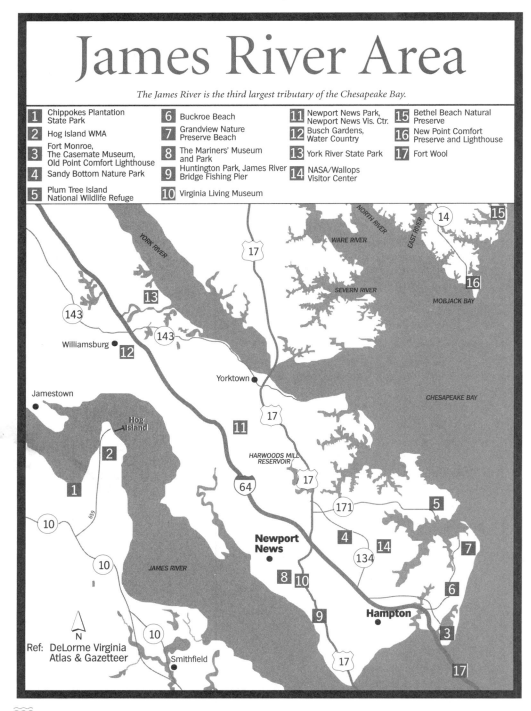

James River Area

The James River is the third largest tributary of the Chesapeake Bay.

1. Chippokes Plantation State Park
2. Hog Island WMA
3. Fort Monroe, The Casemate Museum, Old Point Comfort Lighthouse
4. Sandy Bottom Nature Park
5. Plum Tree Island National Wildlife Refuge
6. Buckroe Beach
7. Grandview Nature Preserve Beach
8. The Mariners' Museum and Park
9. Huntington Park, James River Bridge Fishing Pier
10. Virginia Living Museum
11. Newport News Park, Newport News Vis. Ctr.
12. Busch Gardens, Water Country
13. York River State Park
14. NASA/Wallops Visitor Center
15. Bethel Beach Natural Preserve
16. New Point Comfort Preserve and Lighthouse
17. Fort Wool

Ref: DeLorme Virginia Atlas & Gazetteer

126-year-old renovated church in the Freemason Harbor area. *Inexpensive to moderate. Phone (757) 622-3966.*

GREEN TREES CAFE. 112 Bank Street, Norfolk. Soup and sandwich menu. Outdoor patio. Lunch on weekdays, dinner on Wednesday through Saturday. *Inexpensive. Phone (757) 625-7041.*

SHIPS CABIN. 4110 East Ocean View Avenue at Shore Drive, Norfolk. Fireplace for winter dining, outdoor deck overlooking the Chesapeake Bay for summer visitors. The menu includes Cajun shrimp and crab cakes, oysters bingo, blackened tuna, grilled rockfish. *Inexpensive to moderate. Phone (757) 362-4659.*

WILD MONKEY. 1603 Colley Avenue, Norfolk. Sample the American, Indian, European, and Asian dishes at this popular Ghent restaurant. Lunch on weekdays, dinner on Monday through Saturday. *Inexpensive to moderate. Phone (757) 627-6462.*

LODGING IN THE NORFOLK AREA

Lodging tends to be centered around the Ocean View area, where Norfolk fronts the Chesapeake Bay, and in the historic downtown area. **Chesapeake Campground** (757-485-0149) at 693 South George Washington Highway in Chesapeake is located on the Intracoastal Waterway, 2 miles south of the drawbridge in Deep Creek on US 17.

BIANCA BOAT AND BREAKFAST. 10 Crawford Parkway, Portsmouth. Spend two nights aboard a yacht. The 43-foot motor sailor is docked at Portsmouth's Olde Towne Historic District, a 10-minute ferry ride from Norfolk's downtown. *Expensive. Phone (757) 625-5033 or (800) 695-1487. E-mail innkeeper@pagehouseinn.com.*

NORFOLK MARRIOTT WATERSIDE. 235 East Main Street, Norfolk. A 23-story hotel convenient to downtown attractions. Pool, two restaurants, lounge. *Moderate to expensive. Phone (757) 627-4200 or (800) 228-9290.*

PAGE HOUSE INN. 323 Fairfax Avenue, Norfolk. Renovated Georgian-Revival manse in the Ghent Historic District. Gourmet food. *Expensive. Phone (757) 625-5033 or (800) 695-1487. E-mail innkeeper@pagehouseinn.com.*

TIDES INN. 7950 Shore Drive, Norfolk. Located in the Ocean View area near naval bases, golf courses, and a marina, and 15 minutes from Virginia Beach. Pool. *Inexpensive to moderate. Phone (757) 587-8781 or (800) 284-3035.*

James River

[Fig. 7] The James River is the third largest tributary of the Chesapeake Bay. The watershed is huge, beginning 343 miles to the west. The mighty James starts as a trickle in Virginia's Allegheny Mountains, gains enough strength to carve a formidable gorge through the mountains of the Blue Ridge, and surges over a series of falls at Richmond, where it becomes tidal.

Early explorers noted that the river had paved the way west for them. They used it for transportation, dammed it for power, and built an impressive length of canal beside it in an attempt to join the east side of the Alleghenies to the Mississippi River system. Now many of the old dams are being breached or destroyed to allow anadromous fish such as shad and herring once again to follow their ancestral paths upstream to spawn. The canal system was abandoned after being damaged by war and replaced by railroads.

The James is important to Virginia's history. The first settlers came up the river, establishing their colony on Jamestown Island. Many prosperous plantations sprang up along the riverbanks and people used the river to export crops and obtain necessities. The river was deep enough for ships to go 170 miles inland, taking supplies all the way to Richmond. Military commanders have used the river to transport troops and supplies in wartime, while anglers, boaters, and sunbathers have found more peaceful ways to enjoy the river.

Noted for its healthy largemouth bass population, the lower James River has enticed the Bass Anglers Sportsman's Society (BASS) to hold the annual BASS Classic national fishing tournament on the river for an unprecedented three years.

🟦 RAGGED ISLAND WILDLIFE MANAGEMENT AREA

[Fig. 6(19)] The 1,537 acres of unspoiled brackish marsh and small pine islands at Ragged Island Wildlife Management Area are open to bird watchers, hikers, fishermen, and photographers. Nothing but the James River separates the wild marshes and uplands from the busy downtown areas of Newport News and Hampton. But even though it's a neighbor to metropolitan Tidewater, Ragged Island is so teeming with life that it has been designated a Watchable Wildlife Area.

On higher ground are loblolly pine forests with areas of wax myrtle understory made practically impenetrable by greenbriar tangles. White-tailed deer, raccoon,

WHITE-TAILED DEER
(Odocoileus virginianus)
The whitetail, once almost extirpated in the midwest and atlantic states, has rebounded and is now the most abundant large game animal in the east.

rabbit, red fox, and gray squirrel inhabit these forests. A quiet approach on foot or by boat may flush waterfowl such as black ducks, mallards, scaup, gadwall, ruddy ducks, buffleheads, and goldeneyes from a pond or creek. A boardwalk and interpretive trail financed by the Nongame Wildlife and Endangered Species Program leads over wetlands of saltmarsh cordgrass, marsh mallow, smartweed, and black needlerush where the clapper rail hides.

Typical fish species of the salty lower James such as bluefish, gray trout, spot, croaker, flounder, and striped bass provide seasonal action for anglers. Across the James River Bridge from the area is a public fishing pier.

Directions: The area lies west of Newport News in Isle of Wight County on the southwestern side of the James River Bridge. It is dissected by US 17 (which is also US 258 and VA 32). There are two parking areas on the southeastern side of US 17. The interpretive trail, boardwalk, and viewing platform start on the parking lot that is closest to the river.

Activities: Wildlife observation, boating, seasonal hunting and fishing.

Facilities: Interpretive signs and trail, boardwalk, viewing platform, nearby fishing pier.

Dates: The area is open from sunrise to sunset, year-round.

Fees: None.

Closest town: Newport News is 5.7 miles across the James River.

For more information: Ragged Island Wildlife Management Area, Virginia Department of Game and Inland Fisheries, Region I, 5806 Mooretown Road, Williamsburg, VA 23118. Phone (757) 253-7072.

CHIPPOKES PLANTATION STATE PARK

[Fig. 7(1)] Chippokes Plantation, located on the James River in Surry County, has been continually farmed since 1619—longer than any other farm in America. The plantation was named for an Indian chief who was friendly to the early settlers.

Chippokes Plantation State Park incorporates the plantation croplands, quiet gardens, and spacious lawns surrounding the Chippokes mansion. Tours of this restored antebellum mansion, circa 1854, are held at various times throughout the year, including the Christmas season.

Paved trails are available for hikers and bikers. Two trails—the 1.3-mile (one-way) College Run Trail and the 0.9-mile (one-way) James River Trail—lead to the tidal James River from the mansion parking lot. The 1-mile (one way) Lower Chippokes Creek Trail connects the mansion with Lower Chippokes Creek, a James River tributary. The park also has a farm and forestry museum with five exhibit buildings where antique farm and forestry equipment, tools, and housewares are on display.

The new campground and cabins are especially welcome additions at Chippokes, as places to stay in Surry County are practically nonexistent. Also, the historic **Jamestown Ferry** (800-VA-FERRY) will transport cars and people across the James from Surry County to Jamestown, where there are abundant campgrounds and lodging facilities. The ferry terminus at Scotland, on the Chippokes side, is on VA 31, 4 miles north of Surry and 9 miles west of the park. Four ferries, including the *Pocahontas*, the *Williamsburg*, the *Surry*, and the *Virginia*, operate 24 hours a day, year-round.

Special events highlight various facets of the park's history annually. They include Historic Garden Week in April, the Steam and Gas Engine Show in June, the Fall Crafts Festival in November, and Christmas at Chippokes in December. And in July, the very popular Pork, Peanut, and Pine Festival attracts thousands to eat pork barbecue and peanut pie, go on hay rides, shop for crafts, and check out antique farm equipment in celebration of Surry County's famous industries.

Directions: From Surry, go east on VA 10 for 2 miles. Turn left on VA 634 and go about 3.5 miles to the entrance, on the left.

Activities: Camping, hiking, biking, picnicking, swimming, canoe trips, mansion tours, museum tours, and hunting (by reservation and lottery).

Facilities: Visitor center, formal gardens, restored mansion, farm and forestry museum, rental cottages, campground, pool, snack bar, hiking/biking trails, picnic shelters, two gift shops.

Dates: The grounds are open from 8 a.m. to dusk daily, year-round. Call for hours of mansion, museum, tours, and pool, which may vary.

Fees: There are fees for parking, for touring mansion and museum, and for cabins and campgrounds.

Closest town: Surry is about 5.5 miles west.

For more information: Chippokes State Park, 695 Chippokes Park Road, Surry, VA 23883. Phone (757) 294-3625. Farm and Forestry Museum, phone (757) 294-3439.

HOG ISLAND WILDLIFE MANAGEMENT AREA

[Fig. 7(2)] This state wildlife management area is a 3,908-acre mix of pine forests, tidal marshes, managed ponds, planted fields, and flat, open land on a peninsula formed by a giant horseshoe bend in the tidal James. The area lies across the James River from Williamsburg along VA 650, beginning about 3 miles north of VA 10, between the towns of Smithfield and Surry.

The largest of the three tracts of land that make up the area is the Hog Island tract, located on the peninsula's tip. Nine parking areas line the road in the Hog Island Tract, where there are two wildlife viewing platforms and areas designated for fishing. The pine uplands of the Carlisle tract and the marshlands of the Stewart Tract are on the southeastern side of the peninsula. A boat ramp is at the far (eastern) end of the access road into the Carlisle tract. On the other side of Lawnes Creek from the boat ramp is the Stewart tract.

Bow fishing for carp is a popular springtime activity, and channel and blue catfish provide good eating during much of the year. Other activities include carefully controlled waterfowl hunts in addition to boating and seasonal hunting for deer, dove, quail, squirrel, rabbit, and turkey. Bird watchers may also see eagles and a wide variety of shorebirds.

Directions: From Surry, go about 7 miles southeast on VA 10. Turn left on VA 617 and go a little over 1 mile. Go left on VA 650 and drive about 2.5 miles to the access road to the Carlisle and Stewart tracts (on the right) or 4.5 miles to the Hog Island tract.

Activities: Seasonal hunting and fishing, boating, bird-watching.

Facilities: Two wildlife viewing platforms, boat ramp.

Dates: The area is open from dawn to dusk, year-round.

Fees: None.

Closest town: Surry is about 13 miles southwest of the Hog Island tract.

For more information: Virginia Department of Game and Inland Fisheries, Region I Office, 5806 Mooretown Road, Williamsburg, VA 23118. Phone (757) 253-7072.

Hampton

The city of Hampton wears more than one hat. It is considered an integral part of what is called Hampton Roads, where rivers converge at the mouth of the Chesapeake Bay. It's also part of Virginia's Lower Peninsula, sharing the southeastern tip of the peninsula with its neighbor, Newport News.

Many of Hampton's attractions are centered on three areas—the Coliseum area off I-64 Exit 263B, the downtown waterfront off I-64 Exit 267, and the Phoebus/Fort Monroe area off I-64 Exit 268. To explore Hampton by car, follow the blue Hampton Tour signs from the Hampton Visitor Center or wherever you see a sign.

The **Air Power Park** (757-727-1163) at 413 West Mercury Boulevard, in the Coliseum area in central Hampton, exhibits aircraft from the various military branches. Visitors can observe the wind tunnel exhibit, tour the outdoor air and spacecraft displays, and examine the model airplane collection. The park is free and open from 9 to 4 daily, year-round, except major holidays.

Visitors to Hampton's renovated waterfront district may feel transported to the seventeenth century as they stroll the cobblestone streets of this old seaport. Brick sidewalks and crape myrtle trees add their charm to the shops, pubs, art galleries, restaurants, and waterfront park. The waterfront is the site of the **Royal Customs House** where British ships once brought tea, spices, cloth, and other supplies for the colonists.

Several weekly events foster a party atmosphere in downtown Hampton from May through September. **Mill Point Park**, located at the eastern end of Queens Way on the waterfront, is the site of live rock music each Wednesday evening and live jazz on

Friday nights. The Saturday night **Block Party** at Queens Way features live Top 40 dance bands, street entertainers, and games.

The picturesque **Hampton Visitor Center** is also on the waterfront. It is located next to the Radisson Hotel at 710 Settlers Landing Road, on the western side of the Hampton River. A brochure of the self-guided **Downtown Hampton Walking Tour** is available here. In addition to providing brochures, maps, gift items, and an orientation video, the center is the departure point for the **Miss Hampton II Harbor Tours** and the **Venture Inn II** cruise and fishing boat.

Miss Hampton II Harbor Tours (888-757-BOAT or 757-722-9102) offers narrated cruises of the Hampton Roads harbor and the Chesapeake Bay. The tours aboard a double-decker boat last about three hours, beginning at 10 a.m. daily between April 12 and October 31. From Memorial Day through Labor Day, a second tour begins at 2 p.m. Sunset cruises, dinner cruises, and trips on the James River and Intracoastal Waterway are other options.

The charter yacht, *Venture Inn II* (757-850-8960), takes individuals and groups on saltwater fishing trips (bait and rods provided), whale-watching tours, eco-safaris, fall foliage cruises, and winter holiday tours. Hot food and snacks can be purchased at the onboard galley. The boat heads out of the bay into the Atlantic Ocean to search for whales from late December to March. Fishing in Hampton Roads, the Chesapeake Bay, and over ocean wrecks is available seasonally.

The Hampton Visitor Center is also on the route of the **Hampton Trolley** (757-826-6351 or 757-727-1271). The trolley connects the hotels and Hampton Coliseum to the downtown waterfront where the visitor center, various attractions, and the historic Queens Way district are located.

HarborLink (757-722-9400) is a fast ferry passenger service that opened in 1999 linking the waterfront attractions between Hampton and Norfolk with an entertaining 45-minute ride across Hampton Roads. From the upper and lower decks of the 90-foot luxury ferry, *M/V Zephyr*, passengers can enjoy refreshments while passing by Fort Wool, the U.S. Naval Base at Norfolk, and a submarine docking station.

On the Hampton side, the ferry docks at the public piers behind the Hampton Visitor Center, adjacent to the Radisson Hotel and the Virginia Air and Space Center. On the Norfolk side, the ferry docks on Waterside Drive adjacent to Nauticus. Inquire about combination tickets to the Virginia Air and Space Center and to Nauticus. The service operates daily, morning to evening, year-round, with extended hours during peak seasons. Tickets may be purchased onboard, at Nauticus, or at the Virginia Air and Space Center.

The **Virginia Air and Space Center** has more than 100 exhibits, which include a moon rock and a meteor from Mars. A giant IMAX theater shows realistic films about flight, exploration, and science. During the summer months, tours from the air and space center to NASA Langley Research Center are available. The **NASA Langley Motor Tour** lasts about 1.5 hours and includes the Lunar Landing Research Center and the NASA wind tunnel. The wind tunnel here will produce winds of an incredible 10,000 mph.

The NASCAR Winston Racing Series and ShorTrack Series draw racing fans to **Langley Speedway** (757-865-1100) on Saturday nights from March to October. The track is a 0.395-mile low-banked asphalt oval track located at 3165 North Armistead Avenue across from the NASA wind tunnel. The gates open at 2, qualifying for all divisions is at 5, and racing begins at 7.

The **Grandview Fishing Pier** (757-851-2811) at 54 South Bonita Drive and **Buckroe Beach Fishing Pier** (757-851-9146) at 330 South Resort Boulevard both extend into the Chesapeake Bay from Hampton's eastern shore. Spring, summer, and fall months brings croaker, flounder, pan trout, spot, and other fish within reach of pier anglers.

The Phoebus/Fort Monroe Area is on Hampton's eastern side. Phoebus was once an incorporated town that retains its unique character as a historic village. The community has a colorful past of Revolutionary War skirmishes, runaway slaves, watermen, railroads, resort hotels, soldiers, and saloons.

The American Theatre (757-727-ARTS), located in the Phoebus community, has undergone a $2 million renovation. The 1908 movie house now has a high-tech sound system, modern lighting, and new additions to help make it a center for the arts. Live theater, children's theater, classic movies, lectures, and concerts featuring international artists are in the plans for this upgraded facility.

Directions: For the Hampton Visitor Center, tour boats, fast ferry, and Virginia Air and Space Center, take Exit 267 (west) off I-64 and cross the bridge. The visitor center is on the left. (Follow the blue Hampton Tour signs.)

For more information: Hampton Visitor Center, 710 Settlers Landing Road, Hampton, VA 23669. Phone (800) 800-2202 or (757) 727-1102. Web site www.vgnet.com. Downtown Hampton Chamber of Commerce, 201 Lincoln Street, Hampton, VA 23669. Phone (757-727-1271). Virginia Air and Space Center, 600 Settlers Landing Road, Hampton, VA 23669. Phone (800) 296-0800 or (757) 727-0900. Web site www.vasc.org.

FORT WOOL/FORT MONROE/THE CASEMATE MUSEUM/OLD POINT COMFORT LIGHTHOUSE

[Fig. 7(3), 9(17)] Two companion forts guard the mouth of Hampton Roads— Fort Wool, which sits on a man-made island just east of the Hampton Roads Bridge Tunnel (I-64), and Fort Monroe, about 1 mile to the north on a Hampton peninsula called Old Point Comfort. People on private boats are allowed to disembark and explore the island where Fort Wool sits, now unused. Also, the cruise boat, *Miss Hampton II* (*see* page 58), makes stops at the island when weather permits.

Fort Monroe is the largest stone fort ever built in the country (it was under construction between 1819 and 1834) and the only U.S. Army fort still in use that is encircled by a moat. The star-shaped structure was built following the War of 1812, when ineffectual coastal defense allowed British ships to enter Hampton Roads and sail up the Chesapeake Bay to capture Washington, DC.

Robert E. Lee was stationed at the fort during its completion and Jefferson Davis, president of the Confederate States, was imprisoned in a casemate, or cell, after the Civil War ended. Visitors to the fort's Casemate Museum can see the cell where he was held. The fort tour includes weapons, uniforms, drawings by Frederick Remington, and the U.S. Army's Coast Artillery Museum. The Coast Artillery operated some of the largest weapons in military history at Fort Monroe between 1907 and 1946.

Also on the grounds of the fort is the well-kept Old Point Comfort Lighthouse. Work on the lighthouse was completed in 1802, making it the second oldest on the Chesapeake Bay. (The oldest is Cape Henry, completed in 1792.) A spiral staircase of hand-hewn stone inside the white tower rises 54 feet to the top, where there is a flashing red light. The lighthouse is listed on the National Register of Historic Places.

Directions: From I-64 at the western end of Hampton Roads Bridge-Tunnel, take Exit 268 onto VA 143 and go east just over 1 mile to Fort Monroe.

Dates: Open 10:30 to 4:30 daily, year-round, except major holidays.

Fees: None.

Closest town: The museum is located in Fort Monroe on the eastern side of Hampton.

For more information: Fort Monroe and the Casemate Museum, PO Box 341, Fort Monroe, VA 23651. Phone (757) 727-3391.

SANDY BOTTOM NATURE PARK

[Fig. 7(4)] This 456-acre nature park is an oasis in metropolitan Hampton/ Newport News. Exhibits at the impressive 10,000-square-foot nature center focus on such subjects as the waterfowl, birds of prey, river otter, turtles, deer, rabbits, and squirrels that hikers and bikers see on and around the lakes and park trails. Interpreters explain how the park—now an environmental education center and wildlife management facility—is like the mythical phoenix, rising from its own ashes.

The beautiful gardens, trails, and lakes were created from garbage dumps and mining pits. The park has a fishing pier, a small spring-fed fishing lake stocked with largemouth bass, catfish, crappie, and bream and a larger mile-long lake. Canoes, john boats, paddleboats, and bicycles are available for rent. Since only electric motors are allowed, no roaring bass boats or personal watercraft interrupt the tranquility of a lakeside picnic. A network of trails encircles the lakes and invites nature lovers to explore marsh, stream, and forest. A rehab area at the park is designed for treating injured wildlife.

Resident Canada geese and nesting or wintering waterfowl make use of the lakes and their perimeters. Beavers build dams on Newmarket Creek that separates Hampton from Newport News. Raccoons devise new ways to pilfer the bacon, eggs, and cheese from campers' breakfast coolers.

Directions: The park is located at 1255 Big Bethel Road in northwestern Hampton. From I-64, take Exit 261A onto Hampton Roads Center Parkway. Go right on Big Bethel Road. The park entrance is on the left.

Activities: Hiking, biking, fishing, boating (electric motors only), picnicking, camping (primitive).

Facilities: Two lakes, nature center with gift shop, gardens, picnic tables and shelters, playground, campground (no hookups), rental tent cabins, rental boats and bicycles.

Dates: The park is open from 8 a.m. to sunset, Tuesday through Sunday, year-round, except Christmas Day.

Fees: There are fees for camping, rental boats and bicycles, and rental shelters.

Closest town: The park is in northwestern Hampton.

For more information: Sandy Bottom Nature Park, 1255 Big Bethel Road, Hampton, VA 23666. Phone (757) 825-4657.

PLUM TREE ISLAND NATIONAL WILDLIFE REFUGE

[Fig. 7(5)] The Plum Tree Island National Wildlife Refuge is a winter refuge for wildfowl, a stopover for migrating ducks and geese, and an important nesting ground and nursery for many varieties of marshland birds. The refuge and adjacent privately owned marshlands of Big Salt Marsh in the bordering city of Poquoson make up the largest saline marsh in the lower Chesapeake Bay.

In the early 1900s, the U. S. Army Air Corps used the salt marsh as a bombing and gunnery range. Because of the danger of unexploded ordnance that may still lie buried in the marsh, people are not allowed to go into the interior portions of the refuge. However, anglers and bird watchers may boat around the edges, and may also

RACCOON
(Procyon lotor)

explore Cow Island, the small island on the northwest corner of the area. Boaters may reach the area by launching at the boat landing at the eastern end of VA 171 (Messick Road) in Poquoson. There are no facilities at the refuge, which is a satellite refuge of Back Bay National Wildlife Refuge.

Directions: From I-64 in Newport News, take Exit 256 and go east on VA 171 for about 10.3 miles to the boat landing at Messick Point. The eastern edge of the refuge lies to the northeast, across the small inlet.

Activities: Boating, fishing, bird-watching.

Facilities: Boat ramp.

Dates: The area is open from dawn to dusk, year-round.

Fees: None.

Closest town: Poquoson borders the area of the southern side.

For more information: Back Bay National Wildlife Refuge, PO Box 6286, Virginia Beach, VA 23456. Phone (757) 721-2412.

HAMPTON BEACHES

Hampton's two public beaches are on its northeastern shore, facing the mouth of the Chesapeake Bay.

Buckroe Beach. [Fig. 7(6)] This wide, clean beach on Hampton's Chesapeake Bay has lifeguards during the summer months. Enjoy big band concerts and an outdoor movie series during the summer at the park pavilion. Picnic shelters are available. The beach, which is free and open daily, year-round, is located at the end of Pembroke Avenue at 1st Street. Phone (757) 727-6347.

Grandview Nature Preserve Beach. [Fig. 7(7)] A 2.5-mile stretch of remote beach on the Chesapeake Bay is located at Grandview Nature Preserve. The 578-acre preserve, operated by the Hampton Department of Parks and Recreation, is a haven for birds and wildlife. It is located at the intersection of Beach Road and State Park Drive in northeastern Hampton. Open daily, year-round. Free admission. Phone (757) 727-6347.

Newport News

Newport News has an interesting mix of industry and opportunities for art, culture, and recreation. Several important museums, including the world-famous Mariners' Museum, are located here. Because of its location at Hampton Roads and on the eastern bank of the James River, Newport News also has a rich colonial and Civil War heritage.

Newport News Shipbuilding is a private company that makes nuclear-powered submarines and aircraft carriers such as the USS *Nimitz*. Founded by railroad magnate Collis P. Huntington in 1886, the company is now one of Virginia's largest private employers, with 20,000 employees. Employment peaked at 31,000 during the shipbuilding boom of World War II. The shipyard is located in the southern tip of Newport News at the mouth of the James River.

Considering the fact that Newport News is a highly industrial shipbuilding center and is located on the heavily traveled I-64 corridor between Williamsburg and Virginia Beach, the city is rich in green space. The city has several parks on the James River as well as Newport News Park (*see* page 66), which is the largest municipal park east of the Mississippi.

At the **Virginia War Museum** (757-247-8523) at 9285 Warwick Boulevard (Exit 263A from I-64), visitors will find 60,000 artifacts from wars that have involved Americans from 1775 to the present. Examples include an 1883 brass Gatling gun, a World War I tank, and a blockade runner's uniform from the Civil War. Civil War artifacts are on display at **Lee Hall Mansion** (757-888-3371), an antebellum Italian-ate mansion at 163 Yorktown Road (Exit 247 from I-64). The mansion is one of 12 stops on a self-guided **Civil War Trails** tour. Brochures may be obtained at the **Newport News Visitor Center** (888-4-WE-R-FUN or 757-886-7777) at 13560 Jefferson Avenue. The center is just off Exit 250B of I-64 in northwestern Newport News at the entrance to Newport News Park (*see* page xx).

The **U.S. Army Transportation Museum** (757-878-1115) located at Building 300, Besson Hall, on Washington Avenue (Exit 250A from I-64), focuses on the U.S. Army's two centuries of transportation history. Visitors can examine aircraft, trains, ships, landing craft, and jeeps at two outdoor parks.

The **Peninsula Fine Arts Center** (757-596-8175) at 101 Museum Drive (Exit 258A from I-64) hosts touring collections of historical and contemporary works. Children may enjoy an interactive gallery or attend programs especially for them. The work of local, regional, and national artists is on display.

The **Newsome House Museum & Cultural Center** (757-247-2360) at 2803 Oak Avenue (Exit 3 from I-664) is a restored 1899 landmark housing a black history study collection and exhibits. In addition to changing exhibits, the museum has special events and a permanent exhibit honoring attorney J. Thomas Newsome, one of the first African-Americans to argue before the Virginia Supreme Court.

The restored **Endview Plantation** home (757-887-1862) has both Revolutionary War and Civil War ties, having been used as a resting place by Washington's army on the way to Yorktown during the Revolutionary War and as a hospital for both Union and Confederate forces during the Civil War. Endview Plantation is located at 362 Yorktown Road (Exit 247 from I-64).

For more information: Newport News Visitor Center, 13560 Jefferson Avenue, Newport News, VA 23603. Phone (888) 4-WE-R-FUN or (757) 886-7777.

THE MARINERS' MUSEUM AND PARK

[Fig. 7(8)] Anyone who has ever been enchanted by the sea will enjoy investigating the legacy of mariners at The Mariners' Museum. Artifacts are on display from the famous Civil

War battle of the ironclads, the USS *Monitor* and the CSS *Virginia* (the name of the ironclad after conversion from the USS *Merrimack*). This first test of iron-clad warships was fought on March 8, 1862, in the waters of Hampton Roads off the coast of Newport News.

Collections in 13 galleries at the museum include ship models, navigational instruments, paintings by artists throughout history, and the world-famous August Crabtree Collection of Miniature Ships. Looming over the heads of visitors are marvelous carved figureheads, including women and giant eagles, with eyes that seem still to look out to sea. Children are fascinated with the costumed interpreters, such as an eighteenth century sea captain, who bring to life the challenging work of mariners.

The museum's permanent gallery, *Defending the Seas*, traces the history of the U.S. Navy and includes re-creations of the prow of an eighteenth-century wooden frigate, the turret of the USS *Monitor*, the deck of an aircraft carrier, and the interior of a submarine, among other interactive exhibits.

The museum is located in an urban park containing 550 acres of woods and fields surrounding tranquil Lake Maury. From March through October, canoes and row-boats may be rented for pleasure boating or fishing. The 5-mile Noland Trail encir-cles the 167-acre lake. Picnic tables are also available.

Directions: From I-64 in Newport News, take Exit 258A and drive south 2.5 miles to the museum entrance at the intersection of Warwick and J. Clyde Morris boulevards.

Activities: Museum tour, picnicking, boating, hiking.

Facilities: Museum, gift shop, park, picnic areas, rental boats and canoes, hiking trail, restrooms.

Dates: Open daily from 10 to 5 except Thanksgiving and Christmas.

Fees: There is an admission fee.

Closest town: The museum is in Newport News.

For more information: The Mariners' Museum, 100 Museum Drive, Newport News, VA 23606. Phone (800) 581-SAIL. Web site www.mariner.org.

▓ HUNTINGTON PARK/JAMES RIVER BRIDGE FISHING PIER

[Fig. 7(9)] This park on the James River has a freshwater lake stocked with trout in addition to a boat ramp, public beach, picnic shelters, and the privately operated James River Bridge Fishing Pier. Pier anglers catch nice-sized croaker, spot, trout, and rockfish seasonally.

Directions: The park is located at 9285 Warwick Boulevard. From I-64 in Hamp-ton, take Exit 263A and go west on US 258. The park is on the right just before crossing the James River Bridge.

Activities: Fishing, swimming, boating, picnicking, tennis.

Facilities: Public beach, private fishing pier, freshwater lake, boat ramp, ball fields, picnic shelters, tennis courts.

Dates: The park is open daily, year-round.

Fees: There is a fee for using the pier.

Closest town: The park is located in Newport News on the James River.

For more information: Huntington Park, 361 Hornet Circle, Newport News, VA 23607. Phone (757) 886-7912. James River Bridge Fishing Pier, 7601 River Road, Newport News, VA 23602. Phone (757) 247-0364.

VIRGINIA LIVING MUSEUM

[Fig. 9(10)] The Virginia Living Museum is an excellent place to bring the entire family to view wildlife close up. A 0.25-mile boardwalk leads along a wooded lakeside where raccoons, otters, foxes, bobcats, beavers, eagles, and white-tailed deer are in enclosed habitats. Gardens of native wildflowers attract birds and butterflies spring through fall. The lake also attracts wild ducks and wading birds such as herons and egrets.

The museum has a touch tank where children can stroke a horseshoe crab or pick up a starfish. An indoor aviary has steps that lead from songbirds in the treetops down to ducks and quail around bottomland ponds. A planetarium theater re-creates the skies and delves into the mysteries of the heavens. Solar activity can be viewed through a 14-inch telescope in the museum observatory.

The Wildlife Arts Festival, the museum's annual fund-raiser, attracts some of the area's best wildlife artists and photographers. Check with the museum for the location of this January festival.

Directions: From I-64 in Newport News, take Exit 258A. Go east on US 17 (J. Clyde Morris Boulevard) about 2 miles to the entrance, on the right.

Activities: Wildlife observation, planetarium shows.

Facilities: Boardwalk, 4,000-gallon ocean aquarium, planetarium, native wildflower gardens, aviary, touch tank, observatory.

Dates: The museum is open daily, year-round, except major holidays.

Fees: There is an admission fee, a fee for the planetarium, and combination tickets that include both admission and the planetarium.

Closest town: The museum is in Newport News.

For more information: Virginia Living Museum, 524 J. Clyde Morris Boulevard, Newport News, VA 23601. Phone (757) 595-1900. Web site www.valivingmuseum.org.

HORSESHOE CRAB

(Limulus polyphemus)
More closely related to spiders than to crabs, horseshoe crabs are "living fossils" that have remained essentialy unchanged for several hundred million years.

NEWPORT NEWS PARK/NEWPORT NEWS VISITOR CENTER

[Fig. 9(11)] Sprawling across the northwest corner of Newport News between US 17 and US 60 is the 8,000-acre Newport News Park—the largest municipal park east of the Mississippi. The park abuts Colonial National Historical Park at Yorktown to the east. The portion of I-64 between Exit 247 and Exit 250 crosses the western side of the park. This green space set aside within hailing distance of the Tidewater Virginia metropolitan area offers all kinds of ways to get away from it all—hiking, biking, picnicking, boating, archery, fishing, and year-round camping, to name some. There's also a 36-hole golf course, an 18-hole championship disc golf course, and a 30-acre aeromodel flying field. The park also rents boats and bicycles.

Directions, information, and brochures on area attractions are available at the Newport News Visitor Center located at the park entrance.

Directions: The visitor center and park entrance are just off Exit 250B of I-64.

Activities: Hiking, biking, picnicking, boating, archery, fishing, camping, tennis, golf, disc golf, aeromodel flying.

Facilities: Hiking and biking trails, two freshwater lakes, picnic tables, playground, archery range, golf course, disc golf course, aeromodel flying field, bike and boat rental, visitor center. Campground with hookups, flush toilets, hot showers, camp store, dump station.

Dates: The park, campgrounds, and visitor center are open daily, year-round. The visitor center is closed on Christmas and New Year's Day.

For more information: Newport News Park and Visitor Center, 13560 Jefferson Avenue, Newport News, VA 23603. Park phone, (757) 886-7912. Visitor center phone, (757) 886-8777 or (888) 4-WE-R-FUN.

RESTAURANTS OF NEWPORT NEWS AND HAMPTON

Here are some of the places to get Chesapeake Bay seafood and other specialties in the Newport News/Hampton area.

BILL'S SEAFOOD HOUSE. 10900 Warwick Boulevard, Newport News. Seafood restaurant serving lunch and dinner. *Inexpensive to moderate. Phone (757) 595-4320.*

ARIA FIFTY ONE CAFE. 605 Pilot House Drive, Newport News. American regional cuisine emphasizing seasonal ingredients. *Moderate. Phone (757) 873-2200.*

BOBBY'S AMERICANA. 17 East Queens Way, Hampton. An elegant atmosphere complements the award-winning cuisine and regional specialties. Dinner only, Tuesday through Sunday in winter; and lunch and dinner in summer. *Moderate. Phone (757) 727-0545.*

HERMAN'S HARBOR HOUSE. 663 Deep Creek Road, Newport News. Seafood restaurant serving lunch (Wednesday through Friday) and dinner nightly. *Moderate. Phone (757) 930-1000.*

SECOND STREET RESTAURANT AND TAVERN. 132 East Queen Street, Hampton. Casual atmosphere and large menu featuring fresh local seafood, steaks, chicken, and homemade Italian specialties. Live entertainment on Tuesday, Friday, and Saturday nights. Outside deck. *Inexpensive to moderate. Phone (757) 722-6811.*

LODGING IN NEWPORT NEWS AND HAMPTON

These facilities will provide a base for exploring the Newport News/Hampton area.

BOXWOOD INN. 10 Elmhurst Street, Newport News. Enjoy lunch and high tea at this restored turn-of-the-century home with period furnishings. *Moderate to expensive. Phone (757) 888-8854.*

THE CHAMBERLIN HOTEL. Fort Monroe, Hampton. A historic hotel located at Fort Monroe off I-64 Exit 268. Restaurant and lounge. Pool. *Moderate to expensive. Phone (757) 723-6511 or (800) 582-8975.*

COMFORT INN. 12330 Jefferson Avenue, Newport News. Pool, fitness facilities, adjacent restaurant. Located off Exit 255A of I-64. *Moderate. Phone (800) 368-2477 or (757) 249-0200.*

DAYS INN OYSTER POINT. 11829 Fishing Point Drive, Newport News. Pool, exercise room, adjacent restaurant. *Moderate. Phone (800) 873-2369 or (757) 873-6700.*

RADISSON HOTEL HAMPTON. 700 Settlers Landing Road, Hampton. Located next to the Virginia Air and Space Center and Hampton Visitor Center. Oversized waterfront rooms with view of Hampton Roads Harbor. Outdoor rooftop pool. Waterside dining at Victor's and seasonal outdoor dining at Oyster Alley. *Expensive. Phone (757) 727-9700 or (800) 333-3333.*

RED ROOF INN. 1925 Coliseum Drive, Hampton. Convenient to the Coliseum Central part of Hampton. Pets are allowed and children stay free. *Moderate. Phone (757) 838-1870 or (800) THE ROOF.*

VICTORIA HOUSE. 4501 Victoria Boulevard, Hampton. This restored turn-of-the-century Victorian inn is located in the historic district. *Moderate to expensive. Phone (757) 722-2658.*

Colonial Virginia Area

Every school child who has ever learned history by agonizing rote can appreciate the history-come-to-life world of Jamestown, Williamsburg, and Yorktown. The historic triangle, as the three towns are collectively called, is located on Virginia's lower peninsula between Richmond and Virginia Beach.

The centerpiece is the meticulously restored village of **Colonial Williamsburg**, with its old streets, reconstructed public buildings, restored taverns, and quaint shops where candlemakers and glassblowers carry on old traditions. Williamsburg is connected by the 23-mile **Colonial Parkway** to Jamestown Island to the southwest and to Yorktown to the southeast. The scenic parkway is popular with bicyclists, though traffic can be hard to contend with on weekends and during peak season.

Jamestown, located on Jamestown Island in the James River, is the site of the first permanent English settlement—the beginning of the colonies. Yorktown, on the York River on the other side of Virginia's Lower Peninsula, is the site of the last major battle of the Revolutionary War, which occurred 174 years after Jamestown was settled. The surrender of General Charles Cornwallis at Yorktown marked the end of colonialism and the beginning of America as a nation. To the north of Williamsburg is York River State Park (*see* page 73). To the southeast are Busch Gardens Williamsburg and Water Country USA (*see* page 71).

Williamsburg/Jamestown/Yorktown

[Fig. 7] From 1699 to 1780, Williamsburg was the capital of Virginia. Thomas Jefferson succeeded in lobbying to have the capital moved to Richmond in 1780 and Williamsburg subsequently lost prominence and languished in relative obscurity. With the financial help of John D. Rockefeller Jr. and others, this one-time powerful seat of politics, business, and culture has been restored to its eighteenth century appearance.

Colonial Williamsburg is open daily, year-round, including holidays. Anyone can walk the streets at no charge and shop in the stores. To take the official tour, enter many of the public buildings, or ride the buses that run between the historic area and the visitor center, you'll need a ticket, which can be purchased at the **Colonial Williamsburg Visitor Center**. Highlights of the tour include an orientation walk, the lavish **Governor's Palace**, the **Capitol**, the **Abby Aldrich Folk Art Center**, the **DeWitt Wallace Gallery**, and **Carter's Grove**, a once-thriving James River plantation. Costumed interpreters on street corners or in restored homes portray such figures as Thomas Jefferson and Patrick Henry, inviting the public to join in lively discussions on government and politics. Onlookers can even participate as a jury member or a witness in a mock trial of a witch. Costumed craftsmen such as silversmiths and woodworkers demonstrate eighteenth century skills in various shops.

The scrupulously tended streets and gardens of Colonial Williamsburg make the perfect backdrop for many annual events, including a Garden Symposium in late March and Historic Garden Week in April. A festive Independence Day celebration begins with a military salute by the Fife and Drum Corps, followed by the reading of the Declaration of Independence from the courthouse steps, and culminating in parades, fireworks, and concerts. The winter holiday season is magical with concerts, feasts, tours, programs, old-fashioned decorations, and sparkling lights. Visitors to Williamsburg, especially during peak times, should make reservations and plans well in advance. This tiny town is host to some 4 million people annually.

A 7-mile drive down the Colonial Parkway from Williamsburg leads to

Jamestown. Three organizations are charged with interpreting the history of Jamestown: the National Park Service, the Association for the Preservation of Virginia Antiquities (APVA), and the Jamestown-Yorktown Foundation.

The National Park Service operates the **Colonial National Historical Park**, which includes Jamestown, Yorktown, and the Colonial Parkway. The parkway connects Jamestown and Yorktown to Williamsburg. With the purchase of a ticket, visitors to Jamestown Island can see a short film and tour a museum at the visitor center, take ranger-led tours of the old townsite, watch craftsmen demonstrate the seventeenth century art of glassblowing at *Glasshouse*, and drive or bike a 5-mile wilderness loop on Jamestown Island. The loop leads through the dense forests of the island, with interpretive signs along the way.

The Association for the Preservation of Virginia Antiquities (APVA) is conducting archeological excavations at **Fort James** on Jamestown Island. Uncovered so far are more than 160,000 artifacts, nearly half of which date to the first years of the English settlement. The archeological site and laboratory are included in the admission fee to the Colonial National Historical Park.

On the mainland, within 1 mile of Jamestown Island, is the **Jamestown Settlement**, operated by the Jamestown-Yorktown Foundation. The settlement is a re-creation of that first colony, complete with full-scale replicas of the *Susan Constant*, *Godspeed*, and *Discovery*, the three English ships that came to Virginia in 1607. Interpreters demonstrate, for those who come aboard, the hardships of four months at sea in the seventeenth century. Also at Jamestown Settlement are a re-creation of Fort James, where the colonists learned to adapt to a strange new coastal environment, and Powhatan Indian village, which provides a memorable look at how tribes of Virginia's coastal plains lived at the time the first settlers arrived.

For another perspective—not to mention an enjoyable way to spend two hours—take the narrated **Jamestown Island Explorer Eco Cruise** (757-259-0400) around Jamestown Island National Park. Boats are often able to approach bald eagles, osprey, herons, and deer along the shoreline without alarming them. Cruise participants can pull up crab pots, just as watermen do, and dredge the bottom for marine life. The cruise boat and rental kayaks are located just behind the parking lot at Jamestown Settlement. Cruises begin at 11, 1, and 3.

On the other end of the 23-mile Colonial Parkway, 11 miles southeast of Williamsburg, is Yorktown. This little town was a seventeenth century tobacco port where General Charles Cornwallis brought 7,000 British troops during the Revolutionary War in the hopes of meeting up with British ships. However, General George Washington and General Comte de Rochambeau, who was in command of the colonists' French allies, hurried their armies down the coast to surround Cornwallis and force his surrender by cutting him off from the British ships with their supplies and reinforcements. The rule of British kings over the colonists ended when Cornwallis's men lay down their arms.

Visitors can now take a 7-mile auto tour of the battlefields and a 9-mile auto tour of the encampment areas, viewing trenches and parapets where history was made. They can walk down Main Street where many of the restored colonial dwellings of the eighteenth century remain as private residences, and dine in exquisite restaurants on Water Street on the York River. Also on Water Street is the **Watermen's Museum** (757-887-2641), where tribute is paid to the crabbers and oystermen of the Chesapeake Bay.

The battlefields are part of Colonial National Historical Park, where the National Park Service operates a visitor center and conducts ranger-led tours of the battlefield and colonial Yorktown. The Jamestown-Yorktown Foundation operates the Yorktown Victory Center, where exhibits, a film, and costumed interpreters tell the story of the colonists' struggle for independence. The center includes a re-created Continental Army encampment and an eighteenth century farm site.

Still another highlight of the Williamsburg area is the **Williamsburg Pottery Factory** (757-564-3326), located just off Exit 234 of I-64, 5 miles west of Williamsburg. The Pottery began in 1938 with the sale of eighteenth century, salt-glaze reproductions at low prices. Today, it has expanded to include more than 70,000 items in 32 buildings over 200 acres. Bargain hunters will find aisles upon aisles of candles, ribbons, china, glassware, collector's items, framed prints, baskets, dried flowers, and much more. Other onsite shops include a bakery, a frame shop, a greenhouse, and a woodworking shop. A restaurant and snack bar are also on the premises. The **Fair Oaks Holiday Trav-L-Park** (800-892-0320 or 757-565-2101) is nearby.

Directions: For the Colonial Williamsburg Visitor Center, take Exit 238 from I-64. After exiting, follow the green and white signs to the visitor center. For Jamestown, take Exit 242A from I-64. Follow VA 199 south about 4 miles. Go left on the Colonial Parkway and drive about 8 miles to Jamestown Island. The Jamestown Settlement is on the right, just before the island. For Yorktown, take Exit 242B from I-64. Go 1 mile on VA 199. Go right on VA 641 and go 1.1 miles. Go right on the Colonial Parkway and go 8.9 miles to Yorktown. Also, look for Colonial Parkway signs in Williamsburg to go to either Jamestown or Yorktown.

Activities: Exploring restored towns, bicycling, wagon rides in historic area, scenic driving, eco-cruising.

Facilities: Visitor center, bookstore, bike rental, horse-drawn wagons, restaurants, hotels, shops, theaters, public restrooms, museum, cruises around Jamestown Island.

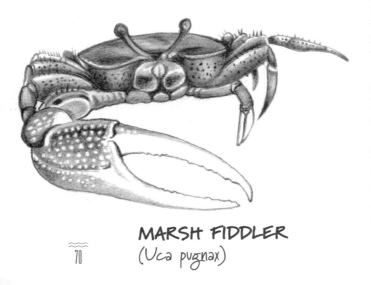

MARSH FIDDLER
(Uca pugnax)

Dates: Jamestown Settlement and Yorktown Victory Center are open from 9 to 5 daily except Christmas and New Year's Day. Colonial Williamsburg is open daily, year-round, including holidays. The Colonial Williamsburg Visitor Center is open 8:30 a.m. to 8 p.m. daily during the summer, with shorter hours during the rest of the year. Buildings in the historic district are generally open from 9 to 5.

Fees: There are admission fees for the Colonial National Historical Park at Jamestown and Yorktown (driving the Colonial Parkway is free), for the Jamestown Settlement and Yorktown Victory Center, and for tours, bus rides, wagon rides, cruises, and admission to many buildings, restored homes, and demonstration shops in Colonial Williamsburg.

Fiddler Crab

Three species of fiddler crab live in Virginia: the red-jointed fiddler (*Uca minax*), the sand fiddler (*Uca pugilator*), and the marsh fiddler (*Uca pugnax*). A pair of low-power binoculars and a bit of time to observe these interesting creatures will reveal their interesting behavior patterns. Males have one very large claw that they wave to show off or to attract a mate. The territorial males will readily fight over burrows, which may reach up to 2 feet and take several days to build. The burrowing and feeding of fiddler crabs plays an important role in the ecology of the marsh, bringing nutrient-rich sediments to the surface and oxygen to plant roots.

Tickets to sites in Colonial Williamsburg may be purchased at the visitor center, Merchants Square Information Center on South Henry Street, and the Lumber House ticket office on Duke of Gloucester Street in the historic area. There are prices for several packages that include most or all of the buildings. The Colonial National Historical Park offers combination tickets that include both the Jamestown Settlement and the Yorktown Victory Center.

For more information: Williamsburg Area Convention and Visitors Bureau, PO Box 3585, Williamsburg, VA 23187. Phone (800) 368-6511. Williamsburg Hotel & Motel Association, PO Box 1515, Williamsburg, VA 23187. Phone (800) 500-4834. Web site www.williamsburgrevfun.com. The Colonial Williamsburg Foundation, PO Box 1776, Williamsburg, VA 23187. Phone (800) HISTORY or (757) 220-7645. Web site www.colonialwilliamsburg.org. Jamestown-Yorktown Foundation, PO Box 1607, Williamsburg, VA 23187. Phone (888) JYF-IN-VA. Colonial National Historical Park, PO Box 210, Yorktown, VA 23690. Phone (757) 898-3400.

BUSCH GARDENS/WATER COUNTRY USA

[Fig. 7(12)] Two theme parks, Busch Gardens Williamsburg and Water Country USA are huge attractions for families and young people who come to the Williamsburg area. Busch Gardens is on US 60, about 1 mile south of Williamsburg. Water Country is about 2.5 miles east of Williamsburg and northeast of Busch Gardens, and about 1 mile east of I-64.

Busch Gardens, voted the country's favorite theme park by the National Amusement Park Historical Association, has thrilling rides and several roller coasters such as the Alpengeist, said to be the world's tallest, fastest, most twisted inverted roller coaster. Young children will enjoy the mini-flume ride, mini-Ferris wheel, three-story treehouse, and children's theater. Eight stage shows include an American Jukebox show, dancing to the big band sounds of the Starlight Orchestra, and the musical extravaganza called *Rockin' the Boat* at the Magic Lantern Theatre.

Handcrafted items such as Italian sculpture and German steins, as well as foods from around the world, make shopping and dining a unique experience at Busch Gardens. The famous Anheuser-Busch Clydesdales are another popular attraction.

Water Country is the place to be on a sizzling summer day when even the beach is too hot. Every imaginable ride—more than 30, in fact—that can keep a body cool and wet has been dreamed up for this park. There are side-by-side water slides for racing against friends, rafts that lead through dark tunnels with laser lighting and other special effects, and water playgrounds for young children.

Packages are available with three or four nights lodging and unlimited general admission to Colonial Williamsburg, the Jamestown Settlement, the Yorktown Victory Center, Busch Gardens Williamsburg, and Water Country USA. Guests of **Kingsmill Resort**, a four-star resort adjacent to Busch Gardens, also have unlimited access to Busch Gardens and Water Country USA (with a minimum stay). Kingsmill has three championship golf courses including the River Course, home to the Michelob Championship on the PGA Tour.

Directions: For Busch Gardens, take Exit 242 from I-64 and go west on VA 199 for about 1 mile. Go left (east) on US 60 and continue about 1 mile to the entrance, on the right. For Water Country, take Exit 242 from I-64 and go east on VA 199. Go less than 1 mile to the entrance, on the right.

Dates: Both parks open at 10 a.m. daily during summer hours. Call for spring and fall hours and for closing times, which vary.

Fees: There are fees for entering the parks and package plans that include hotel stays, visits to Williamsburg-area attractions, and park admission. Rides and shows are included in the admission price.

Closest town: Williamsburg is about 3 miles from each park.

For more information: Busch Gardens Williamsburg or Water Country USA, 1 Busch Gardens Boulevard, Williamsburg, VA 23187-8785. Phone (757) 253-3350. Web site

BUTTERFLY WEED
(Asclepias tuberosa)

www.buschgardens.com or www.watercountryusa.com. For packages, Williamsburg Hotel/Motel Association, PO Box 1515, Williamsburg, VA 23187. Phone (800) 211-7165. Kingsmill Resort, 1010 Kingsmill Road, Williamsburg, VA 23185. Phone (888) 334-4852 or (757) 253-1703.

YORK RIVER STATE PARK

[Fig. 7(13)] York River State Park is about 12 miles northeast of Williamsburg on the tidal York River. A beautiful visitor center overlooking the river has interpretive videos and displays about the complex workings of the estuary, pine forests, and marshes.

The York River and its tributary, Taskinas Creek, are the focal points of this unusual 2,505-acre state park. The York is a Chesapeake Bay tributary formed when the Mattaponi and Pamunkey rivers merge at West Point. The mix of salt water and fresh water of the marshes here provide the perfect nursery for Chesapeake Bay marine life. In fact, 525 acres of the Taskinas Creek and its wetlands are managed as part of the Chesapeake Bay National Estuarine Research Reserve under the auspices of the Virginia Institute of Marine Science (VIMS). The Reserve sponsors important environmental programs at the park such as a workshop on landscaping with native plants at the Native Plant Arboretum.

At the arboretum, which was completed in 1999, you can see plants native to the area such as butterfly weed (*Asclepias tuberosa*), New York aster (*Aster novi-belgii*), and Jerusalem artichoke (*Helianthus tuberosus*). The Jerusalem artichoke is a large sunflower that grows as high as a cornstalk. An Indian squaw prepared the nutritious tubers of the plants for explorers Lewis and Clark in 1805. Today the tubers are sold in health food stores. Many butterflies have particular native plants that, in the caterpillar stage, they rely on for food. The painted lady caterpillar feeds on the Jerusalem artichoke, for instance.

Many who come to the park are fascinated with the fossils of ancient marine life that are commonly uncovered along the banks of the York River. Some 5 million years ago, the land was covered with a shallow sea, brimming with early versions of today's whales, porpoises, sharks, clams, scallops, and snails. Traces of the existence of those early marine forms now show up as fossils on the York River beach.

Canoes are available for exploring the marshes of Taskinas Creek, where the spotted sandpiper (*Acititis macularia*) probes the muddy banks and the American woodcock (*Philohela minor*) performs its amazing courtship displays. A park concessionaire has john boats, paddle boats, and other craft for freshwater fishing on the park's 7-acre Woodstock Pond. Motorboats may be launched from the boat ramp on the York River at Croaker Landing, which is located in the park at the eastern end of VA 605. Hikers have 25 miles of woodland and marsh trails to explore. Bicycles may be rented for the 20 miles of bicycle trails. Several trails are also designated for horseback riding.

Park personnel put a lot of creativity into coming up with new programs and excursions to interpret the park's environment for visitors. The Taskinas Creek marshes are the setting for guided canoe trips by moonlight or starlight, fall foliage canoe trips, and wetland walks. Friday evening ghost hikes are popular in summer and fall, when tales such as *The Lady of the York* and *What Happened to Moody's Wharf* provide spine-tingling adventure. Fishing clinics at the park's Woodstock Pond, fossil hunting on the York River, and a pontoon boat ride on the river provide other ways to enjoy the park.

Directions: From I-64, Exit 231B (Croaker Exit—about 10 miles west of Williamsburg), go north on VA 607 (Croaker Road) about 1 mile. Go right on VA 606 (Riverview Road) about 2 miles to the park entrance, on the left. Drive 3 miles to the visitor center.

Activities: Hiking, biking, fishing, boating, canoeing, horseback riding (bring your own horse), picnicking, volleyball, badminton, horseshoes. Leashed pets are allowed.

Facilities: Visitor center, picnic tables with grills, picnic shelters, boat ramp, observation tower, native plant arboretum, amphitheater, playgrounds, volleyball courts, badminton courts, horseshoe pits, 7-acre pond, restrooms. Hiking, biking, equestrian, and canoeing trails. Rental canoes, rowboats, john boats, paddle boats, hydro bikes (a watercraft that operates like a bicycle), cruiser bikes, and mountain bikes.

Dates: The park is open from 8 to dusk daily, year-round. The visitor center and gift shop are open from 8 to 6 daily from Apr. through Oct.

Fees: There is a nominal fee per vehicle on weekdays and per person on weekends. Some programs and excursions also have a fee. There is also a rental fee for boats, bikes, and other recreational equipment.

Closest town: The park is 13 miles northwest of Williamsburg.

For more information: York River State Park, 5526 Riverview Road, Williamsburg, VA 23188. Phone (757) 566-3036.

RESTAURANTS IN THE COLONIAL VIRGINIA AREA

JOSIAH CHOWNING'S TAVERN. Duke of Gloucester Street, Williamsburg. Menu mixes food typical of British pubs with American cuisine. Located in the historic district. *Moderate. Phone (757) 229-2141 or (800) TAVERNS.*

ROSIE RUMPE'S REGAL DUMPE. Ramada Inn Central, 5351 Richmond Road, Williamsburg. Dinner theater where you're part of the show. A five-course meal is served with, perhaps, a visit from King Henry VIII. *Moderate. Phone (757) 565-4443 or (888) 767-9767.*

SECOND STREET RESTAURANT AND TAVERN. 140 Second Street, Williamsburg. Casual atmosphere. Sports center with nine television screens. Homemade soups, sandwiches, local seafood, steaks, and burgers. Late-night grill. *Inexpensive. Phone (757) 220-2286.*

SHIELDS TAVERN. Duke of Gloucester Street, Williamsburg. The menu features items from local farms, rivers, and the Chesapeake Bay. *Inexpensive to moderate.*

Phone (757) 229-2141 or (800) HISTORY.

THE YORKSHIRE STEAK & SEAFOOD RESTAURANT. 700 York Street, Route 60 East, Williamsburg. The menu includes prime rib, steaks, and fresh seafood from Virginia waters. *Moderate. Phone (757) 229-9790.*

LODGING IN THE COLONIAL VIRGINIA AREA

Motels, hotels, bed and breakfasts, and campgrounds are abundant in the Williamsburg area. Rates are considerably lower in winter. **The Williamsburg Hotel and Motel Association** (800-500-4834) coordinates reservations with some 75 hotels, motels, and B&Bs and offers packages that include area attractions.

The Newport Hospitality Group (800-444-HOST) also offers packages in combination with stays at the Ramada Historic Area, three Quality Inns (one in historic area), two Hampton Inns (one in historic area), and a Comfort Inn. *Moderate to expensive.*

The Official Resort Hotels of Colonial Williamsburg (800-HISTORY) offer packages in combination with stays at **Williamsburg Lodge** (large verandas overlooking gardens, huge fireplace; *expensive*), **Williamsburg Woodlands** (Cascades restaurant, waterfall, pine forest, adjacent to visitor center; *expensive*), and **Governor's Inn** (swimming pool, game room, near historic area; *expensive*).

LIBERTY ROSE B&B INN. 1022 Jamestown Road, Williamsburg. Restored home with gardens, courtyards, and century-old trees on a hilltop. *Expensive. Phone (757) 253-1260 or (800) 545-1825.*

NEWPORT HOUSE B&B. 710 South Henry Street, Williamsburg. Dance on Tuesday evenings in the ballroom of this home that was designed in 1756. Period furnishings, canopy beds. Located a short walk from the historical district. *Expensive. Phone (757) 229-1775.*

THE TRAVELODGE HISTORIC AREA. 120 Bypass Road, Williamsburg. Large outdoor heated pool, volleyball court, picnic area with grills, adjacent restaurant. *Inexpensive to moderate. Phone (757) 229-2000.*

DAYS INN WEST. 90 Old York Road, Williamsburg. Close to Water Country and Busch Gardens. Restaurant, gift shop, pool, picnic tables, attraction tickets available. *Inexpensive to moderate. Phone (800) 635-5366 or (757) 253-6444.*

YORKTOWN MOTOR LODGE. 8829 George Washington Highway (US 17), Yorktown. Pool, nearby restaurants, close to Yorktown attractions. *Moderate. Phone (800) 950-4003 or (757) 898-5451.*

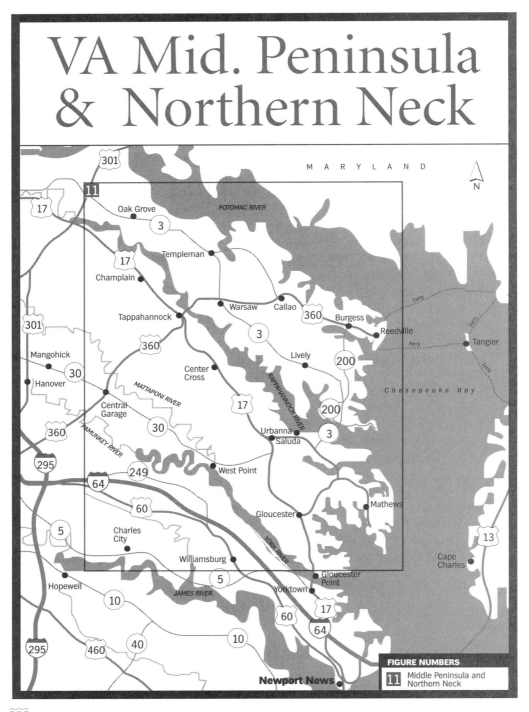

VA Mid. Peninsula & Northern Neck

The Middle Peninsula
and Northern Neck

The peninsulas on the western shore of Virginia's Chesapeake Bay demonstrate how geography influences history and culture.

The James and York rivers define Virginia's Lower Peninsula, where Newport News (*see* page 62) and Hampton (*see* page 57) are located. The York and Rappahannock rivers outline the Middle Peninsula, with the towns of West Point, Gloucester Point, Gloucester, Mathews, Saluda, Urbanna, and Tappahannock. The tidal Rappahannock and Potomac rivers lap at the shores of the peninsula known as the Northern Neck, where the communities of White Stone, Kilmarnock, Windmill Point, Reedville, Heathsville, Montross, and Warsaw are located.

Portions of these rivers or their tributaries—including parts of the Rappahannock, the Piankatank, the Mattaponi, the Pamunkey, and the Chickahominy—comprise what has been called "the heart of the most pristine freshwater complex on

[*Above:* Caledon Natural Area]

77

BALD EAGLES
(Haliaeetus leucocephalus)

the Atlantic Coast" by The Nature Conservancy. The freshwater and tidal marshes along the curves and meanders of these waterways are host to an incredible variety of fish, waterfowl, and wildlife. The detritus-laden ooze of such marshlands is a veritable stew of minute organisms vital to the health of the Chesapeake Bay. It is no accident that the river's banks are inhabited and defended by descendants of early European settlers and by tribes of American Indians who have lived lightly on the lands for many generations.

The tributary tidal rivers reach far inland, creating long peninsulas that were almost as isolated as islands until engineers designed bridges that would span the wide rivers. Consequently, the Indian tribes and early settlers inhabiting these peninsulas had to be resourceful and self-reliant.

The waters that define the peninsulas have also defined the lifestyle of their peoples. The Indians learned well how to harvest the riches of the Chesapeake Bay and its tributaries. The shells and bones of bay creatures and feathers of wetland birds are literally laced into their everyday lives and tribal festivals. As European settlers arrived, they too learned to be watermen, duck hunters, and boat builders. Learning the history and culture of the peninsula may take getting sand between the toes and salt air in the hair.

Even school children are familiar with the Colonial heritage of the Jamestown/Williamsburg area on the Lower Peninsula. The Middle Peninsula and the Northern Neck, however, are not so well known. To mention the Middle Peninsula or Northern Neck is to conjure up thoughts of quaint fishing villages and weathered docks stacked with crab pots. Or maybe thoughts turn to marshes crowded with noisy ducks and geese, or long stretches of back roads where plowed fields bake in the noonday sun and gulls follow the disc on a tractor as it turns up worms and grubs. These images are accurate, of course, but there is more.

Little known to the rest of the world are the strong ties these remote stretches of tidewater have with the early history of the New World. Many people are surprised to learn that Captain John Smith explored far up the tidal rivers that reach inland and define the peninsulas. Also, England established counties and port cities that are older even than Williamsburg. Museums and historic sites commemorating both the European and Native American past are sprinkled throughout the counties, especially on the Northern Neck. But sometimes you may have to go a bit out of the way to find them.

The Middle Peninsula

Six counties on the western shore of Virginia's Chesapeake Bay make up the Middle Peninsula. From east to west, they are Mathews, Gloucester, Middlesex, King and Queen, King William, and Essex. Although the county names have an obvious British influence, many of the river names—Mattaponi, Pamunkey, Piankatank, and Rappahannock—reveal the area's strong Indian heritage.

County and town historians have mapped out several walking and driving tours of historic towns and scenic counties on the Middle Peninsula. The towns include Gloucester in Gloucester County, Urbanna and Saluda in Middlesex County, Tappahannock in Essex County, and West Point in King William County. Both Middlesex and Mathews counties have booklets outlining driving tours.

The main attraction of the **Gloucester Historic Walking Tour** is Courthouse Square, with its jail, debtors prison, and courthouse. The old courthouse was constructed in the 1780s and used for 200 years. The current county offices are in the Botetourt Building, which was formerly the Tavern at Gloucester Courthouse, and was built prior to 1774. Also on the tour are other restored buildings, as well as gift shops, antique shops, and restaurants. Gloucester is also known for its Daffodil Festival (804-693-2355), held on the first weekend in April to coincide with the blooming of thousands of daffodils in area gardens and on daffodil farms. Gloucester farms ship daffodil bulbs to destinations worldwide.

Middlesex County is on the northeastern corner of the Middle Peninsula. The **Middlesex Heritage Tour** has a comprehensive booklet on the driving and walking tours of Saluda, Urbanna, and Middlesex County. The booklet describes the county's older homes and buildings, as well as the lives of the people associated with them.

Urbanna, which is located on the Rappahannock River north of Saluda, served as a port town where tobacco was shipped to England in return for European supplies. The **Urbanna Self-Guided Walking Tour** has several sites listed on the National Register of Historic Places, including the old tobacco warehouse and the courthouse. The tobacco warehouse, which houses a visitor center, was built in 1766 and is one of the oldest surviving mercantile structures in America associated with the sale of tobacco. Soil of the Middle Peninsula produced high quality, aromatic tobacco that was once used as currency. The town was thriving in the early 1800s, sending local produce and supplies on steamboats to Fredericksburg and Baltimore. Canneries were opened to preserve vegetables and seafood that were shipped to cities up and down the East Coast.

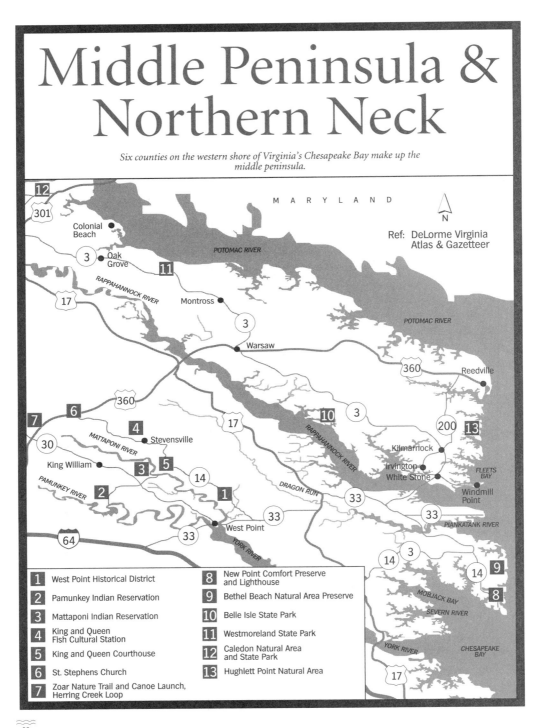

Middle Peninsula & Northern Neck

Six counties on the western shore of Virginia's Chesapeake Bay make up the middle peninsula.

MARYLAND

Ref: DeLorme Virginia Atlas & Gazetteer

POTOMAC RIVER

Colonial Beach

Oak Grove

RAPPAHANNOCK RIVER

Montross

POTOMAC RIVER

Warsaw

Reedville

Stevensville

MATTAPONI RIVER

King William

PAMUNKEY RIVER

RAPPAHANNOCK RIVER

Kilmarnock

Irvington
White Stone

FLEETS BAY

Windmill Point

DRAGON RUN

West Point

YORK RIVER

PIANKATANK RIVER

MOBJACK BAY

SEVERN RIVER

YORK RIVER

CHESAPEAKE BAY

1	West Point Historical District	8	New Point Comfort Preserve and Lighthouse
2	Pamunkey Indian Reservation	9	Bethel Beach Natural Area Preserve
3	Mattaponi Indian Reservation	10	Belle Isle State Park
4	King and Queen Fish Cultural Station	11	Westmoreland State Park
5	King and Queen Courthouse	12	Caledon Natural Area and State Park
6	St. Stephens Church	13	Hughlett Point Natural Area
7	Zoar Nature Trail and Canoe Launch, Herring Creek Loop		

The Courthouse, built in 1748, is one of Virginia's 11 Colonial courthouses still standing. The building underwent architectural modifications, serving for a time as an interdenominational church and, during the Civil War, as a confederate barracks. Visitors to the town love to gaze at the ornate Victorian homes constructed during the town's prosperous days as a summer resort and port city.

The Urbanna Oyster Festival (804-758-0368), usually held on the first weekend in November when the oyster harvest is at its peak, is one of the Middle Peninsula's most popular events. This out-of-the-way village swells in size by some 80,000 revelers who come to sample oysters on the half-shell, oyster stew, oyster casserole, fried oysters, and oyster fritters, as well as clams, crabs, and other Chesapeake Bay specialties. The festival includes a parade, a fine arts exhibit, and the arrival of tall ships.

Deltaville, a Middlesex County fishing village some 17 miles east of Urbanna on VA 33, is the site of two annual rockfish tournaments. The Lower Middlesex Volunteer Fire Department Rockfish Tournament (804-776-6046) is held the weekend before Thanksgiving. The CCA/Greentop Benefit Rockfish Tournament (757-481-1226 or 804-672-1368) is held on the first Saturday in December. Boaters, their families, and visitors come to watch the weigh-in and join in festivities at day's end.

Tappahannock is located about 30 miles upriver from Urbanna and, like Urbanna, was established as a port city by England in the early 1600s. Captain John Smith, who explored much of the Chesapeake Bay and its tributaries, landed here in 1608, but local Indians drove him back to his ship. The name Tappahannock comes from the Indian *Tappahannocke*, meaning "on the rise and fall of water."

The **Tappahannock Walking Tour** takes in 13 homes and buildings with diverse architectural styles of this town that is older even than Richmond and Williamsburg. The sites include Scots Arms Tavern, circa 1680; the Beale Memorial Baptist Church, which was the 1728 courthouse; the debtors prison, built prior to 1769; and the Customs House from the early 1800s.

The **Rappahannock River Cruise** (800-598-BOAT or 804-453-BOAT) begins on the north side of US 360/17 on Hoskins Creek on the southern end of town. The two-decker *Captain Thomas* boat takes passengers on the Rappahannock to tour Ingleside Plantation Winery (*see* page 92) and enjoy the plantation's buffet lunch. Bald eagles (*Haliaeetus leucocephalus*) are frequently spotted along the river.

While in Tappahannock, be sure to stop at **Lowery's Seafood Restaurant** (804) 443-2800 on US 360/17 on the northwestern end of town. The restaurant has been a local landmark since 1938, serving regional fare such as frog legs, quail, fresh seafood, and homegrown vegetables.

For more information: Virginia's Chesapeake Bay, phone (800) 336-3078. Middle Peninsula Travel Council, PO Box 386, Saluda, VA 23149. Phone (800) 217-8912.

THE PIANKATANK AND DRAGON RUN

[Fig. 9] The brackish tidal Piankatank has fisheries such as white perch, bluegill, largemouth bass, catfish, and striped bass typical of its larger tidal-river cousins. Upstream, the Piankatank becomes Dragon Run. The Run, as it's known by those who float or fish it, is relatively unspoiled and incredibly scenic. The water may be high enough in the nontidal portions to float the river only in the spring, but the trip through mysterious cypress swamps and heavy forest cover is well worth the effort to set time aside. Fish populations include redbreast sunfish, crappie, largemouth bass, bluegill, chain pickerel, and some of the best white perch fishing in the state, especially where Dragon Run widens out in the lower portion. The endangered bald eagle (*Haliaeetus leucocephalus*) nests here and many unusual warblers find the thick undergrowth to their liking.

Canoeists who discover this quiet waterway take great pleasure in floating remote stretches of river that have not changed much since the Piankatank Indians launched their own boats. History lies even in the rivers' names. The Piankatank, meaning "winding waterway," was named by Chief Powhatan, who subdued the Piankatank Indians. Captain John Smith, who sailed up the Piankatank on a mapping expedition, named Dragon Run when he reached the headwaters.

A public boat ramp on the Piankatank is on VA 606 at Freeport in northwestern Gloucester County. Dragon Run is accessible to canoeists at places where the highway crosses the river, but permission to park on the shoulder may be required from adjacent landowners.

THE MATTAPONI-PAMUNKEY TRAIL

Perhaps the best way to become acquainted with King William County and the town of West Point is to follow the Mattaponi-Pamunkey Trail. The Mattaponi River on the northeast side and the Pamunkey River to the south define King William County, which is northeast of Richmond and Hanover County. The rivers merge at the county's southeastern tip at West Point to form the York River.

The Mattaponi-Pamunkey Trail, which is more suggested highway routes than an actual trail, was designed to connect the county's main thoroughfares—VA 30 and US 360—with scenic, rural back roads that branch off to historic, cultural, and natural attractions. The main trail is about 30 miles one direction, extending along US 30 from the northwestern border of King William County to the county's southeastern tip, and about 8 miles in another direction, following US 360 across the width of the county. Some of the side branches include all or parts of VA 604, VA 615, VA 600, VA 629, VA 632, and VA 640.

Also on the trail are sites that are on the National Register of Historic Places, such as **King William Courthouse** at King William, **Saint John's Church** at Rose Garden, the **Pamunkey Indian Reservation Archaeological District**, and the **West Point Historical District**. A brochure with a detailed description of the trail is available from West Point town offices, King William county offices, or regional tourism offices. Some of the highlights are listed here:

For more information: King William County, King William, VA 23086. Phone (804) 769-4927. Town of West Point, West Point Chamber of Commerce, PO Box 1035, West Point, VA 23181-1035. Phone (804) 843-4620. Middle Peninsula Travel Council, PO Box 386, Saluda, VA 23149. Phone (800) 217-8912.

WEST POINT HISTORICAL DISTRICT

[Fig. 9(1)] By glancing at a map, the strategic location of West Point becomes obvious. The town was formed where the Mattaponi and Pamunkey converge to form the York River. West Point was first an Indian village and then a Colonial plantation, but in the late 19th century it became a busy commercial port and terminus of the Richmond-York River Railroad.

It would be easy to pass through the town on VA 33 and miss the historic district just a half block away. A turn to the east onto Main Street will lead past old homes, shops, churches, the library, town hall, and post office—structures preserved from the late nineteenth and early twentieth centuries. To take the **Historic District Walking Tour**, visitors can park in the town library lot at 7th and Main streets, then walk along Main Street and parallel Lee Street and the connecting blocks of 1st, 4th, 7th, and 10th. Architectural styles include Victorian Italianate, Queen Anne, and Gothic Revival.

At the eastern end of Main Street (the corner of Main and 1st) is Beach Park on the York River. Facing the York, the Mattaponi River comes in on your left and the Pamunkey River comes in on your right. The park is the former site of the Terminal Hotel, a once-popular destination when West Point was in its heyday.

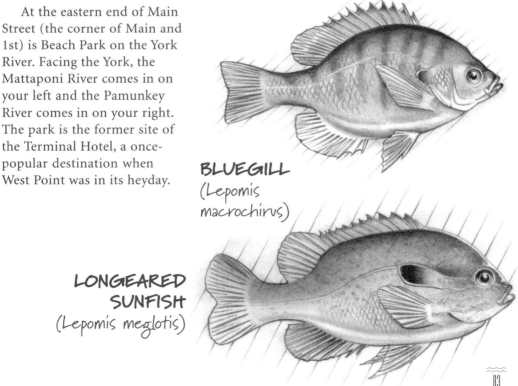

BLUEGILL
(Lepomis macrochirus)

LONGEARED SUNFISH
(Lepomis meglotis)

INDIAN RESERVATIONS

Direct descendants of Chief Powhatan and his Indian tribe, who once hunted and fished the land that is now King William County, still live here. The **Mattaponi Reservation** [Fig. 9(3)] (804-769-2229) and **Pamunkey Reservation** [Fig. 9(2)] (804-843-4740) are each located on the rivers that bear their names. The public is invited to the reservations periodically for cultural events. The **Pamunkey Indian Museum** (804-843-4792) and the **Mattaponi Indian Museum** (804-769-2229) display early relics that help with an understanding of tribal culture from the Ice Age to the present. Call ahead for hours.

MATTAPONI AND PAMUNKEY RIVERS

[Fig. 9] The Mattaponi has the distinction of being one of the cleanest lowland rivers in the Eastern United States. Several rare plants inhabit the marshes of the Mattaponi and Pamunkey rivers. The tropical water-hyssop (*Racopa innominata*), Parker's pipewort (*Eriocaulon parkeri*) and marsh senna (*Chamaecrista fasciculata*) are among examples. Sensitive joint-vetch (*Aeschynomene virginica*)—a globally rare plant—has adapted to the tidal channel edges of the freshwater marshes.

Anglers know both the Mattaponi and the Pamunkey for their fantastic channel catfish and white catfish action, and for the exciting spawning runs of white perch and herring in the spring. Striped bass, blue catfish, yellow perch, and redbreast sunfish also provide sport for fishermen. Public boat ramps are located on the Mattaponi at West Point (VA 33, Glass Island landing), Waterfence, Melrose, and Aylett. The Aylett landing, located on VA 600 just east of Aylett and US 360, has picnic facilities and a paved ramp. On the Pamunkey, landings are located at Lester Manor (VA 672, just downstream from the Pamunkey Reservation), and at West Point's Beach Park (York River access, corner of Main and 1st streets). The rivers may also be accessed wherever they intersect a road, but landowner permission may be required for parking off the shoulder.

ZOAR NATURE TRAIL/HERRING CREEK LOOP TRAIL/ZOAR CANOE LAUNCH

[Fig. 9(7)] The Zoar Nature Trail, Herring Creek Nature Trail, and canoe put-in are on Herring Creek about 2 miles north of Aylett. The parking areas for the trail and launch area are on the eastern side of VA 600, near the creek's confluence with the scenic Mattaponi River on the border of King William and King and Queen counties.

The Zoar Nature Trail is a 1-mile interpretive walk through a 29-acre tract of the 378-acre Zoar State Forest. Several wooden bridges and a gentle footpath lead through forested wetlands and dryer woodlands beneath a canopy formed by magnificent beech, oak, and hickory trees that have escaped the lumberman's axe over the years. Evergreens such as mountain laurel and American holly color the woods even in mid-winter. The shorter Herring Creek Loop Trail climbs above Herring Creek. Brochures for the two trails are located at the parking lot trailheads.

At the canoe launch area, anglers can be seen during the spring spawning run using dip nets to catch herring. Mattaponi Canoe and Kayak (800-769-3545), an

Catch-and-Release Fishing

Pictures of huge stringers of bass or of dripping saltwater fish nailed to boards at the dock are becoming a thing of the past. Too often, the fish in such pictures were not cooked and eaten, but thrown in the trash. More and more, anglers are realizing the joys of catch-and-release fishing, which involves returning the fish to the water to grow even larger and provide sport on another day.

A camera stored in a watertight bag and a tape for measuring the length of the fish provide ways to record the catch. Hooks can be made barbless by mashing the barb with needlenose pliers—a tool also helpful in getting a hook out of the fish with minimal damage to the mouth. Avoid treble hooks. A net will help support the fish while removing the hook. If the fish must be handled, savvy anglers wet their hands first to minimize damage to the fish's protective slime coating and return the fish to the water as soon as possible.

For a fish hooked in the gut or gill, cut the line and leave the hook. Some freshwater hooks are made of material that will dissolve away in time. A stressed fish can often be revived by holding it in the current or moving it slowly forward so that water is forced through the gills.

outfitter at Aylett, provides rental canoes and kayaks and guide service. Look for beaver slides along the banks of the Mattaponi.

Trails: Zoar Nature Trail is an easy 1-mile loop near the Herring Creek confluence with the Mattaponi River. Herring Creek Loop Trail is a shorter loop of easy to moderate difficulty, with views of Herring Creek.

Directions: From US 360 at Aylett, go north on VA 600 about 2 miles. Turn right at the sign for Zoar State Forest. Then go left into the lower parking area for the canoe launch and the Herring Creek Trail or go straight into the upper parking area for the Zoar Nature Trail.

For more information: Zoar State Forest, Virginia Department of Forestry, PO Box 3758, Charlottesville, VA 22903. Phone (804) 977-6555. King and Queen County office, phone (804) 769-1655.

NEW POINT COMFORT PRESERVE AND LIGHTHOUSE

[Fig. 9(8), 7(16)] This 108-acre Nature Conservancy preserve is located at New Point Comfort at the southern tip of Mathews County. The sensitive habitats protected here include a sandy beach, a salt marsh, and a maritime forest. A handicap-accessible boardwalk with interpretive signs leads into the preserve, where more than 200 bird species have been identified.

From the boardwalk observation deck, the New Point Comfort Lighthouse is visible. The lighthouse is on the island at the southern tip of Mathews County, near the entrance to Mobjack Bay. This 63-foot brick tower was completed in 1804, damaged during the Civil War, repaired, and used until the early 1950s. In the 1970s, the lighthouse was named a National Historic Landmark and restored. It is accessible only by water.

Directions: From downtown Mathews on VA 198 in Mathews County, go south on VA 14 for 8.5 miles to Bavon. Turn left (still on VA 14) in Bavon and drive for 0.9 mile (the road becomes VA 600). Bear right when the road forks (still on VA 600) and continue a few hundred yards to road's end at the New Point Comfort boardwalk.

Activities: Nature walk.

Facilities: Boardwalk and observation deck.

Dates: Open dawn to dusk, year-round.

Fees: None.

Closest town: Mathews is 10 miles north.

For more information: The Nature Conservancy, Virginia Chapter, 1233A Cedars Court, Charlottesville, VA 22903-4800. Phone (804) 295-6106.

BETHEL BEACH NATURAL AREA PRESERVE

[Fig. 9(9), Fig. 7(15)] Several rare species have evolved in harmony with the shifting sands of the beach and low dunes that make up much of this 83-acre preserve fronting the Chesapeake Bay east of Mathews.

Least terns (*Sterna antillarum*), dainty birds with black caps and gray backs, lay their nests in shallow depressions in the sand—a trait that leaves them vulnerable to marauding predators and human activity. The federally threatened northeastern beach tiger beetle (*Cicindela dorsalis dorsalis*) is also found on the beach.

The rare sea-beach knotweed (*Polygonum glaucum*) is well suited to the area behind the dunes where overwash at high tide drains into the inlet behind the spit. Look for a whitish waxy coating on the sprawling blue-green plant. The expansive salt marsh west of the dunes is vital as a filter for sediments and pollution, a buffer from wind and waves, and a nursery for many of the estuary's fish and crustaceans. The marsh is also a nesting site of the northern harrier (*Circus cyaneus*), which usually nests farther north.

Leashed pets are permitted.

Directions: From VA 14 at Mathews, go east on VA 611 (Tabernacle Road) for 4.4 miles. Go left on VA 609 and go 2.1 miles to the end of the road. Park near the concrete barricade at the beach.

Activities: Nature and wildlife observation and photography.

Facilities: None.

Dates: The preserve is open year-round, but the southern portion is closed from May 1 through Sept. 15 to protect nesting birds.

Fees: None.

Closest town: Mathews is 6.5 miles west.

For more information: Chesapeake Bay Region Steward, Virginia Department of Conservation and Recreation, Division of Natural Heritage, Gloucester Point, VA 23062. Phone (804) 684-7577.

RESTAURANTS ON THE MIDDLE PENINSULA

A little advance planning might be helpful if you want breakfast or dinner on the Middle Peninsula. Restaurants tend to be few and far between.

ECKHARD'S. VA 3, Topping. German and other foods. Located 1 mile south of the Rappahannock River bridge. *Inexpensive to moderate. Phone (804) 758-4060.*

GALLEY RESTAURANT. Deltaville. Specializes in fresh seafood. *Inexpensive to moderate. Phone (804) 776-6040.*

LOWERY'S SEAFOOD RESTAURANT. 528 Church Lane, Tappahannock. Since 1938, known for fine service and Chesapeake Bay cuisine. Lunch and dinner daily, year-round. *Inexpensive to moderate. Phone (804) 443-2800.*

RIVER'S INN RESTAURANT AND CRAB DECK. 8109 Yacht Haven Drive, Gloucester Point. Specializes in fresh seafood. Located on the York River at York River Yacht Haven. *Inexpensive to moderate. Phone (804) 642-9942.*

SEABREEZE RESTAURANT. Grimstead, Gwynn's Island. Typical Chesapeake Bay fare. Waterfront. Come by car or boat. *Inexpensive to moderate. Phone (804) 725-4000.*

SEAWELL'S ORDINARY. US 17 (George Washington Memorial Highway), Ordinary. Sample foods from the area at this historic restaurant housed in a 1712 residence. Colonial atmosphere. *Inexpensive to moderate. Phone (804) 642-3635.*

VIRGINIA STREET CAFE. Virginia and Cross Streets, Urbanna. Specializes in regional foods. *Inexpensive to moderate. Phone (804) 758-3798.*

LODGING ON THE MIDDLE PENINSULA

To best enjoy the Middle Peninsula, come to stay for awhile at one of these accommodations. The peninsula is rich in bed and breakfast inns, which lend themselves perfectly to settling into the rhythm of the seasons and the tides. The **New Point Campground** (804-725-5120) at New Point in Mathews County has hookups, a beach, boat rentals, a marina, and a pool. Campgrounds are also located at Gloucester Point, New Point, Gwynn's Island, Deltaville, Topping, Urbanna, and King and Queen Courthouse. A complete list of hotels, motels, B&Bs, and campgrounds is available by calling the Middle Peninsula Travel Council at (800) 217-8912.

AIRVILLE PLANTATION. 6423 T. C. Walker Road, Gloucester. National Historic Register plantation with period furnishings, working fireplaces, a pool, a beach, fishing, and a deepwater dock. *Expensive. Phone (804) 694-0287.*

DAYS INN. US 17, Tappahannock Boulevard, Tappahannock. Restaurant nearby. *Inexpensive to moderate. Phone (804) 443-9200.*

DOCKSIDE INN. Highway 33, Deltaville. Efficiencies with small refrigerators and microwaves. *Inexpensive to moderate. Phone (804) 776-9224.*

DRAGON RUN INN. US 17 and VA 602, Church View. A 1913 country farmhouse converted to a B&B . The house was built with cypress from the Dragon Run swamp. *Moderate. Phone (804) 758-5719. Web site www.dragon-run-inn.com.*

THE INN. 250 Virginia Street, Urbanna. Spacious rooms; formal and casual dining. *Phone (804) 758-4852.*

ISLANDER MOTEL. Gwynn's Island. Waterfront location in a sheltered harbor with a marina and a restaurant. Pool, beach, tennis courts. *Moderate. Phone (804) 725-2151.*

The Northern Neck

Four Virginia counties make up the peninsula called the Northern Neck, or simply the Neck by locals. Bounded to the north by the Potomac River, to the south by the Rappahannock River, and to the east by the Chesapeake Bay, the counties include Lancaster, Northumberland, Richmond, and Westmoreland. Depending on who's doing the defining, King George County is sometimes included. King George is less isolated than its eastern neighbors are, but it does have Caledon State Park and Natural Area [Fig. 9(12)] (*see* page 97) in a remote bend of the Potomac where there is a large concentration of bald eagles.

The people who live on the Northern Neck share ancestral traditions of working the salt water that nearly surrounds them, hunting the marshes and woodlands, and farming the rich soil. While harvesting Chesapeake Bay crabs, clams, oysters, and fish, the Northern Neck waterman faces the daily uncertainties of weather—a sudden squall, ice freezing on the boat deck, baking summer sun, and heavy fog, to mention a few. Most watermen come from long lines of watermen before them and take great pride in their ability to wrest a living from the sea.

Before modern game management practices evolved, many game animals were just about wiped out on the Northern Neck, just as they were all across the Commonwealth. Today, however, wild turkeys are abundant and turkey hunting is excellent. Fall also brings deer, quail, and waterfowl hunters to Northern Neck counties.

The Robert O. Norris Jr. Bridge, known locally as the Rappahannock River Bridge, provides a dramatic entry to the southeastern corner of the Northern Neck on VA 3. Far below the 2-mile-long span, anglers in boats pull tasty croaker and spot from around the bridge pilings or from the waters off Parrott Island. Other boats leave V-shaped wakes as they head out of marinas from inlets on both sides of the Rappahannock to fish for pan trout, bluefish, and rockfish off Windmill Point, Stingray Point, the Hole in the Wall, the Cell, and other Chesapeake Bay hotspots.

Stingray Point, by the way, got its name from a fascinating incident involving Capt. John Smith. While exploring the Chesapeake, Smith was stung by a stingray. Pain and swelling became so great that he ordered his men to begin digging his grave and making funeral arrangements. However, local Indians knew of a remedy. By dinnertime, so the account goes, Smith was well enough to join his comrades.

The quiet community of White Stone in Lancaster County is near the northern end of the Rappahannock River Bridge. Quiet, that is, unless the local fire department is holding its Rappahannock River Waterfowl Show (804-435-6355). This March event annually draws thousands of waterfowl and art enthusiasts for a decoy-carving competition, waterfowl art, and photography exhibits. The fire department building and adjacent schoolhouse are filled with the sounds of goose and duck callers and the mixed aroma of barbecue, fried chicken, hot dogs, and fresh popcorn. White Stone also celebrates its Chesapeake Bay heritage with the annual Bay Seafood Festival in early September.

Up the road from White Stone, in nearby Kilmarnock, is the **Lancaster County Visitors Center** (800-579-9102) in the Chesapeake Commons Shopping Center.

On VA 200 between White Stone and Irvington is **Historic Christ Church** (804-438-6855), a National Historic Landmark completed in 1735. It doesn't take an architect to appreciate the exquisite brickwork and unusual roof flare of this Colonial Episcopal church. Costumed interpreters will point out the altarpiece of native walnut, the wainscoted pews, and the triple-decker pulpit with dome top. The church is about 1.5 miles north of Irvington and clearly marked. A museum, small gift shop, and restrooms are on the church grounds.

On Carter's Creek at Irvington is **The Tides** (800-843-3746 or 804-438-5000), recognized by *Condé Nast Traveler* as one of the world's premier resorts. Golf Digest has rated the resort's Golden Eagle course one of Virginia's top ten golf courses. Moonlight, lunch, and dinner cruises are available aboard the 127-foot classic 1926 yacht, the **Miss Ann** (reservations required, phone 804-438-5000). Tennis, biking, sailing, canoeing, fishing, or relaxing on the sandy beach are other options.

At Lancaster on VA 3 is the **Mary Ball Washington Museum** (804-462-7280), honoring George Washington's mother, who was born in Lancaster County. In the museum complex are the Old Clerk's Office from the 1790s and an 1820 jail. The self-guided walking tour of the **Lancaster Courthouse Historic District** highlights the past 350 years in Lancaster County.

The fishing village of Reedville is located on the northeastern tip of the Northern Neck in Northumberland County. Take US 360 northeast out of Richmond, drive 86 miles, and you'll dead-end at this picturesque village of grand old Victorian homes built at the turn of the century by ship captains and wealthy industrialists. Some of the homes have been converted into B&Bs with second- and third-floor rooms where you can watch ships, sailboats, and workboats on the Chesapeake Bay.

The **Reedville Fishermen's Museum** (804-453-6529) is located on Cockrell's Creek in the center of the historic district. On display is a growing collection of typical Chesapeake Bay workboats such as a crabbing skiff, a menhaden striker boat, and a 1929 buyboat pilothouse. Ask for a brochure of the **Reedville Walking Tour** as a guide for the turn-of-the-century Victorian homes lined up on Main Street. Also, the museum has exhibits on Reedville's thriving menhaden industry, which provides jobs for many Northumberland County residents. (On some days, depending on wind direction, the air is filled with a pungent fishy aroma from the local menhaden processing plant.)

Reedville is a premier destination for saltwater anglers. Several charter boats operate out of Cockrell's Creek (*see* Outfitters, Guides, and Suppliers Appendix, page 315). The annual **Reedville Bluefish Derby** in mid-June draws hundreds of boaters in pursuit of big bluefish and big cash prizes. Prizes are also awarded for the largest rockfish (striped bass). Buzzard's Point Marina (804-453-6325) is headquarters. Reedville is also the site of the Blessing of the Fleet on the first Sunday of May.

From May 1 through October 15 (weekends only the first and last two weeks), cruise boats depart Reedville at 10 a.m. daily for Smith Island (*see* page 107) and **Tangier Island**, returning to dock at 3:45 p.m. The **Smith Island Cruise** (804-453-3430) operates out of the KOA Campground. The **Tangier Island Cruise** (804-453-BOAT) operates out of Buzzard's Point Marina.

Tangier Island is in Virginia waters 17 miles out in the Chesapeake Bay east of Reedville. According to legend, Captain John Smith named the island on his exploration of the Chesapeake Bay in 1608, although there is no mention of the name "Tangier" until 1713. The Indians, so the story goes, traded Tangier to an enterprising man named John West in 1666 for two overcoats. The first permanent settlers, John Crockett and his two sons, arrived in 1686. By the 1800s, the island had 100 residents, half of whom were Crocketts.

Tangier—only 1 mile wide and 3 miles long—has been used as pasture for livestock, as a hideout for pirates, as a British base during both the Revolutionary War and the War of 1812, and as a site in the 1800s for huge Methodist camp meetings. The 800 islanders now on Tangier are mostly watermen and their families, who rely on crabs for a living as their ancestors have done for many years. Soft-shell farms maintained along the shoreline produce such an abundant harvest that Tangier is often called the "soft-shell capital of the world." A few cars are on the island, but golf carts, motorcycles, bicycles, and walking are the usual modes of transportation. While mainlanders have cars, the islanders have boats. There are two grocery stores, a post office, and one school with grades K-12.

To avoid summer crowds, spring and fall are good times to arrange a visit to Tangier Island. Or make a reservation at one of Tangier's three B&Bs to enjoy the island at night, after the tour boats have left. The **Chesapeake House** (757-891-2331), located on Main Street near the boat dock, has a restaurant on the premises and is open spring through fall. **Sunset Inn** (757-891-2535) is on the waterfront and is open year-round. Shirley's Bay View Inn (858-891-2396), an 1806 home converted to an inn, is on Ridge Road and is open year-round. In addition to the famous Chesapeake House Restaurant, three other island restaurants also specialize in seafood.

The **Northumberland County Visitor's Center** (804-529-5031) is located at 410

Northumberland Highway at Callao in the northwestern part of the county. Eleven miles west of Callao, VA 3 and US 360 merge at Warsaw, the seat of Richmond County. The **Richmond County Courthouse** is located at the juncture of these two highways. This classical Colonial courthouse was built in 1748 and is still in use. Two buildings down the hill from the courthouse is the **Old Jail**, which houses the **Richmond County Museum and Visitor Center** (804-333-3607). A brochure is available here describing a walk through Warsaw, which includes an 1835 Episcopal church and cemetery, Antebellum and Victorian buildings, and a local nature trail.

The **Rappahannock River National Wildlife Refuge** (804-333-5189) is an 1,100-acre wildlife sanctuary on Cat Point Creek. Trails follow several miles of old farm roads through woods and marshes. The refuge is located on VA 634 off US 360, about 5 miles southwest of Warsaw. No facilities are on the refuge.

Westmoreland County has several attractions of interest. The historic deep-water harbor of Kinsale is a boaters' community between two branches of the Yeocomico River in the southeastern corner of the county on VA 203. Until the early 1900s, when steamboats went the way of the horse and buggy, the town was a commercial shipping hub. Exhibits on the town's past and information on a walking tour of the historic district are available at the **Kinsale Museum** (804-472-3001), housed in what used to be a meat market on the town green.

The **Westmoreland County Visitor's Center** (804-SEE WCVA) is on Courthouse Square at Montross, which lies on VA 3 in the heart of the county. **Westmoreland County Museum and Library** (804-493-8440), also at Montross, has as a centerpiece a life-size portrait of William Pitt, a member of the House of Commons, by well-known artist Charles Wilson Peale.

Atlantic Menhaden

Tourists along the Atlantic coast and Chesapeake Bay often ask what the large ships and spotter planes are doing close to shore. The ships are likely menhaden boats from Reedville, using weighted nets to surround schools of the Atlantic menhaden (*Brevoortia tyrannus*). The oily fish is used to produce fertilizer, food for livestock, pet food, fishmeal, and industrial oil.

The menhaden or bunker, as they are called, is pursued not only by humans, but also by whales, sharks, porpoises, and bluefish. The voracious bluefish attack the thick schools of baitfish in a frenzy, slashing the menhaden to pieces and attracting screaming seagulls overhead—a giveaway to anglers looking for some exciting fishing. The seagulls dive to pick up scraps of menhaden on the surface and anglers cast anything shiny into the melee, often hooking a fish on every cast.

Menhaden are often visible in the surf, their shiny sides flashing as they dart just beneath the surface. There is often audible flapping and splashing as the fish engage in a never-ending attempt to outmaneuver their enemies.

The birthplaces of George Washington, Robert E. Lee, and James Monroe are only about 10 miles apart, as the crow flies, near the southwestern side of the Potomac River. All three birthplaces are off VA 3 in Westmoreland County. The birthplace of Robert E. Lee and George Washington are on either side of Westmoreland State Park (*see* page 94). James Monroe, the fifth president of the United States, was born off VA 205 near Colonial Beach, but little has been done to commemorate the site. A group of concerned citizens has received a grant to develop the site and reconstruct the home.

Lee was born at **Stratford Hall Plantation** (804-493-8038), a massive H-shaped manor house built in the late 1730s, home to many prominent members of the Lee family, and maintained in immaculate condition today. On the grounds are a formal garden outlined in boxwoods and a reconstructed gristmill turned by a giant water-wheel. Three miles of nature trails wind through woods where General Lee once rode horses. From the bluffs overlooking the Potomac River is a magnificent view of the river cliffs where fossils from ancient seas are embedded. Visitors who arrive in the middle of the day can enjoy a plantation lunch served in a log cabin. Stratford Hall, open from 9 to 4:30 daily except major holidays, is maintained and operated by the nonprofit Robert E. Lee Memorial Association. The dining room at Stratford Hall is open for lunch and dinner daily, year-round. To get to the plantation, travel on VA 3, approximately 1 mile east of the entrance to Westmoreland State Park, then go east on VA 214 about 2 miles to the entrance.

George Washington's Birthplace at Wakefield is a national park that leaves more to the imagination than does Stratford Hall Plantation. The actual home where the first United States president was born burned to the ground on Christmas Day in 1779 while Washington was serving with the Continental Army at Morristown, New Jersey. In 1936, the site on Popes Creek was excavated, then covered again for preservation. With no records about the house to go on other than the excavated foundations, the National Park Service has built Popes Creek Plantation house next to the original site in an attempt to replicate an eighteenth century plantation and lifestyle similar to the one Washington was born into. Costumed interpreters invite visitors to temporarily transport themselves back to the world that produced several early U.S. presidents and leaders. The plantation and a marker that serves as a national monument are part of the 538-acre national park, which is located on VA 204 about 2 miles north of Wakefield Corner and VA 3.

Just up the road from the birthplace is **Ingleside Plantation Winery** (804-224-8687). The 2,500-acre plantation has an interesting and varied history, dating back to 1834. It has served as a school for boys, a Civil War fort for Union troops, a temporary courthouse, and a dairy farm before becoming a winery in 1980. Special events held annually at the plantation include Summer Jazz in the Courtyard in June and the Northern Neck Seafood Extravaganza in September. The winery is located on VA 638 between Leedstown and Oak Grove.

From May through September, there are ripe berries of one kind or another at **Westmoreland Berry Farm and Orchard** on VA 637 (800-997-BERRY) west of Oak Grove. Sun-warmed strawberries are delicious from mid-May to early June. Cherries, black and red raspberries, blackberries, and apricots never taste sweeter than when you pick them yourself. You can also shop for already picked berries, as well as fresh peaches and apples, preserves, cookbooks, and gifts. Hikers can enjoy the several miles of trails of the **Voorhees Nature Preserve**, property at the berry farm managed by the Virginia Chapter of The Nature Conservancy. The trails pass through woodlands, opening to views of the Rappahannock River and marshes at several observation points. To find the farm, go 2.5 miles west of Oak Grove on VA 3, turn left (south) on VA 634, and follow signs about 3 miles to the farm.

The town of Colonial Beach is on VA 205 on the tidal Potomac River, about 5 miles north of Oak Grove and VA 3. **Colonial Beach Visitor's Center** (804-224-0732), located on the boardwalk, is open seasonally. The community has a wide, lifeguarded beach (804-244-8145 or 804-224-1781) that is cleaned and smoothed daily during the summer. Restrooms are available.

For more information: Northern Neck Tourism Council, PO Box 1707, Warsaw, VA 22572. Phone (800) 393-6180. E-mail nntc@northernneck.org. Web site www.northernneck.org. Virginia's Chesapeake Bay, PO Box 149, Saluda, VA 23149. Phone (800) 336-3078.

HUGHLETT POINT NATURAL AREA

[Fig. 9(13)] On a secluded Chesapeake Bay peninsula northeast of Kilmarnock, at the mouth of Dividing Creek, is a mix of wetlands, uplands, and sandy beach that comprise Hughlett Point Natural Area. Walking trails, boardwalks, and platforms make the natural area an excellent place for nature observation. Early mornings and dusk are the best times to hear the calls of birds or see critters emerge from the marsh edges, but any time of day has its rewards.

Many visitors to Hughlett Point hope to get a glimpse of a river otter (*Lontra canadensis*) floating on its back, picking the meat from a crustacean, or see a bald eagle (*Haliaeetus leucocephalus*) or osprey (*Pandion haliaeetus*) perched on trees at the marsh edge.

There is also the possibility of seeing a gray fox, great blue heron, snowy egret, clapper rail, or the elegant tundra swan. Bird watchers are familiar with the many migrating and nesting songbirds that find food and cover in the mix of tidal and nontidal wetlands or upland forests of the preserve.

But a creature at least partly responsible for the preservation of the 205-acre natural area is a barely noticeable insect, the northeastern beach tiger beetle (*Cicindela dorsalis dorsalis*) that skitters or flies a short distance away from your approaching steps. The undisturbed beach on the peninsula has all the necessary requirements for this threatened species to complete its two-year life cycle. After hatching from eggs

SNOWY EGRET
(*Egretta thula*)
Snowy egrets have
a black bill,
black legs, and
yellow feet
sometimes referred to as golden slippers.

laid in the sand, larvae of tiger beetles live in burrows, capturing small prey with their large jaws. The agile, predatory adults are about 0.66 inch long, with bronze-green heads, large, pinching jaws, and a white or cream-colored back with dark markings.

According to the Virginia Division of Natural Heritage, which manages the natural area, the species was once found in abundance on beaches from Cape Cod, Massachusetts, to mid-New Jersey, and on the shores of the Chesapeake Bay. Now, however, the protean tidal environment of this sandy beach is one of the few places the federally protected species is found in the northeast.

Directions: From Kilmarnock, go north on VA 200 about 4 miles. Turn right (east) on VA 606 and go about 2 miles. Turn right (south) on VA 605 and go about 2 miles to the parking area on the left.

Activities: Wildlife and wildfowl walks, fishing, crabbing.

Facilities: Walking trails and boardwalks, observation platforms, interpretive signs.

Dates: The preserve is open from dawn to dusk, year-round.

Fees: None.

Closest town: Kilmarnock is about 8 miles southwest.

For more information: Chesapeake Bay Region Steward, Virginia Department of Conservation and Recreation, Division of Natural Heritage, Gloucester Point, VA 23062. Phone (804) 684-7577.

WESTMORELAND STATE PARK

[Fig. 9(11)] Westmoreland State Park was one of Virginia's six original parks built in the 1930s by the Civilian Conservation Corps. The CCC parks are recognizable by their sturdy log cabins, restaurants, and other buildings that have stood the test of time. Even roads had to be dug by hand. Also note the expertly constructed stone walls and arched bridges from the park's early days. The 1,299-acre park is positioned on a high bluff

Westmoreland State Park fishing pier.

above the Potomac River, which is 6 miles wide at this point. From the screened porch of the park restaurant, which sits in a grove of giant tulip poplars, red oaks, and white oaks, the view of the river is breathtaking.

Bald eagles soar beneath the cliffs, easily visible at times from the restaurant and from the back yards of the shaded rental cottages near the cliffs. As eagles continue to recover from their once-depleted numbers, they become an increasingly common sight on the Potomac River.

Seven hiking trails totaling 6.1 miles lead into the mature woods and to swamps around the park and down to the beach below the fossil-rich Horsehead Cliffs. Raccoons, foxes, deer, and owls inhabit the woods, while beavers, nutria, and wood ducks live in the park swamps. Along the cliffs that front the Potomac River is an entirely different habitat favoring waterfowl, shorebirds, and birds of prey such as sandpipers, terns, gulls, and osprey.

Anglers fishing from the surf, pier, or boats can catch striped bass, spot, and bluefish. Rock Spring Pond has freshwater fish, including catfish, bream, bass, and crappie. (Licenses are required.) Rowboats and paddleboats may be rented at the park. Powerboats are also allowed.

Directions: From Montross, drive 6 miles west on VA 3. Turn right on VA 347 and continue about 0.5 mile to the park entrance.

Activities: Hiking, biking (limited to the park roads and Mountain View bicycle route), picnicking, camping, swimming, boating, beachcombing.

Facilities: Hiking trails, campground (some hookups), rental cabins, boat ramp, paddleboat and rowboat rental, marina, fishing pier, pool and concession area, amphitheater, visitor center, restaurant, store, picnic tables and rental shelters, hot showers, restrooms.

Dates: The park is open from 8 a.m. to dark, year-round. The campgrounds, cabins, and restaurant are open from spring through fall. The pool is open from Memorial Day weekend through Labor Day.

Fees: There is an entrance fee, camping fee, and rental fee for shelters.

Closest town: Montross is about 6 miles southeast.

For more information: Westmoreland State Park, Route 1, Box 600, Montross, VA 22520. Phone (804) 493-8821.

BIG MEADOW INTERPRETIVE TRAIL

The Big Meadow Interpretive Trail follows an 1890 logging road at the start. Acorns crunch underfoot. The white oaks, red cedar, sweetgum, hickory, and tulip poplar of a mature forest block the sunlight and provide a fairly open understory dotted with red maples and American holly trees.

The path leads to an overlook on Yellow Swamp, where Indians under the rule of powerful Chief Powhatan once hunted. Then it leads steeply down to the Potomac River. Here, below the fossil-rich Horsehead Cliffs, beachcombers equipped with plastic bags stroll the sands looking for the fossilized remains of the prehistoric Miocene sea that once washed the area. As marine animals died, their remains settled to the bottom and were covered in sediments. Over millions of years, the land rose and the sea retreated. Now, as the Potomac cuts into the cliffs, sharks' teeth, whale bones, and fossils of crustaceans are revealed. Locating fossils can be difficult, and removing them by digging is only allowed with prior permission from the state park administration office in Richmond.

Trail: 1.25-mile (one-way) moderate interpretive path with steep sections, leading through woods to an overlook at Yellow Swamp and to the beach.

BELLE ISLE STATE PARK

[Fig. 9(10)] Belle Isle State Park is being developed from the tidal wetlands and upland fields and forests along Lancaster County's Rappahannock River shoreline. Today, anglers catch spot and croaker and families picnic on the same ground where there was once a village of Moraughtacunds, a tribe under the rule of Chief Powhatan. For many years after the Indians were gone, the Belle Isle peninsula was farmed as a plantation.

The state acquired the 733 acres, including 7 miles of shoreline, in 1993. Call for information on canoe trips, pontoon boat rides, interpretive programs, and environmental education programs.

Directions: From Kilmarnock, go west on VA 3 about 10 miles to Lively. Go left onto VA 201 and drive about 3 miles. Turn right on VA 354 at St. Mary's White Chapel and drive about 4 miles. Go left on VA 683 and continue about 1 mile to the park entrance.

Activities: Hiking, biking, picnicking, fishing, boating.

Facilities: Hiking and biking trails, picnic tables, boat ramp, portable toilets with handicap access.

Dates: The park is open daily, year-round.

Fees: There is an entry fee.

Closest town: Kilmarnock is about 18 miles east.

For more information: Belle Isle State Park, Route 3, Box 550, Lancaster, VA 22503-9425. Phone (804) 462-5030.

TULIPTREE OR
YELLOW POPLAR
(Liriodendron tulipifera)

CALEDON NATURAL AREA AND STATE PARK

[Fig. 9(12)] Bald eagles in one of the largest concentrations on the East Coast are the reason many people make time for a visit to Caledon Natural Area and State Park. So many eagles perch on the bluffs rising above the Potomac River that the park has been designated a National Natural Landmark. One of the best ways to see this magnificent bird of prey is to make a reservation to go on a guided tour, conducted from mid-June to September. Spotting scopes are available.

Even if no eagles are visible, five hiking trails that lead through Caledon's mature forests have their own rewards. Massive poplars, oaks, and beech trees rise 100 feet or more to a high canopy that shades out sunlight and leaves an open understory. The trails adjoin in partial loops. Each trail is about 1 mile or less in length and is criss-crossed with streams and sprinkled with benches and footbridges. The Boyd's Hole Trail to the Potomac River is open only between October 1 and March 21. Sensitive eagle habitat is closed during nesting season.

Directions: From US 301 about 6 miles north of Edgehill in King George County and 4 miles south of the Potomac River Bridge near Dahlgren, go southwest on VA 206 (which is joined by VA 218) for about 3 miles. When VA 206 and VA 218 fork, bear right on VA 218 and continue about 0.6 mile to the park entrance.

Activities: Hiking, guided eagle tours.

Facilities: Hiking trails, picnic tables, visitor center, portable toilets.

Dates: The park trails are open from 8 to sunset daily, year-round. The visitor center is open daily during summer and on weekends during the spring and fall. The trail to the eagle habitat on the Potomac River is open from late Oct. to late March.

Fees: There is an entry fee.

Closest town: Dahlgren is about 5 miles east.

For more information: Caledon Natural Area, 11617 Caledon Road, King George, VA 22485. Phone (540) 663-3861.

RESTAURANTS ON THE NORTHERN NECK

There are some excellent restaurants on the Northern Neck, but some are tucked away on the waterfront on back roads, easier to find by boat than by car.

CHESAPEAKE CAFE. VA 3 North, Kilmarnock. Sunday lunch buffet. Closed Tuesday. *Inexpensive to moderate. Phone (804) 435-3250.*

HORN HARBOR HOUSE. Burgess. This restaurant on the Great Wicomico River is a favorite with travelers and locals. Come by boat or car. *Moderate. Phone (804) 453-3351.*

ELIJAH'S RESTAURANT. 729 Main Street, Reedville. Restored 1800s market with waterfront location. Fresh seafood, beef, homemade soups and salads. *Inexpensive to moderate. Phone (804) 453-3621.*

KINSALE HARBOUR YACHT CLUB RESTAURANT. VA 203, Kinsale. Serving seafood and other fare Apr. through Oct. *Moderate. Phone (804) 472-2514.*

THE PILOT'S WHARF. Cole's Point Plantation, Cole's Point. Fresh seafood, steaks, chef's specials. Come by land or sea. Casual. Seasonal live music and outdoor crab deck. Located on the Potomac River off VA 202. *Inexpensive to moderate. Phone (804) 472-4761.*

SANDPIPER RESTAURANT. VA 3, White Stone. Charbroiled steaks, fresh seafood. Opens at 5 p.m. Tuesday through Saturday. Casual. *Inexpensive to moderate. Phone (804) 435-6176.*

WILKERSON'S RESTAURANT. VA 205, 3900 McKinney Boulevard, Colonial Beach. Crab cakes, rockfish, other fresh seafood, steaks, chicken. Waterfront. Open daily. Buffet Friday through Sunday. *Inexpensive to moderate. Phone (804) 224-7117.*

LODGING ON THE NORTHERN NECK

Although motels may be a bit scarce on the Northern Neck, the peninsula is a haven for those who enjoy B&Bs. Restored ship captains' homes in Reedville are a highlight. Campgrounds and cottages are available at **Heritage Park Resort** in Warsaw (800-335-4464), at the **Reedville KOA** (804-453-3430) where the Smith Island ferry is located, and at **Coles Point Plantation in Coles Point** (804-472-3955), where there is a marina and restaurant.

THE HOPE AND GLORY INN. 634 King Carter Drive, Irvington. Bed and breakfast, built in 1890 as a school. Victorian gardens. Complimentary bicycles for exploring Irvington. Pets and children are welcome in cottages. Named one of the world's best hotels by Europe's *Tatler/Cunard Travel Guide. Expensive. Phone (804) 438-6053.*

BAY MOTEL. US 360, Reedville. Convenient to Reedville fishing activity and cruise boats. *Inexpensive to moderate. Phone (804) 453-5171.*

BEST WESTERN. 4522 Richmond Road, Warsaw. Restaurant nearby. Pool. Small pets allowed. *Moderate. Phone (804) 333-1700.*

THE MORRIS HOUSE. Lower Main Street, Reedville. Restored sea captain's home (1835) on the waterfront in the historic district. Children and pets are allowed with prior notice. Beautiful interior woodwork, antiques. Private dock, complimentary bikes. *Moderate to expensive. Phone (804) 453-7016.*

STRANGERS IN GOOD COMPANY. 170 Bell's Cove Road, Callao. B&B in a secluded 150-year-old farmhouse with large library. Victorian decor. Children and pets are allowed with prior notice. *Moderate. Phone (804) 529-5132.*

THE TIDES. Irvington. Two historic resort hotels. Three restaurants with award-winning cuisine, two golf courses including the top-rated Golden Eagle, marina, tennis courts, swimming pool, exercise room, beach. Closed in winter. *Expensive. Phone (804) 438-5000 or (800) 843-3746.*

WHISPERING PINES MOTEL. VA 3, White Stone. Located on VA 3 just north of White Stone. *Inexpensive to moderate. Phone (804) 453-1101.*

WINDMILL POINT RESORT. VA 695, Windmill Point. Restaurant, 150-slip marina on the Chesapeake Bay, beach, swimming pools, nine-hole golf course, tennis courts, nature trails. *Expensive. Phone (804) 435-1166.*

WHITE OAK
(*Quercus alba*)
White oaks grow to
100 feet and have
rounded tips on their
leaves.

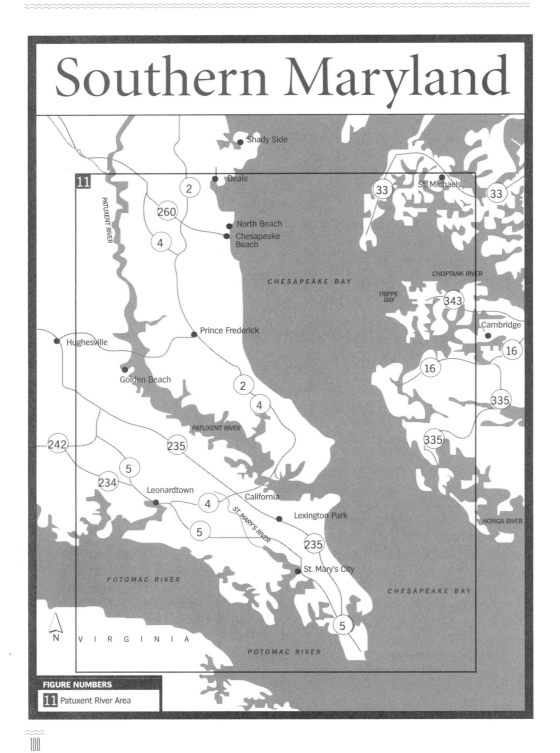

Southern Maryland

11 Patuxent River Area

Shady Side

Deale

2

260

4

North Beach

Chesapeake Beach

PATUXENT RIVER

CHESAPEAKE BAY

33 St. Michaels

33

CHOPTANK RIVER

TRIPPE BAY

343

Cambridge

16

Prince Frederick

Hughesville

Golden Beach

2

4

16

335

PATUXENT RIVER

242

235

5

234

Leonardtown

California

4

ST. MARY'S RIVER

Lexington Park

5

235

335

HONGA RIVER

St. Mary's City

POTOMAC RIVER

CHESAPEAKE BAY

N

VIRGINIA

5

POTOMAC RIVER

FIGURE NUMBERS

11 Patuxent River Area

Southern Maryland

S ince colonial times, the proximity of Southern Maryland to the metropolitan areas of Washington, DC, and Baltimore, Maryland, has meant this pastoral Chesapeake Bay countryside has felt the tread of soldiers' feet, seen the construction of high tech defense and energy facilities, and received wave after wave of city dwellers in search of solitude and renewal.

The counties of Calvert and St. Mary's that border the western side of the bay have somehow managed to keep much of their rural character, their isolated wetlands where a wild goose still calls, their salty watermen who ply the bay in workboats.

A drive along the main routes that follow the county contours southeast/northwest can be deceptive. The riches in parks, preserves, museums, and historic cities hide just off the main route, and a traveler could drive through the counties without learning the human and natural history of Maryland's birthplace.

[*Above:* Chesapeake Bay offers many opportunities for wildlife photography]

Chambers of commerce, county tourist bureaus, and visitor information centers are brimming with information to connect travelers with mouth-watering seafood, to provide anglers and boaters with directions to marinas and boat landings, and to help kayakers and canoeists find flat water and protected coves to explore.

The wide road shoulders and pastoral scenery make Southern Maryland ideal for cyclists. Morning sunshine on tobacco leaves drying inside a red barn is especially beautiful viewed from a bicycle, wind in the face, birdsong all around. Many of the sites mentioned here have roads and trails that invite exploration by mountain bike. A Southern Maryland Bicycle Map is available from the Calvert County Department of Economic Development. Phone (800) 331-9771.

St. Mary's County

An Amish farm boy clutches his hat as he pedals a bicycle down a dusty lane. A woman in a car waves as she passes the plain-clad youngster on her way to work at the technologically sophisticated Patuxent River Naval Air Station. Like much of Maryland's western Chesapeake Bay, St. Mary's County has its own dichotomy of cultures, its own seamless melding of past, present, and future.

The county occupies Maryland's southernmost land on the western side of the bay, bordered by the Patuxent River to the northeast and the lower Potomac River to the southwest. The peninsula formed by these two rivers extended southward like a beckoning finger to the early explorers as they headed north past Virginia and took a left turn into the Potomac River.

For more information: St. Mary's County Travel and Tourism Division, Economic and Community Development, PO Box 653, Leonardtown, MD 20650. Phone (301) 475-4405 or (800) 327-9023. E-mail stmcdecd@mail.ameritel.net.

St. Mary's County Tourist Information Center, located with the St. Mary's County Chamber of Commerce on MD 5 in Mechanicsville. Phone (301) 884-5555.

ST. CLEMENT'S ISLAND AND POTOMAC RIVER MUSEUM

[Fig. 11(1)] Called the birthplace of Maryland, St. Clement's Island was the place Leonard Calvert and his English adventurers first touched Maryland soil. After coming ashore on March 25, 1634, they held the first Roman Catholic Mass of the original colonies. A 40-foot cross was erected three centuries later in 1934 as a reminder of the religious freedom the state's first colonists were seeking.

With its strategic location at the mouth of the Potomac River, 0.5 mile off the coast of St. Mary's County at Coltons Point, St. Clement's Island naturally became involved in the Revolutionary War, the War of 1812, and the Civil War. Today the island is a state park with hiking trails, picnic tables, information boards, and a boat dock and fishing pier. The park is accessible only by boat.

One of the best ways to learn about Maryland's colonization and the Native Americans who hunted and fished the area prior to the arrival of the English is to visit the Potomac River Museum. Located at Coltons Point, the museum has models of the *Ark of London* and the *Dove*, the ships that carried 140 colonists on their four-month voyage across the Atlantic.

A country store from 1890 and the Little Red Schoolhouse from 1820 are also on the museum grounds. During the Blessing of the Fleet event on the first full weekend of October, the museum staff provides boat tours of the island.

Directions: The state park is located on an island in the Potomac River 0.5 mile offshore near St. Clement's and Breton bays. It is accessible only by boat. For museum, from MD 5 at Morganza in north-central St. Mary's County, go south on MD 242 about 12 miles to Coltons Point. Turn left on Bayview Road and follow signs.

Activities: State park: hiking, picnicking, fishing. Group boat trips to park by previous arrangement with the museum.

Facilities: State park: hiking trails, picnic tables, pavilion, restrooms, fishing pier/boat dock. Museum: exhibits, country store, gift shop, pier and dock.

Dates: State park: open sunrise to sunset year-round, except on major holidays. Museum: open Mar. through Sept., 9 to 5 weekdays, 12 to 5 weekends; Oct. through late Mar., 12 to 4 Wednesday through Sunday.

Fees: State park: none. Museum: There is a charge for admission; none for children 12 and under.

For more information: St. Clement's Island State Park, c/o Point Lookout State Park, PO Box 48, Scotland, MD 20687. Phone (301) 872-5688. Potomac River Museum, Coltons Point, MD 20626. Phone (301) 769-2222.

HISTORIC ST. MARY'S CITY

[Fig. 11(2)] Just two days after they landed at St. Clement's Island, the English explorers sailed the *Ark of London* and the *Dove* up what is now called St. Mary's River. They were so taken by the lush river valley, they bought an entire village from the Indians along with 30 square miles of land around it and established Maryland's first permanent settlement, St. Mary's City. The city served as Maryland's capital for the next 60 years.

Today, visitors can reconstruct in their minds the seventeenth-century town that existed here. They can walk among excavations still in progress and reconstructed buildings at Historic St. Mary's City, just south of the little college town of St. Mary's City. The original city was all but forgotten after the capital was moved to Annapolis in 1695.

The tour includes Godiah Spray Tobacco Plantation, a working farm where museum workers representing the Spray family and their indentured servants explain tidewater farming. Other volunteers, also dressed in period costume, work in the city gardens, sew, interpret Indian culture at the Woodland Indian Hamlet, and help to maintain and sail the *Maryland Dove*. This working re-creation of the 1630s square-rigged ship of the colonists is docked on the river below the reconstructed State House of 1676. Farthing's Ordinary and Garden, constructed to resemble a typical 17th century inn, and Farthing's Kitchen are favorite stops on the tour.

Founded by Roman Catholics in search of religious freedom, St. Mary's County became the Mother County of Maryland. Not only did the colony practice religious tolerance, but also the colonists proved they could coexist peacefully with Indians. St. Mary's City witnessed the nation's first black to attain a governmental position and received the first request for women's right to vote.

Directions: The visitor center is on Rosecroft Road, just off MD 5 south of St. Mary's City in southern St. Mary's County.

Facilities: Visitor center, museum tour, restaurant, restrooms.

Dates: Open 10 to 5 Wednesday through Sunday, mid-Mar. through the last weekend in Nov. Closed Thanksgiving Day.

Fees: There is a fee for the museum tour.

Closest town: St. Mary's City is just north of historic city.

For more information: HSMC, PO Box 39, St. Mary's City, MD 20686. Phone (301) 862-0990 or (800) SMC-1634.

POINT LOOKOUT STATE PARK

[Fig. 11(27)] Point Lookout State Park occupies 1,046 acres on a narrow peninsula at the southern tip of St. Mary's County. The peninsula is formed by the Chesapeake Bay on the east side and the mouth of the Potomac River on the west.

A drive down to the point reveals the saltwater focus of this park. To the right is a launch area on salty Lake Conoy, giving canoeists flat water to explore and giving boaters access to the tidal Potomac River and to the Chesapeake Bay via the Potomac. On the left, a popular pier juts 710 feet into the productive fishing waters of the bay. Continuing down the narrowing strip of land, a causeway lined with huge boulders, or riprap, to protect the shore from erosion provides anglers another access point to good fishing waters. From the riprap, fishermen cast spoons and plugs for rockfish and bluefish, while others in small boats cast toward shore for fish that are attracted to the rocks.

On the right of the causeway is a picnic area and public beach. At the peninsula's tip, where the waters of the Potomac finally spill into the bay, is the Point Lookout Lighthouse, built in 1830. Unlike the traditional tower-shaped lighthouses, this one is a small house with a lantern on a rooftop. Except for an occasional open house, the lighthouse is closed to the public. Near the public restrooms and kiosks is one accessible part of the old lighthouse—a tiny, brick outbuilding used by the former keeper of the lighthouse.

But life has not always been so placid at Point Lookout. Today a family opens a picnic basket, pitches a tent or watches a cattle egret take flight where Civil War soldiers were once held prisoner and where smallpox victims and Union soldiers were hospitalized. Some 52,000 Confederate soldiers passed through the Point Lookout prison camp during the war. The point offered a natural barrier to escape.

Scant evidence remains to remind a visitor of the agony of war. Two obelisks stand on MD 5 near the park entrance in memory of the 3,384 who died while imprisoned under deplorable conditions. Despite the risk of being housed with highly contagious patients, some prisoners faked smallpox so they could be sent to the nearby hospital where they might try to escape. Today, the gentle slap of waves on the swimming beach and the feel of sand beneath bare feet are more akin to the peace this retreat afforded in the early 1800s, before the war and before the Battle of Gettysburg in 1863 which spurred the construction of the prison. During the summer, the park operates a visitor center with a small Civil War museum and a nature center. Evening campfire programs expand on the human and natural history of the point.

Fishing and crabbing are allowed at two smaller piers and at designated areas on both the river and bay side of the park. Anglers on the Potomac side of the shoreline do not need a fishing license. Swimming is permitted only at the beach/picnic area. Special events such as Civil War re-enactments, "ghost walks," and other interpretive programs entertain park visitors throughout the year. Leashed pets are allowed only at specified campsites, on the causeway, and on the beach north of the causeway.

During the summer, cruises are available from the park to Smith Island. The cruise boat docks next to the camp store, where anglers can find bait and gear for crabbing or fishing.

Directions: In St. Mary's County, follow MD 5 to its southern terminus at the confluence of the Chesapeake Bay and the Potomac River.

Activities: Camping, picnicking, hiking, limited biking, boating, flat-water canoeing, fishing, crabbing, seasonal hunting, Smith Island cruise.

Facilities: Campground (143 wood sites, 26 with full hook-ups); dumping station; camp store; trails; swimming beach with grills, picnic tables, shower buildings, and playground; visitor center and museum; rental motor boats, canoes and rowboats; boat ramp; cruise boat.

Dates: Gates open year-round except Thanksgiving, Christmas and New Year's Day. Swimming beach: Open Memorial Day through Labor Day. Camp office: Open 8 a.m. to 11 p.m. year-round. Camp store: Open 7 a.m. to 8 p.m. daily, Memorial Day through Labor Day. Visitor Center: open 10 to 6 weekends, Apr. through May and Sept. through Oct., and daily, Memorial Day through Labor Day; closed Nov. through Mar. Cruise to Smith Island: runs 10 to 4 daily, Memorial Day through Labor Day.

Fees: Entrance fee weekends and holidays May-Sept.; fee for camping, use of beach/picnic area, cottage rental, boat launch.

Closest town: Lexington Park is about 16 miles north.

For more information: Point Lookout State Park, PO Box 48, Scotland, MD 20687. Phone (301) 872-5688.

TRAILS OF POINT LOOKOUT STATE PARK

Hiking trails are limited at Point Lookout to the short Periwinkle Point Trail (named for the periwinkle snail found here) and the Railroad Trail. Both are out and back hikes on flat land, heading in opposite directions from the same trailhead at the visitor center. At the trailhead, go left 0.25 mile to Periwinkle Point on Lake Conoy and back. Or, go right 0.5 mile and back for the Railroad Trail.

If a hiker on the Railroad Trail imagines hearing the whistle of a steam engine in the birdsong along this old railroad bed, it's just the product of an overactive imagination. Trains and tracks never made it to Point Lookout, although there were major plans to extend train travel from the nation's capital at Washington, D C, all the way to the point to avoid the more lengthy water route. Following the Civil War, plans were finalized and the bed was cleared. Farther north, workers laid tracks and trains began to operate, including a regular run by the U. S. Navy during World War II. But the railroad continually changed hands, delaying construction. Finally the national decline of railroads spelled the end of this one, too. Hikers and bird watchers finally became the first people to use the railroad bed on the southern end cleared so long ago.

Small ditches on either side of the raised bed usually hold marshy water and breed mosquitoes and other biting insects. A good bug repellent is a must during warm weather. If these two short trails leave you wanting more, the flat, easy roads of the campground loops lead through maritime forests and marshes with more opportunities to spot wildlife, wildflowers, birds, and reptiles.

The finger of Point Lookout points the way south for fall migratory birds along the Atlantic Flyway. September and October are the best months for bird watchers to add new varieties to their sightings lists.

The woods harbor red foxes, white-tailed deer, opossums, and cottontail rabbits. Quiet visitors may surprise a raccoon raiding a duck's nest for eggs. Often, when animals are not seen, droppings, tracks, and burrows in the sand or wet marsh may tell of their presence. Look for the mud holes of fiddler crabs and tiny tracks in the sand from the broad-headed skink or ground skink. Listen for the guitar string "k'tunk" of the green frog or the sudden croak of a great blue heron as it rises from the marsh. Biologists believe there may even be a state endangered nocturnal species here called the Eastern narrow-mouth toad (*Gastrophryne carolinensis*), which hides under rocks and logs. Several varieties of turtles reside at or visit Point Lookout including the Eastern box turtle, common snapping turtle, Eastern painted turtle,

MARSH PERIWINKLE
(*Littorina irrorata*)

Eastern mud turtle, northern diamond-backed terrapin, the federally threatened loggerhead sea turtle, and the federally endangered Kemp's (Atlantic) ridley sea turtle. Both the loggerhead (*Caretta caretta*) and the ridley (*Lepidochelys kempii*) sea turtles gained federal protection in the 1970s, following overharvesting of the reptiles and their eggs, disruption of habitat, and fishnet drownings.

Throughout much of the campground and around the visitor center, a prolific reed grass called phragmites (*Phragmites australis*) astounds visitors with its beauty, while annoying park personnel with its persistence and dominating nature. The reeds form dense stands in marshes, choking out the competition, offering little food for wildlife, and spreading by means of roots or rhizomes up to 30 feet long. In late summer, flower heads composed of feathery plumes of silky hairs undulate in the wind.

Marsh Periwinkle

Climbing the stalks of saltmarsh cordgrass and clinging to rocks at Point Lookout is the common and abundant snail of wetlands, the marsh periwinkle (*Littorina irrorata*). About 1 inch long, the algae-eating periwinkle lays eggs that hatch into larvae, which then develop into small snails during summer.

Trails: Periwinkle: 0.5-mile easy round trip from visitor center to Lake Conoy and back. Railroad: 1-mile easy round trip from visitor center along old railroad bed and back.

SMITH ISLAND CRUISES

A cruise ship is available each Wednesday through Sunday during the summer months to take tourists to Smith Island, a serene land accessible only by boat. A boat departs from the state park at 10 a.m. and returns at 4 p.m. See Somerset County in Eastern Shore, page 289, for a description of Smith Island.

Directions: Enter park on MD 5. Dock is next to camp store.

For more information: Capt. Alan Tyler, PO Box 41, Rhodes Point, MD 21824. Phone (410) 425-2771.

PINEY POINT LIGHTHOUSE MUSEUM AND PARK

[Fig. 11(3)] The Piney Point Lighthouse is one of just four lighthouses still in existence on the Potomac River. Its fixed Fresnel beacon, which could be seen for 11 miles, was housed in a classic tower structure. The brick lighthouse was constructed in 1836 approximately 14 miles upriver from the Chesapeake Bay and retired by the U. S. Coast Guard in 1964.

Sometimes called the Lighthouse of Presidents, Piney Point has been visited by James Madison, Abraham Lincoln, Theodore Roosevelt, and many other presidents and dignitaries. The lighthouse is on the grounds of a 6-acre park with a museum, boardwalk, gift shop, and picnic facilities. The museum depicts the history of Piney Point and other Chesapeake Bay lights.

History exhibits include information about the Black Panther Historic Shipwreck Preserve 1 mile offshore. The *Black Panther* was a German submarine that now serves as Maryland's first underwater park on the bottom of the Potomac. The submarine was taken into United States possession during World War II, sunk off Point No Point in the Chesapeake Bay by a demolition team in 1948, then raised and moved to its present location off Piney Point in 1949.

Directions: From the junction of MD 5 and MD 249 at Callaway in southern St. Mary's County, go 9 miles south on MD 249 and go right on Lighthouse Road to the park.

Dates: Lighthouse grounds: open sunrise to sunset daily, year-round. Museum and gift shop: open 12 to 5, Saturday through Sunday, May through Oct. Call for weekday hours.

For more information: St. Clement's Island Potomac River Museum, phone (301) 769-2222.

PATUXENT RIVER NAVAL AIR MUSEUM

[Fig. 11(5)] Located at Lexington Park, the Patuxent Naval Air Museum presents the history of the United States Navy's aviation research and development, testing, and evaluation since 1911. Just east of Lexington Park is the Patuxent River Naval Air Station, employer of some 16,000 people. The cupola from the Cedar Point Lighthouse, built in 1896, that stood abandoned on an eroding jut of land in the Chesapeake Bay on the east side of the naval air station, is now located on museum grounds. It is not open to the public.

Directions: Museum is on Shangri-La Drive and MD 235 at Lexington Park, just east of the MD 246 and MD 235 intersection.

Facilities: Museum, restrooms.

Dates: Open Wednesday through Sunday, 12 to 5, year-round. Closed Easter, Thanksgiving, Christmas, and New Year's Day.

Fees: None.

For more information: Patuxent River Naval Air Museum, phone (301) 863-7418.

ST. MARY'S RIVER STATE PARK

[Fig. 11(6)] St. Mary's River State Park has a split personality. Two tracts of land make up the park, one with 250-acre St. Mary's Lake as the focal point and one with 2,200 acres of Maryland undeveloped wild lands. Both sections of the park are located in St. Mary's County between MD 5 and MD 235 and between Leonardtown and Lexington Park. The lake and the wild lands are about 0.5 mile apart, separated by a stretch of private land and MD 471.

The Western Branch of St. Mary's River was dammed in the 1970s for flood control, forming a popular freshwater fishing lake. The denuded trunks of hardwood trees that grew in the former river valley poke above the lake surface and are fantastic fish attractors. Today, anglers cast popping bugs into the shallows or play deep-running crankbaits for trophy largemouth bass in the dark green waters. Chain pickerel, crappie, bluegill, and sunfish are also available both to the angler and the occasional predatory bald eagle. Bulletin boards at the boat launch area list current

Fishing is popular in St. Mary's Lake.

regulations. Electric trolling motors up to one horsepower may be used but gasoline motors are prohibited. Camping, swimming, and fires are also banned.

A well-used trail around the lake gives boat-less anglers access to the entire 11.5-mile perimeter of the lake. The imprints of horses' hooves and mountain bike tires indicate other popular uses of the trail.

In the wild lands section of the park, men and women with bow and arrow or firearms still pursue rabbit, squirrel, and white-tailed deer on the same stretch of the St. Mary's River where tribes of Indians such as the Algonquins, Piscataway-Conoy, and the bellicose Susquehannocks once hunted. An alert hunter or hiker sometimes finds evidence of early life along the river in the form of arrowheads, axe heads, or pottery. Runoff from a heavy rain can uncover relics from as far back as 3000 B.C.

Swamp and marsh habitat characterize the river and its tributaries in the central and northern part of the wild lands area. The main river is enlarged at the southern tip of the wild lands area by the western branch tributary, flowing in from St. Mary's Lake. The St. Mary's River empties a 5,600-acre watershed that, before the flood-control lake was created, could and did flood the town of Great Mills regularly. The town took its name from the numerous mills that harnessed the river's power. Cecil's Old Mill (on MD 5 at Great Mills), listed in the National Register of Historic Places, is the last water mill in St. Mary's County. Originally constructed as a textile mill for long-since failed cotton fields, the mill now sells local arts and crafts.

Directions: For St. Mary's Lake, from Great Mills (at junction of MD 5 and MD 246 in south/central St. Mary's County) go 2.5 miles north on MD 5. Go right on Camp Cosoma Road and drive about 0.75 mile to the lake parking lot.

For wild lands area, from Great Mills go 0.2 mile north on MD 5. Turn right on

MD 471 (Indian Bridge Road) and go about 2.5 miles. Turn right into the wild lands area. Visitors can also access the park by following Old Rolling Road from MD 237 at California. Or, from MD 235 at California, go south on MD 237 (Chancellors Run) a little over 1 mile and turn right on Norris Road into the park.

Activities: Freshwater fishing, seasonal hunting, boating (no gasoline motors), hiking, mountain biking, horseback riding, picnicking, playground.

Facilities: Fishing lake, boat ramp, restrooms, picnic tables, playground. There are no facilities at the wild lands section.

Dates: The park is open sunrise to sunset, year-round, except major holidays. The boat ramp is open spring to fall.

Fees: A lake entrance fee is in effect May through Sept.

Closest town: Great Mills is 2.5 miles south of the lake entrance road and about 1.5 miles south of the southern border of the wild lands section of the park. Lexington Park (with stores and motels) is about 5 miles east of the lake entrance. California is 1 mile north of the northern boundary of the wild lands.

For more information: Park Manager, Point Lookout State Park, PO Box 48, Scotland, MD 20687. Phone (301) 872-5688. Cecil's Old Mill, phone (301) 994-1510.

GREENWELL STATE PARK

[Fig. 11(28)] Two bay horses stand in the shade of a white barn, switching their tales. On both sides of the long, dusty lane leading to Rosedale Manor House, yellow-green fields of soybeans soak up the afternoon sun. Driving down the entrance lane to Greenwell State Park, visitors might be able to imagine themselves arriving more than a century ago by horse and buggy at this grand manor house.

The park is part of a 4,000-acre tract formerly called Resurrection Manor that was one of Maryland's oldest land grants. Lord Baltimore made the grant to Thomas Cornwayles in 1650 in appreciation of Cornwayles's service as president of the Provincial Council.

Located on a bluff above the scenic Patuxent River, the manor house that was built by a later owner in the 1830s remains as a focal point of today's park. The house is on Maryland's list of historic properties. The most recent owners of the manor house, John Philip Greenwell Jr. and his sister, Mary Wallace Greenwell, donated their 177-acre farm for use as a state park, with special emphasis on facilities for the physically challenged. The State of Maryland bought an adjacent farm to add to the Greenwell donation to form the current 576-acre park.

Huge red oaks, pin oaks, red cedars, hackberry trees, ginkgoes, magnolias, and walnuts planted by a former owner now shade the picnic area and grounds around the house. Behind the house is a pier reaching into the Patuxent River where people can crab and fish. Swimming is permitted on a nearby beach. Boaters may also launch canoes or kayaks or other nonmotorized craft on the beach to explore the river shoreline. One area of woods is set aside in fall for hunting.

Directions: From the junction of MD 4 and MD 235 (Three Notch Road) at California, go north 4 miles on 235. Turn right on MD 245 East (Sotterley Gate Road) and go 2.5 miles. Turn right onto Steerhorn Neck Road. The park entrance is the second drive on the left (approximately 0.8 mile).

Activities: Hiking, fishing, picnicking, hunting, canoe/kayaking, swimming.

Facilities: Picnic tables, hiking trails, fishing pier, rental manor house for special events.

Dates: Open sunrise to sunset, year-round.

Fees: None for day use; a rental fee is charged for manor house.

Closest town: California is 7 miles south.

For more information: Greenwell State Park, 44828 Steer Horn Neck Road, Hollywood, MD 20636. Phone (301) 373-2731. Or contact Point Lookout State Park, PO Box 48, Scotland, MD 20687. Phone (301) 872-5688.

HIKING TRAILS OF GREENWELL STATE PARK

Five trails, named for the color of their blazes, skirt fields of crops and lead into woods where hikers may get a glimpse red or gray foxes, cottontail rabbits, white-tailed deer, and groundhogs. The Orange Trail is described below.

The wooded White Trail begins across the road from a small parking area located on Steerhorn Neck Road about halfway between MD 245 and the park entrance road. The Gray Access trailhead is on the left side of the entrance road near the entrance and leads to the Blue, Red, Yellow, and White trails. Each trail is shaped like a lasso, with the same beginning and end, and with a loop at the far end. A current park map may be helpful, as trail colors are sometimes changed.

ORANGE TRAIL. Beginning beside a paddock and barn, the Orange Trail is a guided nature walk with weathered signs that are getting increasingly difficult to read. The path leads to a patch of deciduous forest, makes a loop around the woods, touches the Patuxent River shoreline, and then returns by the same trail to the parking lot. Often, a transition area between field and woods is a good place to spot animals that use the woods for cover, venturing into the field to eat. Ducks may glide out from shore in the wetlands of the trail.

In spring and summer, the bright flash of an azure bird may draw your attention to the bluebird boxes along the trail. In fall, look for pokeweed loaded with crimson berries, bright yellow tickseed sunflowers, and a path strewn with the dark husks of walnuts. The Christmas smell of cedar and the red berries of American holly lend their color to a winter hike.

The parking lot for the trailhead is located on the right side of the entrance road, just before the first side road to the right. The trailhead is on the left side of the road. Check with the park for any possible rerouting of this trail.

Trail: A 1.1-mile hike from the parking area to the woods, looping around the woods and returning by the same trail.

Degree of difficulty: Easy, with some challenging terrain through the forest near the river.

Blaze: Orange.

SOTTERLEY PLANTATION

[Fig. 11(29)] This plantation house, built in 1717, is the earliest known post-in-ground structure in the country. It is supported by cedar timbers driven into the ground rather than by a traditional foundation. The intricate latticework, Chippendale staircase, and shell alcoves inside are fine examples of period woodwork. The house has been continually occupied and the land has been a working plantation from the start.

Situated on the scenic Patuxent River, Sotterley was well positioned to become a colonial port of entry and tobacco plantation. Of interest on the grounds are a tobacco shed, a smokehouse where country hams are still cured, and restored slave quarters. The colorful past of Sotterley includes governors and gamblers, and enslaved and later free African Americans.

Directions: From the junction of MD 4 and MD 235 at California, go 4 miles north on MD 235. Turn right (east) on MD 245 and go about 2.5 miles. Turn right on Sotterley Road.

Dates: Grounds are open 10 to 4 Tuesday through Sunday year-round. Manor house tours are conducted May through Oct.

Fees: There is an admission fee.

Closest town: California is about 7 miles south.

For more information: Phone (800) 681-0850.

BEACHES IN ST. MARY'S COUNTY

Several public beaches provide access to the Chesapeake Bay and tributaries in St. Mary's County. There are also beaches at Greenwell (*see* page 110), Point Lookout (*see* page 104), and St. Mary's River (*see* page 108) state parks.

ELM'S BEACH, Forest Road, Dameron. [Fig. 11(7)] This beach in the southern part of the county features picnic tables, a swimming beach, a pavilion, and portable toilets. There is no running water. Open daily Apr. 15 through Oct. 31. Pedestrian access to beach year-round. Phone (301) 475-4572.

ST. INIGOES LANDING. [Fig. 11(8)] This beach, also in the southern part of the county, is located at the end of Beachville Road at the southern end of St. Inigoes Neck. It is southwest of St. Inigoes and MD 5. A boat ramp offers access to St. Mary's River. There is a pier and picnic area. Open dawn to dusk (does not apply to boaters). Phone (301) 475-4572.

MYRTLE POINT PARK. [Fig. 11(9)] Located off MD 4 at the eastern end of Patuxent Beach Road in California, Myrtle Point Park has walking trails, a beach, and picnic tables. Open dawn to dusk. Phone (301) 475-4572.

WICOMICO SHORES LANDING, MD 234, Army-Navy Drive, Chaptico. A ramp at Wicomico Shores Landing in the western corner of St. Mary's County gives boaters access to the Wicomico River. There is also a pier, a beach, a picnic area, and a gazebo on this state scenic river. The area opens at 6 a.m. Closing time varies according to season. Closed Nov. through Mar. Phone (301) 475-4572.

RESTAURANTS IN ST. MARY'S COUNTY

Here are a few of many fine restaurants in St. Mary's County that serve fresh Chesapeake Bay seafood.

SCHEIBEL'S RESTAURANT. MD 5, Wynne Road, Ridge. Fresh seafood, steaks, and chicken. Waterfront dining. Open May through Oct. *Inexpensive. Phone (301) 872-5185.*

STILL ANCHORS AT DENNIS POINT MARINA. Dennis Point Way, Drayden. Steamed crabs, steaks, seafood. Waterfront and outside dining. Closed Mondays. *Moderate. Phone (301) 994-2288.*

YE OLDE RESTAURANT & ICE CREAM PARLOUR. Washington Street, Leonardtown. Home-cooked meals, steak, seafood, sandwiches, and Eat Smart Menu. Open Monday through Saturday. *Inexpensive. Phone (301) 475-3020.*

CLARKES LANDING RESTAURANT. Clarkes Landing Road, Hollywood. Fresh seafood, steak, steamed crabs. Waterfront dining, outside dining. Open daily Memorial Day through Sept. *Inexpensive. Phone (301) 373-8468.*

LODGING IN ST. MARY'S COUNTY

Planning ahead is a good idea for those staying overnight in St. Mary's County. Because of the county's rural character, inns and motels tend to be a little hard to locate. The county can provide a complete listing. Here are a few suggestions.

BARD'S FIELD OF TRINITY MANOR. Pratt Road, Ridge. This historical waterfront house (1798) is an example of Tidewater architecture. It has fireplaces in the living and dining rooms and features access to boating, fishing, crabbing, birdwatching. *Moderate. Phone (301) 872-5989.*

SWANN'S HOTEL/INN. MD 249, Piney Point. 12 rooms, 3 cottages, lounge. *Moderate. Phone (301) 994-0774.*

A&E COMFORT HOTEL. MD 246, Lexington Park. 35 rooms, discounts offered. *Moderate. Phone (301) 863-7411.*

PATUXENT INN. MD 235, Lexington Park. Lounge and restaurant, continental breakfast, two lighted tennis courts, jogging trail, outdoor pool. *Moderate. Phone (301) 862-4100.*

SUPER 8 MOTEL. MD 235, California. Continental breakfast. Pets accepted. *Inexpensive. Phone (301) 862-9822.*

CHARLOTTE HALL MOTEL. MD 5, Charlotte Hall. Outdoor pool. Near restaurants. *Moderate. Phone (301) 884-7411.*

LOGGERHEAD TURTLE
(Caretta caretta)

Calvert County

With just 213 square miles on a peninsula sandwiched between the Chesapeake Bay to the east and the Patuxent River to the west, Calvert County is Maryland's smallest county. Many come here for the excellent opportunities for fishing, crabbing, and enjoying the sandy beaches. The counties' parks, preserves, museums, and harbors also offer visitors many options for learning about and enjoying the natural and human history of the area.

For more information: Calvert County Department of Economic Development, Courthouse, Prince Frederick, MD 20678. Phone (800) 331-9771 or (410) 535-4583. Web site www.co.cal.md.us/cced. E-mail cced@co.cal.md.us.

Calvert County Chamber of Commerce, phone (410) 535-2577.

VISITOR INFORMATION CENTERS

Two information centers have helpful staff, maps, brochures, and restrooms:

FAIRVIEW INFORMATION CENTER (northern Calvert County), 8120 Southern Maryland Boulevard, Route 4, Owings, MD 20736. Phone (410) 257-5381 or (410) 257-0801.

SOLOMONS INFORMATION CENTER (southern Calvert County), MD 2/4 (across from the Calvert Marine Museum), Solomons, MD 20688. Phone (410) 326-6027.

SOLOMONS ISLAND AREA

[Fig. 11] Solomons Island is a major yachting center at the mouth of the Patuxent River. Situated on a peninsula on the western shore of southern Calvert County, the town of Solomons has quaint harbors where colorful yachts bobbing in their slips become subject matter on many a roll of film. Boaters may be attracted to the harbor for the services a good marina can provide, but Solomons also offers gift shops, antique shops, museums, a seafood market, seafood restaurants overlooking the water, and a boardwalk on the Patuxent with modern public restrooms.

Nightlife is available on the island, especially on weekends during the tourist season, at several restaurants and bars grouped together on the main thoroughfare. Sip cocktails in the open air at the Polynesian-style Tiki Bar (410-326-4075), or sample the excellent crabcakes at Bowen's Inn (410-326-9880) while enjoying a live band. The Rhumbline Inn (410-326-3261) features a sports lounge and dance club.

Entertainment is available Wednesdays through Saturdays at the Naughty Gull Restaurant and Pub (410-326-GULL). Catamarans Seafood and Steaks (410-326-8399) often has a DJ or live band. A popular spot for young people is Solomon's Pier Restaurant (410-326-2424).

Charter captains offer cruise boats and fishing excursions from the protected harbors (*see* Appendix A, page 315). The Southern Maryland Sailing Association sponsors many racing events, including the Screwpile Lighthouse Challenge held here in mid-July.

On the tip of the island is the University of Maryland's Chesapeake Biological Laboratory Visitors Center, open from 10 to 4 Tuesdays through Sundays. Friendly staff members invite visitors to learn more about the ecology and natural resources of the Chesapeake Bay. The laboratory is part of the university's Center for Environmental Science, which is housed in 14 nearby buildings. Some of these old "company houses" lining Farren Avenue and Williams Street once housed shuckers and canners of the Isaac Solomon Oyster Packing Company.

The coves of Solomons Island provided protection during the War of 1812 when Commodore Joshua Barney sailed a flotilla here to launch an attack on British boats that had come into the Chesapeake Bay.

Despite the modern yachts and many gift shops, the village retains some of its past character from when Isaac Solomon's Oyster Packing Facility was in its heyday in the 1800s. In the 1800s, local shipyards built schooners and sloops but are best known for the "bugeye," forerunner of the graceful and legendary skipjack. Examples of both the bugeye and skipjack are on display at the Calvert Marine Museum.

For more information: Calvert County Department of Economic Development, Courthouse, Prince Frederick, MD 20678. Phone (800) 331-9771 or (410) 535-4583.

Solomons Information Center, MD 2/4 (across from the Calvert Marine Museum), Solomons, MD 20688. Phone (410) 326-6027.

Chesapeake Biological Laboratory Visitors Center, PO Box 38, Solomons, MD 20688. Phone (410) 326-7232.

Southern Maryland Sailing Association, phone (410) 326-4364 or (310) 862-3100.

CALVERT MARINE MUSEUM

[Fig. 11(10)] The incredibly complex workings of an estuary are creatively demonstrated at the Calvert Marine Museum. Exhibits designed to intrigue both children and adults interpret the marine paleontology of Calvert Cliffs and the estuarine biology of the Patuxent River and Chesapeake Bay. A 15-tank "Estuarine" provides a close-up view of underwater life that results when salt water and fresh water mix. A Discovery Room with a "please touch" policy invites children to dig for fossils, look through microscopes, build model sailboats, and try on costumes.

Outside the main exhibition hall, visitors can watch river otters at play, meander along a boardwalk through a re-created living salt marsh, visit the Lore Oyster House, and see traditional Chesapeake Bay log canoes, Smith Island crab scrapes, and deadrise workboats.

Also part of the museum complex open to the public is the restored cottage-style Drum Point Lighthouse. The original prefabricated structure was built in 33 days in 1883 at the confluence of the bay and the Patuxent River at a cost of $25,000, decommissioned in 1962, and moved to the museum grounds in 1975. The Drum Point Light is one of just three remaining screwpile lighthouses out of 45 that were built on the Chesapeake and is listed in the National Register of Historic Places.

A one-hour cruise from the museum harbor aboard the bugeye *William B. Tennison* offers views of the busy Solomons inner harbor, the Chesapeake Biological Laboratory, and the Patuxent River estuary. Built in 1899, the *Tennison* is the oldest Coast Guard-licensed passenger vessel on the Chesapeake Bay and has been called the third oldest in the country. Made of nine logs, the bugeye or buyboat was originally a sailing craft used in the oyster industry, but it was converted to power in the early 1900s.

Directions: Located at Solomons on the east side of MD 2/4.

Activities: Museum tour, explore lighthouse, harbor cruise.

Facilities: Marine museum, marsh boardwalk, restored lighthouse, cruise boat, restrooms.

Dates: Museum open daily 10 to 5, closed New Year's Day, Thanksgiving, and Christmas. Cruises offered May through Oct., Wednesday through Sunday, 2 p.m.; there is an additional cruise at 12:30 p.m. Saturday and Sunday, July through Aug.

Fees: Entrance fee (nominal), cruise boat fee.

For more information: Calvert Marine Museum, PO Box 97, Solomons, MD 20688. Phone (410) 326-2042.

ANNMARIE GARDEN

[Fig. 11(11)] Just north of Solomons Island is Annmarie Garden, where nature and sculpted gardens intermingle along quiet walkways bordering St. John's Creek. The garden was the inspiration of Francis L. Koenig, who named it for his wife and donated it to the county in appreciation of the many enjoyable years he spent in the area. One of the garden's highlights is an impressive sculpture of a Chesapeake Bay waterman called *Tribute to the Oyster Tonger*.

Enjoy the serendipitous discovery, one by one, of the garden's 12 benches created by an artist with the help of Calvert County's elementary students. Inlaid ceramic tiles on the bench seats depict Southern Maryland's native plants such as bloodroot, dogwood, loblolly pine, pawpaw, and rose mallow. The garden gateway is a piece of art itself, constructed with 7 tons of ceramics in 630 colorful pieces. Development of the garden is ongoing as donations and funding allow.

Directions: From the east side of Governor Johnson Memorial Bridge at Solomons, go north 1.5 miles on MD 2/4. Turn right on Dowell Road. The garden entrance is less than a mile down on the left.

Dates: Open 10 to 4 daily, year-round.

Fees: None.

For more information: Annmarie Garden, 175 Main Street, Prince Frederick, MD 20678. Phone (410) 326-4640.

COVE POINT LIGHTHOUSE

[Fig. 11(12)] Built in 1828, Cove Point Lighthouse is about 4.5 miles north of Solomons off MD 2/4 at the eastern end of MD 497 (Cove Point Road.) The brick tower can be seen from a gate, but it is not open to the public.

Calvert Cliffs offers 14 miles of hiking trails, including the Red Trail above.

CALVERT CLIFFS

The Cliffs of Calvert must have been an impressive sight when Capt. John Smith first sailed up the Chesapeake Bay in 1608. For 30 miles these marvelous cliffs are exposed along the western shore of the bay in southern Calvert County. The cliffs were formed during the Miocene Era, when the land was covered with warm, shallow seas. As marine animals died, their remains built up on the bottom of the sea, layer after layer. Over the millennia, the waters receded. Wave and sand action began to erode the sedimentary layers. As soil and sand washed away, fossils from marine vertebrates and bivalves that existed 10 to 20 million years ago were again exposed to sunlight.

Travelers have several opportunities along MD 2/4 to view the imposing cliffs or learn about their natural and human history. Two of these are at Calvert Cliffs State Park and Flag Ponds Nature Park. Cove Point Lighthouse and Coast Guard Station is at the southern end of the cliffs. The lighthouse has not been open to the public, but it is being given to the Calvert Marine Museum and may be open in the future.

CALVERT CLIFFS STATE PARK

[Fig. 11(13)] Today, many visitors come to Calvert Cliffs State Park to take a 2-mile (round-trip) hike to the beach adjacent to the cliffs to strain wet sand for teeth of ancient

Red Salamander

The 3-to-7-inch red salamander (*Psuedotriton ruber*) lives in crevices and debris in cold streams or in leaves and under logs in the woods. Like many salamanders, it changes color as it matures. The young are reddish orange with many black spots. Adults are purplish brown or dark orange, with larger spots that run together. It has yellow eyes, unlike the similar mud salamander (*Pseudotriton montanus*), which has brown eyes.

sharks, crocodiles, and dolphins, or to search the shifting sands for oyster shells, clam shells, or any of 600 species of fossils that have been identified. The 45-minute walk to the beach along the Red Trail has its own rewards (*see* page 120). Also, the cliffs are as remarkable as when Indians and early settlers viewed them. No climbing on the steep slopes is allowed because of the danger of slides, but the cliffs can be seen from the beach or from a boat.

A family graveyard inside the park contains the remains of Basil Dixon, a Quaker and physician dating from 1812. His descendants live across the waters in Talbot County on the Eastern Shore. Before Dixon's time, details of ownership are sketchy, although historians believe the park property was part of a land grant by the King of England in the late 1600s. A courthouse fire that burned county records in the mid-1800s makes it impossible to know for sure.

At the parking lot are a picnic area, a recycled tire playground, and a 1-acre fishing pond that contains bass, bluegill, and catfish. Saltwater anglers can also carry gear to the beach to try for spot, croaker, and bluefish. A pavilion is available for rent and a camping area for organized youth groups may also be reserved.

During the summer, park rangers conduct guided nature walks, show fossils from the cliffs, and explain the interesting natural history of Calvert Cliffs. Much of the maintenance of the park is carried on by volunteers from The Friends of Calvert Cliffs State Park who stepped in to help when budget cuts threatened the continuing operation of the facility.

Those who like to travel with the family dog should plan ahead, as pets are not allowed in the park. Anyone who can't hike the 2-mile round trip to the cliffs may wish to visit nearby Flag Ponds Park, located about 3 miles north of the entrance to the state park (*see* page 121).

Directions: From Prince Frederick in Calvert County, go south on MD 2/4 approximately 14 miles to the park entrance, on the left.

Activities: Hiking, fossil hunting, picnicking, freshwater and saltwater fishing, biking (service road only), youth group camping, seasonal hunting for rabbit, squirrel, and deer.

Facilities: Picnic tables and grills, 13 miles of hiking trails, pavilion (reservations required), fishing pond, recycled tire playground, youth group campground (reservations required), restrooms.

Dates: Open 8 a.m. to sunset daily, year-round. The beach area closes at 5:30 p.m.

Fees: Entrance donation requested. There is a fee to reserve the picnic pavilion and a youth camping fee.

Closest town: Prince Frederick is 14 miles north; Solomon's Island is 5 miles south.

For more information: Point Lookout State Park, PO Box 48, Scotland, MD 20687. Phone (301) 872-5688. Or contact Friends of Calvert Cliffs State Park, PO Box 1042, Lusby, MD 20656.

HIKING TRAILS AT CALVERT CLIFFS STATE PARK

Fourteen miles of trails named for the color of their blazes lead through woodlands, fields, and pine and hardwood forests, and provide the only access to the cliffs. A variety of loop hikes are possible by combining connecting trails. Hikers should carry their own water.

The 1.8-mile Red Trail, which leads to the beach and cliffs, is the most used. The 3.7-mile (one-way) Orange Trail, which runs through hardwood forests, has a wooden walkway across a wet area and features heart-pumping climbs. It can be combined with the service road or the Red Trail for a loop of about 5 miles. Grover Creek runs beside the Orange Trail, then spreads out into a wooded marsh with beavers, muskrats, amphibians, reptiles, and wetland birds and plants. The 2.6-mile White Trail follows openings that serve as firebreaks. Mature beech trees, American holly, and mountain laurel are common along the path.

The Silver Trail makes a 1.2-mile circuit off the Red Trail through a climax forest of oak and hickory. The 1.5-mile Yellow Trail and the 2.2-mile Blue Trail take off to the right as one path between the parking lot and the pond bridge. The Yellow Trail breaks off to the left, passes through a pine forest and field, crosses Gray's Creek, and reconnects with the Red Trail. The Blue Trail meanders into a wooded marsh, then returns to the Red Trail.

Horses are allowed on the Red, Yellow, or Blue trails (except during hunting season) and bicycles are restricted to the service road. Some trails are closed during hunting season.

The variety of habitats, including fields, freshwater ponds, dry woods, freshwater wooded marsh, tidal wetlands, saltwater marsh, and sandy beach is home to a wide range of plant and animal life. Besides the white-tailed deer, wild turkey, gray squirrel and raccoon that inhabit most eastern forests, you may also see frogs such as the bullfrog (*Rana catesbeiana*), green treefrog (*Hyla cinerea*), gray treefrog (*Hyla chrysoscelis*), southern leopard frog (*Rana sphenocephala*), and spring peeper (*Hyla crucifer*). Other amphibians identified at Calvert

SPRING PEEPER
(*Hyla crucifer*)

Cliffs include the tiny broadhead skink (*Eumeces laticeps*), five-lined skink (*Eumeces fasciatus*), and red salamander (*Pseudotriton ruber*). The Red Trail has some of the wettest areas, making it one of the best places to spot these amphibians.

Freshwater marshes such as those at Calvert Cliffs typically produce more variety of plants than saltwater marshes. Some plants are adapted to growing in water at varying depths while others grow only along the damp edges. The arrow arum (*Peltandra virginica*), with its large arrow-shaped leaves, is one that sprouts from beneath the surface. Visitors to the park in late spring or early summer will see stalks of white flowers, while those who come later will see the green berries that form after the bloom, causing the stalk to droop. Look for this plant on the lower Red Trail and lower Orange Trail.

Among the great variety of plants that thrive in freshwater marsh habitats is the coast pepperbush (*Clethra alnifolia*), a deciduous member of the heath family This shrub produces dense spikes of small, bell-shaped white flowers from July through September.

An abundance of bird life accompanies the wide variety of plants in freshwater marshes. Several gulls, including the great-black-backed gull (*Larus marinus*), herring gull (*Larus argentatus*), laughing gull (*Larus atracilla*), and ring-billed gull (*Larus delawarensis*) are found here. Owls that lend their haunting calls to the woodland night are the great horned owl (*Bubo virginianus*), screech owl (*Otus asio*), and barred owl (*Strix varia*).

Long-legged birds such as the great blue heron (*Ardea herodias*), snowy egret (*Egretta thula*), and green-backed heron (*Butorides striatus*) wade the shallows in search of a meal. Keeping birds, small mammals, and rodents alert are such predators of the marshes and woodlands as the osprey or fish hawk (*Pandion haliaetus*), Cooper's hawk (*Accipiter cooperii*), sharp-shinned hawk (*Accipiter striatus*), sparrow hawk or kestrel (*Falco sparverius*), red-tailed hawk (*Buteo jamaicensis*), and red-shouldered hawk (*Buteo lineatus*). Cliff swallows (*Petrochelidon pyrrhonota*) wheel and turn as they chase insects above the steep bluffs.

THE RED TRAIL.

A 1.8-mile (one-way) walk along this path takes visitors from the parking lot to the cliffs and beach on the Chesapeake Bay. A boardwalk at the beginning crosses the marshy edge of a 1-acre fishing pond lined with wetland vegetation, black willow, mimosa, and alder. Past the pond, the hard-packed sandy trail temporarily coincides with a wide service road where large tulip poplar, oak, shagbark hickory, and scrub pine shade an understory that includes mountain laurel, deerberry, and pawpaw. A huge chestnut oak leans across the path here. After the trail leaves the service road, it leads by a beaver dam and large freshwater marsh before it ends at a sandy beach on the Chesapeake Bay. Fossil-laden Calvert Cliffs are in full view from the beach.

Trail: 1.8-mile walk (one-way) to beach and view of cliffs; 3.6-mile round trip.

Degree of difficulty: Moderate, with uphill climb from the beach on the return trip.

▓ FLAG PONDS NATURE PARK

[Fig. 11(14)] An ever-changing variety of habitats at Flag Ponds Nature Park highlights the protean nature of the Chesapeake Bay estuary. Over the years, nature has repeatedly sculpted the streams, wetlands, cliffs, and sands. Today, boardwalks and observation platforms give the visitor access to two freshwater ponds. The sandy beach with its view of Calvert Cliffs is only 0.5 mile from the parking lot. A pier off the beach brings anglers above waters that hold spot, croaker, flounder, trout, and other saltwater species.

Longer trails and boardwalks invite exploration of the park's wetlands and woods. Wild turkeys, red foxes, white-tailed deer, river otters, and muskrats inhabit the forests. Wildflowers found here include the blue flag iris (*Iris versicolor*), which gave the park its name. Those familiar with the tall bearded iris that grows from a bulb in many domestic gardens will recognize this small, delicate member of the same family. *Iris versicolor* opens its violet-blue petals in summer, adding color to the park's moist areas. Rose mallow (*Hibiscus palustris*), another species that favors coastal marshes, also blooms in summer. A spring bloomer to look for in the park woodlands is columbine (*Aqualegia canadensis*), with its nodding red tubular flowers and protruding yellow stamens. Ruby-throated hummingbirds seek out the columbine for its nectar.

A shanty called Buoy Hotel, one of three such shanties that housed fishermen in the early 1900s, remains on the property, housing an exhibit on the former pound-net fishery for croaker, trout, and herring.

This park provides a pleasant alternative for those who can't hike the Calvert Cliffs State Park trails because they have a pet (not permitted at the state park) or don't have time. Leashed pets are allowed here and the beach is accessible without a long hike. Beach parking is available for the handi-capped.

Directions: From Prince Frederick, go south 10 miles on MD 2/4 and look for the entrance sign on the left.

Activities: Hiking, picnicking, fishing, fossil hunting on beach.

Facilities: Hiking trails, wetlands boardwalk and observation platform, picnic tables and grills, two ponds, fishing pier, visitor center, exhibits, restrooms.

Dates: Open 9 to 6 Monday through Friday and 9 to 8 on weekends Memorial Day through Labor Day; open 9 to 6 on weekends only for the remainder of year.

Fees: There is an entrance fee.

Closest town: Prince Frederick is 10 miles north.

For more information: Flag Ponds Nature Park, Calvert County Courthouse, Prince Frederick, MD 20678. Phone (410) 586-1477 or (410) 535-5327.

PAWPAW
(Asimina triloba)

CALVERT CLIFFS NUCLEAR POWER PLANT VISITORS CENTER

[Fig. 11(15)] Juxtaposed with the bucolic countryside of Southern Maryland is the state's only nuclear power plant, which provides 45 percent of the electricity for customers of Baltimore Gas & Electric. Tours through the power plant must be prearranged, but a nineteenth-century working tobacco barn has been renovated into an information center, which is open from 10 to 4 daily (except on major holidays). Highlights include exhibits on agriculture and archaeology, and a hands-on exhibit on energy and nuclear power.

An overlook provides views of the power plant and a splendid view of the Eastern Shore across the Chesapeake Bay. The entrance to the power plant is on MD 4 in Calvert County, 10 miles south of Prince Frederick.

Directions: From Prince Frederick, go south on MD 2/4 approximately 10 miles to the entrance on the left.

Activities: Exhibits, overlook.

Facilities: Visitor center, restrooms, overlook.

Dates: Open 10 to 4 daily, except holidays.

Fees: None.

Closest town: Prince Frederick is 10 miles north.

For more information: Calvert Cliffs Nuclear Power Plant Visitors Center, 1650 Calvert Cliffs Parkway, Lusby, MD 20657-4702. Phone (410) 495-4673.

JEFFERSON PATTERSON PARK AND MUSEUM

[Fig. 11(16)] The human history of the Chesapeake Bay area is under scrutiny by the experts at Jefferson Patterson Park and Museum. Located on 544 scenic acres on Calvert County's southwestern border with the Patuxent River, this state museum of history and archeology is studying 70 archeological sites with evidence of human habitation over the past 9,000 years.

The staff of the museum makes concerted efforts to share their finds with the public and even to involve the public in their work. For instance, in the summer of 1998, volunteers joined archeologists in the survey and excavation of a colonial house site dating to the 1690s. In addition to changing exhibits, the park's visitor center features a permanent exhibit called "12,000 Years in the Chesapeake: An Archaeological Story." A Discovery Room at the visitor center invites hands-on exploration by children. Listed on the National Register of Historic Places, the property also has a Woodland Nature Trail and Riverside Archeology Trail. Pets are allowed on leashes.

Also on the museum grounds is the 23,000-square-foot state-of-the-art facility of the Academy of Natural Sciences' Estuarine Research Center. Free public tours of the facilities—including butterfly, hummingbird, and wildlife gardens and changing art exhibits—are available by appointment from 9 to 11 a.m. on the first Friday of each month. Group tours can also be arranged. The center is closed on legal holidays.

Directions: From Prince Frederick, go about 3 miles south on MD 4. Turn right on MD

264 (Broomes Island Road) and go 2 miles. Turn left on MD 265 (Mackall Road) and drive 6 miles to the museum entrance on the right. For the Academy of Natural Sciences' Estuarine Research Center, after turning into the park entrance, follow the park road to a T intersection and turn left. Go through the first parking lot to a brick building on the right.

Activities: Touring visitor center, picnicking, hiking.

Facilities: Visitor center, cultural exhibits, family Discovery Room, gift shop, restrooms, nature trail, archaeology trail, picnic area and pavilion.

Dates: Open to the public 10 to 5, Wednesday through Sunday, Apr. 15 through Oct. 15.

Fees: None, except for a fee for group use of pavilion.

Closest town: Prince Frederick is 11 miles northeast.

For more information: Jefferson Patterson Park and Museum, 10515 Mackall Road, St. Leonard, MD 20685. Phone (410) 586-8500. Pavilion rental, phone (410) 586-8501; volunteer opportunities and historic preservation information, phone (410) 586-8555. Academy of Natural Sciences' Estuarine Research Center, 10545 Mackall Road, St. Leonard, MD 20685. Phone (410) 586-9700. E-mail hatch@acnatsci.org.

WILD TURKEY
(Meleagris gallopavo)

ONE ROOM SCHOOLHOUSE

[Fig. 11(17)] Not far from Battle Creek Cypress Swamp is Port Republic School Number 7, restored by the Calvert Retired Teachers Association to its appearance in the early 1900s. Here children sat at wooden desks, learning from their McGuffy Readers and writing their lessons on wooden slates. The schoolhouse sits in a shady grove on the grounds of Christ Church in Port Republic on MD 264 (Broomes Island Road), and it is open to the public from 2 to 4 p.m. on Sundays during summer months.

For more information: One Room Schoolhouse, 2416 Azalea Road, Port Republic, MD 20676. Phone (410) 586-0482 or (410) 586-0109.

CHESAPEAKE BEACH RAILWAY MUSEUM

[Fig. 11(18)] In the northeastern corner of the county are North Beach and Chesapeake Beach, two communities that were the center of a thriving resort in the early 1900. The Chesapeake Beach Railway Museum, located in a train station remaining from that time, provides a look back in time to the days when steam engines carried people from Washington, DC, and Baltimore, Maryland, to the bayside resort. The museum, located on MD 261 in Chesapeake Beach, is open from 1 to 4 p.m. daily, May to September, and on weekends, April and October. Admission is free.

For more information: Chesapeake Beach Railway Museum, 4155 Mear's Avenue, PO Box 783, Chesapeake Beach, MD 20732. Phone (410) 257-3892.

⬚ BATTLE CREEK CYPRESS SWAMP SANCTUARY

[Fig. 11(19)] Step into the mysterious dimness of this cypress swamp and the hurried pace of the outside world is shed as water from a cypress knee. Battle Creek Cypress Swamp Sanctuary is best known as the country's northernmost refuge of the baldcypress (*Taxodium distichum*). The Nature Conservancy acquired the 100-acre preserve in 1957 and Calvert County built a 0.25-mile boardwalk through the swamp.

Today, children ask about the strange "knees" of the baldcypress roots that emerge from the calm, brackish water along the self-guided nature walk. Fossilized knees, cones, and stumps have been preserved in clay beds that date back 100,000 years—a time when cypress swamps were common and wooly mammoths lumbered over the land.

Adults admiring the present-day trees that soar to 100 feet above the water wonder why cypress trees found a home in the Battle Creek stream valley 5,000 to 15,000 years ago when the Pleistocene glaciers retreated, but not in other stream valleys of Southern Maryland. The question is one that scientists are still trying to answer. Whatever the reason, today's Southern Maryland baldcypress trees are thought to be descended from those ancient swamps.

But the swamp has other interesting features besides its impressive cypresses. The damp habitat is ideal for muskrats, frogs, salamanders, reptiles, and many varieties of insects. The rich vegetation is an excellent example of a coastal plain swamp. Some aquatic plants grow from beneath the water. Sweetgum, ash, spicebush, and southern arrowwood are found in the moist areas of Battle Creek Cypress Swamp. Arrowood is a *Viburnum* that was used by the Indians because its strong, straight, symmetrical branches made excellent arrows. The southern arrowwood (*Viburnum dentatum*) has egg-shaped to round, coarse-toothed leaves and is distinguished from other arrowwoods by the velvety hairs on its twigs.

On the ridges of the stream valley are trees more characteristic of drier areas, including the tulip tree (yellow poplar), mountain laurel, and Virginia or scrub pine. In the transition area between wet and dry habitat, such animals as white-tailed deer, red fox, raccoon, and opossum may leave tracks that give away their presence. Observant hikers occasionally come across an owl casting. These cylindrical

BALDCYPRESS
(*Taxodium distichum*)

packages of fur, teeth, and bones may resemble a cocoon but are actually the undigested parts of an owl's last meal.

Early morning is an excellent time for bird-watching any time of year on both the swamp boardwalk and on an upland trail. Woodpeckers give notice that mating season has arrived by seeking out the most resonant hollow tree for a noisemaker. Spring and summer birders have identified breeding warblers includ-

Baldcypress

The baldcypress (*Taxodium distichum*), with its swollen, fluted trunk, is the Spanish-moss-draped tree of southeastern swamps. Despite the evergreen appearance of its needles, the tree is not evergreen. The needles turn brown in autumn and fall off with the twigs.

ing the Kentucky, worm-eating, prothonotary, parula, and hooded varieties. Fall warblers search the canopy for insects or flit through the understory on their way south.

A flower identification book is a help when spring-beauties (*Claytonia*), mayapples (*Podophyllum*), pink lady's slippers (*Cypripedium acaule*), and violets (*Violaceae*) blanket the northern part of the swamp. Cardinal flowers (*Lobelia cardinalis*) color the damp edges with their late summer fire.

A nature center expands on the natural and cultural heritage of Battle Creek. The Natural Resources Division of Calvert County also schedules outdoor activities and programs throughout the year.

Directions: From MD 2/4, 2 miles south of Prince Frederick, go right (west) on MD 506 (Sixes Road). Drive about 1.8 miles and turn left on Grays Road. The sanctuary is 0.25 mile down on the right.

Activities: Hiking, guided tours for groups by reservation.

Facilities: Swamp and upland hiking trails, visitor center, restrooms.

Dates: Open Apr. through Sept., 10 to 5 Tuesday through Saturday, 1 to 5 Sunday; Oct. through Mar., 10 to 4:30 Tuesday through Saturday, 1 to 4:30 Sunday; closed Mondays, Thanksgiving, Christmas, and New Year's Day.

Fees: None.

Closest town: Prince Frederick is 5 miles north.

For more information: Battle Creek Cypress Swamp Sanctuary, c/o Calvert County Courthouse, Prince Frederick, MD 20678. Phone (410) 535-5327.

BEACHES AND RECREATION AREAS IN CALVERT COUNTY

Calvert County has public beaches on the Chesapeake Bay at the communities of (south to north) Breezy Point, Chesapeake Beach and North Beach. There are also beaches at Calvert Cliffs State Park (*see* page 49) and Flag Ponds Nature Park (*see* page 121).

BREEZY POINT BEACH AND CAMPGROUND. [Fig. 11(24)] Located on Breezy Point Road off MD 261, Breezy Point features 0.5 mile of sandy beach on the Chesapeake

River Otter

This large, playful member of the weasel family makes a den with an underwater entrance in stream banks. Fish, frogs, snakes, crayfish, blue crabs, and even young muskrats are on the menu for this web-footed aquatic mammal. Although not as agile on land as its weasel cousins, river otters (*Lutra canadensis*) will cross large land expanses to reach another lake or river with better hunting opportunities. Slick troughs in snow or mud on a river bank will sometimes give away the presence of this secretive critter.

Bay, picnic tables, restroom facilities, a playground, and a fishing pier. The county-operated beach and campground are open Apr. 15 through Oct. 15. There are admission and camping fees. The Breezy Point office is open mid-Apr. through mid-Oct., phone (410) 535-0259. At all other times, contact the county Parks and Recreation office at (410) 535-1600 or (310) 855-1243, ext. 225.

BAY FRONT PARK. [Fig. 11(25)] This uncrowded beach and fishing pier is at Chesapeake Beach in the northeastern part of the county. It is open during daylight hours. There is no admission fee. Pets are not allowed. Phone (410) 257-2230.

NORTH BEACH PUBLIC BEACH. [Fig. 11(26)] This beach features a free swimming beach (nettle nets provided), snack bar, boardwalk, and a fishing/crabbing pier. The beach is located in the community of North Beach in northeastern Calvert County. The pier and beach close at midnight. No pets. Phone (410) 257-9618 or (301) 855-6681.

RIVER OTTER
(Lutra canadensis)

RESTAURANTS IN CALVERT COUNTY

Here are some of the restaurants in Calvert County that specialize in seafood.

ROD'N REEL RESTAURANT. Route 261 and Mears Avenue, Chesapeake Beach. Bay-view dining features fresh seafood, live entertainment. Open daily. Sunday breakfast buffet. *Moderate. Phone (410) 257-2735 or (301) 855-8351.*

STONEY'S SEAFOOD HOUSE (two locations). 3939 Oyster House Road, Broomes Island, phone (410) 586-1888 and Solomons Island Road North, Prince Frederick, phone (410) 535-1888. Specializes in crabcake sandwiches and seafood. Open daily. *Moderate.*

CAPTAIN'S TABLE. 275 Lore Road, Solomons. Located across from the information center and behind the Comfort Inn, this seafood restaurant overlooks a beautiful yacht harbor. Excellent soft-shell crab, crabcakes, and coleslaw. Decorated with paintings of local lighthouses and Amish farm country. Open year-round for breakfast, lunch and dinner. *Moderate. Phone (410) 326-2772.*

LIGHTHOUSE INN. 14640 Solomons Island Road South, Solomons. Steak and seafood. Daily specials. Fine dining overlooking the harbor. *Moderate. Phone (410) 326-2444.*

DRY DOCK RESTAURANT. Between C Street and Back Creek in Zahniser's Yachting Center, Solomons. Fresh seafood, prime rib, chicken. Great view of Solomons Harbor. *Moderate. Phone (410) 326-4817.*

THE C. D. CAFÉ. 14350 Solomons Island Road, Avondale Center, Solomons. Fresh pastries, espresso and innovative cuisine. *Inexpensive. Phone (410) 326-3877.*

LODGING IN CALVERT COUNTY

Most motels and inns in Calvert County are located in the vicinity of Solomons in the southern part of the county. Here is a sampling of places to stay. Contact information services for other listings.

COMFORT INN. Lore Road at Beacons Marina, Solomons. Captains Table restaurant, outdoor pool, Jacuzzi suites, cable TV. *Moderate. Phone (410) 326-6303.*

HOLIDAY INN SELECT. 155 Holiday Drive, Solomons. 9-acre waterfront retreat. Maryland Way restaurant and lounge, conference center, marina, outdoor pool, ballroom, amphitheater, tennis courts, cable TV. *Moderate to expensive. Phone (410) 326-6311 or (800) 356-2009.*

BACK CREEK INN BED & BREAKFAST. Alexander and Calvert streets, PO Box 520, Solomons. This waterfront inn, built in 1880 and completely restored, is bordered by gardens and furnished with antiques. Private suites, fireplaces, and full breakfast included. Dock at the inn's private pier. *Moderate to expensive. Phone (410) 326-2022.*

SOLOMONS VICTORIAN INN. 125 Charles Street, PO Box 759, Solomons. Gracious Queen Anne Victorian structure overlooking Solomons harbor. 5 guestrooms and 3 suites with double whirlpools. Private baths, no pets. Full breakfast. *Moderate to expensive. Phone (410) 326-4811.*

Patuxent River Area

The Patuxent River is the longest river entirely within the state of Maryland.

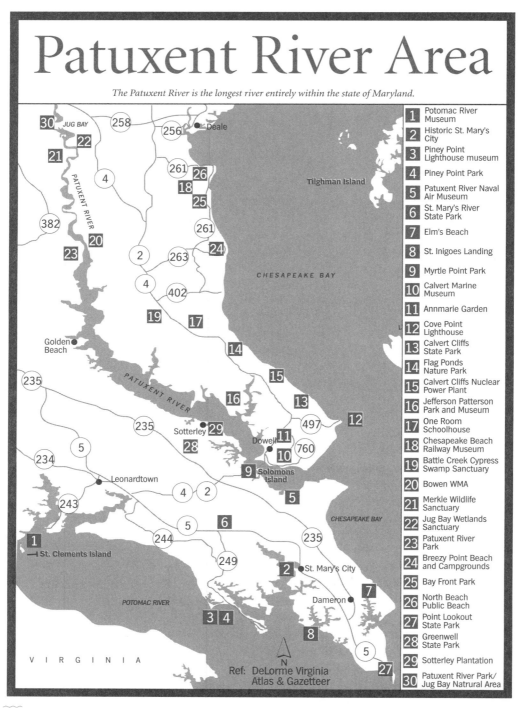

1	Potomac River Museum
2	Historic St. Mary's City
3	Piney Point Lighthouse museum
4	Piney Point Park
5	Patuxent River Naval Air Museum
6	St. Mary's River State Park
7	Elm's Beach
8	St. Inigoes Landing
9	Myrtle Point Park
10	Calvert Marine Museum
11	Annmarie Garden
12	Cove Point Lighthouse
13	Calvert Cliffs State Park
14	Flag Ponds Nature Park
15	Calvert Cliffs Nuclear Power Plant
16	Jefferson Patterson Park and Museum
17	One Room Schoolhouse
18	Chesapeake Beach Railway Museum
19	Battle Creek Cypress Swamp Sanctuary
20	Bowen WMA
21	Merkle Wildlife Sanctuary
22	Jug Bay Wetlands Sanctuary
23	Patuxent River Park
24	Breezy Point Beach and Campgrounds
25	Bay Front Park
26	North Beach Public Beach
27	Point Lookout State Park
28	Greenwell State Park
29	Sotterley Plantation
30	Patuxent River Park/ Jug Bay Natrural Area

Ref: DeLorme Virginia Atlas & Gazetteer

Patuxent River

[Fig. 11] With its headwaters at Parr's Ridge where Carroll, Howard, Frederick, and Montgomery counties meet, and its mouth some 110 languid miles to the southeast at Solomons on the Chesapeake Bay, the Patuxent River is the longest river entirely within the state of Maryland. The watershed of this State Scenic River drains one-tenth of the state, including the southern end of the Washington, DC, and Baltimore suburban corridor.

The Patuxent has become important as a demonstration area for showing how strategies to control nutrients and pollution might apply to coastal areas elsewhere. Some 6,700 acres of wetlands, mostly in the coastal plain in the middle portion of the river, naturally filter the Patuxent's water. These lands also attract birds and wildlife in tremendous numbers and variety. Several preserves, parks, and sanctuaries make excellent use of the Patuxent's ecosystem for research and/or recreation. Because of environmentally sensitive areas, permission is required to enter some sites. Although the Patuxent reaches well above Southern Maryland into Central Maryland (subject of the next section of this book), all of the sites of interest along the river are covered here for the sake of consistency.

BOWEN WILDLIFE MANAGEMENT AREA

[Fig. 11(20)] Named for Harry L. Bowen, who sold this 330-acre tidal marsh to the state for $1 in 1955, Bowen Wildlife Management Area provides a refuge for migrating and wintering waterfowl that is priceless. Buffleheads, wood ducks, lesser scaup, American wigeon, and black ducks are just a few of the ducks that wildlife observers might see here. Mammals that make use of the marsh habitat include minks, muskrats, and river otters. Because of the wet terrain, Bowen is accessible only by boat. Hunters traditionally use push boats to search for elusive sora and Virginia rails that feed among the river grasses. In fact, waterfowl hunting is a popular pursuit. Free permits for use of the permanent blinds are available from the Myrtle Grove Wildlife Office. White perch, catfish, carp, and rockfish lure anglers to the area. Crabbers and trappers also use the marsh.

Bowen is not just for those who hunt, trap, crab, or fish. Equipped with a canoe and a free afternoon, anyone who enjoys observing wildlife in a river tidal wetland will have fun poking about Bowen's many creeks.

Directions: For Magruders Ferry Landing, from US 301 at Rosaryville in Prince Georges County, go southeast on MD 382 (Croom Road) about 12 miles. Turn left on Magruders Ferry Road and continue about 1 mile to boat ramp.

Activities: Canoeing, boating, seasonal hunting, fishing, trapping, crabbing.

Facilities: Boat ramp.

Dates: Open year-round.

Fees: None.

Closest town: Rosaryville is about 13 miles northwest.

For more information: Myrtle Grove Work Center, phone (301) 743-5161.

MERKLE WILDLIFE SANCTUARY

[Fig. 11(21)] The 1,678 acres of Merkle Wildlife Sanctuary were set aside as a refuge for Canada geese. Beginning in 1932, conservationist Edward Merkle began an attempt to reintroduce geese to the area. From a few breeding pairs in 1932, the flocks have gradually increased to include an estimated 10,000 wintering geese—the largest population on the western bay. A visitor center provides information about Edward Merkle, Canada geese, and Chesapeake Bay wildlife. The 5 miles of marked trails and gardens in the sanctuary are open daily, year-round.

Directions: From US 301 and MD 4 at Upper Marlboro, go south on US 301. Turn left (south) on MD 382. Turn left on St. Thomas Church Road and go left again at the park entrance.

Activities: Hiking, biking, fishing, picnicking.

Facilities: Trails for hiking, biking. Gardens, picnic tables, visitor center, gift shop, restrooms.

Dates: Open 7 to sunset daily, year-round, with occasional trail closures to protect feeding and nesting wildlife. The visitor center is open 10 to 4 weekdays and winter weekends.

Fees: There is a parking fee.

Closest town: Rosaryville is 6 miles northwest.

For more information: Merkle Wildlife Sanctuary and Visitor's Center, 11704 Fenno Road, Upper Marlboro, MD 20772. Phone (301) 888-1410 or (800) 784-5380.

JUG BAY

[Fig. 11] Jug Bay is the name of a bulge of the Patuxent River just north of the point where Calvert, Anne Arundel, and Prince Georges counties meet. The bay is surrounded with one of the largest tidal freshwater wetlands on the East Coast. Tidal fresh water is water that rises and falls with the tides but is not salty. The habitat provides conditions favorable to spawning white perch and developing rockfish (striped bass) and other species.

Jug Bay's location on the Atlantic Flyway makes it perfect for the more than 200 species of birds that have been identified here. Bald eagles, huge flocks of tundra swans, Canada geese, and green-winged teal find protection here from winter winds. Bird watchers here have sighted the peregrine falcon, loggerhead shrike, Swainson's thrush, mourning warbler, and dark-eyed junco, to mention a few.

The lush vegetation of tidal wetlands is the envy of many who try to establish water gardens in their yards. Rose mallow (*Hibiscus coccineus*) displays its huge crimson blossoms. Pickerelweed (*Pontederia cordata*) has pretty heart-shaped leaves and blue summer blooms. Adding summer color is a yellow pond lily called spatterdock (*Nuphar luteum*), with heart-shaped leaves that rise above the water at low tide. All plant life is dominated by wild rice (*Zizania aquatica*), a valuable food source for many seed-eating birds. Wild rice grows as high as a basketball hoop, waving its shimmering gold fronds in late summer breezes.

Some 25,000 waterfowl are estimated to feed on the rice and on seed-bearing plants such as Walter's millet (*Echinochloa walteri*) and dotted smartweed (*Polygonum punctatum*) during winter months. The ripening of these seeds coincides perfectly with the fall migration of waterfowl, bobolinks, sora rails, red-winged blackbirds, and many other birds. Several endangered plants such as downy bushclover (*Lespedeza*) and smooth tick trefoil (*Desmodium*) also are suited to the wetland habitat.

Loggerhead Shrike

Open grassland with scattered trees is perfect habitat for the loggerhead shrike (*Lanius ludovicianus*), a pale gray bird with white undersides and a black mask. Unlike most songbirds, the shrike preys on small birds and rodents, in addition to insects. It has no talons, but impales its victim on a thorn before tearing it apart, a technique that earns it the common name, butcher bird.

Where the Piscataway Indians once hunted and gathered, two sanctuaries, a natural area, and a county park provide protection for and access to this bird watchers' paradise.

PATUXENT RIVER PARK AND JUG BAY NATURAL AREA

Patuxent River Park and Jug Bay Natural Area comprise 2,000 acres of tidal freshwater wetlands. The park has a visitor center, nature study area, and 8 miles of hiking trails. Call ahead to rent a canoe, which is probably the best way to get close to waterfowl. A boardwalk and an observation tower that rises above the tops of the wild rice marsh provide another way to view wildlife and birds. Don't forget binoculars.

The park is also the starting point for the 4-mile Chesapeake Bay Critical Area Driving Tour, which extends south across Mattaponi Creek to the Merkle Wildlife Sanctuary. Allow extra time to take advantage of the observation towers and pull-offs along the way. The tour is open on Sundays only.

Directions: From the junction of US 301 and MD 4 at Upper Marlboro, go south on US 301. Turn left (south) on MD 382. Turn left at Croom Airport Road and follow it to the park entrance.

Activities: Canoeing, hiking, crabbing, fishing, horseback riding, camping.

Facilities: Observation towers, canoe rental, 8 miles of trails, campground, restrooms.

Dates: Sunrise to sunset, year-round.

Fees: There is a camping fee and canoe rental fee.

Closest town: Upper Marlboro is about 8 miles north.

For more information: Patuxent River

LOGGERHEAD SHRIKE
(*Lanius ludovicianus*)

Park, 16000 Croom Airport Road, Upper Marlboro, MD. 20772. Phone (301) 888-1410 or (301) 627-6074.

JUG BAY WETLANDS SANCTUARY

[Fig. 11(22)] On the Patuxent River where Anne Arundel County operates this 640-acre sanctuary, sweeping expanses of wild rice, cattail, and other aquatic plants spread as far as the eye can see. The wetlands support a rich variety of wildlife, including invertebrates, fish, amphibians, reptiles, mammals, and more than 250 species of birds.

Seven miles of boardwalks and trails give visitors an intimate look at various habitats, which include—in addition to wetlands—hardwood forests, nontidal wetlands, agricultural fields, streams, and seasonal ponds. An observation deck overlooks the wetlands and the wide Patuxent. Osprey and occasional bald eagles soar above the water. Fast-flying ducks move to and fro between feeding and resting areas. Muskrats and beavers occasionally make appearances. Several varieties of turtles and snakes may also reveal their presence to patient observers in wildlife observation blinds.

In 1991, the sanctuary became part of the Chesapeake Bay National Estuarine Research Reserve. Naturalists study water quality, rare plants, and plant succession at Jug Bay. Amphibians, turtles, songbirds and fish populations are also subjects of interest. Nature tours, canoe trips, and winter bird walks give interpreters the opportunity to explain some of their research, ranging from the intricacies of tidal freshwater wetland plants to fluctuations in migratory bird populations. Jug Bay has given up evidence of continuous human habitation for the past 8,000 years. During colonial times, ships involved in the lucrative tobacco trade came up the Patuxent to Bristol Landing, just north of Jug Bay. Displayed at the visitor center are Indian projectile points, axe heads, and artifacts from colonial times that have been uncovered at the sanctuary.

Directions: From MD 2 about 18 miles south of Annapolis in southern Anne Arundel County, go west about 4 miles on MD 258. Go west on Wrighton Road and follow signs.

Activities: Hiking, canoeing, wildlife and wildfowl observation. No fishing or boat launching.

Facilities: Visitor center, interpretive exhibits, hiking and canoe trails, restrooms.

Dates: Open year-round by reservation only, from 9 to 5 on Wednesday and weekends (closed Sunday, Dec. through Feb.).

Fees: There is an entrance fee. Prior reservation required.

Closest town: Annapolis is about 23 miles north.

For more information: Jug Bay Wetlands Sanctuary, 1361 Wrighton Road, Lothian, MD 20711. For permission to visit, contact Anne Arundel County Department of Recreation and Parks, phone (410) 741-9330.

PATUXENT RESEARCH REFUGE

This national wildlife refuge lies along the Patuxent River between the metropolitan areas of Washington, DC, and Baltimore, Maryland. Created primarily for research, the refuge is perhaps best known for discovering the horrific consequences of the use of DDT as a pesticide. Rachel Carson based her influential book, *Silent Spring*, on the researchers' findings that DDT in the food chain of birds caused their eggs to become thin-shelled. Eggs would break, resulting in an alarming decline of bald eagles, peregrine falcons, ospreys, and many other birds.

Researchers use records from long-term monitoring of migratory birds to detect population trends. Work at the refuge has also helped dwindling populations of Mississippi sandhill cranes to recover. Fortunately, the interests of the public are not forgotten at Patuxent Research Refuge. Parts of the refuge are geared to inform visitors about ongoing projects. Visitors are treated to the rare sight of captive colonies of endangered whooping cranes. By studying the cranes, researchers hope to find ways to help save them from extinction. Refuge exhibits describe rescue efforts for other wildlife such as wolves, sea otters, and condors. A state-of-the-art visitor center emphasizes the scientific bent of the refuge with stunning arrays of lights and sounds, interactive displays, moving scenery, and replicas of wildlife in meticulous detail. Allow at least an hour for the Wisdom of Wildness exhibit hall and the gift shop. Near the visitor center is Redington Lake and the 1.4-mile Cash Lake Trail. The refuge has a total of nearly 4 miles of trails. The North Tract of the refuge has watchable wildlife at wetlands, including a 3-acre open pond with two nesting islands and 20 acres of forested wetlands. Fishing, birding, photography, jogging, horseback riding, and bicycling are allowed in selected areas.

Directions: From the Baltimore-Washington Parkway (MD 295), for the visitor center, take Powder Mill Road Exit. Go east and follow signs. For North Tract, take MD 198 Exit off MD 295 and go east toward Fort Meade. Go right at the refuge sign just before the ball field on the right.

Activities: Hiking, jogging, horseback riding, fishing, bicycling, seasonal tram tours, seasonal hunting on North Tract (must pass hunter safety course and shooting test).

Facilities: Visitor center, auditorium, gift shop, nature trail, tram, restrooms.

Dates: Visitor center open 10 to 5:30 daily, year-round, except Christmas. North Tract open 8 to 4:30 (or later) daily, year-round, except Thanksgiving, Christmas, New Year's Day.

Fees: There is a small fee for tram rides.

For more information: Patuxent National Wildlife Refuge Visitor Center, 10901 Scarlet Tanager Loop, Laurel, MD 20708-4027. Phone (301) 497-5760. Patuxent Research Refuge North Tract, 230 Bald Eagle Drive, Laurel, MD 20724-3000. Phone (410) 674-3304 for North Tract.

PATUXENT RIVER STATE PARK

[Fig. 11(23)] This 6,648-acre undeveloped park encompasses 12 linear miles of the Patuxent River valley in Howard and Montgomery counties between MD 27 and MD 97, north of Gaithersburg. Highlights include an Environmental Study Area, self-guided nature trail, trout stream, and hunting opportunities.

For more information: Patuxent River State Park, c/o Seneca Creek State Park, 11950 Clopper Road, Gaithersburg, MD 20878. Phone (301) 924-2127.

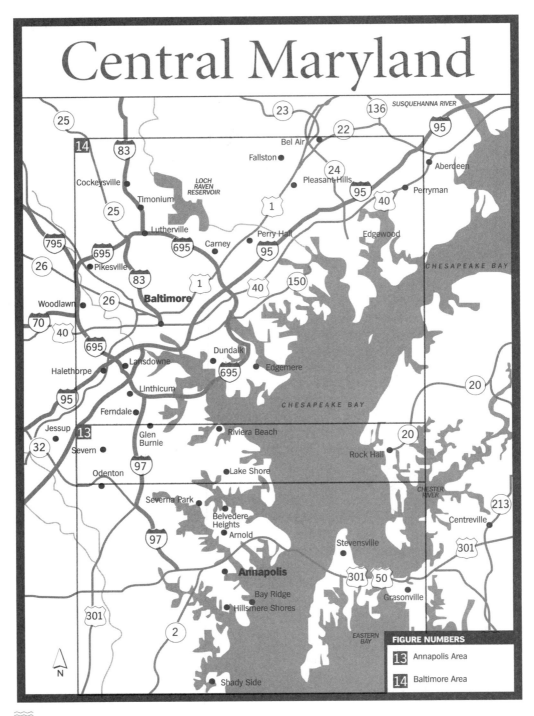

Central Maryland

FIGURE NUMBERS

13	Annapolis Area
14	Baltimore Area

Central Maryland

T he part of Central Maryland close to the Chesapeake Bay is a multifaceted land. The capital city of Annapolis and the metropolitan area of Baltimore are replete with historical and cultural attractions, entertainment possibilities, dining experiences, fishing opportunities, sailing and yachting adventures, and guidance for visitors. Their location on the Chesapeake Bay has helped these cities grow to prominence.

But the proximity of areas of high population to the highly sensitive waters of this valuable estuary also is cause for concern. The watershed of the bay includes not just the urban area in and around Baltimore but also that of Washington, DC, just 25 miles west of the bay. Researchers in state-of-the-art facilities continually seek ways to enable so many people to enjoy the benefits of the bay without destroying its ecosystems.

Despite urbanization, the cities and the surrounding counties of Anne Arundel and

[*Above:* Red foxes are found in natural areas around Chesapeake Bay]

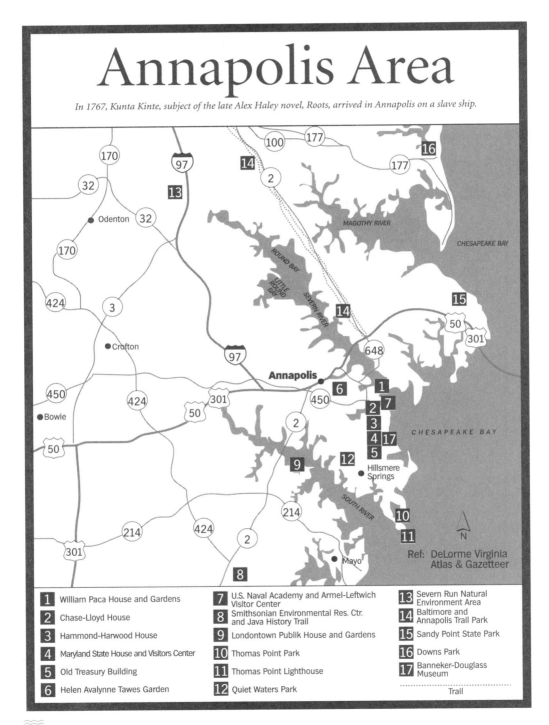

Annapolis Area

In 1767, Kunta Kinte, subject of the late Alex Haley novel, Roots, arrived in Annapolis on a slave ship.

170
97
32
Odenton
32
170
424
3
Crofton
450
424
50
Bowie
50
214
424
301
214

100
177
14
2
16
177
MAGOTHY RIVER
CHESAPEAKE BAY
ROUND BAY
LITTLE ROUND BAY
SEVERN RIVER
14
15
50
301
648
Annapolis
450
6
1
2 7
3
4 17
5
2
12
9
Hillsmere Springs
CHESAPEAKE BAY
10
11
Mayo
8

N

Ref: DeLorme Virginia
Atlas & Gazetteer

SOUTH RIVER

1 William Paca House and Gardens

2 Chase-Lloyd House

3 Hammond-Harwood House

4 Maryland State House and Visitors Center

5 Old Treasury Building

6 Helen Avalynne Tawes Garden

7 U.S. Naval Academy and Armel-Leftwich Visitor Center

8 Smithsonian Environmental Res. Ctr. and Java History Trail

9 Londontown Publik House and Gardens

10 Thomas Point Park

11 Thomas Point Lighthouse

12 Quiet Waters Park

13 Severn Run Natural Environment Area

14 Baltimore and Annapolis Trail Park

15 Sandy Point State Park

16 Downs Park

17 Banneker-Douglass Museum

Trail

Baltimore have out-of-the-way treasures—places of inestimable beauty, sometimes subtle, often memorable. Estuarine rivers such as the West, Rhode, South, Severn, and Magothy are like miniature versions of the great Chesapeake. Every cove and marsh has its own collection of grasses, flowering plants, amphibians, fish, birds, mammals, and insects.

Fog settling in a pine forest can be as rewarding as a shimmering sunrise backlighting a tall sailboat. There are piers where a piece of meat on a string dropped in the dark water will produce a blue crab. There are wetlands where the only sound is the rustle of wild rice swaying in the wind, and there are trails where horseback riders and joggers share the outdoors with youngsters on roller blades and skate boards.

What attracts many to this part of the Chesapeake is the combination of the estuary's beauty and the benefits and pleasures of city life. A vacationer can dine on the finest seafood and sleep in the plushest inn after spending the day fishing the bay, hiking a preserve, or exploring a marsh in a sea kayak. One could do worse.

Annapolis

[Fig. 13] Annapolis, at the heart of Anne Arundel, is Maryland's capital, known for its quiet charm and its understated elegance. The city has a small-town flavor, and offers some of the Chesapeake Bay's best dining and shopping in a historical setting. In many cases, walking is all the transportation you'll need to enjoy theaters, museums, festivals, and quaint waterfront pubs with a variety of musical entertainment.

Stop by the visitor information booth at Annapolis City Dock (May through September) to learn about this port, famous internationally as a yachting center. The visitor booth and waterfront park are located on the site of a former colonial port that was surrounded by warehouses, taverns, and a shipbuilding business. In 1767, Kunta Kinte, subject of the late Alex Haley's novel, *Roots*, arrived at the dock on a slave ship.

Today skippers tend to their boats tied along the wharf at Market Square and Dock Street where Chesapeake Bay watermen have docked for generations. Visitors, townspeople, and the smartly dressed midshipmen from the U. S. Naval Academy mingle on historic city streets. The aroma of fresh-baked breads and Chesapeake Bay seafood fills the air. At the waterfront, seagulls swoop to catch bits of bread children toss into the air.

Annapolis is brimming with opportunities to explore. Several organizations offer tours on foot, by boat, or on wheels (*see* Appendix A, page 315). Old homes, museums, the City Dock, State Circle, seafood restaurants, shops, and the scenic waterfront are fine places to poke about by oneself, too. At the waterfront, book a fishing charter, rent a sea kayak or powerboat, or climb aboard a sailing schooner, cruise boat, or yacht to tour the Chesapeake Bay. Dine outside on the City Dock after picking up a pizza, fried chicken, or seafood sandwiches at **The Market House on the City Dock** (410-269-0941).

Three eighteenth-century mansions (the Hammond-Harwood, Chase-Lloyd, and William Paca houses) are located near each other in the downtown historic district. On the campus of St. John's College is the Liberty Tree, so named because it served as a meeting place for the Sons of Liberty prior to the Revolutionary War. St. John's College, which traces its origins to King William's College founded in 1696, is one of the nation's oldest colleges. The Victorian-style **Government House** (410-974-3531) at State Circle and School Street, with its collection of Maryland art and antiques, is the official residence of Maryland's governor.

Each October, this "Sailboat Capital of the United States" celebrates its maritime heritage with a sailboat show, followed by a powerboat show (410-268-8828).

Most of the nightlife at Annapolis is in or near the historic district. **Ram's Head Tavern** (410- 268-4545) at 33 West Street is home of the only local micro-brewery. Many folks come to this English-tavern-style restaurant especially for Ram's Head on Stage where local and national bands perform nightly during peak seasons.

King of France Tavern (410-263-2641) in the Treaty of Paris Restaurant at 16 Church Circle features live jazz on weekends. The tavern belongs to an association called Historic Inns of Annapolis. **Middleton Tavern** (410-263-3323) at 2 Market Space is an historic tavern featuring an oyster bar, other traditional Maryland fare, and live entertainment in an eighteenth-century setting on the city dock.

Club Hollywood (410-974-6888) at 30 Hudson Street is open six nights a week. It has pool tables, video games, live music, and disc jockeys. Come for swing night on Monday and a dance called DC hand-dancing on Wednesday.

Just outside the historic district at 2072 Somerville Road is an excellent place for families called **Jillian's Billiard Club and Cafe** (410-841-5599). In addition to live entertainment, Jillian's has video games, billiards, and table hockey.

For more information: Annapolis & Anne Arundel County Conference & Visitors Bureau, 26 West Street, Annapolis, MD 21401. Phone (410) 280-0445.

WILLIAM PACA HOUSE AND GARDEN

[Fig. 13(1)] William Paca, signer of the Declaration of Independence and former governor of Maryland, built this Georgian mansion on Prince George Street between 1763 and 1765. Note period furniture from England and the original pine floors and door. On the 2-acre grounds are four parterres, or flower beds and paths that form patterns, in addition to a wilderness garden and an herb and vegetable garden.

Dates: Open daily, Mar. through Dec. Open Friday through Sunday in Jan. and Feb. Hours are 10 to 4 daily except noon to 4 Sunday. Closed major holidays.

Fees: There is an admission fee.

For more information: William Paca House and Garden, 186 Prince George Street, Annapolis, MD 21401. Phone (410) 263-5553.

CHASE-LLOYD HOUSE

[Fig. 13(2)] Samuel Chase, U. S. Supreme Court justice and signer of the Declaration of Independence built this Georgian townhouse at 22 Maryland Avenue between 1769 and 1773.

It is noted for such fine details as a Palladian window and a cantilevered stairway.

Dates: Open 2 to 4, Tuesday through Saturday, Mar. through Dec., and Thursday through Saturday in Jan. and Feb.

Fees: There is an admission fee.

For more information: Phone (410) 263-2723 (day) or (410) 268-8005 (evening).

HAMMOND-HARWOOD HOUSE

[Fig. 13(3)] Built in 1774 for Maryland legislator Mathias Hammond, this Georgian structure at 19 Maryland Avenue was designed by architect William Buckland and is an exquisite example of late Colonial architecture.

Dates: Open 10 to 4 daily, noon to 4 Sunday. Closed major holidays.

Fees: There is an admission fee.

For more information: Hammond-Harwood House, 19 Maryland Avenue, Annapolis, MD 21401. Phone (410) 269-1714.

MARYLAND STATE HOUSE AND VISITORS CENTER

[Fig. 13(4)] Construction on Maryland's capitol building at State Circle was begun in 1772, interrupted during the Revolutionary War, then completed in 1779, making it the oldest state house in the country in continuous use by a legislature. The Maryland State House was the site of Washington's resignation as commander-in-chief and the ratification of the Treaty of Paris. It served as the nation's capital from 1783 to 1784. The visitor center is on the first floor.

Dates: Open 9 to 5 daily year-round, except Christmas Day. Free 30-minute walk-in tours at 11 and 3.

Fees: None.

For more information: Maryland State House, phone (410) 974-3400.

OLD TREASURY BUILDING

[Fig. 13(5)] On the same circle with the Maryland State House is the Old Treasury Building, a cross-shaped brick structure that serves as the historic Annapolis Foundation Research Center. Built between 1735 and 1737, this is the oldest public building in the state. Open by appointment.

For more information: Phone (410) 267-8149.

HELEN AVALYNNE TAWES GARDEN

[Fig. 13(6)] Open daily from sunrise to sunset, this 6-acre garden on Taylor Avenue and Rowe Boulevard, located among the state office buildings, has plantings that characterize the state's natural communities. Included are a forest of the mountainous western part of the state, a stream-side environment, and the sandy soil of an Eastern Shore peninsula.

Dates: Open daily, sunrise to sunset year-round. The gift shop is open 9 to 3, Monday through Friday.

Fees: None.

For more information: Helen Avalynne Tawes Garden, Maryland Department of Natural Resources, Tawes State Office Building, Annapolis, MD 21401. Phone (410) 260-8189.

U. S. NAVAL ACADEMY AND ARMEL-LEFTWICH VISITOR CENTER

[Fig. 13(7)] Annapolis is the home of the U. S. Naval Academy, where men and women learn to become professional officers in the U. S. Navy and Marine Corps. See occasional full-dress parades and, during warm weather, noon formation. At the visitor center, learn about Naval Academy history and traditions, view the award-winning film *To Lead and to Serve*, find out about the life of a midshipman, and take a guided walking tour of the Yard.

Directions: The Naval Academy is on King George Street and Parker Road. The visitor center is located inside Gate 1. The museum is in Preble Hall.

Facilities: Interactive exhibits, pictorial displays, theater, gift shop, snack bar, museum, restrooms.

Dates: Guided tours of Naval Academy grounds are held daily on the hour or half-hour, year-round except Thanksgiving, Christmas, and New Year's Day. Call for opening and closing hours, which vary according to season.

Fees: There is no admission fee for the visitor center or museum. There is a tour fee.

For more information: Armel-Leftwich Visitor Center, 52 King George Street (Gate 1), Annapolis, MD 21402. Phone (410) 263-6933. U.S. Naval Academy Museum, 118 Maryland Avenue, Annapolis, MD 21402. Phone (410) 293-2108.

BANNEKER-DOUGLASS MUSEUM

[Fig. 13(17)] Housed in the old Mount Moriah Church at 84 Franklin Street, the Banneker-Douglass Museum preserves Maryland's African-American culture. The museum is named for Benjamin Banneker and Frederick Douglass, two prominent black Marylanders. The Victorian-Gothic building is on the National Register of Historic Places.

Dates: Open 10 to 3, Tuesday through Friday; 12 to 4, Saturday.

Fees: None.

For more information: Banneker-Douglass Museum, 84 Franklin Street, Annapolis, MD 21401. Phone (410) 974-2893.

GUIDE SERVICES AND TOURIST INFORMATION

DISCOVER ANNAPOLIS TOURS. One-hour minibus tours depart from the Annapolis visitor center at 26 West Street. Call for times. Operates daily Apr. through Nov and weekends Dec. through Mar. Phone (410) 626-6000.

THREE CENTURIES TOURS OF ANNAPOLIS. Located at 48 Maryland Avenue. Tours of historic Annapolis and the U. S. Naval Academy by guides in colonial attire. Operates twice daily Apr. through Oct. and Saturdays Nov. through Mar. Phone (410) 263-5401.

STATE HOUSE VISITORS CENTER, State Circle, Annapolis, MD 21401. Phone (410) 974-3400.

RESTAURANTS IN ANNAPOLIS

Not surprisingly, fresh Chesapeake Bay seafood is a specialty at many Annapolis restaurants. Here are several popular spots.

CARROL'S CREEK RESTAURANT. 410 Severn Avenue, Annapolis. Eat fresh seafood indoors or out. Downtown location on Restaurant Row. Called one of America's top waterfront restaurants by *Bon Appetit* magazine. *Moderate to expensive. Phone (410) 263-8102.*

MCGARVEY'S SALOON AND OYSTER BAR. 8 Market Space, Annapolis. Serving seafood, steaks, and hamburgers. Located a block from the City Dock. *Moderate. Phone (410) 263-5700.*

SAM'S WATERFRONT CAFÉ. 2020 Chesapeake Harbour Drive, Annapolis. Lighthouse-shaped restaurant modeled after Thomas Point Lighthouse. Enjoy waterfront views and local seafood, indoors or out. Jazz on weekends. *Moderate to expensive. Phone (410) 263-3600.*

O'LEARY'S SEAFOOD RESTAURANT. 310 Third Street, Annapolis. Specializing in fresh seafood including Maryland crabs, mahi mahi, wahoo, halibut, and sea bass. *Moderate. Phone (410) 263-0884.*

49 WEST. 49 West Street, Annapolis. European-style cafe features light fare such as soups and sandwiches. Live jazz. *Inexpensive. Phone (410) 626-9796.*

HARRY BROWNE'S. 66 State Circle, Annapolis. Historic restaurant and lounge with lavish lunches, brunches, and dinners. *Expensive. Phone (410) 263-4332.*

Other crab houses near Annapolis are at Kent Narrows across the Chesapeake Bay Bridge—easy to get to by continuing east on US 50 for 20 minutes, exiting at Kent Narrows Bridge. Look for restaurants just off the highway on the left and right. Expect highway delays for east-bound traffic on Fridays and Saturdays in spring and summer.

LODGING IN ANNAPOLIS

Many historic and elegant inns offer the perfect way to experience Annapolis hospitality.

LOEW'S ANNAPOLIS HOTEL. 126 West Street, Annapolis. Area's only AAA four-star hotel. Known for excellent service, and one of few hotels that caters to pet owners. Features Starbucks Coffee Bar and The Corinthian dining room (moderate to expensive) with fine food and atmosphere. Located in the historic area close to attractions and waterfront. *Expensive. Phone (410) 263-7777 or (800) 526-2593.*

STATE HOUSE INN. 25 State Circle, Annapolis. Relax in a Jacuzzi in this elegant inn. The Maryland State House and Chesapeake Bay are visible from some rooms. *Expensive. Phone (410) 990-0024.*

ANNAPOLIS ECONO LODGE. 2451 Riva Road, Annapolis. In-room whirlpools, free HBO. Within 2 miles of Annapolis Harbor, 3 miles of U. S. Naval Academy. *Inexpensive to moderate. Phone (410) 224-4317.*

Anne Arundel County

Anne Arundel County lies along the western shore of the Chesapeake Bay east of Washington, DC, and south of Baltimore. Its western border is defined by the scenic Patuxent River, a Chesapeake Bay tributary important for its aquatic ecosystems protected and studied by various research centers, parks, and preserves. In fact, Anne Arundel is intersected and bordered by several important Chesapeake Bay tributaries, including the lovely Severn River, which passes by the city of Annapolis on its way to a confluence with the bay. A total of 400 miles of waterfront provides endless opportunities for sportfishing, boating, touring, swimming, sunbathing, photography, nature study, and dining with outstanding views. On weekends from Labor Day weekend through October, the Maryland Renaissance Festival draws some 200,000 visitors to Crownsville, about 4 miles northwest of Annapolis. A 22-acre re-creation of a sixteenth century English village offers entertainment, foods, and shopping. Jousting, Maryland's state sport, takes center stage.

SMITHSONIAN ENVIRONMENTAL RESEARCH CENTER

[Fig. 13(8)] In the wetlands of Muddy Creek, where the brackish Rhode River receives an influx of fresh water, scientists from the Smithsonian Institution carry on environmental research. The 2,600-acre research center, located across the South River from Annapolis in Anne Arundel County, includes coastal plain forests in varying stages of succession, agricultural fields, freshwater wetlands and marshes, and open waters where salt water and fresh water mix.

Guides lead visitors on hikes or Saturday canoe trips (call ahead to arrange) into the marshes and forests of poplar, river birch, sycamore, and oak. The 1.5-mile Discovery Trail follows Muddy Creek through forests of tulip poplar and sweetgum. A boardwalk allows exploration of a marsh and leads to Hog Island, where the trail is shaded by groves of mountain laurel. The Java Trail is described on page 143.

Canoeists and hikers sometimes see white-tailed deer, wild turkey, and beaver. Birds in the marshes include osprey, snowy egrets, great blue herons, swans, and even bald eagles. Birders have also identified many varieties of ducks, songbirds, and spring and fall warblers.

Interpreters explain the food value to wildlife and wildfowl of estuaries such as this one. Runoff from agricultural fields contains nutrients such as nitrogen and phosphorous. Through photosynthesis, plants that grow in the shallow water convert these nutrients into food for small animals. The entire food chain benefits.

This rich resource attracted Native Americans to the area many thousands of years ago. Middens, or garbage heaps of discarded clam and oyster shells, help

NARROW-LEAVED CATTAIL
(Typha augustifolia)

archaeologists unravel the mysteries of the lifestyles of various Indian tribes. The Piscataways, the Choptank, and the Mattaponi once hunted where the scientists now carry on their studies.

By the time explorers arrived, warring Susquehannocks from the north and Powhatans from the south had made the area too dangerous for other Indians. The lack of resident tribes had an interesting result—relatively few rivers and creeks in this part of Maryland have Indian names.

Following long use as a tobacco farm, the land's soil was further depleted by a dairy farming operation between 1915 and 1947. By the time the Smithsonian acquired Java Farm in 1965, vandals had destroyed buildings and the Smithsonian came close to selling the property. A committee of scientists from the institute, however, saw promise in the land, and encouraged the Smithsonian to establish a research center in the Rhode River watershed. In the ensuing decades, nature has seriously begun restoring the health of wetlands and forests.

Narrow-leaved Cattail

Native Americans devised many uses for cattails. The long stems could be woven into mats for shelter or for ground cloths. The roots were eaten raw or boiled. Red-winged blackbirds expertly weave their nests onto the close-growing cattails. The narrow-leaved cattail (*Typha augustifolia*) is the only variety that can stand brackish water.

Directions: From MD 2 south of Annapolis, go east on MD 214, right on MD 468 south, and left at the Smithsonian sign. The visitor center is the modern brick building on the right.

Activities: Hikes and guided canoe trips by appointment.

Facilities: Education center, hiking trails, canoe waters.

Dates: Open 8 to 4 weekdays year-round by appointment. Guided 2-hour canoe trips are offered on Sat.

Fees: There is no entry fee. There is a fee for guides.

Closest town: Annapolis is about 8 miles north.

For more information: Phone (410) 269-1412.

JAVA HISTORY TRAIL

[Fig. 13(8)] This 1.3-mile trail leads from the Reed Education Center past exhibits depicting the area's history. Included are a depiction of pre-colonial Native American culture, description of slave life on a tobacco plantation, remains of the Java mansion, an exhibit on the dairy farm that operated here in the first part of the 1900s, and a demonstration of natural processes that slowly reclaim cultivated land.

The trail features the Piscataway Indians, one of three tribes known to have hunted in the area during late summer and fall. White-tailed deer, cottontail rabbit, black bear, geese, ducks, wild turkey, muskrat, and river otter supplied them with food, clothing, and tools. The Indians found many uses for wetland plants such as pickerelweed, wild rice, and duck potatoes.

Trail: 1.3-mile easy loop from education center.

LONDONTOWN PUBLIK HOUSE AND GARDENS

[Fig. 13(9)] This National Historic Landmark was constructed in the late 1750s to provide food and lodging for passengers who would take the ferry across the South River to Annapolis. With changing fortunes, including the silting of the river and declining popularity of the ferry, much of the original community of Londontown has disappeared, with the notable exception of The Publik House. Archaeologists still search for other evidence of the lost town.

Eight acres of woodland gardens with scenic river frontage feature paths with themes such as a Spring Flower Walk and an American Wildflower Walk. On special occasions, interpreters dressed in colonial attire lead tours.

Directions: From Annapolis, go south on MD 2. One mile past South River bridge, turn left on MD 235 (Mayo Road). Go 1 mile and turn left on Londontown Road; drive to the end of the road.

Facilities: Historic house, gardens, museum shop, restrooms.

Dates: Grounds are open 10 to 4, Monday through Saturday; 12 to 4, Sunday. House tours are conducted hourly. Closed Jan. and Feb.

Fees: There is an admission charge.

For more information: Londontown Publik House, 839 Londontown Road, Edgewater, MD 21037. Phone (410) 222-1919

THOMAS POINT PARK

[Fig. 13(10)] This 44-acre county park, acquired in 1962 for recreation and conservation, sits on a narrow peninsula in the Chesapeake Bay at the mouth of the South River, southeast of Annapolis. Perhaps the park's small size gives it a low profile. Maybe most people are looking for more excitement than walking, jogging, watching birds, fishing, or enjoying the scenery. Whatever the reason, this little gem remains largely undiscovered by the throngs that occupy many other public areas. The park offers a magnificent view of the Chesapeake Bay, with the Bay Bridge to the north and, to the east, Thomas Point Lighthouse and the Eastern Shore.

The bay's excellent fishing waters surround the park. Because of its small size, limited parking, and sensitive natural environment, which includes a wildlife refuge and marsh, recreation is limited to passive activities and vehicle permits are required. Walkers and bikers may enter without a permit. Swimming and wading are not allowed. Leashed pets are permitted.

Directions: From MD 2 at Annapolis, go southeast on Forest Drive to the junction with Bay Ridge Road. Turn right on Arundel on the Bay Road, bear right on Thomas Point Road and continue to the park entrance.

Activities: Walking, biking, jogging, fishing, picnicking. Camping for organized youth groups. No swimming or wading is allowed.

Facilities: Picnic tables, rental pavilion, youth group campground, restroom.

Dates: Open 8 to sunset daily, year-round. The office hours are 10 to 12, Wednesday through Sunday, closed Monday and Tuesday.

Fees: There is a vehicle permit fee, but no fee for walkers or bikers. There is a fee for youth group camping and pavilion rental.

Closest town: Annapolis is about 5 miles to the north.

For more information: Thomas Point Park, 3890 Thomas Point Road, Annapolis, MD 21403. Phone (410) 222-1969.

THOMAS POINT LIGHTHOUSE

[Fig. 13(11)] Located at the mouth of the South River, southeast of Annapolis, Thomas Point Lighthouse is one of the few surviving offshore screwpile lighthouses still in use by the U. S. Coast Guard. It was built in 1875, the third lighthouse on this site, and was among the last Chesapeake Bay lighthouses with a keeper. The first lighthouse was so poorly constructed that it lasted only a short time. Severe shoaling caused the second one to be abandoned. The current wooden hexagonal structure is slated to become a National Historical Landmark.

The lighthouse, accessible only by boat, is not open to the public, but it can be seen—and photographed—from Thomas Point Park. With its attractive red roof and white sides, it has become one of the most loved and most photographed lighthouses on the bay.

QUIET WATERS PARK

[Fig. 13(12)] South of Annapolis on the South River is Quiet Waters Park, where a looping trail leads for several miles past flowering dogwood (*Cornus florida*), pink azalea or pinkster flower (*Rhododendron*

Black Skimmer

People are inevitably amazed the first time they see a black skimmer (*Rynchops niger*) flying just over the water, with lower mandible cutting the surface. When the skimmer connects with a fish, the head snaps down and the beak closes on the prey. This skillful flyer is black above and white below, with a red beak tipped with black. The black skimmer is the only bird to have a lower mandible longer than the upper. Undisturbed nest sites can be difficult to find because eggs are laid right on sandbars and beaches, usually among shell litter.

BLACK SKIMMER
(*Rynchops niger*)

Osprey

This large raptor has a dark back, white undersides, and a wingspread of 5.5 feet. The osprey (*Pandion haliaetus*) dives into lakes, rivers, and oceans feet first for its prey. Many such dives are fruitless. But after rising into the air with a successful catch, the bird shakes itself off, lines the fish up head first to reduce air drag, and flies to a perch or nest. On occasion, the osprey has been known to sink its talons deeply into a fish too big to lift, which then pulls the great bird beneath the surface.

nudiflorum), tall pines (*Pinus*), and majestic white oaks (*Quercus alba*). In a beautiful natural setting, including trellised benches, trail users can enjoy views of the South River. An outdoor rink is popular among ice skaters.

A concessionaire offers opportunities to explore Chesapeake Bay natural history by sea kayak, canoe, and pedal boats. Sea kayaking instruction is available.

Natural history lectures held from time to time at the park's Blue Heron Center are sponsored by the Anne Arundel Bird Club, Friends of Quiet Waters Park, Severn River Association, Sierra Club, and Anne Arundel County SPCA. Various experts talk about mysterious creatures of the marsh, or where to find particular wildflowers on area trails and in parks and marshes. Listeners learn how to help save the Chesapeake Bay, beginning in their own backyards. On another night they might hear about the breeding biology and feeding habits of the black skimmer (*Rynchops nigra*).

Directions: From Forest Drive (bordering Annapolis on the southwestern side), go south. Turn right on Hillsmere Drive, then right into the park.

Activities: Hiking, seasonal ice skating, canoeing, sea kayaking.

Facilities: Hiking trail, formal gardens, outdoor ice rink, cafe, canoe/kayak concession.

Dates: The park is open 7 to dusk daily. The park office is open 9 to 4 weekdays, 10 to 4 weekends. The park and office are closed Tuesdays.

Fees: There is a vehicle entry fee. Admission is free to bikers, hikers, and roller bladers. There are also fees for boat rental and for the ice rink.

Closest town: Forest Drive and the southern edge of Annapolis are about 1.5 miles north.

For more information: Quiet Waters Park, 600 Quiet Waters Park Road, Annapolis, MD 21403. Phone (410) 222-1777. Boat rental or instruction: Amphibious Horizons, phone (410) 267-8742.

THE SEVERN RIVER AND SEVERN RUN

The 23-mile-long Severn River and its 9 miles of headwaters in Severn Run have figured prominently in Maryland's history. The area remained relatively unchanged during thousands of years of use by Native Americans. Puritans who came up the Chesapeake Bay and turned into the Severn in the 1650s established a brisk tobacco trade out of the Annapolis harbor. But as soils became depleted, the tobacco port shifted to Baltimore, while

Annapolis re-established itself as a political and military center. The U. S. Naval Academy opened its doors on the banks of the Severn in 1845. Today, a fourth of Anne Arundel County's population lives within the 70 square miles of the Severn watershed, but about half the land remains forested and undeveloped.

With a growing population depending on good water quality, the Severn River was designated a National Wild and Scenic River in the 1970s, and its waters now receive protection under federal and state laws. The designation was a natural. The Severn's steep ravines and stands of huge tulip poplars and oaks provide beautiful surroundings in addition to protecting the watershed. Fascinating wetlands with names such as Sullivan's Cove

OSPREY
(*Pandion haliaeetus*)

Marsh and Round Bay Bog are home to black ducks, mallards, pintails, great egrets, green-backed herons, ospreys, muskrats, and several species of frogs. Standing water in the acidic soil of Round Bay Bog provides a niche for cranberry bushes (*Vaccinium*) and the Virginia chain fern (*Woodwardia virginica*).

On Severn Run, the part of the Severn watershed that's above the fall line, red maples and river birches color the riverbanks with red and yellow fall color. The banks of the Run, as it's called, are home to many plant species, including a rare climbing fern (*Lygodium palmutum*). This plant has unfernlike leaflets divided into two hand-shaped parts.

As the water crosses the fall line into the Severn River and flows toward the Chesapeake, it collects an increasing number of boaters, fishermen, crabbers, and others seeking recreation on coves, creeks, and river. Oyster gatherers would also be competing for space, but the supply of oysters has dwindled with increasing pollution and siltation.

In late winter, the winter flounder (*Pseudopleuronectes americanus*) spawns at the mouth of the Severn and other major rivers of the upper Chesapeake.

SEVERN RUN NATURAL ENVIRONMENTAL AREA

[Fig. 13(13)] The 1,600 acres of Severn Run Natural Environmental Area in western Anne Arundel County are divided into six tracts along the Severn River, varying in habitat from marsh to mature forest. The land is owned by the state and managed as a buffer zone to protect the water quality and scenic value of the Severn River.

The riverine habitat is ideal for many species of wildlife. Great blue herons have established a rookery in the area. In spring, a horseback rider may watch several deer browsing at the edge of woods. Canoeists might see mallards, black ducks, or wood ducks clatter into the air as they approach. Hikers sometimes spot raccoons, red foxes, gray squirrels, and cottontail rabbits. They also may find the furred or feathered remains of a hawk's or an owl's dinner.

Anglers enjoy catching perch, largemouth bass, and stocked trout from Severn Run. A well-defined trail with walkways and bridges originates where Dicus Mill Road crosses Severn Run and provides access to Severn Run during trout season. Dicus Mill Road goes west from MD 3, about 1.5 miles north of the junction with MD 32 at Millersville.

There are several other unmarked trails and many footpaths throughout the area, where pink lady's slipper (*Cypripedium acaule*) grows in shaded woodlands in May and trailing arbutus (*Epigaea repens*) provides a bit of green among the dead leaves in winter.

A 1-mile unmarked loop trail provides scenic views of the upper Severn River. The trail is located at the end of Indian Landing Road in Millersville, northwest of Annapolis. A 3-mile horse trail leads from New Cut Road toward Quarterfield Road southeast of Ridgeway.

The Severn Run Natural Environmental Area has no developed picnic areas or overnight camping facilities except for a campground for organized youth groups. For permission to explore the variety of hiking trails here and for a map, contact Sandy Point State Park, which oversees recreation in the Natural Environmental Area.

Activities: Hiking, seasonal fishing.

Dates: Open dawn to dusk, year-round. Obtain information from Sandy Point Park, open 8:30 to 5, weekdays.

Fees: None.

Closest town: Millersville is just south of the area.

For more information: Sandy Point State Park, 1100 East College Parkway, Annapolis, MD 21401. Phone (410) 974-2149.

BALTIMORE AND ANNAPOLIS TRAIL PARK

[Fig. 13(14)] On the north side of the Severn River, the Baltimore and Annapolis Trail Park extends arrowlike for 13.3 miles along an old railroad bed. Hikers, bikers, joggers, equestrians, roller bladers, moms with strollers, and wheelchair users pass through urban areas, small towns, fields, wetlands, and forests as they follow the route of the old Baltimore and Annapolis Railroad from Glen Burnie south to Annapolis. The paved path is a comfortable 10 feet wide. Wildlife such as gray squirrels, raccoons, rabbits, great horned owls, and a great variety of songbirds find suitable habitat in the 66-foot wide park.

The trail is busiest on weekends, holidays, and during after-school hours. Peak use occurs during spring and fall, with heaviest traffic in the middle of the trail around Severna Park. The rural southern end of the trail across the bridge from Annapolis affords the most solitude. Markers placed at 0.5-mile intervals begin with Mile 0 at the southern end.

Trail users can thank the folks associated with the national Rails to Trails Conservancy for their ongoing work to transform abandoned railroad beds like this one into trails the public can enjoy. Also, many volunteers help by maintaining the trail, planting flowerbeds, building benches and bulletin boards, preserving railroad history, and patrolling the park. Evidence of the historical significance of this route remains in old railroad switch boxes, track sections, and the Severna Park Railroad Station. On Thursday evenings in summer, the B&A Trail Porch Pickers entertain from the front porch of the park ranger station at Earleigh Heights.

Directions: Several parking areas are available along the trail, including these two operated by the park:

For the ranger station at Earleigh Heights (Mile 7), from US 50 at Annapolis, cross the Severn River Bridge and take Exit 27B. Go 7 miles north on MD 2 (Ritchie Highway). Turn left at Earleigh Heights Road and go 0.25 mile. The ranger station is the yellow building with red trim on the left.

For the parking lot at the southern end (Mile 0), from US 50 at Annapolis, cross the Severn River Bridge and take Exit 27, turning south on MD 450 toward the Naval Academy. Go 0.1 mile to the first right, and turn into the driveway of the parking lot.

Parking is available at shopping centers and public lots including the Jones Station Park & Ride lot on MD 2 at Jones Station Road in Arnold, the Marley Station Mall parking lot on MD 2 at Mountain Road in Glen Burnie, the Harundale Mall parking lot on MD 2 in Glen Burnie, and the Glen Burnie parking garage at the North Arundel Court House.

Facilities: Restrooms are at Earleigh Heights ranger station. Picnic tables, benches, water fountains, and public telephones are spaced along the trail. Access for wheelchair users is at Earleigh Heights.

Activities: Hiking, jogging, biking, horseback riding, roller blading.

Dates: Open dawn to dusk daily, year-round. The ranger station is open 8:30 to 3 daily except Fridays.

Fees: None.

Closest town: Trail goes from Glen Burnie to Annapolis.

For more information: B&A Trail Park, PO Box 1007, Severna Park, MD 21146. Phone (410) 222-6244.

Trailing Arbutus

Trailing arbutus (*Epigaea repens*) is one of the subtle rewards of undisturbed soil. The tiny sweet-scented pink and white blossoms of this evergreen creeper hide among the leaf litter in early spring. Occurrences are fairly scarce because the plant does not fare well in soil that has been cultivated or grazed.

TRAILING ARBUTUS (*Epigaea repens*)

🏞 SANDY POINT STATE PARK

[Fig. 13(15)] Sandy Point is one of Maryland's older state parks, developed during the 1950s to give people recreational opportunities on the Chesapeake Bay. The park's sandy beaches are the prime attraction, affording sun worshipers and builders of sand castles a picture-postcard view of the Chesapeake Bay Bridge suspended above sailing regattas, ocean-going freighters, and smaller working boats.

Adding its own ambiance to the scene is Sandy Point Shoal Lighthouse. The lighthouse is a solar facility built on a caisson foundation in 1858, and is still operated by the U. S. Coast Guard. On clear days, Baltimore Light, which guides boats toward the entrance of Baltimore Harbor, is visible to the north. Both lighthouses have a caisson foundation, are accessible only by boat, and are not open to the public.

Located as it is next to the bridge, a mere 32 miles east of metropolitan Washington, DC, and just 8 miles east of the state capital at Annapolis, Sandy Point receives nearly 1 million visitors annually. Crowded conditions can be expected on the 600-acre park and 1-mile stretch of beach when school is out. For more solitude, avoid peak seasons or schedule trips for weekdays when possible. Even in summer, however, most people head for the park's beaches, leaving the beautiful marshes and pine forests to those who wish to explore.

Except for birders, who come from all over the world for the spring nesting season and to see migrant birds of prey, shorebirds, and waterfowl in fall and winter, few people are aware of the park's beauty in the off-season. A morning stroll along the beach or a picnic lunch is a fine way to unwind on a spring weekday. Spring is also the time to collect winter's bounty of driftwood deposited on the beach, scope out the peregrine falcons nesting on the bridge, and listen to the wild calls of Canada geese and tundra swans. Take a fishing rod in a rental boat on a fall afternoon and try a new lure for scrappy bluefish. A quiet, snow-covered beach in winter offers an experience totally different from the shoreline on a raucous summer afternoon. Beautifully sculpted driftwood also rewards beachcombers who come after winter storms.

Winter is also the time to hear the haunting calls of the great-horned (*Bubo virginianus*), barred (*Strix varia*), and long-eared (*Asio otus*) owls in the park's pine forests. Ducks such as the canvasback (*Aythya valisineria*), redhead (*Aythya valisineria*), and lesser scaup (*Aythya valisineria*) find refuge in the sheltered waterways.

Presently undergoing a makeover is the park mansion, Sandy Point Farmhouse, which dates

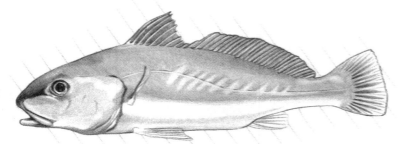

ATLANTIC CROAKER (*Micropogonias undulatus*)

back to 1815 when the property was used as a farm for the cultivation of seaweed.

White perch attract anglers to the 25-acre Mezick Pond fishing pier. With 23 public ramps providing public access to the pond, summer fishing is usually not possible from a boat. Off the beaches and in the brackish water of the Chesapeake Bay, however, striped bass (rockfish), white perch, channel catfish, flounder, bluefish, spot, and croaker provide plenty of action.

Hiking is perhaps an afterthought at Sandy Point State Park, where the longest trail takes just 20 minutes to walk or even less time to travel by mountain bike. However, the staff also oversees two more wild places, the nearby 200-acre Corcoran Tract, a Nature Conservancy holding with very limited hiking and birding possibilities (call the park office for permission), and the 2,500-acre Severn Run Natural Environmental Area, separated into six parcels (*see* page 147).

Atlantic Croaker

This bottom feeder dines on shrimp, crabs, worms, and mollusks. The Atlantic croaker (*Micropogonias undulatus*) moves into the Chesapeake Bay in spring and leaves in the fall for the deeper, warmer waters offshore. Anglers, drift fishing or at anchor, match these foods by casting peeler crab, sea clam, shrimp, bloodworms, and squid to catch hardheads, as they are called. Occasional croakers of 3 and 4 pounds are recorded, but most are smaller. These members of the drum family make a loud croaking noise when caught.

Overnight camping (except by organized youth groups with reservations) is not permitted at Sandy Point State Park or at many other places south of Baltimore. One option for campers is the Capitol KOA Campground (410-923-2771) 20 minutes south of the park at Millersville. Many campers go to Point Lookout State Park, several hours south, in Saint Mary's County.

Directions: From US 50/301 east of Annapolis, take Exit 32 before crossing Chesapeake Bay Bridge and follow signs to the park.

Activities: Swimming, picnicking, fishing, crabbing, bird-watching, roller blading, beachcombing, boating, kayaking, sailing, cross-country skiing, hiking, biking, youth group camping (reservation required).

Facilities: Guarded swimming beach with bathhouses, food concession and beach store, picnic tables with grills and comfort stations throughout the park (handicapped facilities available), 12 large group shelters (reservation required), marina with motorboat and rowboat rental (Chesapeake Bay sport-fishing license required), docking facilities for day use, 22 boat ramps, 5 miles of hiking trails in the park plus 6 miles in the Corcoran Environmental Area.

Dates: Gates are open daily year-round, except major holidays. Hours are 6 to 9 during summer, but vary according to the length of day the rest of the year. The swimming beach and food concession are open Memorial Day through Labor Day. The marina store is open on weekends during spring rockfish season and daily Memorial Day through Labor Day. The launch ramp is open 24 hours a day from mid-May to mid-Sept.

Fees: There is an entrance fee, varying in amount according to the time of the week and the time of year (free in winter). There is a fee for rental boats.

Closest town: Annapolis is 8 miles west and Washington, DC, is 32 miles west.

For more information: Sandy Point State Park, 1100 East College Parkway, Annapolis, MD 21401. Phones: office (410) 974-2149, marina (410) 974-2772.

DOWNS PARK

[Fig. 13(16)] On the eastern end of a Chesapeake Bay peninsula formed by the Severn and Magothy rivers between Baltimore and Maryland is 231-acre Downs Park, a great getaway for hikers and bikers. Five miles of wide, paved trails are perfect for walking, jogging, biking, and roller blading.

A 3.5-mile path, looping all the way around the perimeter of the park, has red markers every tenth of a mile. A 1.8-mile senior exercise trail, with green markers, begins at the information center, follows the perimeter trail to the gatehouse, then loops back to the start. Several miles of easy natural paths wind through the park woodlands, where the clear, flutelike call of the tufted titmouse rings from tall oaks.

Fishermen enjoy casting from the shore of the Chesapeake Bay and in the freshwater pond at the north end of the park. Saltwater and freshwater fishing licenses are available at nearby sport-fishing stores. Swimming and boating are not permitted. Pets are permitted in the park on a leash.

During summer months, a bayside concert series draws listeners to the park amphitheater on Saturday evenings to hear music as varied as honky-tonk swing, Dixieland, ragtime, country, chamber, zydeco, and big band. U. S. Navy and Air Force bands also entertain as bay waters reflect the changing colors of sunset.

The park's North Overlook is where the crumbling remains of Bodkin Island Lighthouse were once visible. Built in 1822 and abandoned in 1855, this lighthouse is now nothing more than a "navigational hazard" on current maps.

Directions: From I-695 on the south side of Baltimore, go south on MD 10 (Arundel Freeway) until it merges with MD 100 East. Follow MD 100 until it merges with MD 177 East (Mountain Road). Follow Mountain Road about 3.5 miles. The park entrance is on the right, about 1 mile past Chesapeake High School.

Activities: Hiking, biking, picnicking, tennis, basketball, handball, softball, volleyball, horseshoes. Camping for organized youth groups.

Facilities: Hiking and biking trails, interpretive trail, picnic areas with tables and grills, rental pavilions, garden, tennis courts, basketball courts, handball courts, softball fields, volleyball court, horseshoe pits, information center, concession stand, bayside amphitheater, conference room, youth camping area, comfort stations.

Dates: The park is open 9 to dusk daily year-round, except closed Tuesday. The office is open 9 to 4. Call for hours on holidays.

Fees: There is a vehicle entry fee. There are rental fees for pavilions and for youth campground.

Closest town: Pasadena is about 5 miles west.

For more information: Downs Park, 8311 John Downs Loop, Pasadena, MD 21122. Phone (410) 222-6230.

▓ RESTAURANTS IN ANNE ARUNDEL CO.

Most restaurants in Anne Arundel County are in the environs of Annapolis. Here are a few of Anne Arundel County's fine eateries.

Brown pelicans beg for a free lunch from a Chesapeake fisherman

CANTLER'S RIVERSIDE INN. 458 Forest Beach Road. Located on Mill Creek, about 20 minutes southeast of Sandy Point State Park. Specializes in fresh crabs and other seafood, which arrives by boat. Accessible by boat or car. Waterfront view. Casual dress. *Inexpensive to moderate. Phone (410) 757-1311.*

GARRY'S GRILL. California cuisine at two locations, one at 914 Bay Ridge Road at Bay Ridge, southeast of Annapolis, and one at 533-A Baltimore and Annapolis Boulevard in Saverna Park. *Inexpensive. Phone (410) 626-0388.*

WOODFIRE. 580-P Ritchie Highway, Saverna Park. Upscale, somewhat formal steak house, operated by owners of Garry's Grill. *Inexpensive to moderate. Phone (410) 626-0388.*

▓ LODGING IN ANNE ARUNDEL COUNTY

An eclectic assortment of inns and motels are spread about this sometimes rural, sometimes suburban, county. Here is a sampling.

THE BARN ON HOWARD'S COVE. 500 Wilson Road. This beautifully restored 150-year-old horse barn is on 6.5 waterfront acres on a Severn River tributary just outside Annapolis. *Moderate to expensive. 410-266-6840.*

HERRINGTON HARBOR MARINA RESORT. 7161 Lake Shore Drive, Friendship. Beachfront inn in the southern part of the county, overlooking the Chesapeake Bay. Restaurant on premises. *Moderate to expensive. Phone (410) 741-5100, (410) 213-9438, extension 100.*

HOLIDAY INN-BWI AIRPORT. 890 Elkridge Landing Road. Located near airport south of Baltimore. Features affordable weekend getaway packages. Pets allowed. *Moderate to expensive. Phone (410) 859-8400.*

Baltimore

Since its founding, Baltimore has been intimately tied to the Chesapeake Bay. Mills located at the fall lines of many bay tributaries near the city and the natural harbor on the Patapsco River combined to help establish Baltimore as a valued port early in its history. Today, Baltimore is the 15th largest city in the U. S. and it ranks fifth among the nation's ports.

Following the urban flight that many cities experienced during the 1950s and 1960s as people abandoned downtown areas and moved to surrounding counties, Baltimore's downtown retail district suffered. Shops stood abandoned. Warehouses were torn down. Piers and wharves deteriorated. However, an inspired urban renewal that began in the 1970s attracted major hotels, office buildings, and bright new facilities such as Harborplace (1980) and the National Aquarium (1981). The citizens of Baltimore are justifiably proud of the remarkable renaissance of their city.

Baltimore's many historic and cultural attractions, parks, gardens, and museums attract visitors as feeding rockfish attract seagulls. Tourists flock to the city by car, boat, plane and train. All Amtrak (800-USA-RAIL) runs between Washington, DC, and Boston, MA, stop at Baltimore's Penn Station.

There's far too much to see in a day. Better to pick and choose a few highlights and allow time to fully enjoy them. A mass transit system (410-539-5000) helps the unfamiliar negotiate the city.

One way to explore the sites of the Inner Harbor or Fells Point National Historic District while avoiding the anxiety of fighting traffic and finding parking places is to travel by water. Even water taxis are available, with boats running continually every 15 to 40 minutes depending on the season, stopping at various landings to provide access to some of Baltimore's most popular attractions. (See Appendix A, page 315 for additional cruise information.) Boat landings in the Baltimore area provide access to the multistoried National Aquarium, the Maryland Science Center, and the recently restored *U. S. Frigate Constellation*.

Baltimore's number one attraction, Harborplace, is an internationally acclaimed, glass-enclosed marketplace with an eclectic mix of locally owned shops, nationally known merchants, waterside cafes, kiosks, and restaurants. Across the street is The Gallery, with 75 more shops and restaurants in a vaulted six-story atrium with cascading escalators and a grand view of the harbor.

The Inner Harbor is also the location of the **Baltimore Maritime Museum** (410-396-3453) at Pier 4 and Pratt Street, with a three-ship exhibit that includes the lightship *Chesapeake*, the World War II submarine USS *Torsk*, and the USS *Taney*, the only ship still afloat that survived the bombing of Pearl Harbor.

On the 27th floor of the **World Trade Center** (410-837-4515) at 401 East Pratt Street is an impressive observation level with a panoramic view of Baltimore's skyline, the Inner Harbor, and in the distance, the Chesapeake Bay. A multimedia presentation depicts the city's history. This 30-story structure is the largest pentagonal building in the world.

South of Eastern Avenue on Broadway are the cobblestone streets of **Fells Point Historic District** (410-675-6756), one of the nation's oldest surviving maritime communities. Fells Point was the hub of the nation's shipbuilding industry during the late 1700s and early 1800s. Some 350 original structures remain, including tiny shops, galleries, pubs, and restaurants, adding their charm to this harbor neighborhood.

Among historic homes in Baltimore are the **Babe Ruth Birthplace** at 216 Emory Street (410-727-1539), the **Evergreen House**, an 1850s Italianate mansion at 4545 North Charles Street (410-516-0341), and the **home of the writer and "Sage of Baltimore," H. L. Mencken** at 1524 Hollins Street (410-396-3523). The **Edgar Allan Poe House** at 200 North Amity Street (410-396-6932) is the place where "The Master of the Macabre" wrote much of his early work.

The **Star-Spangled Banner Flag House and 1812 Museum** at 844 East Pratt Street (410-837-1793) was the home of Mary Pickersgill, seamstress of the 30-by-40-foot flag for Fort McHenry that inspired Francis Scott Key to write the words for *The Star Spangled Banner* during the War of 1812.

The **Baltimore Museum of Art** (410-396-7137) at North Charles and 31st streets is the state's largest art museum, housing the world-famous Cone collection, including works by Picasso, Cezanne, and Matisse. The **Walters Art Gallery** (410-547-ARTS) at Charles Street and Centre Street has a world-renowned collection on five floors. Included in addition to paintings are Egyptian artifacts, jeweled Faberge eggs, and medieval armor.

Baltimore is also the home of the **Pimlico Race Course** (410-542-9400), where the middle jewel of thoroughbred racing's Triple Crown is run. Other attractions include the **The Baltimore Opera Company** (410-625-1600), the **Baltimore Symphony Orchestra** (800-442-1198), a new interactive children's museum called **Port Discovery** (410-727-8120), the shops of **Antique Row** (410-383-2881) in the 800 block of North Howard Street, and of course, **Oriole Park at Camden Yards** (410-685-9800), home of the Baltimore Orioles baseball team.

Most of Baltimore's night life is concentrated in the downtown area, where the shimmering lights of the Inner Harbor add their own magic to an evening on the town. The Comedy Factory, located upstairs at **Burke's Cafe** (410-752-4189), draws top comedians to entertain Baltimore audiences. The restaurant and comedy club is at 36 Light Street at the intersection with Lombard Street. Reservations are required.

Sports enthusiasts and families with children will want to check out the **ESPN Zone** (410-685-ESPN). The new restaurant/bar/arena complex at the upper end of the Inner Harbor has a sports theme. On the second floor is a game arena that is open into the wee hours. There are batting cages, a cage for shooting basketball, and many family-oriented activities. One popular game involves sitting in a chair and driving a simulated racecar or speed boat.

The ESPN Zone is in the Power-plant Building at 601 East Pratt Street, a renovated building that also houses the **Hard Rock Cafe** (410-347-7625), featuring American food,

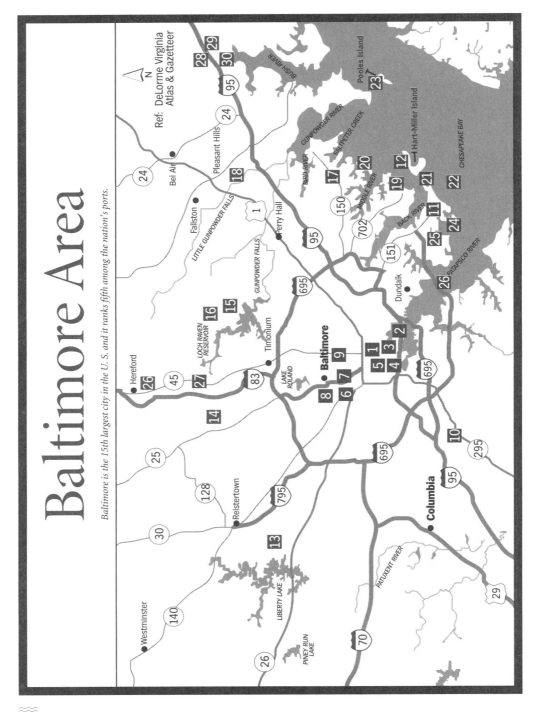

Baltimore Area

Baltimore is the 15th largest city in the U. S. and it ranks fifth among the nation's ports.

Ref: DeLorme Virginia Atlas & Gazetteer

1 Baltimore Area Visitors Center
2 Fort McHenry
3 National Aquarium
4 Maryland Science Center and Davis Planetarium
5 U. S. Frigate Constellation
6 Druid Hill Park
7 Baltimore Zoo
8 Cylburn Arboretum
9 Sherwood Gardens
10 Patapsco Valley State Park

11 North Point State Park
12 Hart-Miller Island State Park
13 Soldiers Delight Natural Environmental Area
14 Oregon Ridge Park and Nature Center
15 Loch Raven Fishing Center
16 Gunpowder Falls State Park
17 Hammerman/Dundee Creek Area
18 Little Gunpowder Trail and Horse Trail Loop
19 Rocky Point Beach and Park
20 Miami Beach

21 Craighill Channel Range Lighthouse-Rear
22 Craighill Channel Range Lighthouse-Front
23 Pooles Island Lighthouse
24 Craighill Channel Upper Range Lighthouse-Front
25 Craighill Channel Upper Range Lighthouse-Rear
26 Gunpowder South Trail
27 Northern Central Rail Trail (NCR Trail)
28 Stoney Forest Demonstration Area
29 Maryland Information Center
30 Bush Declaration Natural Resources Management Area

Southern Stingray

Anyone who wants to see a southern stingray (*Dasyatis americana*) anywhere near Baltimore will have to go to the National Aquarium because this square-shaped ray cannot tolerate the brackish water in the upper Chesapeake. The southern stingray is fairly common, however, near the mouth of the bay. Rays move by undulating their giant winglike fins, a kind of underwater slow-motion flight. They are armed with a poisonous spine near the end of their whiplike tails.

rock 'n' roll memorabilia, live entertainment, dining, and dancing.

A breathtaking view of the harbor is part of the glamorous atmosphere of the **Pisces Restaurant** (410-685-2835) on the top floor of the **Hyatt Regency Baltimore** (800-233-1234). This seafood restaurant is one of many places that offer live music on some nights. The 14-story hotel, which has an atrium and 486 rooms, is located at 300 Light Street.

Live entertainment is also a weekend attraction at **Planet Hollywood** (410-685-STAR) at 201 East Pratt Street, a restaurant with a movie theme.

BALTIMORE GUIDE SERVICES AND TOURIST INFORMATION

[Fig. 14(1)] **BALTIMORE AREA VISITORS CENTER,** 301 East Pratt Street, Baltimore, MD 21202. Phone (410) 837-4636 or (800) 282-6632.

BALTIMORE AREA CONVENTION AND VISITORS ASSOCIATION, 100 Light Street, Baltimore, MD 21202. Phone (800) 343-3468 or (410) 659-7300.

WATER TAXI, HARBOR BOATING, INC. Hire a taxi for a relaxed visit by water to attractions of your choosing such as the National Aquarium, Harborplace, Maryland Science Center, and Fells Point. Operates Monday through Saturday. Phone (410) 563-3901 or (800) 658-8947.

HARBOR SHUTTLE. This is the lowest-cost water transportation system of the inner harbor, with free van service to Fort McHenry. Phone (410) 675-2900.

MARYLAND TOURS, INC. Narrated tours Apr. through Oct. Shuttle service May through Sept. Phone (410) 685-4288.

FORT McHENRY

[Fig. 14(2)] Although the Chesapeake Bay is valued for its shipping channels in times of peace, it also has permitted warships to penetrate America's coastline all the way to Baltimore. This threat by sea spurred the construction in 1803 of Fort McHenry on the tip of the peninsula defending Baltimore's outer harbor.

The flag flying over the fort during the War of 1812 during a British bombardment was the inspiration for the words to *The Star Spangled Banner* penned by Francis Scott Key. The words were later set to music and chosen as the national anthem. A visit to the star-shaped fort (accessible by water taxi and car) will bring to life the fascinating details of the 25 hours Key spent detained aboard a British ship while some 1,500 to 1,800 bombs, rockets, and shells were fired. Key, a Maryland attorney, had boarded the vessel to obtain the release of a friend when the battle began.

Dates: Open 9 to 8 daily, late June through Labor Day, and 9 to 5 daily for the remainder of the year.

Fees: There is a charge for admission.

For more information: Phone (410) 962-4290.

THE NATIONAL AQUARIUM

[Fig. 14(3)] Even for those whose time is limited, the National Aquarium in Baltimore is a must-see. State-of-the-art habitats help visitors feel they're on the coast of Iceland or inside a misty rain forest with golden tamarins, multicolored parrots, and two-toed sloths that seem to move in slow motion. Extraordinary fish in every imaginable color poke about a realistic Atlantic coral reef in a tank that rises several stories high. Stingrays appear to move to music in the 265,000-gallon pool they share with several species of sharks and a hawksbill sea turtle.

At the Marine Mammal Pavilion, Atlantic bottlenose dolphins put on daily shows. A mountains-to-the-sea exhibit, an outdoor seal pool, and an Icelandic exhibit are other highlights.

Directions: From I-95 in south Baltimore (just south of Fort McHenry Tunnel), take Exit 53/I-395 to Pratt Street. Turn right on Pratt Street. The aquarium is on the right.

Facilities: Exhibits, gift shop, cafe, restrooms, handicap access.

Dates: Open 9 to 8 daily July and Aug. Open 10 to 5 Saturday through Thursday and 10 to 8 Friday, Nov. through Feb. Open 9 to 5 Saturday through Thursday and 9 to 8 Friday, Mar. through June, Sept. and Oct.

Fees: There is a charge for admission.

For more information: National Aquarium, Pier 3/501 East Pratt Street, Baltimore, MD 21202. Phone (410) 576-3800. Ticketmaster: In Baltimore, (410) 481-SEAT; in District of Columbia, (202) 432-SEAT; in Northern Virginia, (703) 573-SEAT; out of state, (800) 551-SEAT.

SOUTHERN
STINGRAY
(Dasyatis
americana)

MARYLAND SCIENCE CENTER AND DAVIS PLANETARIUM

[Fig. 14(4)] Enjoy the science center's three floors of exhibits and demonstrations, the Davis Planetarium, and the IMAX Theater. A refurbished antique telescope enables skywatchers to observe planets, comets, and solar and lunar eclipses. The computerized telescope will turn automatically to Mars, Jupiter, or the setting of your choosing. IMAX Theaters are known for their incredible three-dimensional movies on screens that are several stories high.

Directions: Located at 601 Light Street (on the Inner Harbor).

For more information: Maryland Science Center and Davis Planetarium, phone (410) 685-5225.

U. S. FRIGATE *CONSTELLATION*

[Fig. 14(5)] After nearly three years of restoration work at the Fort McHenry shipyard, this first ship commissioned by the U. S. Navy has returned to its dock at Pier I and Pratt Street on the Inner Harbor, where visitors may stroll the decks, check out the battle stations, and discover how crewmen lived at the beginning of the Civil War. The *Constellation*, called the best-known artifact in Baltimore, was first launched in 1797 from Baltimore's Fells Point and served in the War of 1812.

For more information: U. S. Frigate *Constellation*, phone (410) 539-1797.

BALTIMORE PARKS AND ZOO

For those who like to search out green oases in a busy city, Baltimore has several that surely qualify.

DRUID HILL PARK. [Fig. 14(6)] Located at 2600 Madison Avenue, just north of US 1 (North Avenue), is scenic Druid Hill Park. With 744 acres, Druid Hills is the second largest urban park in America. This historical site, which dates back to 1688, has pavilions, picnic facilities, a playground, ball fields, tennis courts, hiking trails, and woodlands. The Baltimore Zoo is also located here.

For more information: Druid Hill Park, 2600 Madison Avenue, Baltimore, MD 21217. Phone (410) 396-6106.

BALTIMORE ZOO. [Fig. 14(7)] On the grounds of Druid Hill Park on Druid Avenue is Baltimore's 168-acre home to 1,500 birds, mammals, and reptiles. Extraordinary natural-looking habitats include the African watering hole, the river otter pond, and the African plains exhibit. Black-footed penguins, the 3-acre elephant exhibit, and hippopotamuses are also popular. The children's zoo, with farm animals, a swinging bridge, and a carousel, was voted the nation's finest. The Maryland Wilderness Exhibit highlights the state's native animals.

Dates: Open 10 to 4:20 daily, year-round, with hours extended in summer. Closed on major holidays.

Fees: There is a charge for admission.

For more information: Baltimore Zoo, phone (410) 366-LION.

CYLBURN ARBORETUM. [Fig. 14(8)] North of Druid Hill Park on Greenspring Avenue is Cylburn Arboretum, where well-tended grounds provide a lovely backdrop to the oaks, magnolias, Japanese maples, and viburnums at this center for environmental education and horticulture. Nature trails and gardens add interest to the Cylburn Mansion, which now serves as home to a Nature Museum and the Maryland Ornithological Society Museum.

Dates: The museum and gift shop are open 10 to 3 Tuesdays and Thursdays, year-round. **Fees:** None.

For more information: Cylburn Arboretum, phone (410) 396-0180.

SHERWOOD GARDENS. [Fig. 14(9)] In late April, the 7 well-groomed acres of Sherwood Gardens feature the spectacular bloom of thousands of tulips. Azaleas and other spring-bloomers continue well into May.

Directions: The gardens are located in northern Baltimore at Stratford Road and Greenway, off Saint Paul Street.

Dates: Open dawn to dusk.

Fees: None.

For more information: Sherwood Gardens, phone (410) 323-7982.

LAKE ROLAND. Located just north of the Baltimore city limits off MD 25, Lake Roland has 98 acres of bass and bluegill fishing waters.

For more information: Lake Roland, phone (410) 974-3211.

▓ RESTAURANTS IN BALTIMORE

The proximity of the Chesapeake Bay is evident in the many seafood appetizers and entrees on the menus of Baltimore's restaurants.

PHILLIPS AT LIGHT STREET PAVILION. Inner Harbor, Baltimore. Children's menu, authentic Maryland seafood, award-winning crab cakes, waterfront dining, seafood buffet. *Inexpensive to moderate. Phone (410) 685-6600.*

O'BRYCKIS CRAB HOUSE. 1727 East Pratt Street. Well-known crab house for half a century. *Moderate to expensive. Phone (410) 732-6399.*

KISLING'S TAVERN. 2100 Fleet Street, Fells Point/Canton. Great crab cakes. Water taxi access. *Inexpensive to moderate. Phone (410) 327-KISS.*

MCCORMICK AND SCHMICK'S SEAFOOD RESTAURANT. 711 Eastern Avenue. Sample the fresh seafood at this lively bistro on the Inner Harbor at Pier 5. Spectacular view of the waterfront. Full service bar. *Inexpensive to moderate. Phone (410) 234-1300.*

RUSTY SCUPPER. 402 Key Highway. "The best crabs in Baltimore" is the claim of this Inner Harbor restaurant, which is accessible by water taxi. Fresh seafood and sizzling steaks are accompanied by a magnificent view of the harbor. Dine indoors or out. *Inexpensive to moderate. Phone (410) 727-3678.*

BOHAGER'S BAR AND GRILL. 515 South Eden Street. Called "Baltimore's Best Tropical Crab Deck" by the *Baltimore Sun.* Entertainment nightly. Located in Fell's Point section of Baltimore, about 3 blocks from Inner Harbor. *Inexpensive to moderate. Phone (410) 563-7220.*

▨ LODGING IN BALTIMORE

Finding lodging is no problem in Baltimore. Expect to pay considerably more for lodging in the popular downtown/Inner Harbor area. Less expensive hotels and motels are on the outskirts of town or in Baltimore County, often with connections to the downtown by **Light Rail** (410-539-5000). Here are some of the most popular places to stay.

DAYS INN INNER HARBOR. 100 Hopkins Place, Baltimore. Economical motel within three blocks of the Inner Harbor and attractions. Restaurant, bar, pool. *Moderate. Phone (410) 576-1000.*

DELUXE PLAZA MOTEL. 6401 Pulaski Highway, Baltimore. Within 5 miles of downtown and Inner Harbor. *Inexpensive to moderate. Phone (410) 485-3600.*

OMNI INN HARBOR HOTEL. 101 West Fayette Street, Baltimore. Twin towers with 707 rooms, excellent restaurants, pool, fitness center. Pets allowed. *Moderate to expensive. Phone (410) 752-1100.*

INN AT HENDERSON'S WHARF. 1000 Fell Street. View the waterfront and stroll the courtyard garden at this historic landmark inn. Built in the 1800s, the structure once served as a tobacco warehouse for the railroad. Water taxi to Inner Harbor available. *Expensive. Phone (410) 522-7777 or (800) 522-2088.*

INNER HARBOR MARRIOTT. Pratt and Eutaw Streets. Views of nearby Inner Harbor and Camden Yards are available from some rooms in this elegant 10-story hotel. Features include restaurant and bar, indoor pool, sauna and exercise room. *Expensive. Phone (410) 962-0202 or (800) 228-9290.*

MR. MOLE B&B. 1601 Bolton Street. A four-star B&B with suites on historic Bolton Hill near symphony, Antique Row, museums, and Inner Harbor. *Expensive. Phone (410) 728-1179.*

Baltimore County

World-famous horse farms and historic towns tucked into the rolling hills of rural Maryland offer serenity just minutes from the busy downtown of Baltimore. Baltimore County has several public beaches, six public golf courses, and 10,000 acres of county parkland. Several magnificent state parks afford access to the county rivers and to some of the county's 173 miles of Chesapeake Bay frontage. The county has the third largest area of thoroughbred race horse farms in the country. For those who enjoy shopping, the largest mall in the state—Towson Town Center—is here. Light rail and subway offer easy transport into Baltimore County from many locations.

Many opportunities for nightlife are spread about Baltimore County. **Padonia Station** (410-252-8181) is a restaurant and bar with a great game room, including video games, virtual reality games, and batting cages. It is located at Padonia, which is on MD 45 north of Timonium and Baltimore.

Nashville's (410-321-6595) is a country music dance club at the Holiday Inn Select at Timonium. The **Towson Dinner Theater** (410-321-6595) provides entertainment while you dine. Towson is along MD 45 just north of Baltimore.

For more information: Baltimore County Conference and Visitors Bureau, 435 York Road-Towson Commons, Towson, MD 21204. Phone (800) 570-2836 or (410) 583-7313. Web site www.visitbacomd.com.

Baltimore County Promotion and Tourism, 400 Washington Avenue, Towson, MD 21204. Phone (410) 887-8040.

PATAPSCO VALLEY STATE PARK

[Fig. 14(10)] Patapsco Valley State Park protects floodplain and provides public access to green areas along the Patapsco River. The park's 14,000 acres embrace the river for 32 miles, crossing parts of Carroll, Howard, Baltimore, and Anne Arundel counties. From Liberty Dam on the North Branch and Skyesville on the South Branch, the park extends downriver southeastward to Baltimore Harbor's Middle Branch. The Patapsco River winds through a steep and narrow canyon in the park, where ancient rock outcroppings have been exposed by the action of rushing water over the millennia. The fresh water of the Piedmont then crosses the fall line and ceases to flow as it becomes influenced by the tides of the coastal plain. This far north in the Chesapeake Bay, the water is only slightly salty.

The park—Maryland's first—was established in 1907. Its forests contain old second-generation stands of oaks, tulip poplar, and beech with an understory of maple and dogwood. Giant sycamores lean out over the river, reflecting their splotchy brown-and-white bark in the dark water. Anadromous fish such as yellow perch and shad leave the brackish water of the bay and climb fish ladders at four dams to spawn here in the fresh water of the Patapsco. Great blue herons prowl the shallows for the spawn, while soaring osprey look for larger prey. Much more common than these Chesapeake Bay fish that must survive the polluted water in Baltimore Harbor and negotiate fish ladders are the freshwater fish such as trout, bass, and perch that draw anglers to the river. Upriver, water quality of the Patapsco is relatively good, but in sluggish areas it decreases, especially in the lower river below Elkridge and into Baltimore Harbor.

White-tailed deer, raccoons, red foxes, rabbits, and gray squirrels inhabit the woodlands of Patapsco Valley State Park. The sudden slap of a tail on the water as a beaver sounds an alarm can catch a hiker off guard. Even if the beaver disappears beneath the water, the conical, chiseled stumps along the bank give away the rodent's presence. A flock of wild turkeys may not even fly when a canoeist glides silently into view, though a kingfisher may chatter irritably as it zips farther downriver to escape an approaching boat. Wood ducks, Canada geese, great blue herons, and other birds are common sights. Many species of warblers and neo-tropical migrating birds use the park on their long journeys. Campers, before they drift off to sleep inside their tents, may hear the low-throated hoot of a great horned owl or the high-pitched, descending call of a screech owl.

Great Horned Owl

The great horned owl (*Bubo virginianus*) has a reputation as a fierce hunter, sometimes attacking birds as large as great blue herons or osprey. The four to seven low hoots of this large owl will silence any smaller owls that may be calling. From a distance, the great horned owl may sound like a barking dog. One of the best ways to locate this common predator is to locate raucous crows and hurry to the scene. Crows consider it their business to harass and mob any great horned owl they find.

GREAT HORNED OWL
(*Bubo virginianus*)

In spring, large colonies of mayapple (*Podophyllum peltatum*) carpet the understory, their nodding white flowers hidden beneath the deeply lobed, umbrella-like leaves. Patches of bright yellow trout lily (*Erythronium americanum*) catch the eye. The mottled purplish leaves, said to resemble the markings of a brook trout, are unmistakable. The flower bulb, which resembles a canine tooth, is responsible for one of the flower's common names, dog's-tooth violet.

Recreation is available in five general regions of the park. The first region, beginning at the park's southern end, is located near Relay and Elkridge (southwest of Baltimore) and consists of three recreation areas: Avalon, Glen Artney, and Orange Grove. Next is the Hilton Area near Catonsville, then the Hollofield Area east of Ellicott City, then the Pickall Area (strictly for groups with reservations) near US 70 and Baltimore beltway Exit 17, and finally, the McKeldin Area 4 miles north of Exit 83 on I-70 and east of Sykesville. Camping is available at the Hilton and Hollofield areas. The park headquarters are at the Hollofield Area off the cloverleaf on the westbound side of US 40.

Directions: The park office is at the Hollofield Area adjacent to US 40 off the cloverleaf on the westbound side of US 40 (on the west side of the river and the railroad tracks and northeast side of Ellicott City). Avalon, Glen Artney, and Orange Grove areas: From US 1 at South Street near Relay and Elkridge, turn onto South Street at the plumbing shop and follow the road to the park. Hilton Area: From I-695 (Baltimore beltway), take Exit 13 west on MD 144 and turn left on South Rolling Road, go one block, continuing straight onto Hilton Avenue, and drive 1.5 miles to the park entrance, on the right.

Hollofield Area: From I-695, take Exit 15 onto US 40 west and drive about 2 miles to the park. McKeldin Area: From I-695, take Exit 16 west on I-70, take Exit 83 north on Marriottsville Road, and go about 4 miles to the park entrance, on the right. Call park for use of Pickall group area.

Activities: Picnicking, family camping (Hilton and Hollofield areas), camping for organized youth groups (Hilton and McKeldin), hiking, biking, horseback riding, fishing, flat-water canoeing, whitewater canoeing (seasonal), cross-country skiing, disc golf (McKeldin), and orienteering courses (beginning at Avalon, advanced at McKeldin).

Facilities: Picnic tables and shelters; trails for hiking, biking, horseback riding; 84 improved campsites (electric hookups, dump station, pet loop at Hollofield Area only). Playgrounds in all areas. History and Conservation Visitor Center at Avalon Area (call to be sure renovations are completed).

Dates: Day use for all except Pickall Area, 10 to sunset daily, year-round; Pickall large group area, May 1 through Sept. 30, weekends only (reservations required). Campgrounds: Hollofield, Apr. 1 through Oct. 30; Hilton, Memorial Day through Labor Day. Mini-cabins: Hilton, Apr. 1 through Oct. 31.

Fees: There is a charge for day use, camping, shelters, pavilions, mini-cabins, and interpretive programs.

Closest town: Baltimore is 15 to 30 miles east and northeast of the various areas of the park.

For more information: Patapsco Valley State Park, 8020 Baltimore National Pike, Ellicott City, MD 21043. Phones: Headquarters, (410) 461-5005; Avalon, Glen Artney, and Orange Grove, (410) 747-2133; Hilton, (410) 747-2133; Hollofield, (410) 465-3287; Pickall, (410) 465-3287; McKeldin, (410) 442-1454. To reserve camping and picnic shelters, phone (888) 432-CAMP.

NORTH POINT STATE PARK

[Fig. 14(11)] North Point State Park's 1,320 acres lie at the end of a peninsula that extends like a foot from downtown Baltimore into southeastern Baltimore County. Park property meets the Chesapeake Bay on the east side and Back River to the north. Fort Howard, which is Federal property and not part of the park, lies at the peninsula's southern tip.

More than half the park is the Black Marsh Wildlands, a state designation that guarantees protection of 667 acres of forest, fields, and marsh from development and intrusion in perpetuity. The 250-acre Black Marsh within the wild lands is the largest protected tidal marsh on the western shore of the Chesapeake Bay. It is also considered one of the finest examples of a tidal marsh still remaining on the upper bay. A pair of bald eagles nests here. To ensure the eagles remain undisturbed, no trails offer access to the nest site.

The land that now makes up North Point State Park has its share of human history. Much of it has been continuously farmed for nearly 350 years. In the War of 1812, gunshots rang across the fields and marshes during skirmishes between local colonists

Spotted Salamander

This fossorial salamander, though common, is not well known because it hides or burrows in soft mud. However, it leaves the safety of its burrow to lay eggs at night following the first warm rains of spring. The spotted salamander (*Ambystoma maculatum*) has yellow spots in two rows down its charcoal-colored back.

and British troops invading Baltimore from the southeast. The route to Baltimore, which passed through what is now park property, came to be called the Defenders Trail.

In the early 1900s, Friday and Saturday nights meant dancing, bowling, or dining at Bay Shore Park, a grand amusement park constructed in 1906 where North Point State Park is now. Summer days brought people from Baltimore to walk the garden pathways of the park, fish from the pier, admire the Edwardian architecture, play games on the midway, swing a partner in the dance hall, try out the newest carnival ride, and listen to the music at the bandstand.

Until 1947 when the park was closed, trolleys rumbled between it and Baltimore. Today, remains of Bay Shore Park are still visible. The restored trolley barn has been converted to an open air pavilion available for rent. After a 50-year hiatus, the fountain has also been restored and is once again spraying water. A small visitor center located near the shore of the bay has exhibits on local history and displays on the park's flora and fauna.

The park's master plan includes new parking lots, picnic areas, permanent restrooms, and a new visitor center. In planning a trip to North Point, travelers should take into consideration that ubiquitous biting flies make the marsh an unpleasant place when they hatch in early summer.

Directions: From I-695 south, take Exit 42 (Edgemere/Fort Howard). Get in the left lane and turn left at the first traffic light onto MD 20 south (North Point Road). Or from I-695 north, take Exit 43 and follow signs to MD 20 south. After getting on MD 20 south, travel approximately 2 miles to the park entrance on the left (0.5 mile past Miller Island Road).

Activities: Wading in Chesapeake Bay, crabbing, bay sport-fishing, hiking, biking, bird-watching, picnicking, canoeing, waterfowl hunting by permit during season.

Facilities: Beachfront, hiking and biking trails, picnic tables, rental Trolley Station for group picnics, visitor center, portable toilets.

Dates: Open 6 to 6 daily, May1 through Oct. 31, and 8 to 4 daily, Nov. 1 through Apr. 30.

Fees: There is a day use fee from May 1 through Oct. 31.

Closest town: The community of Edgemere is 2 miles away and the city of Baltimore is 6 miles northwest of the park.

For more information: North Point State Park, PO Box 176, Fort Howard, MD 21052. Phone (410) 477-0757. Or contact Gunpowder Falls State Park (North Point is operated as an area of Gunpowder Falls), 2813 Jerusalem Road, PO Box 480, Kingsville, MD 21087. Phone (410) 592-2897.

WILDLANDS TRAIL

This 2-mile trail, offering one of the best ways to observe the flora and fauna of Black Marsh, passes through hardwood forest, tidal wetland, and open meadow. Notice how time and nature are reclaiming the meadows where farmers once plowed their fields. A multitude of small sweetgum (*Liquidambar sytraciflua*), greenbriar (*Smilax*), and multiflora rose (*Rosa multiflora*) are quick to claim space in disturbed soil. During spring months, look for spotted salamander egg masses in vernal ponds along the trail.

The trail climbs to an expansive view of the bay from a cliff, where lucky hikers are occasionally treated to a sight of one of the park's nesting bald eagles (*Haliaeetus leucocephalus*). The path also passes by an old booster station for the trolley that once ran here. A trail spur provides access to an observation platform over Black Marsh where great blue herons, ducks, and other wildfowl feed and find shelter.

The American bittern (*Botarus lentiginosus*) can freeze its brown-streaked body and upturned head and beak, nearly disappearing in plain view among the marsh grasses that camouflage it. In contrast, the common egret (*Casmerodius albus*), with its gracefully curved neck, long legs, and white plumage, stands out like a bridal gown on a rack of dark suits.

Directions: The first trailhead is just off the first parking lot as you enter the park on Bay Shore Road, on the left. The second trailhead is about 0.75 mile down the road from the first. A new road providing park access from North Point Boulevard is being developed. Access will change. Call the park for additional information.

Trail: A 2-mile, moderate, one-way path through park wild land. A loop is formed by connecting the two ends of the trail with the park road.

WETLANDS TRAIL

This nature trail skirts a man-made wetland mitigation area, a habitat created to compensate for the loss of wetlands elsewhere. Signs along the way interpret the flora and fauna. Among the birds that have taken a liking to this wetland and nearby Black Marsh are numerous ducks such as buffleheads, mallards, and blue and green winged teal. Visitors also can see mute swans, kestrels (sparrow hawks), northern harriers (marsh hawks), bitterns, barred owls, great horned owls, great blue herons, green-backed herons, and numerous songbirds.

Early in the morning, an observant hiker might spot the secretive, mostly nocturnal eastern mud turtle (*Kinosternon subrubrum*), with its yellowish brown shell, foraging for mollusks or vegetation just beneath the surface. These wetlands create the perfect habitat for this turtle, found abundantly here, that grows to only 4 or 5 inches long.

Directions: Trailhead is off the main road into the park (Bay Shore Road), about 1 mile past the entrance, on the right.

Trail: 0.75-mile, easy, interpretive loop around wetland.

HART-MILLER ISLAND STATE PARK

[Fig. 14(12)] A boater lifts his engine and drifts onto the sands of Hart Miller Island. The isolation and quiet are the first things he notices. Sandpipers diddle back and forth on the beach, foraging between lapping waves. It's a September weekday, and he seems to have the 1,000-plus acres of the island to himself.

In the morning mist he imagines buried treasure and yellowed maps that supposedly reveal the whereabouts of chests of gold. The gentle surf whispers rumors about old Joseph Hart who may have buried a fortune here, but took his secret to the grave.

Hart-Miller Island has its legends, its tales of wealth beneath the shifting sands. Rumors persist of buried treasure and valuable coins dating from the early 1800s. But today, this island neighbor to North Point State Park is valuable as a state park.

Hart-Miller Island used to be part of the mainland peninsula and the community of Miller's Island. In recent years, Hart Island and Miller Island became separated by water from each other and from the mainland to the southwest. The two islands were joined as one again in 1981 with the construction of a dike on their east side and a sandy beach on the west side. More land is surfacing as the impoundment between the dike and the island is continually filled with dredge material from Baltimore Harbor and surrounding tributaries.

Hart-Miller Island is a separate state park, though less than 1 mile of water separates it from North Point State Park. The watery separation however, is critical. Because visitation at Hart-Miller is limited to those with boats, the island has become a boater's haven.

Some people come to the island to sunbathe in relative seclusion and swim or look for shells on the 0.5 mile of sandy beach. Other popular activities are hiking, picnicking, fishing, and watching osprey dive for fish. Camping is allowed from May 1 through September 1 on this island and the smaller Pleasure Island between Hart-Miller and North Point state parks. Leashed pets are permitted only on Pleasure Island.

Hiking opportunities are limited to two short trails. The Miller Island Trail is a 0.5

RED FOX
(Vulpes fulva)

mile out and back, and begins just south of the park building complex behind the campsites. The path goes through woods to an observation platform. The even shorter Hawk Cove Beach trail is on the south end of the island.

Red foxes and raccoons prowl among the willow oak, sweetgum, and sassafras on Hart-Miller. Bird watchers make note of cormorants, ducks, gulls, terns, sandpipers, and even peregrine falcons that frequent the island.

Directions: From I-695 to the boat launch at Rocky Point Park in southeastern Baltimore County, take Exit 36 to MD 702 south and follow it about 3.5 miles to Back River Neck Road south. Continue south on Back River Neck Road for 2 miles. Turn left onto Barrison Point Road and follow signs to the ramps. Hart-Miller Island is 1 mile to the east across the water.

Red Fox

Visitors to Hart-Miller Island are more likely to find the tracks of the red fox (*Vulpes fulva*) than to see this canny subject of legend and folklore. The tracks are 2 to 2.5 inches long, round, and dainty—somewhat like those of a large cat except that the imprint of the toenails shows in the fox track, but does not ordinarily show in the track of the domestic cat. When the fox is trotting at its usual pace, the tracks are often in direct register—that is, with the back foot falling squarely in the track of the front foot. The fox's diet includes mice, rabbits, insects, berries, and other fruits. Unlike its smaller woodland cousin, the gray fox, the red fox does not climb trees.

Another launch area is at Bill's Rowboat and Outboard Motors on Miller's Island Road, which turns off North Point Road 0.5 mile north of the entrance to North Point State Park.

Activities: Swimming, beachcombing, hiking, picnicking, fishing, camping. Seasonal waterfowl hunting by permit. Day use and camping also permitted on nearby Pleasure Island.

Facilities: Swimming beach; 22 primitive campsites with table, lantern post, and grill (first come, first served); restrooms on west side of island.

Dates: Gates are open May 1 through Sept. 30, sunrise to sunset for day use, registered campers only after sunset. Waterfowl hunting by permit after Sept. 30. Boaters may anchor offshore and spend the night on their vessels.

Fees: None for day use. For camping there is a charge, which is collected after campers set up at night.

Closest town: Rocky Point Park boat ramp is 1 mile across the water to the west. Community of Edgemere is about 4 miles to the southwest.

For more information: North Point State Park, PO Box 176, Fort Howard, MD 21052. Phone (410) 477-0757. Or Gunpowder Falls State Park (Both North Point and Hart-Miller state parks are areas of Gunpowder Falls), 2813 Jerusalem Road, PO Box 480, Kingsville, MD 21087. Phone (410) 592-2897.

🏛 SOLDIERS DELIGHT NATURAL ENVIRONMENTAL AREA

[Fig. 14(13)] The desolate expanses of grasses and stunted blackjack oaks, post oaks, and Virginia pines at Soldiers Delight mark a rare microenvironment called a serpentine barren. Serpentine rock, named for its resemblance to snakeskin, is yellow, green, or brown in color, often mottled with red. Serpentine barrens are rare in the East and are thought to be pieces of the earth's mantle thrust up and over the crust when continents collided and built the Appalachian Mountains some 250 million years ago.

The massive exposed areas of this metamorphosed igneous bedrock at Soldiers Delight are composed of minerals that form nutrient-poor soil toxic to most plants. The soil is high in magnesium and iron, but low in calcium and phosphate. Many of the plants that eke out a scrabbly existence by adapting to the harsh conditions are rare or far more common in the arid West.

More than 39 rare, threatened, or endangered plant species, along with rare insects, rocks, and minerals can be found here. Among the rare wildflowers is the federally endangered fringed gentian (*Gentiana crinita*) and blazing-star (*Liatris*), with its fuzzy rose-purple flower heads blooming from midsummer to fall. The arid soil also supports prairie grasses such as Indian grass, purplish three-awn, and little bluestem.

Seven miles of hiking trails lead into the barrens and surrounding woodlands. The 3-mile Yellow Trail and the 2-mile Orange Trail (named for the color of their blazes) begin as one trail and lead across the bedrock toward the woods. After they separate, they loop back to the starting point. Hikers can easily tell where the serpentine bedrock ends by the surrounding border of lush woodlands. The stunted trees growing in the serpentine barren are about 65 years old—the same age as the more erect, healthy looking trees that surround the barren.

At the visitor center, helpful volunteers explain several opinions of how Soldiers Delight was named. The center has a nature shop, a collection of Native American artifacts, and a reference library on serpentine ecosystems and the natural history of the area.

Directions: From I-695 on the west side of Baltimore, take Exit 18. Go west on MD 26 (Liberty Road) for 5 miles. Turn right on Deer Park Road and drive 3.4 miles to a parking lot and overlook on the left. The environment area is on both sides of road. Or from I-795, exit on Franklin Boulevard west; go left on Berrymans Lane, then left on Deer Park Road.

Activities: Hiking, fishing, boating, cross-country skiing, swimming.

Facilities: Hiking trails, boat launch, boat rental, snack bar, picnic facilities, visitor center, playground, shelters.

Dates: Open dawn to dusk, year-round. Visitor center, open 9 to 4 daily, year-round, except major holidays.

Fees: None.

Closest town: Randallstown is about 3 miles southeast.

For more information: Soldiers Delight Natural Environmental Area, 5100 Deer Park Road, Owings Mills, MD 21117.

OREGON RIDGE PARK AND NATURE CENTER

[Fig. 14(14)] Located north of Baltimore in Cockeysville is 1,000-acre Oregon Ridge Park, with a nature center run by full-time naturalists and volunteers. Many species of birds, wildlife, and wildflowers are suited to the diverse habitats here, including woods, meadows, streams, swamps, and ponds. Investigate rocky outcrops and iron pits, explore the marble quarry, or join a naturalist on a moonlight hike, bird walk, bee-keeping demonstration, or for maple syrup making. Archeological digs in the park have turned up artifacts that are displayed at the nature center.

Around a cold, spring-fed lake is a beach area with both shallow and deep water for swimming.

Directions: From I-83 at Cockeysville, take Exit 20-B. Go west 1 mile on Shawn Road. Turn left on Beaver Dam Road, bear right at fork and follow signs.

Activities: Hiking, swimming, sand volleyball, horseshoes, summer concerts by the Baltimore Symphony Orchestra.

Facilities: Nature trails, nature center, beach, concession stand, bathhouse, pavilion, sand volleyball court, horseshoe pits, playground, restrooms.

Dates: Open 9 to 5, Tuesday through Sunday.

Fees: None.

Closest town: Cockeysville is 2 miles east.

For more information: Oregon Ridge Nature Center, 13555 Beaver Dam Road, Cockeysville, MD 21030. Phone (410) 887-1818 or (410) 887-3818.

Fringed Gentian

Fringed gentians (*Gentiana crinita*) are late-bloomers, providing their bluish purple blossoms from August to November. The fringes serve as a deterrent to crawling insects, but flying insects that are necessary for pollination are able to push past the fringe.

LOCH RAVEN FISHING CENTER

[Fig. 14(15)] This is a user-financed county facility located on the Loch Raven Reservoir 0.5 mile east of Timonium, a half-mile east of the #2 bridge on Dulaney Valley Road. Fish for largemouth and smallmouth bass, chain pickerel, northern pike, crappie, channel catfish, and sunfish. There is a boat ramp (electric motors only), bait and tackle nearby, picnicking, and handicap access.

Facilities: Boat ramp, picnic facilities, handicap access.

Dates: Open at 6 a.m. daily, Apr. through Oct.

Fees: There is a charge for use.

Closest town: Timonium is across Loch Raven Reservoir to the west.

For more information: Loch Raven Fishing Center, phone (410) 887-7692 or Department of Recreation and Parks, phone (410) 887-3813.

LIGHTHOUSES OF BALTIMORE COUNTY

Several lighthouses have guided sailors approaching Baltimore's harbors and outer islands over the years. East of the city limits of Baltimore is Fort Carroll Lighthouse, a wooden frame tower on the Patapsco River just east of the Francis Scott Key Bridge and US 695. It is accessible only by boat but is privately owned and not open to the public.

Four more lighthouses surround the southeastern end of the Patapsco River Neck peninsula (south and east of Edgemere). The Craighill Channel Upper Range—Rear [Fig. 14(25)] is an iron pyramidal tower that is not open to the public. Permission must be obtained to view it from Sparrows Point. The Craighill Channel Upper Range—Front [Fig. 14(24)] is an octagonal brick tower off the southern tip of the peninsula at Fort Howard Park.

The Craighill Channel Range—Front [Fig. 14(22)] is a round lighthouse on a caisson foundation, located in the Chesapeake Bay 2 miles east of North Point State Park. A lower light works in conjunction with a range light while an upper light could be spotted by navigators coming from outside the range. The lighthouse is not open to the public.

The 105-foot pyramidal skeleton tower of Craighill Channel Range—Rear [Fig. 14(21)] is one of the highest towers in the Chesapeake Bay. This light is located off Swan Point at the northeastern corner of North Point State Park.

GUNPOWDER FALLS STATE PARK

[Fig. 14(16)] In 1959, Marylanders gained access to land along the Big Gunpowder Falls River and the Little Gunpowder Falls River when the state gave park designation to thousands of acres. The park designation was designed primarily to protect this important water source for the city of Baltimore.

The riverside greenways have a spin-off value that is priceless for those with wanderlust who yearn to follow the bends and twists of a river as it makes its way to the sea. Beginning at the Pennsylvania line and extending southeastward to the Chesapeake Bay, Gunpowder Falls State Park is a segmented linear park that covers 18,000 acres of two river valleys that join in Baltimore County northeast of Baltimore.

More than 100 miles of trails, including the 20-mile-long Northern Central Rail Trail (NCR Trail), meander through the river valleys, giving hikers, bikers, and horseback riders access to the premier trout streams, tidal marshes, and dense woodlands of the park. Available along the rivers as they flow toward a confluence with the Chesapeake Bay are tidewater and freshwater fishing opportunities, whitewater for canoeing and kayaking, wetlands for bird-watching and wildlife observation, swimming holes, pleasant inner tube floats, and places to launch a sailboat or motorboat. White-tailed deer, groundhogs, and beaver surprise hikers topping a hill. Ducks rise from the river with a clatter of wings as a canoeist rounds a bend. Wading birds and diving birds cause visitors to dig the binoculars from the back of the car.

The park has no single entrance since the land spreads out along the river and is accessible in many places from local roads. In addition to road access points, several distinct park areas offer facilities and sylvan surroundings along the Gunpowder Falls rivers for picnickers, swimmers, anglers, tubers, boaters, and canoeists.

The most-developed area is the Hammerman Area at the mouth of the river near the Chesapeake Bay with a popular life-guarded beach, wetlands, and waterfowl. To the north, along the Little Gunpowder Falls River on the Harford/Baltimore county line, is the Central Area with the park headquarters, a historic mill and village, and trails. The Central Area also includes a Wildlands Area along the Big Gunpowder Falls River in Baltimore County near Perry Hall. To the northeast on the Big Gunpowder Falls River is the remote Hereford Area defined by its Piedmont forests, rocky outcroppings, and the famous NCR Trail.

Camping in the park is available only for organized youth groups, by reservation. However, there is a commercial campground, **Morris Meadows Recreation Farm** (800-643-7056), at Freeland, near the northern end of the park.

Also considered part of Gunpowder Falls State Park are North Point State Park (*see* page 165) and Hart-Miller Island State Park (*see* page 168), located south of the other areas and southeast of Baltimore.

Stories passed down through the years offer several explanations for the rivers' names. Did the name come from a mill that operated before the Revolutionary War and made gunpowder from the coals of burnt willow branches? Or was it inspired from the gunpowder an early settler gave the Indians who planted it to see if it would grow? Still another tale involves Guy Fawkes, an Englishman who plotted to blow up Parliament. In November of 1605, relatives of the leaders of the "gunpowder plot" named the rivers to commemorate the plan, according to some accounts. Speculation is interesting, but no one knows for sure.

The "falls" part of the Gunpowder Falls name comes not from any waterfalls on the river, but because the river crosses the fall line. The fall line is a geological boundary separating the flowing water on the gentle slopes of the Piedmont and the flat water of the Coastal Plain, where the rise and fall of the tides influence water.

Directions: Access is available from many roads along the Big Gunpowder Falls and Little Gunpowder Falls rivers.

Activities: Freshwater fishing, tubing, boating, canoeing (including whitewater), sea kayaking, hiking, mountain biking (except in designated wild lands), horseback riding, jet skiing, wind-surfing, historical tours, deer and duck hunting by permit, camping for organized youth groups.

Facilities: Visitor center, historic train station, nature center, hiking/biking/horseback riding trails, nature trails, fishing streams and rivers including four designated trout streams, picnic areas, youth group campgrounds, marina with boat rental, playground, ball diamonds, food concession, changing rooms, archery ranges, mini-cabins.

Dates: Undeveloped areas of the park are open sunrise to sunset, year-round. For developed areas, see the sections that follow.

For more information: Gunpowder Falls State Park, 2813 Jerusalem Road, PO Box 480, Kingsville, MD 21087. Phone (410) 592-2897.

HAMMERMAN/DUNDEE CREEK AREA

[Fig. 14(17)] Where the slow-moving Gunpowder River becomes tidal and mixes its waters with the salty Chesapeake Bay east of Baltimore, the Hammerman/Dundee Creek Area offers weary city-dwellers an escape. This most developed part of Gunpowder Falls State Park encompasses about 640 acres on a peninsula in eastern Baltimore County. It is well known for its 1,500-foot swimming beach with beach house, concession area, picnic pavilions, ball fields, and playgrounds, as well as for nearby **Dundee Creek Marina** with its store and facilities for boaters. These areas easily receive the most visitors in the 18,000-acre linear park. Those who seek solitude and quiet should visit these areas during the off season or try a less-popular part of the Gunpowder Falls rivers.

Bird-watching is popular at the Hammerman Area throughout the seasons, including winter when the marshes fill with wintering waterfowl. Park rangers lead spring peeper walks and night hikes. Participants on guided canoe trips learn about egrets, osprey, and migrating and resident ducks. Northern harriers or marsh hawks (*Circus cyaneus*) and green-backed herons (*Butorides striatus*) are fairly common. Tundra swans (*Cygnus columbianus*), Canada geese (*Branta canadensis*), black ducks (*Anas rubripes*), and other waterfowl make their winter home on the lower Gunpowder. Small cabins called mini-cabins were added in 1998. Pets are not allowed in the Hammerman Area.

Directions: From I-95 east of Baltimore and just north of the I-695 beltway, take Exit 67A and go east on MD 43 (White Marsh Boulevard) about 1 mile to MD 40 east. Go about 0.5 mile on MD 40 east. Turn right at the first light onto Ebenezer Road and go 4.5 miles to the Hammerman entrance on the left. Dundee Creek Marina is just past the Hammerman entrance, on the right.

Activities: Fishing, swimming, hiking, archery, boating, sailing, sea kayaking, wind surfing, picnicking.

Facilities: Picnic tables and grills, pavilions (phone 888-432-CAMP for reservations), beach with paved ramp, restrooms, recycled tire playground (new in 1997), ball diamonds, food concession, changing rooms, hiking trails, archery range (located near Dundee Creek Marina and available when not in use by the group that maintains it), new mini-cabins (call for reservations). Most areas are wheelchair accessible. Dundee Creek Marina has small motorboat rentals, slip rentals, dry storage, a store, and restrooms. Hammerman has rental catamarans, jet skis, and sea kayaks.

Dates: Open 8 a.m. to sunset, year-round. The marina launch area is open 5 a.m. to 10 p.m. daily, Mar. 1 through the end of rockfish season. The marina store is open 5:30 a.m. to 2 p.m., Apr. 1 through May 1, and 5:30 a.m. to 7 p.m., May 1 through the end of summer. Call (410) 335-9390 for fall hours.

Fees: There is a small service charge (half price on Wednesday). There is a service charge for use of the pavilion, mini-cabins, boat launch, and boats.

Closest town: Baltimore is about 11 miles southwest.

For more information: Gunpowder Falls State Park, 2813 Jerusalem Road, PO Box 480, Kingsville, MD 21087. Phone (410) 592-2897.

CENTRAL AREA

The Central Area of Gunpowder Falls State Park is located along both the Little Gunpowder Falls River and the Big Gunpowder Falls River northeast of Perry Hall. On the Little Gunpowder where the river divides Harford and Baltimore counties west of Fallston are the Pleasantville, Sweet Air, and Days Cove areas in addition to the park headquarters and **Jerusalem Mill Visitor Center**. A variety of well-marked, blazed trails on these park lands connect the Little Gunpowder to the open fields, forests, and ponds that characterize the Central Area. The park headquarters, housed at Jerusalem Mill, take visitors into an eighteenth-century village that includes a covered bridge, blacksmith shop, gunsmith shop, gristmill, general store, and tenant houses.

Directions: For Jerusalem Mill Visitor Center (park headquarters), from I-95, take exit 74 to MD 152 west (Mountain Road) toward Fallston. Go 2 miles and turn left onto Jerusalem Road. Go 1.1 mile to Jerusalem Mill, on the left. Parking is on the right, just before the mill.

For Pleasantville, take Exit 74 from I-95 and go west on MD 152 toward Fallston for 11 miles. Go left on MD 165 (Baldwin Mill Road). Continue straight on MD 165 until it crosses the Little Gunpowder Falls. Roadside parking pull-outs provide trailhead access.

For Sweet Air, take Exit 74 from I-95 and go west on MD 152 toward Fallston for 11 miles. Go left on MD 165 (Baldwin Mill Road). After less than 0.5 mile, go right on Green Road. Go just over 1 mile and turn right on Moores Road. Go about 0.3 mile and go left onto Dalton-Bevard Road to a parking lot at the road's end. Contact the headquarters about Days Cove, which is open by reservation for pre-scheduled programs.

Activities: Fishing, swimming, hiking, horseback riding, canoeing, tubing, nature trails, hunting by permit, and camping for organized youth groups.

Facilities: Hiking/biking/ horseback riding trails, nature trails, waterfowl blinds (permit required), youth group camping area, visitor center.

Dates: The park is open sunrise to sunset, year-round. The park headquarters are open 8-4:30, weekdays, year-round. The Jerusalem Mill Museum is open 1 to 4 p.m. Saturday and Sunday year-round.

Fees: None (donations welcome).

Closest town: Jacksonville is just over two miles west of the area on MD 145. Kingsville is 2 miles southwest of the park headquarters at Jerusalem Road and US 1.

For more information: Gunpowder Falls State Park, 2813 Jerusalem Road, PO Box 480, Kingsville, MD 21087. Phone (410) 592-2897.

LITTLE GUNPOWDER TRAIL AND HORSE TRAIL LOOP. [Fig. 14(18)] From the trailhead at Jerusalem Mill, follow the white-blazed Little Gunpowder Trail downriver through hills and valleys along the west bank of the Little Gunpowder Falls River. The path loops around the historic village, meeting the yellow-blazed horse trail at the Jericho covered bridge. Return via the horse trail through farmland and a pine plantation (1-mile round trip). Those who wish a longer hike can follow the Little Gunpowder Trail downstream, returning by the same path.

Trail: White-blazed moderate 1-mile loop hike along Little Gunpowder Falls River formed by combining the Little Gunpowder Trail and horse trail.

WILDLANDS AREA. The Wildlands section of the Central Area of Gunpowder Falls State Park is a 2-by-1.5-mile area located along the lower Big Gunpowder Falls River, down river from Loch Raven Reservoir. In addition to the white-blazed **Big Gunpowder Trail** which runs through the wild lands along the south side of the river, there are several interconnecting trails that traverse the Wildlands Area on the north side of the river, forming loop hikes of varying lengths. Bicycles are not allowed. The trailhead begins at the parking lot where Bel Air Road (US 1) crosses the river northeast of Baltimore and Perry Hall.

Once hikers enter the woods, leaving the highway behind, the peace of the riverbank settles in. A stealthy approach may reveal a solitary great blue heron, poised motionless above a fish. A muskrat may slip into the water off the bank, making a V as it swims across the river. Wild creatures such as these seem far removed from the busy streets of Baltimore just a few miles away.

The outermost parts of three trails combine to form an easy 4.6-mile loop, beginning at the parking lot. For this loop, take the blue-blazed **Stocksdale Trail** upriver from the parking lot. Make an immediate right turn onto the pink-blazed **Wildlands Trail**, which rejoins the Stocksdale Trail after about 1.2 miles. Go right again on the Stocksdale Trail and continue for 0.8 mile. Turn right on the yellow-blazed **Sweathouse Trail**. This 1.7-mile trail is named for the Big Gunpowder Falls tributary it crosses called Sweathouse Branch, once the site of Indian sweat lodges.

Although no evidence indicates there were any permanent Indian camps in Baltimore County, Susquehannock Indians may have traveled from the Susquehanna River south through the county to Algonquin camps. The construction of sweat lodges indicates the Indians were apparently just as captivated by the verdant banks of the boulder-tossed stream valleys as hikers are today. The Sweathouse Trail also circles back to the Stocksdale Trail. A right turn and a 0.8-mile trek take you back to the trailhead at the parking lot.

For a shorter loop, take the blue-blazed Stocksdale Trail upriver from the parking lot and take an immediate right onto the pink-blazed Wildlands Trail. Turn left onto the Stocksdale Trail and go back to the start. The total hike is about 2.3 miles.

Directions: From the I-695 beltway on the northeast side of Baltimore, go north on US 1 about 5.5 miles. Trailhead parking is on the right, immediately after crossing the Big Gunpowder Falls River.

HEREFORD AREA

On the upper Big Gunpowder Falls River is the 3,800-acre Hereford area of the park, where I-83 intersects the Big Gunpowder Falls River after it leaves Prettyboy Reservoir about 14 miles north of Baltimore in Baltimore County. Cool swimming holes and great tubing and canoeing waters offer a refuge from summer heat. Some of the state's best trout fishing challenge the fly fisherman here. Twenty miles of paths open the woodlands to explorers on foot or horseback. Bicycles are prohibited. Especially recommended for scenic beauty are **Raven Rock Falls, Panther Branch**, and the area between Falls Road and Prettyboy Reservoir. Maryland has two designated wild lands in this area—one near Prettyboy Dam and one at Panther Branch. The historic 19-mile **Northern Central Railroad Trail** passes through the area. An archery range is available for the public except when tournaments are scheduled. A small picnic area is at **Camp Wood** on Bunker Hill Road. Seasonal bow hunting for deer is available by permit.

Directions: Trailheads are located where the Big Gunpowder Falls River crosses Falls Road, Masemore Road, Bunker Hill Road, York Road, and Big Falls Road. A popular spot for fly fishermen is at Camp Wood on Bunker Hill Road off MD 45 north of Hereford.

Activities: Fishing, swimming, hiking, horseback riding, canoeing/tubing, archery, picnicking, nature trails, cross country skiing, camping for organized youth groups, bow hunting for deer (permit required). Contact the park for alternative trail for bicyclists.

Facilities: Horse and hiking trails, trout streams, archery course, picnic tables, nature trails, youth camping area.

Dates: Park trails are open sunrise to sunset.

Fees: None.

Closest town: Hereford is just south of the Hereford Area at the junction of MD 45 and MD 138.

For more information: Gunpowder Falls State Park, 2813 Jerusalem Road, PO Box 480, Kingsville, MD 21087. Phone (410) 592-2897.

GUNPOWDER SOUTH TRAIL. [Fig. 14(26)] This white-blazed trail provides access to trout waters and some of the most scenic areas of the park, passing through lush evergreen groves of hemlock and mountain laurel in the **Hereford Wildlands**. Hikers can make a loop by taking the more southerly Highland Trail on the return trip. Bicycles are prohibited. Rangers recommend the 2.4-mile stretch of the Gunpowder South Trail from Masemore Road westward toward **Prettyboy Dam**. About 0.25 mile past Falls Road, the trail leaves state park property and enters City of Baltimore property just below Prettyboy Dam. The trail on city property up to the dam is rugged and not well marked, but it is very scenic.

The trail also extends eastward from Masemore Road about 3.5 miles to Big Falls Road. The Gunpowder North Trail is on the other side of the river.

Directions: From I-83 at Hereford, take Exit 27 and go west on Mount Carmel Road about 0.5 mile. Turn right on Masemore Road and go just over 1 mile to the parking area on the right, before crossing Big Gunpowder Falls River.

Trail: Recommended scenic stretch is a 2.4-mile one-way moderate hike westward through lush heath forest.

NORTHERN CENTRAL RAIL TRAIL (NCR TRAIL)

[Fig. 14(27)] This 19.7-mile, 10-foot-wide trail follows the old railroad bed of the Northern Central Railroad. From 1838 to 1972, from the headwaters of the Chesapeake Bay to the Pennsylvania line, small towns such as Ashland, Phoenix, Sparks, Glencoe, Monkton, White Hall and Freeland sprang up beside the busy steel rails that connected Baltimore with York,

Pennsylvania. Products such as flour, paper, coal, milk, grains, and the US Mail rumbled to and from these towns.

Union soldiers traveled the Northern Central during the Civil War and President Abraham Lincoln rode it to deliver the Gettysburg address. Use of this railroad and other rail lines across the country dwindled after automobiles and trucks began to carry people and goods on ever-improving highways. In 1972, when the flooding rains of Hurricane Agnes washed out bridges and rails, the line was not needed enough to warrant repairs. The Maryland Department of Natural Resources converted the abandoned railroad into a multiuse trail in 1972.

The NCR Trail begins in Ashland, passes several historic towns, the **Monkton Train Station**, **and Sparks Bank Nature Center** on its meandering way north, and ends at the Pennsylvania line where it joins the York County Heritage Trail. Heading upriver, the trail follows the Big Gunpowder River to just north of MD 138 east of Hereford, at the mouth of the Little Falls River (not to be confused with Little Gunpowder Falls). Then the trail follows the Little Falls and finally Beetree Run to the Pennsylvania line.

The surface of crushed stone is wheelchair accessible. Hiking, jogging, biking, and horseback riding are permitted. Pets must be leashed. Plan to carry out your trash, as there are no containers. The trail also provides access to the Loch Raven watershed and more than 8 miles of managed trout stream on the Big Gunpowder River and the Little Falls River.

Hikers make frequent discoveries of wildlife and wildflowers along the way. On the banks and woodlands beside the boulder-strewn Big Gunpowder, look for the purple petals and grasslike leaves of slender blue flag (*Iris prismatica*), and the nodding, three-petaled nodding trillium (*Trillium cernuum*).

Monkton Station, located along the NCR Trail, was a Pennsylvania Railroad Company stop from 1898 to 1972. Listed on the National Register of Historic Places, the old station features artifacts from the days when commuters to and from Baltimore would stop here. Now the renovated structure serves as a quieter stop for bicyclists and hikers along the Northern Central Railroad Trail.

NORTHERN
HARRIER
(*Circus cyaneus*)

Directions: From I-83 at Ashland in Baltimore County, take Exit 20 and go east about 0.5 mile to York Road. Turn right (south) on York Road and go about 0.25 mile. Turn left on Ashland Road and go 0.5 mile to the dead end at the parking lot and trailhead. During the busy seasons when the parking lot may be full, hikers can go to a more northern access point and hike south. For the Freeland trailhead at the northern end of the trail, from MD 45 (York Road), just south of the Maryland/Pennsylvania line, go west on Freeland Road, and go 2 miles to the parking lot and trailhead.

Northern Harrier

This large hawk with a 42-inch wingspan is a fairly common sight soaring above meadows and marshes. The male is pale gray above and white below, while the female is brown above and streaked with brown on her undersides. The distinctive white rump and banded tail make identification easier. The northern harrier, or marsh hawk, (*Circus cyaneus*) feeds chiefly on rodents and builds a nest close to or on the ground.

For Sparks Bank Nature Center, from I-83 North, take Exit 24 and turn right on Belfast Road. Turn right on MD 45 (York Road). Take the second left onto Sparks Road, cross the NCR Trail, and the nature center will be on the right. For Monkton Station, from I-83 North, take Exit 27 and turn right on Mt. Carmel Road. Go right on York Road, then take an immediate left on Monkton Road. After crossing the NCR Trail, Monkton Station is on the left.

Restrooms are at Paper Mill, Phoenix, Glencoe, Monkton, White Hall, Bentley Springs, and Freeland. Water is available at Sparks, Monkton, White Hall, and Freeland.

Activities: Hiking, jogging, biking, horseback riding, trout fishing. Camping is available for organized youth groups.

Facilities: Horse and hiking trails, 8 miles of trout streams, archery course, Monkton Train Station, park offices, history museum, gift shop, restrooms, Sparks Bank Nature Center, picnic tables, nature trails, youth camping area.

Dates: The trail is open sunrise to sunset year-round. The Monkton Train Station is open 9 to 5 on Saturday and Sunday, Apr. through May and Sept. through Oct., and 9 to 5 Wednesday through Sunday, June through Aug. Sparks Bank Nature Center is open 10 to12 Saturday and 1 to 3 Sunday, Apr. through Oct.

Fees: None.

Closest town: Sparks Bank Nature Center is at Sparks Station, about 4 miles north of Cockeysville. Monkton Station and park trails are near Hereford on I-83.

Trail: Easy 19.7-mile linear path following old railroad bed.

BEACHES IN BALTIMORE COUNTY

In addition to state park beaches and the beach at Oregon Ridge Park (*see* page 171), swimming is allowed from Memorial Day through Labor Day when lifeguards are on duty at the following two beaches located east of Baltimore. There is an admission charge.

ROCKY POINT BEACH AND PARK. [Fig. 14(19)] This is the largest waterfront park in the county, with over 700 feet of white sandy beach. It is the home of the Baltimore County Sailing Center. Sailing lessons are available.

Directions: From MD 150 at Essex (east side of Baltimore), go east on Back River Neck, left on Barrison Neck Road, and right on Rocky Point Road to the park.

Activities: Swimming, picnicking, fishing from shoreline or pier.

Facilities: Bathhouse, concession stand, volleyball court, horseshoe pits, playground, boat ramps (open year-round), pavilion for group rental.

For more information: Rocky Point Beach and Park, phone (410) 887-0217 or (410) 887-3818.

MIAMI BEACH. [Fig. 14(20)] Located on a peninsula just north of Rocky Point Park, the beach is on the Chesapeake Bay.

Directions: From MD 150 at Bowleys Quarters (east side of Baltimore), go southeast about 2 miles on Bowleys Quarters Road. Turn left into the park.

Activities: Swimming, picnicking, taking nature walk.

Facilities: Beach front, pavilion, bathhouse, concession stand, playground, self-guided nature tour on wooden boardwalk.

For more information: Miami Beach, phone (410) 887-5939 or (410) 887-3818.

RESTAURANTS IN BALTIMORE COUNTY

Dining opportunities in Baltimore County range from upscale fast food restaurants to famous fine eateries. There are several dinner theaters with excellent productions and gourmet menus. Here are a few of the many fine places to dine.

FISHERMAN'S INN. Fifth Street and Miller Island Road, Edgemere. Located across the water from Pleasure Island at North Point State Park. Outstanding crabcake sandwiches. Overlooks Chesapeake Bay. *Inexpensive to moderate. Phone (410) 477-2528.*

DRIFTWOOD INN. 203 Nanticoke Road, Middle River. Located on Hopkins Creek. Dock your boat at the restaurant while dining. Steak, fresh seafood. *Moderate. Phone (410) 391-3493.*

TIMONIUM DINNER THEATER, 9603 Deereco Road, Timonium. Dine and watch first-class productions. *Moderate. Phone (410) 560-1113.*

CAROLINA GARDENS. 1625 Holly Tree Road, Bowleys Quarters. Located east of Baltimore at mouth of Middle River. Eat fine seafood inside or on outside deck. Live entertainment on weekends. *Moderate. Phone (410) 335-7775.*

WILD DUCK CAFÉ. Frog Mortar Creek at Maryland Marina, Bowley's Quarters. Enjoy the waterfront view of Frog Mortar Creek off Middle River while sampling steamed crabs and other fresh seafood. Open seasonally. Casual atmosphere. Complimentary docking available. *Moderate. Phone (410) 335-2121.*

THE CRAB SHANTY. 3410 Plum Tree Drive, Ellicott City. Voted one of area's best seafood restaurants, The Crab Shanty is in Howard County, just west of the Baltimore County line. Seafood, chicken, pasta in casually elegant atmosphere. *Inexpensive. Phone (410) 465-9660.*

THE ELKRIDGE FURNACE INN. 5745 Furnace Avenue, Elkridge. Dine in elegance at this historic manor home in Howard County near the Baltimore County and Anne Arundel County lines. French cuisine. *Moderate to expensive. Phone (410) 379-9336.*

LODGING IN BALTIMORE COUNTY

Motels along the interstates in Baltimore County offer an economical alternative to the more expensive restaurants of downtown Baltimore. **Light Rail** (410-539-5000) connects the northern and southern outskirts of Baltimore to the downtown area. Most former bed and breakfast inns in the county have been reverted to private residences.

HAMPTON INN WHITE MARSH. 8225 Town Center Drive, Baltimore. This inn off I-95, Exit 67B, just northeast of the Baltimore city limits, has 127 rooms, a pool, and nearby restaurants. *Moderate. Phone (410) 931-2200.*

COMFORT INN NORTHWEST. 10 Wooded Way, Pikesville. Located off I-695, Exit 20. Restaurant and pool are featured in this newly-renovated inn. Pimlico Race Track is 5 miles. Pets allowed. *Moderate. Phone (410) 484-7700.*

BAUERNSCHMIDT MANOR BED AND BREAKFAST. 2316 Bauernschmidt Drive. Located on the Middle River east of Baltimore, this B&B features outstanding views of the Chesapeake Bay, a pool, and a gourmet breakfast. *Expensive. Phone (410) 687-2233.*

MARRIOTT'S HUNT VALLEY INN. 245 Shawan Road, Hunt Valley. Located off I-83 north of Baltimore at Hunt Valley; 390 rooms. Pets allowed. *Moderate to expensive. 410-785-7000.*

HOLIDAY INN SELECT. 2004 Greenspring Drive, Timonium. Easy Light Rail ride to Baltimore Inner Harbor, National Aquarium, and Oriole Park at Camden Yards. Features Music City Grille, Nashville's Country Western Bar, Toucan's Lounge. *Expensive. Phone (800) 289-4499 or (410) 252-7373.*

SHERATON BALTIMORE NORTH. 903 Dulaney Valley Road, Towson. Located off Exit 27A of I-695 Baltimore Beltway. On premises is Carnegie's Restaurant, featuring buffet meals. Pets allowed. *Expensive. Phone (410) 321-7400 or (800) 433-7619.*

EMBASSY SUITES BALTIMORE/HUNT VALLEY. 213 International Circle, Hunt Valley. Located off I-83, Exit 20A (Shawan Road), north of Baltimore. Hunt Valley Grille is in hotel atrium; other restaurants and Hunt Valley Mall across street. Close to Timonium Fairgrounds where Preakness thoroughbred race is held. MTA and Light Rail available into Camden Yards, National Aquarium, Inner Harbor. Pets allowed. *Expensive. Phone 410-584-1400.*

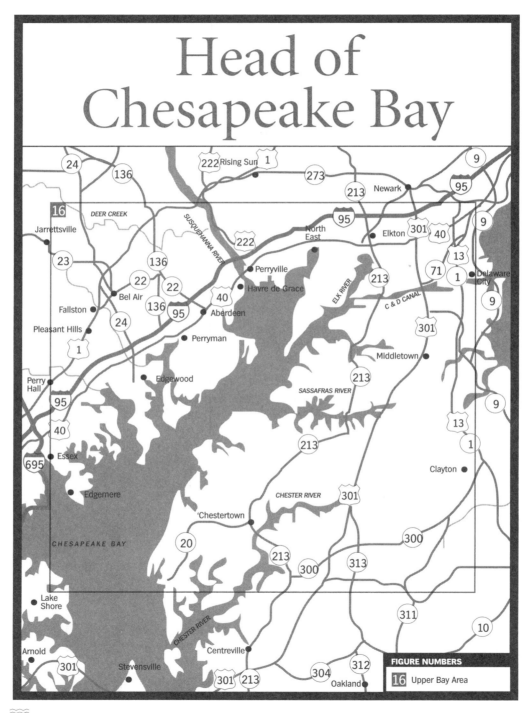

Head of Chesapeake Bay

Head of the Chesapeake Bay

Travelers who breeze across the head of the Chesapeake Bay on I-95 between Baltimore and Philadelphia may be oblivious to the rich natural and historical resources just minutes off the highway along the way. Five major rivers, two counties, and several historic towns are full of possibilities.

The five rivers that form the head of the Chesapeake Bay converge at Turkey Point on Cecil County's Elk Neck. From west to east, they are the Susquehanna, the North East, the Elk, the Bohemia, and the Sassafras. The surge of fresh water into the upper bay provides prime spawning grounds for anadromous fish—fish such as striped bass (rockfish), white perch, herring, and shad that return from the salty sea in spring to spawn in fresh water.

The two counties of the upper Chesapeake—Harford and Cecil—are known for their quiet nature, picturesque harbors, historic bed and breakfast inns, and waterfront

[*Above:* American goldfinch]

restaurants. Here are remote places where a person can cast a lure, watch a heron, listen to a chorus of marsh frogs, or just sit on the edge of a pier and feel the lap of waves on bare feet.

Positioned at the head of the Chesapeake Bay are two information centers for travelers on I-95. **Maryland House Information Center** (410-272-0176) is in Harford County between Exits 80 and 85, west of Aberdeen. **Chesapeake House Information Center** (410-287-2313) is in Cecil County between Exits 93 and 100, between Perryville and North East.

Harford County

In typical Maryland fashion, Harford County adroitly balances its quiet rural nature and its Chesapeake Bay history with modern advances including state-of-the-art estuarine research laboratories (Otter Point Creek), testing grounds for high-tech weapons (Aberdeen), luxurious golf courses, and fine restaurants.

History is preserved at Havre de Grace, where museums pay tribute to decoy carvers, oyster tongers, and Chesapeake Bay boat builders. At the **Ladew Topiary Gardens** (410-557-9570) in Monkton, native vegetation blends with sculpted trees and shrubs in a water garden, a berry garden, and flower gardens on 22 acres. The gardens adorn the grounds of a Manor House with a room called the Oval Library, which was selected as one of the 100 Most Beautiful Rooms in America.

Near the center of the county is Bel Air, the county seat, where a variety of restaurants and quaint shops line historic Main Street. The Palladian structure called **Liriodendron Mansion** (410-879-4424 or 410-838-3942), built at 502 West Gordon Street in 1898, is now maintained as a Bel Air museum.

Between Havre de Grace and Bel Air on US 40 is Aberdeen, a town closely linked to the **Aberdeen Proving Ground**, which is a military reservation on the large peninsula just south of town. The citizens of Aberdeen are as proud of their past, however, as they are of their military connections. Artifacts and memorabilia from the social, economic, and cultural development of the city are displayed at **Aberdeen Rooms Archives and Museum** (410-273-6325) at 58 North Parke Street.

For those who want to experience the Chesapeake Bay firsthand, charters and tours are available. The skipjack **Martha Lewis** (800-406-0766 or 410-939-3998) is available for cruises from the Havre de Grace lighthouse pier. This V-bottom, two-sail bateau is one of the few remaining dredge boats of the once-thriving Chesapeake Bay oyster fleet.

For more information: Discover Harford County Tourism Council, 121 North Union Avenue, #B, Havre de Grace, MD 21078. Phone (800) 597-2649, (410) 939-3336. Maryland House Travel Center (I-95, 3 miles southwest of junction with MD 132 at Aberdeen), Aberdeen, MD 21001. Phone (410) 272-0176.

🐟 MARINER POINT PARK

[Fig. 16(1)] Just east of the Baltimore County line in Joppatowne is Mariner Point Park, with 38 acres that provide an inviting place to fish, spread a picnic blanket, hike a trail, or launch a boat in the Gunpowder River. The park also has pavilions that may be rented as well as playgrounds and a fishing pier.

Directions: The park is located off Joppa Farm Road in Joppatowne. From US 40, go south on Joppa Farm Road about 2.5 miles. Turn right on Kearney Road and go 100 yards into park.

Activities: Hiking, picnicking, fishing, boating, volleyball, horseshoes.

Facilities: Fishing pier, boat launch, picnic tables, rental pavilions, playgrounds, volleyball courts, horseshoe pits.

Dates: Open Memorial Day through the end of Oct.

Fees: There is a rental charge for the pavilions.

For more information: Harford County Department of Parks and Recreation, phone (410) 612-1608, or to reserve pavilions, phone (410) 612-1606.

Striped Bass

This popular game fish, known as rockfish by Chesapeake Bay anglers, is dependent on the water quality of tidal fresh water in the upper bay and bay tributaries for successful spawning. After centuries of abundance, the striped bass (*Morone saxitilis*) suffered a serious setback in the 1980s because of over-fishing in combination with high acidity and pollution in its spawning grounds. After a fishing moratorium and some progress in bay cleanup, the fish has made an astounding comeback. Fishing is once again allowed, with size and possession limits that encourage catch-and-release fishing.

🐟 OTTER POINT CREEK, LEIGHT PARK, & MELVIN G. BOSLEY CONSERVANCY

[Fig. 16(2)] Just south of the busy I-95 and US 40 corridor in southern Harford County, between Edgewood and Aberdeen, is the sensitive ecosystem of Otter Point Creek, which joins Bush River at the head of the Chesapeake Bay. The creek's habitats are studied at the 672-acre

STRIPED BASS
(Morone saxitilis)

Canvasback

The wedge-shaped head and bill profile distinguish the canvasback (*Aythya valisineria*) from the redhead duck (*Aythya americana*). The webbed feet are near the rear of this pochard, or diving duck, enabling it to swim underwater with ease. However, what helps it underwater is a hindrance on land—a characteristic that keeps the ungainly canvasback from straying far from water's edge.

CANVASBACK
(*Aythya valisineria*)

Otter Point Creek component of the **Chesapeake National Estuarine Research Reserve** (NERR). The reserve is one of three in Maryland that are part of the national reserve system. (Jug Bay and Monie Bay are the other two).

The 350-acre Melvin G. Bosley Conservancy and 61-acre Leight Park are part of the reserve. There is limited access to the conservancy, but it is a good place to see beaver, songbirds, waterfowl, and wildflowers. Interpretive programs are available by request. The county has a public boat landing at nearby Otter Point Landing.

At Leight Park is the new Anita C. Leight Estuary Center where the staff is putting together exhibits about the Chesapeake Bay and its environs. The center, open year-round on weekends, has a discovery room with interactive displays and live animals, a library, an auditorium, and a laboratory.

Nature trails and canoe trails on the reserve provide access to a diversity of upper Chesapeake Bay habitats including creeks, rivers, lagoons, tidal marshes, scrub and shrub wetlands, and forested uplands—a diversity that attracts a tremendous variety of birds and wildlife. Spring warblers travel from Central and South America to nest in the park's forests.

The various ecosystems are also ideal for a wide range of vegetation. Rooted aquatic plants such as water milfoil (*Miriophyllulm spicatum*) and wild celery (*Vallisneria americana*) grow in the shallow water at the front of the marsh. Common marsh plants such as pickerelweed (*Pontederia cordata*), arrow arum (*Peltandra virginica*), and spatterdock, or yellow pond lily (*Nuphar luteum*), dominate the marsh, while the higher elevations give way to stands of cattail (*Typha lattifolia*) and sweet flag (*Acorus calamus*).

Several plants rare to the region or to Maryland have been identified on Otter Point Creek, including grass-like beak rush (*Rhynchospora globularis*) and Baltic rush (*Juncus balticus*).

Canoeists may catch glimpses of river otters, beaver, muskrats, and raccoons. Large marsh birds such as herons and egrets are common, as are black ducks, Virginia rails, canvasbacks, and spotted sandpipers. Bird-watchers have also sighted the American bittern and upland sandpiper.

Other marsh critters include snapping turtles and painted turtles, the American eel, blue crabs, bay anchovies, and spottail shiners.

The reserve is administered nationally and managed by the state with cooperation from county and volunteer organizations. Research conducted on site provides a better understanding of the Chesapeake Bay ecosystem. Scientists share their knowledge with the community through workshops, cultural history presentations, and research seminars. They also work with high school and college students to monitor estuary waters and help solve pollution problems.

Directions: Conservancy: From I-95, Exit 77A, go south on MD 24 toward Edgewood. At the fourth traffic light, turn left onto MD 775 (Edgewood Road). Go left onto Hanson Road, then left onto Perry Avenue, and look for the conservancy parking lot, on the left. Park: From I-95, take Exit 77A and go south on MD 24 toward Edgewood. Turn left at the third traffic light and follow the signs to US 40 East. Turn east on MD 40 and go 1.5 miles to Otter Point Road. Turn right on Otter Point Road and go about 1 mile to the park entrance, on the right.

Activities: Conservancy: hiking, fishing, wildlife viewing. Park: canoeing, nature hikes, viewing exhibits, nature programs.

Facilities: Conservancy: hiking trails, nearby boat ramp. Park: canoe waters, hiking trails, Estuary Center.

Dates: Conservancy: call ahead for permission to enter. Park: open 10 to 5 Saturdays, 12 to 5 Sundays, year-round.

Fees: None.

Closest town: Edgewood is on the south side.

For more information: Melvin G. Bosley Conservancy, phone (410) 612-1688. Anita C. Leight Estuary Center, 700 Otter Point Road, Abingdon, MD 21009. Phone (410) 612-1688.

U.S. ARMY ORDNANCE MUSEUM

[Fig. 16(3)] The U. S. Army Ordnance Museum is located at the Aberdeen Proving Ground, where artillery has been tested since 1917. With 8,000 artifacts, the museum has what has been called the most extensive collection of combat vehicles, artillery, small arms, ammunition, and military material in existence. On display are body armor, the Gatling gun, and Gen. John Pershing's Locomobile from World War I. At the Proving Ground, visitors can also explore the Army's 25-acre Tank and Artillery Park and drive the Mile of Tanks. In commemoration of Armed Forces Day, the Army fires artillery and parades its military vehicles through Aberdeen every third Saturday in May.

Directions: From I-95, take Exit 85 and go east on MD 22 to the museum at the junction of Maryland and Aberdeen boulevards.

Dates: Open 10 to 4:45 daily, year-round, except major holidays.

Fees: None.

For more information: U. S. Army Ordnance Museum, Aberdeen Proving Ground B2601, Aberdeen, MD 21005. Phone (410) 278-3602.

POOLES ISLAND LIGHTHOUSE

[Fig. 16(4)] This stone tower is on Pooles Island in the middle of the Chesapeake Bay off the southern tip of Harford County's Gunpowder Neck. The island takes its name from Nathaniel Powell, one of the men accompanying Captain John Smith when he landed on the island in 1608. Over the centuries, the name Powell underwent several transformations until it became Poole.

This lighthouse resembles the white granite tower of the Concord Point light at Havre de Grace and many others built by a local contractor, John Donohoo. This one was erected in 1825, automated in 1917, and closed in 1939. It is part of Aberdeen Proving Ground and not open to the public.

SUSQUEHANNA MUSEUM (LOCK HOUSE)

[Fig. 16(5)] Barges loaded with coal and farm products and pulled by mules once carried goods 45 miles up the Susquehanna and Tidewater Canal between Havre de Grace and Wrightsville, Pennsylvania. The museum is located at the southern end of the canal, which is no longer in use. The 1836 lockhouse, built in 1840, has been restored. Demonstrations show how the lock worked.

Dates: Open 1 to 5, Saturday and Sunday, Apr. through Dec.

Fees: There is an admission fee.

For more information: Susquehanna Museum, Erie and Conesto Streets, Havre de Grace, MD 21078. Phone (410) 939-1800, (410) 939-5780.

STEPPINGSTONE MUSEUM

[Fig. 16(6)] Watch the sparks fly as a blacksmith hammers hot iron into shape at this turn-of-the-century farm museum with a stone farmhouse. There is also a replica of a canning house. A cooper, a weaver, and several other tradespeople in period dress demonstrate their crafts. The museum is located on a bluff overlooking the Susquehanna River. Special events include Civil War remembrances, the Scottish Festival, a fall harvest festival, and a Christmas open house.

Dates: Open 1 to 5, Saturday and Sunday, May through Sept.

Fees: There is an admission fee.

For more information: Steppingstone Museum, 461 Quaker Bottom Road, Havre de Grace, MD 21078. Phone (410) 939-2299.

HAVRE DE GRACE DECOY MUSEUM

[Fig. 16(7)] This famous museum features excellent examples of Chesapeake Bay working decoys. An annual Duck Fair in September draws decoy carvers, artists, duck callers, and decoy buyers from up and down the East Coast.

Dates: Open 1 to 5, Tuesday through Sunday, year-round, except major holidays.
Fees: There is an admission fee except for children age 8 and under.
For more information: Havre De Grace Decoy Museum, 215 Giles Street, Havre de Grace, MD 21078. Phone (410) 939-3739.

HAVRE DE GRACE MARITIME MUSEUM

[Fig. 16(8)] Learn the history of local seafarers and see artifacts and photographs from Colonial times to the present. Museum expansion includes more exhibit area, lecture rooms, library, and a gift shop.
Dates: Open 1 to 5, Saturday and Sunday, May through Oct.
Fees: There is an admission fee.
For more information: Havre de Grace Maritime Museum, 1010 Cairns Run Road, Aberdeen, MD 21001. Phone (410) 734-6357 or (410) 939-4800.

CONCORD POINT LIGHTHOUSE

[Fig. 16(9)] Go to the foot of Lafayette Street in Havre de Grace to see one of the oldest lighthouses still in operation on the East Coast. Concord Point—once known as Point Conquest—marks the place where the powerful flow of the Susquehanna meets the tidal Chesapeake Bay. The treacherous currents spurred the General Assembly of Maryland to authorize construction of the lighthouse in 1826.

The Concord Point's tower, constructed of Port Deposit Granite and now restored to original condition, was built in 1827, manned from 1829 to 1920, and remained in use until 1975. It was originally lighted by nine whale-oil lamps with tin reflectors.

Visitors may climb the 36-foot tower for views of the bay and Havre de Grace. The lighthouse keeper's home—a stone house across the street from the light tower—is undergoing restoration.
Dates: Open 1 to 5, Saturdays, Sundays, and holidays, Apr. through Oct.
Fees: None.
For more information: Phone (410) 939-1498.

RESTAURANTS OF HARFORD COUNTY

Listed here are a few of many fine restaurants near the Chesapeake Bay in Harford County.

GABLER'S SHORE RESTAURANT. 2200 Perryman Road, Aberdeen. Known for its plain atmosphere and perfectly seasoned steamed crabs. Beer on tap. Voted Baltimore's Best Crab House five years by *Baltimore Magazine*. Open seasonally. *Inexpensive to moderate. Phone (410) 272-0626.*

MACGREGOR'S. 331 St. John's Street, Havre de Grace. Seafood and crab cakes are the specialties of this restaurant overlooking the bay. The decor includes carved decoys and old prints of the town. *Moderate. Phone (410) 939-3003 or (800) 300-6319.*

BAYOU RESTAURANT. 927 Pulaski Highway (MD 40), Havre de Grace. A local

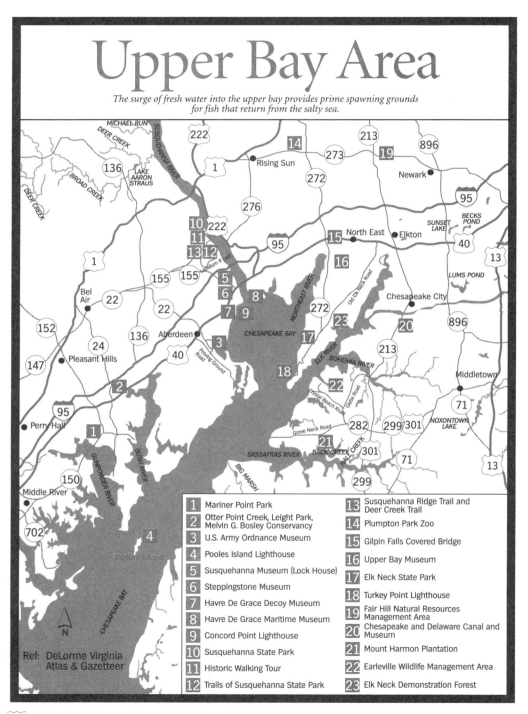

Upper Bay Area

The surge of fresh water into the upper bay provides prime spawning grounds for fish that return from the salty sea.

1. Mariner Point Park
2. Otter Point Creek, Leight Park, Melvin G. Bosley Conservancy
3. U.S. Army Ordnance Museum
4. Pooles Island Lighthouse
5. Susquehanna Museum (Lock House)
6. Steppingstone Museum
7. Havre De Grace Decoy Museum
8. Havre De Grace Maritime Museum
9. Concord Point Lighthouse
10. Susquehanna State Park
11. Historic Walking Tour
12. Trails of Susquehanna State Park
13. Susquehanna Ridge Trail and Deer Creek Trail
14. Plumpton Park Zoo
15. Gilpin Falls Covered Bridge
16. Upper Bay Museum
17. Elk Neck State Park
18. Turkey Point Lighthouse
19. Fair Hill Natural Resources Management Area
20. Chesapeake and Delaware Canal and Museum
21. Mount Harmon Plantation
22. Earleville Wildlife Management Area
23. Elk Neck Demonstration Forest

Ref: DeLorme Virginia Atlas & Gazetteer

favorite for over 40 years, this restaurant specializes in fresh seafood, steaks, and veal. Homemade pies are baked daily. Work of local artists is featured. *Moderate. Phone (410) 939-3565.*

TIDEWATER GRILLE. 300 Foot of Franklin Street, Havre de Grace. This three-star restaurant has a waterfront location where the Susquehanna River meets the Chesapeake Bay. Accessible by car and boat. Authentic regional American fare. *Moderate. Phone (410) 939-3313 or (410) 575-7045.*

🏵 LODGING IN HARFORD COUNTY

Most motels and inns near the Chesapeake Bay are located along the I-95 corridor at Edgewood, Aberdeen, and Havre de Grace. B&Bs are mostly in historic Havre de Grace.

BEST WESTERN INVITATIONAL INN. 1709 Edgewood Road (Exit 77A off I-95 at SR 24), Edgewood. Complimentary deluxe continental breakfast, outdoor pool, exercise facility, 3-diamond rating. *Moderate. Phone (410) 679-9700.*

DAYS INN. 2116 Emmorton Park Road, Edgewood. Conveniently located at Exit 77A of I-95, this motel is newly renovated. Pets are welcome. *Inexpensive to moderate. Phone (410) 671-9990.*

4 POINTS HOTEL BY SHERATON. I-95 and MD 24, Aberdeen. This Sheraton hotel is convenient for travelers on I-95. *Moderate. Phone (410) 273-6300.*

QUALITY INN & SUITES. 793 W. Belair Avenue, Aberdeen. Free continental breakfast, outdoor pool, 4 miles from Chesapeake Bay public access, 5 miles from Ripken Museum. *Inexpensive to moderate. Phone (410) 272-6000.*

CURRIER HOUSE B&B. 800 South Market Street, Havre de Grace. The granddaughter of the original owner of this historic B&B is the innkeeper. The inn has a waterfront view and is near antique shops and a golf course. *Moderate. Phone (410) 939-7886 or (800) 827-2889.*

SPENCER SILVER MANSION B&B. 200 South Union Avenue, Havre de Grace. This restored Victorian mansion has elegant waterside accommodations in the heart of the historic district. *Expensive. Phone (410) 939-1097.*

VANDIVER INN. 410 South Union Street, Havre de Grace. This three-story structure, built in 1886, is listed on the National Register of Historic Places. Rooms are furnished with antiques. Breakfast is included in the affordable rates. Close to Chesapeake Bay. *Moderate. Phone (410) 939-5200 or (800) 245-1655.*

The Susquehanna River

[Fig. 16] When we speak of rivers, we speak of how green or wide they are, of the bass or brook trout that swim beneath the surface, or the scenery that makes a canoe trip memorable. But with the Susquehanna River at the head of the Chesapeake Bay, a few numbers will help round out the river's story.

The Susquehanna River enters Maryland from Pennsylvania, forming the boundary between Harford and Cecil counties. After draining a 13-million-acre watershed—the second largest drainage area in the East—the river enters the upper Chesapeake Bay at Havre de Grace. This 444-mile-long river, which begins near Cooperstown, New York, and flows by Harrisburg, Pennsylvania, dumps an incredible 19 million gallons of fresh water into the bay every minute. The flow makes up more than half the fresh water received by the Chesapeake Bay in an average year.

The statistics have meaningful consequences for those who live in the river's watershed and below it. Because of the large volume of water the river adds to the bay, the quality of that water is of vital importance to the bay's health. Everyone in the river's drainage basin who plows a field, fertilizes a lawn, or takes trash to a landfill impacts the bay's plankton, oysters, crabs, striped bass, shad, waterfowl, and wetlands.

The huge volume of the Susquehanna's flow provides power for turbines in hydroelectric plants and the river provides millions of people with clean water with a turn of a faucet. The same river that cools uranium rods in nuclear power plants north of Maryland also cools swimmers and tubers on a sweltering August day.

Those who live on the river's banks are well acquainted with the dangers of flooding. History records more than 40 major floods since 1736. Port Deposit's three-story-high structures built on the side of the Susquehanna's granite cliffs are testament to the river's power. During high water, the cliff-side residents of this historic Cecil County town can climb outside steps that zigzag up the cliffs to a higher floor.

For many, however, the dangers of living in the floodplain are overcome by the benefits of beautiful scenery and outstanding recreation in the form of boating, canoeing, inner-tubing, and fishing.

Maryland boat landings at Tydings Park, at Jean Roberts Memorial Park, at Frank Hutchins Park in Havre de Grace, off Main Street in Port Deposit, and at Lapidum Landing at Susquehanna State Park give anglers access to the river's largemouth and smallmouth bass, striped bass, chain pickerel, crappie, perch, and sunfish.

SUSQUEHANNA STATE PARK

[Fig. 16(10)] Early-morning sunlight on the Susquehanna River traces the curve of fishing line as a lone angler in a john boat casts a bucktail for striped bass. Two elderly hikers on a park trail stop to admire the way the same gold light bathes a massive rock outcrop. A father who has taken his 10-year-old daughter on her first camping trip scrambles eggs in a pan over a propane stove.

Susquehanna State Park has variety enough to interest the young and the old, the fisherman, canoeist, and hiker. The land is located in southeastern Harford County on the west bank of the Susquehanna River. With 3,600 acres of heavy forest cover, stream and river access, interesting geology, and a historic walking tour complete with a working gristmill, the park is full of things to do. The 74-site campground has no hookups, but does have hot showers and restrooms in each loop. The Deer Creek Picnic Area is near

Deer Creek, where swimming, tubing, and freshwater fishing for smallmouth bass, catfish, and rockfish provide warm-weather fun. At the Rock Run Grist Mill, which is a highlight of the park's historic area, corn-grinding demonstrations take place on summer weekends.

Even night fishing is possible from Lapidum Landing, a boat launch on the Susquehanna that is open 24 hours a day. Hikers, horseback riders, bikers, and pets on leashes are allowed on the park's 12 miles of hiking trails. Visitors sometimes get glimpses of white-tailed deer, rabbits, or maybe even a red fox or coyote. On occasion, the sight of a bald eagle soaring above the trees, wings spread a full 6.5 feet, provides the memory of a lifetime. In a quiet moment, a hiker or a fisherman might be struck with the realization that the Susquehannock Indians once prowled the same dense forests, were inspired by the same impressive boulders and outcroppings, and fished the same Deer Creek in the park that now bears their name.

Park headquarters for Susquehanna State Park is located at 855-acre Rocks State Park in Harford County about 30 miles north of Baltimore on MD 24.

Directions: From Interstate 95, take Exit 89 and go west on MD 155 about 3 miles to MD 161. Turn right on 161, go 0.4 mile, and turn right on Rock Run Road. Follow signs to the park.

Activities: Hiking, historic walk, biking, horseback riding, boating and canoeing, tubing, camping, picnicking, cross-country skiing.

Facilities: Picnic area with tables and grills, restrooms, boat launch, hiking trails, pet trail, playground; campground with table and fire ring at each site (no hookups); showers with hot water and flush toilets.

Dates: The park is open from 9 to sunset, year-round. The campground is open from Memorial Day to Sept. 30.

Fees: There are fees for camping and launching boats.

Closest town: Havre de Grace is 3 miles southeast of the park.

For more information: Susquehanna State Park, c/o Rocks State Park, 3318 Rocks Chrome Hill Road, Jarrettsville, MD 21084. Phone (410) 557-7994.

HISTORIC WALKING TOUR

[Fig. 16(11)] A visit to Susquehanna State Park would be incomplete without taking the time for this fascinating look into Harford County's days of gristmills and manor homes. A brochure details interesting history along the way. The 45-minute easy walk begins at **Rock Run Grist Mill**, a restored four-story structure built in the late 1700s to harness the power of Rock Run before it empties into the Susquehanna River. Note the 12-ton water wheel that turns as water fills the buckets. Such a mill was crucial to community life. Rather than taking cash for grinding the farmer's grain, the miller would take a portion or "pottle" of the grist to use to barter among the townspeople for his own necessities.

The walk also includes a spring house, mill race and mill pond, carriage house, 13-room restored manor home (**Archer House**, built in 1804) with wine cellar and indoor smoke house, and the restored **Jersey Toll House**, which housed the toll collector for a

1-mile-long bridge that once spanned the Susquehanna River.

Views of stonework and ditches that are the remains of the once-significant **Susquehanna and Tidewater Canal** are near the end of the walking tour. The canal extended from Havre de Grace 45 miles westward to Wrightsville. Locks built of granite were constructed at intervals to raise the water level and boats from 20 feet above sea level at Havre de Grace to 1,000 feet at Wrightsville. Remnants of three locks are on park property.

TRAILS OF SUSQUEHANNA STATE PARK

[Fig. 16(12)] Twelve miles of blazed trails varying from easy to difficult access the park's river frontage, forests, fields, and ridges. The light-blue-blazed **Mason-Dixon Trail**, an Appalachian Trail spur, uses park trails along the Susquehanna River to connect the AT to Havre de Grace. Hikers should stay on blazed trails to protect the park's environmentally sensitive areas. Pets are not allowed in the Deer Creek Picnic Area and must be on a leash elsewhere. Trails close at sunset.

SUSQUEHANNA RIDGE TRAIL. [Fig. 16(13)] Outstanding views of the Susquehanna River valley await those who make the 3-mile trek along the river ridge between Deer Creek Picnic Area and Lapidum Road, just west of the boat landing.

Trail: 3-mile, moderately difficult red-blazed path along ridge, with difficult climbs, connecting picnic area and boat landing.

DEER CREEK TRAIL. [Fig. 16(13)] Take this 2-mile loop from the picnic area for its inspiring views and to observe huge oaks and tulip poplars.

Trail: 2.1-mile green-blazed loop, of moderate difficulty, that begins in the picnic area.

Cecil County

With the Susquehanna River on its western border and the Sassafras River on its southern border, Cecil County is partially defined by waters that flow to the Chesapeake Bay. Also, the uppermost rivers that feed the bay—the North East, Elk, and Bohemia—and their tributaries penetrate the county like the fingers of a hand, dividing it into many large and small peninsulas.

Tidal wetlands and forested uplands on these water-wrapped lands are home to a great variety of birds and wildlife. Much of the waterfowl, wildfowl, and wildlife reside in the state-operated park, in the demonstration forest, in the managed hunting areas in the southeastern part of the county, or at Fair Hill Natural Resources Management Area in the northeastern corner.

This watershed of the upper bay harbors wonderful things to do and places to go, from aristocratic manor homes to restored mill houses, from thoroughbred horse racing to Winston drag racing, and from sailing the Chesapeake at sunset to attending a Civil War re-enactment at Rising Sun. A day might begin with crab omelets at a country B&B,

progress to a picnic lunch at Elk Neck State Park, and end with waterfront dining on the C&D Canal at Chesapeake City.

The county sits in Maryland's northeast corner, bordered by Pennsylvania to the north and Delaware to the east. The I-95 corridor that connects Baltimore with Wilmington, Delaware bisects the county from west to east. Off the busy freeway are the quiet back roads that lead to eighteenth and nineteenth century towns, Revolutionary War and Civil War history, fields and forests, and the thoroughbred farms that characterize the countryside at the head of the Chesapeake Bay. Some of Cecil County's highways have wide, paved shoulders that invite bicycle touring.

Several historic towns lure travelers interested in learning about the county's past. On the banks of the Susquehanna River, several miles north of Perryville, is Port Deposit, where nineteenth century architecture combines with a stunning river setting. **The Union Hotel** (410-378-3503) on Main Street (MD 222) was built of hemlock logs around 1790, with V-notched construction chinked with mud and stone. Waiters dressed in colonial garb serve period food.

In the center of the county on the North East River is Charlestown. Established in 1742, Charlestown is the county's oldest incorporated town. A **walking tour** (410-287-8793) features the eighteenth century taverns and houses that keep this town much as it was in colonial times.

Both Rising Sun, formerly called Summer Hill, in the northwestern corner of the county and Elkton on the eastern side were Revolutionary War crossroads between Baltimore and Philadelphia. Rising Sun also has a Civil War past, which is celebrated with a re-enactment each October. Continental and British troops sometimes camped at Elkton during the Revolutionary War. Such leaders as Howe, Lafayette, and Rochambeau passed through.

Perryville, located across the Susquehanna River from Havre de Grace, is known for the restored **Perryville Train Station**, built about 1904, and the **Principio Furnace**, constructed in 1722 and used to make iron cannon balls during the Revolutionary War.

George and Martha Washington used to ferry across the Susquehanna and visit **Rodgers Tavern** at Perryville on trips between Mount Vernon and points north. The restored tavern, located on MD 7 (Old Post Road/Philadelphia Road), features architecture representative of its time. Perryville is also the location of the **B&O Holly Tree**, a 127-year-old, 55-foot holly on Jackson Station Road. On the first Saturday of each December, a day of festivities culminating in a tree-lighting ceremony commemorates a tradition started by the B&O Railroad in 1948.

In addition to these attractions and the ones mentioned below, Cecil County has historic manor homes, eighteenth century churches, and beautiful back roads that await discovery by curious travelers.

For more information: Cecil County Department of Tourism, 129 East Main Street, Elkton, MD 21921. Phone (800) CECIL-95 or (410) 996-5300.

PLUMPTON PARK ZOO

[Fig. 16(14)] The Plumpton Park Zoo, called a "family-friendly zoo," is about 3 miles east of Rising Sun. This small but popular country zoo attracts some 50,000 people annually.

Both children and adults can view North American animals that are difficult to see close up in the wild, such as a barred owl, red-tailed hawk, white-tailed deer, cougar, and bear. Exotic species among the 250 animals include zebra, giraffe, monkey, gibbon, alligator, camel, and the latest addition, a beautiful Siberian tiger. The zoo has a nature trail and picnic facilities on Northeast Creek, where wild geese and ducks announce their presence with honks and quacks.

Directions: From I-95, take Exit 100 and go north on MD 272 to the second traffic light at the intersection of MD 272 and MD 273. Go left onto MD 273 and drive 1 mile to the park, on the left.

Dates: Open 10 to 5 daily, year-round, weather permitting.

Fees: There is an entry fee.

Closest town: Rising Sun is 3 miles west.

For more information: Plumpton Park Zoo, 1416 Telegraph Road, Rising Sun, MD 21911. Phone (410) 658-6850.

NORTH EAST

[Fig. 16] This little town, with the flavor of Main Street USA, sits at the head of the North East River, about 9 miles east of Havre de Grace. Visitors stroll along the streets licking double-dip ice cream cones and investigating shops filled with antiques and collectibles. Favored attractions include **Cramer's 5 & 10** and the **Day Basket Factory**. At the 5 & 10, shelves are filled with penny candy and other items from the 1950s. At the Day Basket Factory on the corner of Main Street and Irishtown Road, artisans make split-oak baskets that have been traditional for more than a century. Also popular are the antiques and collectibles of the **Shoppes of Londonshire**.

From March through November, Winston series drag racing draws fans to the **Cecil County Dragway** at 1573 Theodore Road (410-287-9105). The popular North East Water Festival is held in July. In October, anglers come to North East Town Park, headquarters for the Upper Bay Rockfish Tournament, and carvers come to North East Middle School to exhibit their amazing decoys in the Upper Shore Decoy Show.

For more information: Cecil County Department of Tourism, phone (410) 996-5300 or (800) CECIL-95. Information and event hotline, phone (410) 287-2658.

GILPIN FALLS COVERED BRIDGE

[Fig. 16(15)] About 5 miles north of North East, where North East Creek intersects MD 272, is Gilpin Falls Covered Bridge. Built about 1860, the 119-foot restored wooden structure has withstood the elements longer than any other covered bridge in the state. The much-photographed bridge is visible and easily accessible from MD 272.

UPPER BAY MUSEUM

[Fig. 16(16)] Boating, hunting, and fishing artifacts used by upper Chesapeake Bay residents are on display at this museum located on Walnut Street in the town of North East.

Directions: The museum is located in North East Community Park. From MD 272 at MD 40, go south on MD 272 approximately 1 mile. Turn right on Walnut Street and follow it to the park.

Dates: Open Sundays, Memorial Day through Labor Day.

Fees: None, but donations are appreciated.

For more information: Upper Bay Museum, phone (410) 287-5909 or (410) 287-0672.

ELK NECK STATE PARK

[Fig. 16(17)] Campers, hikers, swimmers, bird-watchers, boaters, and anglers all have reason to seek out Elk Neck State Park. The park is in southwestern Cecil County on a peninsula formed by the Chesapeake Bay and Elk River. The 2,188 acres of the park are composed of coastal terrain with small valleys and high wooded bluffs overlooking the bay and North East River on the park's western edge.

Motorboats, rowboats, and Jet Skis may be rented and launched in the Elk River at a concession on the east side of the peninsula. A waterfront area on the North East River offers unguarded swimming.

Canoeists enjoy paddling along the riverbanks, habitat for the unique flora and fauna that inhabit the fresh tidal marshes of the upper Chesapeake Bay. White-tailed deer, gray squirrel, beaver, and raccoon are just a few of the wild animals that may make an appearance along water's edge. Anglers and crabbers in rowboats and motorboats or on the riverbanks have a number of options, including blue crabs, largemouth bass, striped bass, shad, channel catfish, pickerel, crappie, yellow perch, and sunfish.

In spring, a tiny red flag flashing in the reeds at water's edge could turn out to be a male red-winged blackbird opening and closing his wings to announce his presence. Blue crabs begin arriving from the deeper, more saline waters of the lower bay to begin mating, and the anadromous striped bass returns from the sea to spawn.

In summer, the waters of the bay around the park are full of life, as the young of many species grow to adulthood. Under the slate-gray surface, the waters teem with life, mostly unseen. Bottom fishermen may pull up strange creatures such as the hogchoker.

Lanterns glowing along the banks in summer and fall mark the places that catfish anglers sit and wait for a bite. On a January day, two hikers hear only the crunch of snow beneath their boots and their own rhythmic breathing as they enjoy having the park to themselves—except, of course, for thousands of wintering wildfowl.

Whatever the season, Elk Neck State Park is an excellent place to learn the ecology of the upper Chesapeake Bay while enjoying the outdoors. Many amenities exist thanks to the energy and expertise of the young men of the Civilian Conservation Corps in the 1930s who constructed the trails, picnic areas, rustic cabins, and roads that remain in use today.

Camping is available year-round at Elk Neck. Cabins require advance reservations.

Hogchoker

Because the hogchoker (*Trinectes maculatus*) is not often caught, this flatfish may confuse anglers. However, the lack of pectoral fins is a giveaway. Also, the lower jaw slightly overlaps the upper jaw and the fish has no snout. The name hogchoker comes from the days when this stiff, bony, scaly fish was used as food for hogs. This shallow-water species found mostly in brackish water prefers muddy or mud-and-sand bottoms.

Pets are allowed in most areas.

Directions: From I-95 in north-central Cecil County, take Exit 100 and go south on MD 272 approximately 11 miles to the park entrance.

Activities: Hiking, picnicking, camping, swimming, mountain biking, fishing, seasonal deer hunting, flatwater canoeing, boating, bird-watching.

Facilities: Boat ramp, rental motorboats and john boats, picnic tables, rental picnic shelters, hiking trails, pet trail, playground, 302 campsites (some with hookups), cabins, camp store, dumping station, conference center, nature center, park office, bathhouses with restrooms.

Dates: The grounds are open from 8 to sunset, year-round. Some parts of the park are closed in winter, but the campground loop with hookups and all hiking trails remain open. The park office is open from 8 to 4 daily. The boat ramp is open 24 hours a day from Memorial Day to Labor Day. The camp store opens the first weekend in Apr.; call for closing dates.

Fees: There is a fee for camping, cabins, boat rental, boat launching, and rental of the conference center.

Closest town: North East is 9 miles north.

For more information: Elk Neck State Park, 4395 Turkey Point Road, North East, MD 21901. Phone (410) 287-5333.

BIRD-WATCHING AT ELK NECK STATE PARK

Several peninsulas along the Atlantic Flyway such as the one at Elk Neck State Park act as natural funnels for migrating birds, which prefer to stay over land whenever possible. At Turkey Point on the southernmost tip of the peninsula, where the highest concentration of migrating birds occurs at Elk Neck, the Ornithological Society of Cecil County has established a regular fall hawk watch. Daily tallies are kept on such hawks as sharp-shinned (*Accipiter striatus*), Cooper's (*Accipiter cooperii*), red-shouldered (*Buteo lineatus*), broad-winged (*Buteo platypterus*), and rough-legged (*Buteo lagopus*).

Also recorded are the northern harrier (*Circus cyaneus*), goshawk (*Accipiter gentilis*), merlin (*Falco columbarius*), black vulture (*Coragyps atratus*), and turkey vulture (*Cathartes aura*). Golden eagles (*Aquila chrysaetos*), bald eagles (*Haliaeetus leucocephalus*), and peregrine falcons (*Falco peregrinus*) are occasionally spotted. In each of the first two seasons of record keeping, the club counted more than 3,000 birds of prey in just 100 hours of bird-watching

With many bird clubs keeping similar watches along the flyway, flight patterns, preferred flying conditions, dates of migration, and numbers of birds can be compared from year to year. Scientists can then use the data in studying the status of migrating birds, even sharing it with other countries on the southern or northern ends of the migration routes.

Hawks, though perhaps the best known and most easily observed of spring and fall migrants, are not the only winged creatures that come across Turkey Point. Warblers cross the water here in astounding numbers. Butterflies are also known to use this portion of the flyway.

Campers and hikers spot wild turkeys year-round, in addition to several varieties of terns, herons, and gulls.

HIKING AT ELK NECK STATE PARK

Short hiking trails named for the color of their blazes lead through Coastal Plain marshes and hardwood forests, affording good opportunities to spot birds and wildlife.

The 1.5-mile **Red Trail** loops through a deciduous hardwood forest with a canopy of oak, hickory, beech, maple, locust, and tulip poplar. Mountain laurel and flowering dogwood bring the understory to life with their pink and white blooms in spring. Patches of ferns, mosses, and wildflowers add to the beauty. The trail is of moderate difficulty and connects the North East Beach entrance road off MD 272 with the chapel at the Mauldin Mountain area.

The 1-mile **Green Trail** is an easy hike between the visitor center and the Bohemia camping loop that goes through a hardwood forest and by a freshwater pond. Spring peepers (*Hyla crucifer*) shrilly announce their presence on spring evenings, while a bullfrog (*Rana catesbeiana*) adds its low thrum to a summer night. Look for the tracks of a raccoon at water's edge. The front feet look much like tiny human hands.

A quiet approach in winter may give hikers a glimpse of a common goldeneye (*Bucephala clangula*), a bufflehead (*Bucephala albeola*), or a hooded merganser (*Lophodytes cucullatus*).

The **Black Trail** is a 2-mile hilly loop of moderate difficulty featuring a hardwood forest, a marsh, and beaches of the Elk River. Tracks of the web-footed, playful river otter may be located along water's edge. The trail is accessible across from site 12 in the Susquehanna campground or in the Wye camping area between sites Wye-2 and Wye-3.

The 2-mile, easy **Blue Trail** leads to a loop at Turkey Point Lighthouse, with views of the bay and Elk River. Overgrown fields give hikers the best opportunity to find wildflowers.

HOGCHOKER
(*Trinectes maculatus*)

Common Goldeneye

An observer who gets a bit too near this duck may be treated to the loud whistling of wings as it runs across the water to pick up speed and become airborne. More often, the goldeneye (*Bucephala clangula*) will dive beneath the surface to avoid an intruder. Note the dark, round head and white wing patch. The female has a white collar while the male has a round white patch in front of its distinctive yellow eye.

The trailhead is at the southern end of MD 272, where a chain blocks the road. The parking area is on the left.

TURKEY POINT LIGHTHOUSE

[Fig. 16(18)] Perched on a 100-foot bluff, the 35-foot tower of the Turkey Point Lighthouse stands as high above the bay waters as any other light. Built in 1833, this is one of the oldest lighthouses in continual operation. The last keeper before automation was Fannie Salter, who lived at the lighthouse from 1925 until her retirement in 1947. The U. S. Coast Guard tore down the keeper's house. Only the oil house and white tower with its flashing light remain. The lighthouse appears in the Clint Eastwood movie *Absolute Power*. The lighthouse is not open to the public.

FAIR HILL NATURAL RESOURCES MANAGEMENT AREA

[Fig. 16(19)] In northeastern Cecil County, Memorial Day brings thoroughbred race horses, steeplechase events, horse racing, and pari-mutuel wagering. The turf track and the Fair Hill Training Center for race horses at Fair Hill Natural Resources Management Area attract those who enjoy the thunder of hooves and the sight of magnificent thoroughbreds. During the fall, Fair Hill hosts the impressive Fair Hill International, a three-day equestrian event.

The state's natural resource management areas are managed for multiple uses—uses that include both environmental protection and public recreation—and this one is no exception. In addition to equestrian events, Fair Hill annually hosts Scottish Games, the Cecil County Fair, and a popular mountain bike race in July. Hikers, bikers, and horseback riders share 40 miles of trails and 35 miles of dirt roads through hardwood forests, along streams, and through fields where bluebirds sit on fence posts, singing a soft, plaintive song. Trail users sometimes spot red foxes and red-tailed hawks, which both prey on the prolific voles in the fields.

Birders come during spring breeding season to spot birds that inhabit both fields and woods. The uncommon cerulean warbler (*Dendroica cerulea*) has been seen in the bottomland woods. The male's head and back are the color of blue sky.

Grassland bird species found here include the Eastern meadowlark (*Sturnella magna*), grasshopper sparrow (*Ammodramus savannarus*), and bobolink (*Dolichonyx oryzivorus*). The bobolink, a bird suffering from habitat loss, benefits from Fair Hill's practice of delaying the harvest of hayfields. Nighttime predators that inhabit the woodlands beside Big Elk Creek include the barred owl (*Strix varia*) and screech owl (*Ostus asio*), whose haunting calls can bring a sleepy youth-group camper sitting bolt upright.

Anglers armed with a Maryland fishing license cast their lures into 5 miles of Big Elk Creek, which runs the length of the 5,613-acre area from the Pennsylvania border on the north to Elk Mills near the southern border. Bluegill, redbreast sunfish, smallmouth bass, white sucker, and stocked rainbow and brown trout reward some 2,500 fishermen annually. The state's largest managed deer hunt (with shotgun) is held in January.

The nonprofit Fair Hill Environmental Foundation, Inc. operates the Fair Hill Nature and Environmental Center on the property, a hub for nature tours for visitors and day camps for children. Groups of youth campers are asked to carry out an environmental project in appreciation for using the campground. Some 200 volunteers help maintain Fair Hill, organize events, and raise money.

Near the center is the **Big Elk Creek Covered Bridge**, one of just five covered bridges in the state. The bridge was built in 1860 at a cost of just $1,165, then heavily damaged in 1938 and again in 1950 when trucks broke through the flooring. The cost of a 1992 reconstruction was $152,000—130 times the original construction price 132 years earlier. The bridge received the state's Historic Civil Engineering Landmark Award in 1994.

A Fair Hill brochure, a trail map, and a calendar of events are available at the visitor center.

Directions: From Elkton, go 8 miles north on MD 213. Go right on scenic MD 273. Fair Hill NRMA is on both sides of the highway along MD 273. The race track is on the right. The office is on the east side of MD 213 at the junction with MD 273.

Activities: Steeplechase and flat races with pari-mutuel wagering, fox chasing on horseback, hiking, freshwater fishing, mountain biking, camping for organized youth groups, seasonal hunting by permit.

Facilities: Equestrian center with stables, turf race course, visitor center, nature center, trails, trout stream, youth-group campground, tea barn, food concession, picnic pavilion, activity building (new).

Dates: The grounds are open sunrise to sunset, year-round. Races are generally scheduled for Memorial Day and in the fall. A three-month bow-hunting season runs from Sept. 15 to Jan. 31 on a designated 650 acres. A managed deer hunt (with shotgun) is held in Jan.

Fees: There is a parking fee and a rental fee for many buildings, including stables, a tea barn, and a picnic pavilion.

Closest town: Elkton is 8 miles south.

For more information: Department of Natural Resources–Fair Hill, 376 Fair Hill Drive, Elkton, MD 21921. Phone (410) 398-1246.

CHESAPEAKE & DELAWARE CANAL AND MUSEUM

[Fig. 16(20)] In the 1700s, the water route between the Delaware River and the port of Baltimore was a long trip south around the Delmarva peninsula. A glance at a map will make obvious why map maker Augustine Herman proposed as early as the mid-1600s building a

Osage-orange

The Osage-orange (*Maclura pomifera*) is a member of the mulberry family (Moraceae), and is best known by children for its bumpy greenish fruits that are much better for throwing than for eating. The tree is native to the Osage Indian country in Texas, Oklahoma, and Arkansas. Because of its thorny nature, the Osage-orange was planted extensively for fencing on the Eastern Shore and in many other places before the invention of barbed wire.

canal across the narrow 14-mile stretch of land at the northern neck of the peninsula, thereby cutting 300 miles off the voyage.

Construction finally began in 1804. But the proposal was easier imagined than done. Lack of funds and the difficulties of digging through swampy marshlands for meager pay were among the obstacles of completing the project. The dream did not become a reality until the canal was opened for business in 1829 at a construction cost of $2.5 million.

Today, the much-improved C&D Canal is the busiest in the United States and third busiest in the world. Guests at inns and restaurants along the canal watch tankers, barges with tugboats, and small boats navigate up and down the 450-foot-wide waterway. The canal, which is owned by the U. S. Army Corps of Engineers, is listed on the National Register of Historic Places and is a National Historic Civil Engineering and Mechanical Engineering Landmark.

The C&D Canal Museum at Chesapeake City displays artifacts from the canal's beginnings. The main attraction is the two-story steam engine—the oldest of its type still in existence—on its original mount. Interactive videos and a television monitor provide current locations of ships in the canal. Within a short walking distance of the museum is a full-size replica of the 30-foot Bethel Bridge Lighthouse. Before 1927, when improvements made the entire canal sea level, the Bethel Bridge Lighthouse was one of many wooden lighthouses along the canal that warned of locks and bridges.

Directions: The canal is located in eastern Cecil County and western Delaware. It passes through Chesapeake City. The museum is located on Second Street and Bethel Road in Chesapeake City.

Dates: The museum is open 8 to 4, Monday through Saturday, year-round.

Fees: None.

Closest town: The canal passes through Chesapeake City, where the museum is located.

For more information: C&D Canal Museum, phone (410) 885-5622.

CHESAPEAKE CITY

[Fig. 16] Picturesque Chesapeake City on the C&D Canal has been featured in *Southern Living* magazine. The rooftops of the colorful homes are visible from the MD 213 bridge that crosses the canal, dividing the town in two. A side trip into town reveals dozens of restored homes with beautiful gardens, antique and gift shops, art galleries, four bed and breakfast inns, and five restaurants.

Many buildings and houses are steeped in history. Most are located on George Street and Bohemia Avenue, which are on the southern side of the canal and the eastern side of MD 213. **The Bayard House Restaurant** (circa 1780) at 11 Bohemia Avenue is one of the oldest buildings in the city. Today, visitors can sample both traditional and innovative Eastern Shore fare year-round at a moderate price as they watch boats navigate the canal.

For more information: Historic district and walking tour, phone (410) 885-2795 or (410) 885-2997. Bayard House Restaurant, phone (410) 885-5040.

MOUNT HARMON PLANTATION

[Fig. 16(21)] This eighteenth-century tobacco plantation is on a peninsula in Back Creek on Cecil County's southern border. Back Creek is a tributary of the Sassafras River, which enters the Chesapeake Bay some 5.5 miles west of Mount Harmon.

The brick manor house, open to the public for guided tours, was built about 1730 and restored to its early appearance in the 1960s. Driving down the winding, 2-mile entrance lane under a canopy of Osage-orange (*Maclura pomifera*), the Georgian-style structure finally comes into view—impressive, isolated on a hill, and nearly surrounded by water. "World's End," it was called on early maps. And it's no wonder.

More than 200 acres of the plantation are still farmed. Formal boxwood and wisteria gardens have been restored, complete with serpentine brick walls and a fountain. Among many important botanical plantings are 200-year-old English yews (*Taxus baccata*)—possibly the oldest in the country—located between the boxwood gardens and the plantation house.

The plantation is also a nature preserve. Natural Lands Trust, Inc., a nonprofit land conservation organization, manages the property for the owner, the National Trust for Historic Preservation. Several well-marked nature trails provide access to fields, ponds, and creeks where observant hikers might spot bald eagles that nest in the area. Among the wildflowers on Mount Harmon property is the American lotus or water chinaquin (*Nelumbo lutea*), cousin to the water lily. The lotus, rare in Maryland, is the largest wildflower in the United States. Its pale yellow, fragrant blossoms extend above the water, sometimes measuring as much as 10 inches across, while its bowl-shaped leaves are 1 to 2 feet wide.

Directions: From the junction of MD 213 and MD 282 at Cecilton, go just under 4 miles west on MD 282 (Grove Neck Road). Look for Mount Harmon sign and entrance, on the left.

Facilities: Plantation house, colonial kitchen, tobacco house, formal gardens, nature trails, mooring space.

Dates: Open 10 to 3, Tuesday and Thursday, 1 to 4 Sunday, or by appointment.

OSAGE-ORANGE
(Maclura pomifera)

Fees: There is an entrance fee for nonmembers and a rental fee for special events.

Closest town: Earleville is about 2.5 miles north.

For more information: Mount Harmon Plantation, PO Box 65, Earleville, MD 21919. Phone (410) 275-8819.

WILDLIFE AND WILDFOWL AREAS

Several forests and wetlands on the peninsulas of southeastern Cecil County are managed to provide habitat for wildlife and wildfowl. Hikers, bikers, horseback riders, bird watchers, and hunters (seasonally) are permitted to use the unmarked trails in these areas.

In the vicinity of Chesapeake City are four managed hunting areas—**Elk Forest** (242 acres, 2 miles west of town), **Welch Point** (77 acres, 6 miles west), **Courthouse Point** (315 acres, 4 miles southwest), and **Bethel** (400 acres, just east). Elk Forest and Welch Point are on the north side of the canal, while the other two are on the south side. Hiking and seasonal hunting for waterfowl, squirrel, and deer are offered on all three areas.

The Elk Forest Area, which borders the C&D Canal, has two ponds that attract a variety of songbirds, waterfowl, and wildlife. Courthouse Point is a favorite among bird watchers in February and March when ducks, geese, and swans stop to rest and feed on the expansive mud flats during their spring migration.

In addition to the wildlife management areas, Elk Neck Demonstration Forest has 3,500 acres open for recreation (*see* page 206).

Directions: The Elk Forest area is 2 miles west of Chesapeake City off MD 213 via Boat Yard Road. Another way to access the area is to go 2 miles north on MD 213 and go left on Elk Forest Road about 1.5 miles to the area.

For Welch Point, go about 2 miles north of Chesapeake City on MD 213 and turn left on Elk Forest Road. Go about 4 miles to area.

For Courthouse Point, go 2 miles south of Chesapeake City on MD 213 and turn right on Courthouse Point Road. Go just over 2 miles. The area is on the left side of the

BEAVER
(Castor canadensis)
Beaver grow to 100 pounds and 5 feet long.

road. The area may also be reached by continuing another 1.5 miles on MD 213 and turning right on Shortcut Road. Go 0.5 mile and turn left on Town Point Road. Look for signs into the area after about 1 mile.

The Bethel area is on the right side of Bethel Road just east of Chesapeake City on the south side of the canal, extending along the canal into Delaware.

Activities: Hiking, hunting, bird watching.

Facilities: Unmarked trails.

Dates: Open sunrise to sunset, year-round. Call for hunting seasons.

Fees: None.

Closest town: Chesapeake City.

For more information: Maryland Department of Natural Resources Forest Service, Cecil County, phone (410) 287-5777.

Beaver

Evidence of dam building along with felled trees and the remaining chiseled, conical stumps give away the presence of this large, fascinating rodent at Elk Neck Demonstration Forest. The web-footed tracks of the beaver (*Castor canadensis*) rarely escape complete annihilation by its wide, flat tail that drags behind. Beavers do not always build lodges, but often excavate ground beneath tree roots or burrow into the stream bank. They also leave slippery U-shaped escape routes down stream embankments, much like an otter's slide.

EARLVILLE WMA

[Fig. 16(22)] This former fish hatchery in southern Cecil County consists of 190 acres managed especially as habitat for game animals such as white-tailed deer, cottontail rabbits, wild turkey, and bobwhite quail.

Besides the obvious appeal Earlville WMA has for hunters (permit required), it also attracts bird watchers, hikers, and naturalists who enjoy Maryland's less-developed and less-visited outdoor places. The unmarked trails are open to both hikers and mountain bikers. The Maryland Ornithological Society also conducts a Christmas Bird Count here.

The property is bisected by Cabin John Creek, which flows into the Elk River near its confluence with the Chesapeake Bay. Beavers have built several dams along a branch of the creek, backing up water into ponds that are popular with wood ducks. Bobwhite quail—ground-dwelling birds that increasingly are losing their habitat in the East—call their own name on spring and summer mornings from the overgrown fields. When a hiker stops to check a topo map, a rabbit bursts from cover, white tail flagging its getaway route.

Parts of the management practices involve planting new fields beside old abandoned ones and varying strips of short and long grasses. Wildlife thrives in such areas, which offer a mix of food and cover.

Directions: From Cecilton in southern Cecil County at the junction of MD 213 and 282, about 3 miles north of the Kent County line, go west on MD 282 (Grove Neck Road) about 3.5 miles. Turn right on Glebe Road and go about 2 miles. Go left on Fingerboard Schoolhouse Road and travel about 1.5 miles to the area.

Activities: Hunting (permit required), hiking, mountain biking, fishing, fox chasing (permit required), trapping (permit required), dog training, Christmas Bird Count.

Facilities: Two unmarked trails, disabled access.

Dates: Open from sunrise to sunset daily, year-round.

Fees: None.

Closest town: Cecilton is about 10 miles southeast.

For more information: Millington Work Center, phone (410) 928-3650.

ELK NECK DEMONSTRATION FOREST

[Fig. 16(23)] Elk Neck Demonstration Forest between North East and Elkton is made up of 3,500 acres of forest on poor, sandy soil. Once known as Elk Neck State Forest, Elk Neck was reclassified in 1983 to demonstrate wise forest management to owners of private woodlots.

The depleted soil, once subject to frequent fires, is being reclaimed by the state-managed forest. Fortunately for outdoor lovers, the uplands and bottomlands of Elk Neck are also open for recreational use, which includes hiking, archery, shooting, hunting, and primitive camping.

Directions: For the primitive camping area, from MD 213 south of Elkton, go west on US 40 approximately 1.8 miles. Turn left on Old Elk Neck Road and go 3.9 miles. Turn right on Irishtown Road and go 2.3 miles. Turn right into the entrance and go 0.9 mile on graveled Forest Trail 2. Turn right on Forest Trail 1 and go 1.6 miles to the camping area 1C, on the right.

Activities: Hiking, archery, shooting, hunting, primitive camping.

Facilities: Overlook tower, hiking trail, archery range, shooting range (permit required), primitive campground.

Dates: Open sunrise to sunset, year-round. Campground opens Apr. 1. Call for closing date.

Fees: None.

Closest town: North East is on the west side, and Elkton is a couple of miles northeast.

For more information: Elk Neck Demonstration Forest, phone (410) 287-5675, or Elk Neck State Park, phone (410) 287-5333.

RESTAURANTS OF CECIL COUNTY

The county's location at the head of the Chesapeake Bay is reflected in the many fine seafood restaurants here. A few are listed here.

HOWARD HOUSE RESTAURANT. 101 West Main Street, Elkton. Fine dining in a historic building, circa 1846. *Moderate. Phone (410) 398-4646.*

BAYARD HOUSE RESTAURANT. 11 Bohemia Avenue, Chesapeake City. Sample traditional Eastern Shore cooking with a hint of the Southwest. The restaurant overlooks the Chesapeake & Delaware Canal. Maryland crab cakes and Eastern Shore crab imperial are favorites. Serving lunch and dinner daily. *Inexpensive to moderate. Phone (410) 885-5040.*

CHESAPEAKE INN RESTAURANT & MARINA. 605 Second Street, Chesapeake City. Enjoy lunch or dinner overlooking the Chesapeake & Delaware Canal. Continental cuisine with Italian flare. Accessible by boat. *Moderate. Phone (410) 885-2040.*

WOODY'S CRAB HOUSE. 29 South Main Street, North East. One of Maryland's top 10 restaurants for steamed crabs and crab cakes. Voted Best of the Bay in 1997 by *Chesapeake Bay Magazine.* Features local art, casual atmosphere. Open Mar. through Dec. *Moderate. Phone (410) 287-3541.*

FAIR HILL INN. Fair Hill, Elkton. Lunch and dinner are served at this old inn (circa 1714), which is on the National Register of Historic Homes. Located at MD 273 and MD 213. *Moderate. Phone (410) 398-4187.*

LODGING IN CECIL COUNTY

Cecil County is well equipped with lodging facilities, including several historic inns. Here are a few suggestions of places to stay:

COMFORT INN. 61 Heather Lane, Perryville. Complimentary continental breakfast, weight room. *Moderate. Phone (410) 642-2866 or (800) 228-5150.*

CRYSTAL INN. 1 Center Drive, North East. Close to I-95, Exit 100. Indoor pool and hot tub, microwave and refrigerator in suite, restaurant. *Moderate to expensive. Phone (800) 631-3803.*

THE MILL HOUSE. 102 Mill Lane, North East. Built about 1710 for a mill owner and for quarters for his servants, this inn is on the Maryland Register of Historic Sites and is fully furnished with antiques. *Moderate. Phone (410) 287-3532.*

NORTH BAY YACHT B&B. 9 Sunset Drive, North East. Waterside, marina facilities. Sailing charters. *Moderate. Phone (410) 287-5948.*

THE BLUE MAX INN. 300 Bohemia Avenue, Chesapeake City. This Georgian Federal-style B&B is in the heart of the historical district of a city that was the hub of construction of the Chesapeake & Delaware Canal. Built in 1854, the inn is named for one-time owner Jack Hunter who wrote the bestseller, *The Blue Max.* Enjoy the spacious porches, fireside dining, and a solarium overlooking a fish pond. *Moderate to expensive. Phone (410) 885-2781.*

INN AT THE CANAL B&B. 104 Bohemia Avenue, Chesapeake City. Watch ships and boats from the waterside porch and from three of the rooms. A family that operated tugboats on the Chesapeake & Delaware Canal once owned the charming Victorian house. *Moderate to expensive. Phone (410) 885-5995.*

SHIP WATCH INN. C&D Canal, Chesapeake City. Located on the C&D Canal, this inn has contemporary decor and rooms with Jacuzzis. *Expensive. Phone (410) 885-5300.*

The Eastern Shore

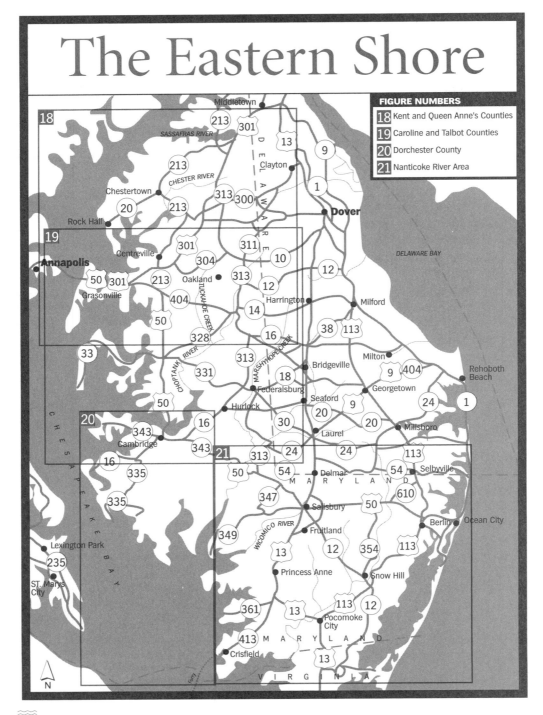

FIGURE NUMBERS

18	Kent and Queen Anne's Counties
19	Caroline and Talbot Counties
20	Dorchester County
21	Nanticoke River Area

The Eastern Shore: Maryland

The words Eastern Shore bring to mind a land of marshes, unbroken expanses of wild rice, loblolly pine forests, villages of hardy watermen, grand waterfront estates of ship captains, and the midnight calls of migrating geese, ducks, and swans. This version of the Eastern Shore does exist, but a traveler sometimes has to go out of the way to find it.

The Eastern Shore is comprised of several Maryland and Virginia counties located on what is called the Delmarva Peninsula, separated from the mainland to the west by the Chesapeake Bay, and washed by Delaware Bay and the Atlantic Ocean on the east. In addition to portions of Maryland and Virginia, the peninsula also contains the entire state of Delaware—hence the tri-state name, Delmarva.

Two modern bridges across the Chesapeake Bay now span the gap both physically and culturally between the Eastern Shore and the mainland of Maryland and Virginia.

[*Above:* Eastern Neck National Wildlife Refuge]

American Oyster

The American oyster (*Crassostrea virginica*) that lives in colonies in the Chesapeake Bay is best eaten during September through April, or during months that have the letter r in their name. Proper cooking completely destroys the bacterium *Vibrio vulnificus* that causes a risk to some people who eat raw oysters. The dangerous bacterium is more likely to be present during warm months. During late spring and summer, the quality and taste of the oyster deteriorates as this bottom dweller uses stored energy to produce spawn, and becomes thin and watery. For the uninitiated, eating this rather gelatinous sea creature *any* time may be a challenge. Said Jonathan Swift, "He was a bold man that first ate an oyster."

AMERICAN OYSTER
(*Crassostrea virginica*)

In 1952, the 4-mile William Preston Lane Jr. Memorial Bridge (usually called the Bay Bridge) replaced the ferry between Annapolis on the western shore and Queen Anne's County on the Eastern Shore. The 17.6-mile Chesapeake Bay Bridge-Tunnel at the mouth of the bay brought the nearly forgotten southern tip of Virginia's Eastern Shore in contact with mainland Virginia at Norfolk when it opened to traffic in 1964. With the bridges have come affluence, development, and new ideas, spilling out as from a cornucopia to this once isolated and fiercely conservative land.

Those who cruise north up the Chesapeake Bay may find themselves imagining how the land on this peninsula looked to early explorers. Captain John Smith, who left Jamestown in 1608 to explore the bay, named the Eastern Shore. He sailed north as far as the Sassafras River, which separates Cecil and Kent counties on what came to be called the Upper Shore.

Some 23 years later, people with a spirit of adventure began one of the Eastern Shore's first permanent settlements on Kent Island, the largest island in the Chesapeake Bay, and now part of Queen Anne's County. Surrounded by rich fishing waters, and with soil suitable for many kinds of farming beneath their feet, these pioneers began a long tradition of making a living from the sea and the soil, with little reliance on outsiders.

Other fishermen and farmers began to populate "The Shore" as it is known locally. But with no way to keep in touch with the outside world but by boat, people developed their own culture and traditions. The hardy individualism and even the British accent can still be found among the descendants of the first settlers. Generally, they reside in small fishing villages and on farms away from the city of Salisbury, Maryland, away from the resort town of Ocean City, Maryland, and away from the bridges and modern highways that are synonymous with change.

Maryland's claim to the Eastern Shore lies in the southeastern part of Cecil County (described in the previous section on Head of the Chesapeake Bay, page 194,) and in the counties of (from north to south) Kent, Queen Anne's, Caroline, Talbot, Dorchester, Wicomico, Somerset, and Worcester.

Several major waterways and innumerable tributaries wind their way through the lowlands of Maryland's Eastern Shore, offering abundant recreation opportunities to those equipped with fishing rods, crabbing gear, canoes, sailboats, motorboats, yachts, water-skis, Jet Skis, duck calls, binoculars, or cameras.

Major ports of call, full-service marinas, and a liberal sprinkling of boat ramps offer access to the rockfish, catfish, bass, pickerel, crappie, crabs, oysters, clams, and other riches of Eastern Shore waters. Many rivers and creeks take their colorful names from the Native Americans who fished these waters before white settlers arrived—names such as Choptank, Nanticoke, Wicomico, Manokin, Big Annemessex, and Pocomoke.

Highways on the peninsula are mostly level and many have wide, paved shoulders. Bicyclists, walkers, and joggers enjoy exploring the countryside using the designated shoulders, passing fields of soybeans, corn, tomatoes, peas, beans, cucumbers, canta-loupes, and melons.

Nature lovers, hikers, and bird watchers can find solitude in the wetlands and forested uplands of the abundant parks, preserves, wildlife management areas, and refuges on Maryland's Eastern Shore. Among the most well-known natural areas are the Eastern Neck Island National Wildlife Refuge (Kent County), the Horsehead Wetlands Center of the Wildfowl Trust of North America (Queen Anne's County), Blackwater National Wildlife Refuge (Dorchester County), Pocomoke River State Park (Worcester County), and Assateague Island National Seashore (Worcester County).

An incredible number of wildlife management areas—18 in the southern four counties of Maryland's Eastern Shore alone—provide habitat for birds and animals on islands, in the reeds and rushes of tidal wetlands, and in the oak and loblolly pine forests.

Tourist facilities such as restaurants and lodging can be found, among other places, at Chestertown in Kent County, in the Kent Island area of Queen Anne's County, in Easton and St. Michaels in Talbot County, in Cambridge in Dorchester County, in Salisbury in Wicomico County, in Princess Anne in Somerset County, and in Pocomoke City and Ocean City in Worcester County.

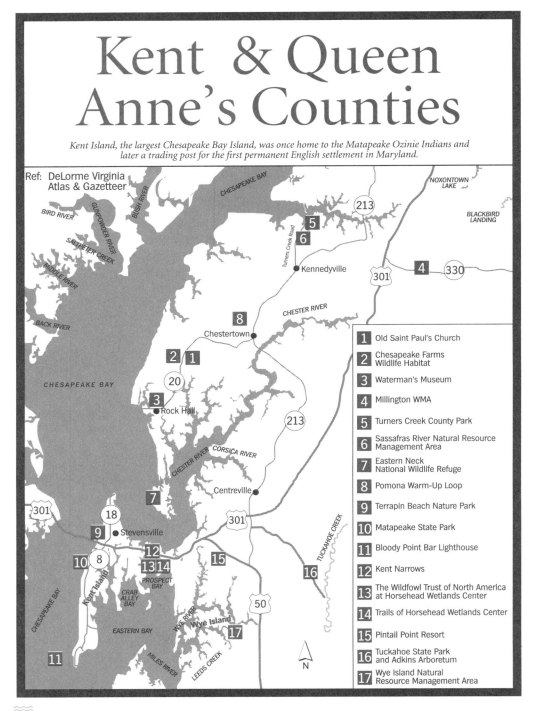

Kent & Queen Anne's Counties

Kent Island, the largest Chesapeake Bay Island, was once home to the Matapeake Ozinie Indians and later a trading post for the first permanent English settlement in Maryland.

Ref: DeLorme Virginia Atlas & Gazetteer

NOXONTOWN LAKE

BLACKBIRD LANDING

CHESAPEAKE BAY

BIRD RIVER

GUNPOWDER RIVER

BUSH RIVER

SALTPETER CREEK

MIDDLE RIVER

BACK RIVER

Turners Creek Road

213

5
6

Kennedyville

301
4
330

CHESTER RIVER

8

Chestertown

2 1

20

CHESAPEAKE BAY

3

Rock Hall

213

CHESTER RIVER

CORSICA RIVER

Centreville

7

301

301

18

9 Stevensville

10 8

12

13 14

15

PROSPECT BAY

CRAB ALLEY BAY

Kent Island

EASTERN BAY

WYE RIVER

Wye Island

17

LEEDS CREEK

MILES RIVER

50

TUCKAHOE CREEK

16

N

11

1	Old Saint Paul's Church
2	Chesapeake Farms Wildlife Habitat
3	Waterman's Museum
4	Millington WMA
5	Turners Creek County Park
6	Sassafras River Natural Resource Management Area
7	Eastern Neck National Wildlife Refuge
8	Pomona Warm-Up Loop
9	Terrapin Beach Nature Park
10	Matapeake State Park
11	Bloody Point Bar Lighthouse
12	Kent Narrows
13	The Wildfowl Trust of North America at Horsehead Wetlands Center
14	Trails of Horsehead Wetlands Center
15	Pintail Point Resort
16	Tuckahoe State Park and Adkins Arboretum
17	Wye Island Natural Resource Management Area

Kent County

On the Chesapeake Bay, between the Sassafras and Chester rivers on the part of the Eastern Shore known as the Upper Shore, is Kent County. The small and large boats resting in many back yards, tied to piers, and being pulled down the highway are testament to the fact that this county is embraced by water on three sides. Despite being Maryland's smallest county, Kent has 31 public boat landings.

The county's coastline varies from historic waterfront towns dotted with marinas to stretches of low, rolling farmland broken only by the tidal Chesapeake Bay rivers. Several cruising, sailing, and kayak operations take advantage of the scenery along the rivers and bay. Fishing charters and boat-rental facilities provide other options. Marinas are located in Chestertown, Georgetown, Galena, Great Oak, Tolchester, Worton, and Rock Hall. Rock Hall is a major port of call on the Eastern Shore. A brochure on cruising the waters of Kent County is available from the county's tourism office.

Automobile travelers seek out parks, wildlife preserves, small museums, and historic sites. Bicyclists pedal down country roads between expanses of fields and farms broken only by the occasional house, barn, and silo. Sporting clay ranges entice marksmen who wish to test their skills. A campground outside of Rock Hall offers a place to pitch a tent or park the family camper.

In addition to fantastic saltwater fishing opportunities, freshwater fishing is available at Urieville Lake off MD 213 about 5 miles north of Chestertown. This lake, which covers approximately 35 acres, has recently been undergoing restoration, but is scheduled to reopen in 2001. Largemouth bass, pickerel, crappie, yellow perch, white perch, and bluegill challenge the skills of anglers here. Facilities include car-top boat access, a fishing pier, and restrooms.

A comprehensive brochure describing a 110-mile self-guided driving tour is available from the Kent County Office of Tourism. The two-part historic tour includes 19 sites from Chestertown to Rock Hall and 17 sites in the upper county.

For more information: Kent County Office of Tourism, 100 North Cross Street, Chestertown, MD 21620. Phone (410) 778-0416. Kent County Public Works, information and permits to use public landings, phone (410) 778-7439.

CHESTERTOWN AREA

Chestertown, the county seat for Kent County, is located on the Chester River and MD 213 just north of the Queen Anne's County line. Court records date back to the 1640s. The town became a busy port of entry in the 1700s, with a tremendous influx of colonists. It also became known for its shipbuilding industry.

On a quiet corner at 346 Cannon Street, tucked between colonial houses with their brick sidewalks, is the **Schooner Sultana Shipyard** (410-778-6461). Today, in the tradition of craftsmen from the past when great shipyards lined the banks of the Chester River and ships from around the world anchored at local harbors, shipbuilders and their students may be found creating authentic reproductions of the 1767 schooner *Sultana*. This eighteenth century schooner is one of the few American-built vessels from the Colonial period for which extensive documentation has survived. Year-round, the public is invited to witness the work of hewing frames, steaming planks, forging iron, and sewing sails.

Another fine way to get the flavor and historic value of Chestertown is to sail up the Chester River. Along the banks are the grand multistoried homes of eighteenth and nineteenth century merchants who built along the waterfront. Chestertown is also an attractive sight to motorists crossing the Chester River on the MD 213 bridge, where black lampposts stand out against the stately homes on the far side.

Attractions include the **Hynson-Ringgold House** with its antler staircase, and **Widehall**, noted for its magnificent gardens and Georgian architecture dating from 1769. Both are on Water Street. Beside the public dock at the bottom of High Street is the old **Customs House**, built in the 1740s, with its exquisite Flemish Bond brickwork.

Visitors who come in September can take the Candlelight Walking Tour, sponsored by the Kent County Historical Society, to gain entrance into many historic homes. Tours are also offered in October and December. The elegant walled gardens of some of these homes are opened to visitors in spring and summer when flowering dogwoods, azaleas, tulips, and daffodils stand out against evergreen trees and well-groomed hedges.

Those looking for live entertainment in Chestertown can find it every Thursday through Saturday night, beginning at 9:30, at **Andy's** (410-778-6779) at 337-1/2 High Street. Evening concerts are held on summer evenings beside the antique fountain in the town square.

The **Visitor Center** at the county tourism office at 100 North Cross Street can provide information on self-guided walking, biking, and driving tours of the county, and a walking guide to the shady, brick streets of the Chestertown historic district.

For more information: Kent County Office of Tourism, 100 North Cross Street, Chestertown, MD 21620. Phone (410) 778-0416.

OLD SAINT PAUL'S CHURCH

[Fig. 18(1)] On Sandy Bottom Road between Chestertown and Rock Hall, beneath the shade of ancient oaks, is an Episcopal church that is the oldest continuously used church in the state. Some of the huge, gnarled trees are more than 300 years old, including the massive Maryland Bicentennial Tree at the edge of the parking lot. Actress Tallulah Bankhead is buried in the cemetery, where gravestones date to the 1600s. The church is open 9 to 5 daily, year-round. Friendly parishioners enjoy chatting about the restored Vestry House, which was built in 1766. A millpond down the hill from the church is full of chattering ducks and geese in winter.

Directions: From Chestertown, take US 20 about 7 miles west. Go left on Sandy Bottom Road to the junction with Ricauds Branch-Langford Road. The church is on the left.

For more information: Old Saint Paul's Church, phone (410) 778-3180 or (410) 778-1540.

CHESAPEAKE FARMS WILDLIFE HABITAT

[Fig. 18(2)] Drive through this 3,000-acre wildlife and agricultural demonstration area set aside by the Du Pont Company to protect soil, water, wildlife, and waterfowl. The area is located on both sides of MD 20, about 8 miles west of Chestertown. On the 5-mile Wildlife Drive that leads off from the north side of MD 20, a visitor might see a kestrel hovering above its prey in a cutover field or a young bald eagle making ungainly attempts at flight. Early mornings and evenings in spring are good times to hear the sound of bobwhite quail. Osprey construct huge nests of sticks in tall trees, while kingfishers build in holes on the side of dirt banks.

Sanctuary Pond Drive is a short road on the south side of MD 20 that goes by a pond and comes back to the highway. It's the place to catch quacking ducks and honking geese as they land and take off from the pond.

Directions: Chesapeake Farms is located on the north side of MD 20, about 8 miles west of Chestertown. Look for signs indicating Wildlife Drive on the north side of the highway and Sanctuary Pond Drive on the south side.

Activities: Wildlife observation.

Facilities: Two scenic drives.

Dates: Wildlife Drive is open sunrise to sunset daily, from Feb. 1 to Oct. 10. Sanctuary Pond Drive is open sunrise to sunset daily, year-round.

Fees: None.

Closest town: Chestertown is 8 miles east.

For more information: Chesapeake Farms Wildlife Habitat, 7319 Remington Drive, Chestertown, MD 21620. Phone (410) 778-8400.

ROCK HALL

[Fig. 18] Rock Hall is located on a harbor on Kent County's Chesapeake Bay frontage where MD 20 meets MD 445 north of Eastern Neck Island. With its 15 marinas, excellent seafood restaurants, June rockfish tournament, and Party on the Bay in August, Rock Hall attracts pleasure boaters from all over the Chesapeake.

The community has several sailing and powerboat charters, fishing boat charters, and a kayak outfitter. Options include half-day, sunrise, and sunset trips, as well as overnight charters to Chestertown, Great Oak, or Georgetown. Weekend and weeklong destinations include the ports of Annapolis, St. Michaels, and Baltimore's Inner Harbor. *See* Appendix A, page 315, for charter operators.

This historic town, where George Washington, Thomas Jefferson, and James Madison used to disembark on their journeys to Philadelphia, is also a popular destination for motorists. Its comfortable bed and breakfast inns, its gift shops and restaurants at **Oyster Court**, and its festivals draw people back year after year for relaxation, shopping, dining, and fun.

Among the colorful shops and restaurants on Main Street is **Durding's Store**, a restoration of an ice cream parlor that opened in 1872. Also, at the intersection of MD 20

American Woodcock

The American woodcock (*Phylohela minor*) seems to have been made by a committee. The stubby body has almost no tail, a head too small for its body, and a long beak that seems out of proportion. When flushed, however, the woodcock darts and weaves through the woods with incredible agility, quickly putting distance between itself and the intruder. Perhaps its most amazing show is the spring courtship flight, which usually takes place in the evening, just before complete darkness. The male circles a field making a nasal "peent" sound, then climbs in spirals high in the air and plummets down, chittering all the while.

AMERICAN WOODCOCK
(*Philohela minor*)

and MD 445 is the **Rock Hall Snack Bar**, a small, plain building on the outside. However, the restaurant opens at 4 a.m., providing customers time to get breakfast and make it to the Eastern Neck Wildlife Refuge for an early morning bird walk. The short-order cook is excellent, and the pancakes are so large they overflow the platter. A visitor who comes a second time is likely to have a cup of coffee waiting on the counter when he or she opens the door. An outdoor store with hunting and fishing supplies is located on MD 20, just east of town.

WATERMAN'S MUSEUM

[Fig. 18(3)] Exhibits on oystering, crabbing, and fishing depict the hard life of the Chesapeake Bay waterman at this museum. Historical photographs, local carvings, and a reproduction of a shanty house help bring to life a fascinating existence. Visitors can also investigate authentic workboats.

Directions: The museum is located on MD 20 in Rock Hall, next to Haven Harbor Marina.

Dates: Open 10 to 5 daily, year-round, except major holidays. If the museum is locked, obtain a key from the marina next door.

Fees: None.

For more information: Waterman's Museum, 20880 Rock Hall Avenue, Rock Hall, MD 21661. Phone (410) 778-6697.

MILLINGTON WILDLIFE MANAGEMENT AREA

[Fig. 18(4)] Four miles north of Millington on Kent County's eastern border is the state's 3,800-acre Millington Wildlife Management Area. Here, anglers can try their luck at four farm ponds stocked with bass, bluegill, and crappie. Hunters—and people who enjoy watching wildlife—come for the white-tailed deer, gray squirrels, red foxes, raccoons, rabbits, ducks, geese, bobwhite quail, wild turkeys, mourning doves, and woodcocks.

Trails take hikers, mountain bikers, horseback riders, and hunters into woods where Lenni Lenape Indians once stalked their prey. Bird watchers who look in mature oak trees may spot the black-and-white pileated woodpecker (*Dryocopus pileatus*) with its brilliant red crest. Nesting warblers are well hidden in brushy undergrowth or distant treetops, but their distinctive territorial and courtship songs aid in identification. Bluebirds check out nesting cavities in spring. Baltimore orioles and bald eagles may also be sighted.

Trails are somewhat rough—what managers call "underdeveloped." An excellent map of the area, showing the location of trails, roads, and ponds, is available at the main parking area. During hunting seasons, any nonhunters should wear blaze orange for safety.

Directions: From Massey, in eastern Kent County, go east on MD 330 (Massey-Delaware Line Road) approximately 1.5 miles. The main parking area and an information box with map and permits are on the left.

Activities: Fishing, hunting, hiking, mountain biking, horseback riding.

Facilities: Hiking trails, fish ponds.

Dates: Open sunrise to sunset, year-round. Hunting seasons run dawn to dusk, Monday through Saturday, from Sept. through Jan. and from mid-Apr. to mid-May. Call for dates for specific game.

Fees: None.

Closest town: Massey is 1.5 miles from the western edge of the area.

For more information: Millington Wildlife Management Area, Route 1, Box 552, Massey MD 21650. Phone (410) 928-3650 or (410) 778-1948.

TURNERS CREEK COUNTY PARK

[Fig. 18(5)] Hikers and wildlife observers enjoy this park for the 147 acres of nature trails, the open fields, and the waterfront bluff overlooking the Sassafras River at the scenic mouth of Turners Creek. The area is located at the north end of Turners Creek Road off MD 298 about 4 miles north of Kennedyville and 11 miles north of Chestertown.

A public boat ramp gives anglers access to the river's good fishing. Canoeists and kayakers enjoy the unspoiled scenery of the high cliffs on the western side of the creek. Picnickers can use a pavilion surrounded by water. The park has a volleyball area, a play area for children, and horseshoe pits. The **Kent County Farm Museum** is located on Turners Creek Road just south of the park. The museum houses artifacts that demonstrate farming practices from past to present. In August, a Threshing Day Dinner is held at Turners Creek Landing to raise funds for the museum's operation.

Directions: From Chestertown, go north on MD 213 about 7 miles to Kennedyville. Turn left on Turners Creek Road and drive about 4 miles to the boat landing at the end of road. The museum is located just south of the boat landing.

Activities: Hiking, fishing, boating, picnicking, volleyball, horseshoes.

Facilities: Hiking trails, boat ramp, picnic pavilion, volleyball area, children's play area, horseshoe pit, restrooms in basement of historic Latham House, nearby farm museum.

Dates: The boat landing is open daily, year-round. The Latham House and restrooms are open seasonally. The museum is open on the first and third Saturday of each month, from Apr. through Oct.

Fees: There is a pavilion rental fee for groups and an admission fee for the farm museum.

Closest town: Kennedyville is 4 miles south and Chestertown is 11 miles south.

For more information: Turners Creek County Park, phone (410) 778-1948. Kent County Farm Museum, phone (410) 348-5721.

SASSAFRAS RIVER NATURAL RESOURCE MANAGEMENT AREA

[Fig. 18(6)] The 1,000-acre Sassafras River Natural Resource Management Area is one of the most recent acquisitions of the state Forest and Park Service. This former cattle farm borders the west side of Turners Creek (*see* page 217) and the Sassafras River in northern Kent County, about 3.5 miles north of Kennedyville.

Old roads and trails lace the area, and work is beginning on a new trail system for hikers, mountain bikers, and horseback riders that will lead into the 1,000 acres of rolling farmland, sandy beaches, marshes, a tidal pond, and hardwood forests. The different habitats provide a great variety of wildlife and plants. White-tailed deer, gray squirrels, and chipmunks live in the relatively mature forests of oak, sycamore, tulip poplar, sweetgum, and hickory. Muskrats and beaver roam the marshes, while groundhogs, rabbits, and red foxes prefer the field habitat.

Geese and ducks are abundant, as are songbirds and shorebirds, including the elegant great blue heron. Bald eagles nest in the area, but observers are asked to give them a wide berth. Eagles often abandon nest sites when disturbed.

A killdeer (*Charadrius vociferus*) may suddenly run ahead of a hiker, dragging an apparent broken wing. The big act is a necessity for this plover that builds its nest on open ground, its eggs an easy target for any fox, raccoon, skunk, or domestic cat that happens upon them. Once the predator is lured away by the seemingly wounded bird, the killdeer flies off, screaming its own name.

Visitors to the management area should not go near the high cliffs on the western side of the area. The unstable cliffs could give way under a person's weight. The manager also asks that visitors stay away from any old structures. Vehicles are restricted to the parking area. Access is limited to hikers, bikers, horseback riders, anglers, and hunters. Blaze-orange clothing is recommended for all nonhunters using the area during hunting season.

Directions: From Chestertown, drive north on MD 213 about 7 miles. Turn left on MD 292 (Turners Creek Road) and drive about 3.5 miles to parking area, on left.

Turners Creek County Park (*see* page 217) is less than a mile farther, at the end of the road.

Activities: Hiking, biking, horseback riding, picnicking, fishing, limited camping for organized youth groups, seasonal deer hunting by lottery.

Facilities: There are trails for hiking, biking, and horseback riding, and a youth camping area.

Dates: Open 8 a.m. to sunset, year-round.

Fees: None.

Closest town: Kennedyville is about 3.5 miles south and Chestertown is about 10 miles south.

For more information: Sassafras River Natural Resource Management Area, c/o Tuckahoe State Park, 13070 Crouse Mill Road, Queen Anne, MD 21657. Phone (410) 820-1668.

EASTERN NECK NATIONAL WILDLIFE REFUGE

[Fig. 18(7)] Like the dot on an exclamation point, Eastern Neck Island is located south of the long finger of land called Eastern Neck in the southwestern corner of Kent County. The tidal Chester River and the Chesapeake Bay surround it. Most of the traveling public passes through Rock Hall and arrives on Eastern Neck Island by way of the MD 445 bridge on the northern end. There are no bridges to connect the island to Kent Island, just 3 miles south. Three miles—not much in distance, but a long way in attitude.

Kent Island, connected to the mainland of Maryland by the Bay Bridge and US 50/ 301, has become a bedroom community for commuters and an enticement for multitudes of people from the western shore who want a great seafood meal, a sunset cruise, a weekend in a plush hotel, or a fishing adventure.

The only residence on Eastern Neck Island, on the other hand, is occupied by staff of the Eastern Neck National Wildlife Refuge. That, plus a few birdhouses.

Over the millennia, on its way to becoming a wildlife refuge, 2,285-acre Eastern Neck Island has worn quite a few hats. Some 4,000 years ago, it served the needs of Woodland Period Indians. Ozinie Indians of the Nanticoke-speaking Algonquin tribe were collecting shells from the area to craft their exquisite beads about the time of Capt. John Smith's arrival in 1608. In the mid-to-late 1600s, a grand mansion called Wickliffe was the hub of a tobacco plantation here. The island may have even served as the county seat for a time.

Smaller farms ruled in the 1800s and a fishing village sprang up at Bogles Wharf on the eastern side. In the early 1900s, the tremendous concentration of wintering waterfowl in the inlets, ponds, and marshes brought hunters to the island. When a developer subdivided Eastern Neck Island into small lots for a housing development, concerned citizens prompted the U. S. Fish and Wildlife Service to acquire the valuable land in the 1960s to protect its wildlife and wildfowl.

Beneficiaries of the acquisition that was to become the wildlife refuge include the endangered Delmarva fox squirrel (*Sciurus niger cinereus*), the threatened southern bald eagle (*Haliaeetus leucocephalus*), and the threatened peregrine falcon (*Falco peregrinus*).

Delmarva Fox Squirrel

The endangered Delmarva fox squirrel (*Sciurus niger cinereus*) may be 30 inches long—much larger than the far more common Eastern gray squirrel. Also, the fox squirrel rarely leaps from tree to tree like its more agile cousin. The secretive mammal spends a great deal of time on the ground foraging for nuts in the open forests of mature oak and pine that it inhabits. As it ages, the fox's silver-gray fur may turn almost white. Despite the differences, the endangered squirrel may still be hard to identify with certainty, silhouetted against the sky, high in a scrub pine.

Also, some 40,000 waterfowl find protection on the island at peak times, including an estimated 20,000 Canada geese (*Branta canadensis*), 7,000 tundra swans (*Olor columbianus*), and 15,000 canvasbacks (*Aythya valisineria*). Mallards, wigeons, black ducks, lesser scaups, buffleheads, green-winged teal, blue-winged teal, pintails, and redheads swim in the coves and fill the skies with sight and sound.

Marsh and shorebirds including long-legged herons and tiny sandpipers thrive in the refuge. The woods, cornfields, and undergrowth attract woodpeckers, flycatchers, swallows, wrens, finches, warblers, bluebirds, hawks, and owls.

Around marshy areas during the day are muskrats and several varieties of turtles and frogs. White-tailed deer materialize in the fields at dusk. The nocturnal red fox, beaver, raccoon, and opossum may sometimes be spotted in the early or late part of the day.

And finally, the people who visit the refuge are beneficiaries. Nearly 6 miles of trails, including three wildlife trails and a handicapped-accessible boardwalk, lead into some of the 500 acres of forest, the 1,000 acres of brackish tidal marshes, and the 700 acres of croplands and grasslands where these birds and animals live. Binoculars are a huge help, especially on the boardwalk trail. Dogs are permitted on leash.

Any time of year will provide rewards. Waterfowl are especially abundant from late September until the last of March. Unusual sightings such as a cinnamon teal may bring birders from 100 miles away for a chance to add something to a life list.

Bald eagles and great horned owls establish territories in late fall and early winter, build their nests in January, lay eggs in February, and usually begin feeding nestlings in April. Woodcocks perform their mating ritual over fields in late winter and early spring. Many species of songbirds pass through the refuge on their migration routes in both spring and fall.

White-tailed fawns, young foxes, and other baby animals can be seen from spring through summer. The plantings of the new butterfly garden near the refuge office attract a variety of butterflies in spring, summer, and fall. The handicapped-accessible stone-dust trail to the garden and the garden itself were completely built by volunteers.

Ingleside Landing Recreation Area on the northwest side of the island is available seasonally for crabbing, car-top boat launching, and picnicking. **Bogles's Wharf** is on the east side of the island. Those who have a county permit (not available at the refuge) may launch trailered boats here. Anglers may fish from the bridge across Eastern Neck Narrows at the refuge entrance. A john-boat rental, open from June 1 to September 30, is located just north of Eastern Neck Narrows.

Directions: From Rock Hall, go south on MD 445 about 6 miles across the bridge at Eastern Neck Narrows onto Eastern Neck Island, where the refuge begins.

Activities: Wildlife and wildfowl observation, hiking, boating, fishing, crabbing, seasonal hunting by permit.

Facilities: Hiking trails, car-top boat ramp, picnic tables, observation towers, visitor center/office, restrooms.

Dates: The refuge is open from a half-hour before sunrise to a half-hour after sunset daily, year-round. There are about five Mondays, five Fridays, and one Saturday in fall that the refuge is closed for managed hunts. The bookstore and office are open from 7:30 to 3:30 on weekdays. The boat launch and picnic area are open May 1 through Sept. 30. The boat rental store outside the refuge is open from 6 to 6 daily, June 1 through Sept. 30.

Fees: None.

Closest town: Rock Hall is about 6 miles north.

For more information: Eastern Neck National Wildlife Refuge, 1730 Eastern Neck Road, Rock Hall, MD 21661. Phone (410) 639-7056. Eastern Neck Boat Rental, phone (410) 639-7100 or (410) 639-7017.

HIKING AT EASTERN NECK NATIONAL WILDLIFE REFUGE

The easy, level hiking trails provide access into each of the refuge's habitats. Insect repellent and/or protective clothing are a must during warm months.

The **Boxes Point Trail** is a 1.2-mile round trip to open ponds and a marsh at Boxes Point on Eastern Neck Narrows on the island's northeastern corner. The trailhead is on the left, 0.7 mile from the refuge entrance.

The **Tubby Cove Boardwalk Trail**, observation platform, and restrooms are 0.8 mile from the entrance. The beautifully constructed boardwalk is handicapped-accessible. The trail is a 0.25-mile round trip.

Signs emerging from the marsh on either side of the boardwalk describe the values of a marsh in controlling sedimentation, filtering water, sheltering birds and animals, and providing vegetation that small organisms feed on in an important first step in the aquatic food chain.

Vegetation growing from the marsh includes Olney three-square (*Scirpus olneyi*), which has three-sided stems, narrow-leaved cattail (*Typhus augustifolia*), and saltmarsh cordgrass (*Spartina

DELMARVA FOX
SQUIRREL
(*Sciurus niger cinereus*)

alterniflora). Saltmarsh cordgrass, which dominates the marsh, is the most important species of marsh plant in the Chesapeake Bay estuary. As the tides flood the marsh and recede, the waters flush out enormous amounts of decaying plant detritus from the cordgrass, along with accompanying algae and bacteria that are important to the complex life cycle of the bay.

At the far end of the boardwalk is a short, pine-strewn path to two observation towers. A grove of scrub pines allows an observer to walk the ramp to the tower without being seen by marsh birds and animals.

For the **Duck Inn Trail**, go left on Bogles Wharf Road about 1.25 miles from the refuge entrance and park at the trailhead on the left. This 1-mile trail (round-trip) leads through a marsh to the Chester River. Bogles Wharf Landing is at the end of Bogles Wharf Road.

The **Wildlife Trail** parking area is on the left, about 1.7 miles from the entrance. This 0.5-mile path loops through a mature forest of white oak, blackjack oak, red oak, tulip poplar, and loblolly pine. White-tailed deer browse the understory, helping to keep the undergrowth down. The open woods with nearby cornfields and grassy areas provide perfect habitat for the Delmarva fox squirrel. An annual deer hunt helps keep the population in check so a burgeoning deer herd doesn't completely consume the same mast that the squirrels need for survival.

BICYCLING KENT COUNTY

Like much of the Eastern Shore, the flat, lightly traveled roads of Kent County are a cyclist's dream. As a bonus, the scenery includes expansive farmland, pine and hardwood forests, wetland ponds and marshes, historic villages, and sunlit sails out on the Chesapeake Bay.

The Baltimore Bicycle Club has developed route descriptions for several bicycle trails, all beginning and ending at Washington College on MD 213 in Chestertown. Parking is available on MD 213 at Washington Square, north of the college. The rides range from the 11-mile **Pomona Warm-Up** that winds through the countryside around Chestertown to the 81.5-mile **Pump House Primer**, which extends north to the Chesapeake & Delaware Canal in Cecil County. The route descriptions give the accumulated mileage at each turn. Tips on where to find food and lodging are included. The route descriptions and a detailed bicycling map are available from the county office of tourism.

The 36-mile **Kent and Queen Anne's Loop** crosses the Chester River at Millington and returns to Chestertown via Queen Anne's County, passing an excellent lunch spot at Unicorn Community Lake. The 50-mile Rock Hall ramble takes in historic Rock Hall and the Eastern Neck Wildlife Refuge.

POMONA WARM-UP LOOP

[Fig. 18(8)] This 11-mile loop leads through countryside west of Chestertown, passing fields where red foxes hunt for voles and mice. On Brices Mill Road, elegant homes sit at the end of driveways lined with old cedars, and horses graze in large paddocks. Mock-orange trees drop their nubby green fruits beside the road. Along Langford-Pomona Road are wide-open fields backed by dark pine forests, and the closest thing to a ringing phone is the meadowlark singing its country song atop a telephone pole.

Trail: 11-mile easy bicycle loop on paved county roads on the western side of Chestertown.

Directions: Go north from Washington College on MD 291 for 0.4 mile. On the north side of Chestertown, turn left on MD 291. Go 0.6 mile and turn right on MD 20. Go 1.2 miles and turn left on Brices Mill Road. Go 1.9 miles and turn left on Lankford-Pomona Road. Go 0.4 mile and turn right, still on Lankford-Pomona Road, at the Airy Hill sign. Go 1.5 miles and turn left on MD 289 (Quaker Neck Road). Go 4.2 miles and turn left on High Street. Go 0.1 mile and turn right on Cross Street. Go 0.1 mile and turn left on MD 213. Go 0.6 mile to Washington College.

For more information: Kent County Bicycle Tour, Kent County Office of Tourism, 100 North Cross Street, Chestertown, MD 21620. Phone (410) 778-0416. Bike repairs are available at Bikework, 208 South Cross Street, Chestertown. Phone (410) 778-6940.

BEACHES IN KENT COUNTY

There are two public beaches in Kent County, one at Betterton, and one at Rock Hall.

BETTERON BEACH. This sandy beach is at a 3.2-acre park at the northern end of MD 292 at Betterton. Betterton is located on the Chesapeake Bay at the mouth of the Sassafras River. There are picnic areas and a pavilion, volleyball courts, a bathhouse, a stone fishing jetty, and a boat ramp. Lifeguards on weekends. Nettle-free swimming in summer. Free parking. Phone (410) 778-1948.

ROCK HALL TOWN BEACH. This small swimming beach and gazebo, known locally as Ferry Park, is located on Beach Road at Rock Hall. Picnic tables, barbecue stands, pavilions. Outstanding view across Chesapeake Bay to western shore.

RESTAURANTS IN KENT COUNTY

Most of Kent County's restaurants are in the towns of Chestertown and Rock Hall.

THE KENNEDYVILLE INN. 11986 Augustine Herman Highway (MD 213), Kennedyville. This restaurant features pit barbecue and micro-brewed beers, house-made pasta and desserts, daily seafood specials, and light fare items. Excellent wine list. Open for dinner Wednesday through Sunday. *Moderate. Phone (410) 348-2400.*

IMPERIAL HOTEL AND RESTAURANT. 208 High Street, Chestertown. Chesapeake foods such as duck, crab, and oysters are exquisitely prepared at this Victorian inn. *Moderate. Phone (410) 778-5000.*

THE OLD WHARF. Cannon Street, Chestertown. Make reservations for this popular waterfront restaurant. Steaks and Chesapeake Bay seafood are on the menu. *Moderate. Phone (410) 778-3566.*

AMERICA'S CUP CAFE. 745 Main Street, Rock Hall. This coffee house and sidewalk cafe features Miss America's Crab Cakes on its light-fare menu. *Inexpensive. Phone (410) 639-7361.*

THE BAY WOLF. 21270 Rock Hall Avenue, Rock Hall. Local favorite known for its varied cuisine and excellent service. The menu includes fresh catch of the day, crab cakes, surf and turf, Austrian pork roast, and Wiener Schnitzel. *Inexpensive to moderate. Phone* (410) 639-2000

OLD OARS INN. Main Street, Rock Hall. This old inn was converted into a restaurant. Located in the colorful historic district. Try the grilled catfish sandwich or spicy perch sandwich. *Inexpensive. Phone (410) 639-2541.*

WATERMAN'S CRABHOUSE. Sharp Street Wharf, Rock Hall. This seafood restaurant overlooks Rock Hall Harbor. Shuttle service is available to local marinas. Fresh seafood includes crab cakes, soft-shell crab, crab imperial, oysters, flounder, and more. *Inexpensive to moderate. Phone (410) 639-2261.*

LODGING IN KENT COUNTY

Here is a sampling of the excellent historic bed and breakfasts, country inns, and motels in Kent County.

CHESAPEAKE INNS. PO Box 609, Chestertown, MD 21620. This is an association of inns in the Chestertown area that have historic and/or architectural significance. Included are Great Oak Manor, The Inn at Rolphs's Wharf, Hill's Inn, and The Harbor Inn at Rock Hall. *Expensive. Phone (in-state) (301) 778-INNS, or (out-of-state) (800) 662-INNS.*

THE PARKER HOUSE B&B. 108 Spring Avenue, Chestertown. Located in Chestertown's Historic District, this three-room inn has a relaxing atmosphere, and is filled with bright and airy furnishings. *Moderate to expensive. Phone (410) 778-9041.*

BRAMPTON BED AND BREAKFAST INN. 25227 Chestertown Road, Chestertown. This former plantation house, listed on the National Register of Historic Places, dates back to the mid-1800s. Note the 3.5-story walnut-and-ash staircase. On the 35-acre grounds between the Chester River and the Chesapeake Bay are 100-year-old trees and boxwoods. *Expensive. Phone (410) 778-1860.*

THE MARINER'S MOTEL. 5657 South Hawthorne Avenue, Rock Hall. This landmark motel combines proximity to the town center with tranquility. It has a pool, picnic gazebo, dog walk area, horseshoes, bike rentals, and a playground. *Moderate. Phone (410) 639-2224.*

NORTH POINT MOTEL AND MARINA. 5639 Walnut Street, Rock Hall. Sunsets on the Chesapeake Bay are a highlight of this motel with bay-front rooms, a swimming pool, and a covered picnic area. *Moderate. Phone (410) 639-2907.*

BAY BREEZE INN. 5758 Main Street, Rock Hall. Dates from the 1920s, when goose hunters would stay at what was then called the Old Crosby Property. Read by the fire in the library and have breakfast on the patio. Located on restored Main Street. *Expensive. Phone (410) 639-2061.*

THE INN AT OSPREY POINT. 20786 Rock Hall Avenue, Rock Hall. This luxurious inn is located on 30 acres of tranquil waterfront in the village of Rock Hall. A gourmet restaurant and marina facilities are next to the inn. *Expensive. Phone (410) 639-2194.*

SWAN HAVEN BED AND BREAKFAST. 20950 Rock Hall Avenue, Rock Hall. This waterfront inn, complete with a dock, is a short walk from Rock Hall's restaurants and shops. Explore protected inlet waters by canoe, kayak, or motorized john boat or dinghy. *Moderate to expensive. Phone (410) 639-2527.*

Queen Anne's County

A visitor arriving on the Eastern Shore by way of the Bay Bridge and US 50/301 from Annapolis and points west will be greeted with a very different first impression of Queen Anne's County than someone entering the county on either one of those highways from the north or from the south.

The Bay Bridge has brought not only tourism and accompanying lodging and eateries to Maryland's Eastern Shore, but also permanent residents who live on scenic Kent Island and commute to work across the bridge to the west. Coming into the county from the north on US 301 or MD 213, or from the south on US 50, however, motorists are greeted to views of woodlands and peaceful farm country, the quiet villages of watermen and farmers, historic churches, and restored homes built by early traders and ship captains.

Residents are justifiably proud of their attractions on Kent Island and the western side of the mainland. But there's more.

To the north, the Chester River separates Queen Anne's County from Kent County. Anglers put in at boat landings off MD 544 north of Kingstown and Chestertown in pursuit of largemouth bass, striped bass, pickerel, crappie, channel catfish, and bluegill.

On the east side, the county borders Kent County, Delaware, and Caroline County, Maryland. The calm, shaded waters of Tuckahoe Creek between Queen Anne's and Caroline counties are perfect for canoeing. Tuckahoe State Park is tucked into the southeastern corner of the county.

To the south, the Queen Anne Highway (MD 404) and a tributary of the Wye River called the Wye East River separate Queen Anne's County from Talbot County. The Wye River, which penetrates the county north to Queenstown, gained international fame in 1998 as the site where the Wye River Accord was signed between the Palestinians and the Israelis.

At the headwaters of the Wye East River is the small **Wye Mills Community Lake**, with largemouth bass, crappie, pickerel, and bluegill fishing. A picnic area and restrooms are available. The lake is located in a triangle created by US 50, MD 404, and MD 213.

Queen Anne's County has a total of nine public boat ramps and 11 more carry-down landings for car-top boats. Call (410) 758-0835 for the necessary permit. Several hunting preserves are spread across the county, and boat rentals and charters for crabbing and fishing are plentiful. The county's Office of Tourism can provide an up-to-date list.

For more information: Queen Anne's County Office of Tourism, 425 Piney Narrows Road, Suite 3, Chester, MD 21619. Phone (410) 604-2100 or (888) 400-RSVP; E-mail tourism@qac.org. Queen Anne's County Chamber of Commerce, 1561 Postal Road, PO Box 511, Chester, MD 21619. Phone (410) 643-8530, E-mail qacchamber@friend.ly.net.

CENTREVILLE

[Fig. 18] With a strategic location at the head of the Corsica River, Centreville once engaged in a brisk shipping trade. The old homes and quiet tree-lined streets of this county seat are Americana—the kind of place many people would like to spend their childhood. Typical of many Eastern Shore towns, Centreville's colonial past has left a mix of architecture ranging from examples of the stark and simple Federal period to ornate Victorian homes with spacious porches.

The **County Courthouse** at 100 Courthouse Square has been in continuous use since 1792—longer than any other courthouse in the state. Note the bronze statue of the county's namesake, Queen Anne, on the courthouse lawn. Queen Anne was the British monarch when the county was founded in 1706.

One of the oldest houses in town is the **Tucker House**, built about 1792, at 124 South Commerce Street, where the smell of fresh bagels causes visitors to make a detour into the bakery next door. The Tucker House with its six fireplaces and herb gardens once served as a town house. **Wright's Chance** (circa 1744) was built as a plantation house, then moved to its present site at 119 South Commerce Street and restored. Highlights inside include exquisite Hepplewhite and Chippendale furniture. These buildings are open for tours by request.

At Front and Corsica streets is the **old wharf** where ships used to dock, now a public landing. The row of homes at the wharf was built by a ship captain for members of his crew and their families.

Of particular interest to those interested in Chesapeake Bay lore is the **Queen Anne's Museum of Eastern Shore Life** at 126 Dulin Clark Road. Artifacts the visitor may examine here give a glimpse into the area's history of agriculture, transportation, and watermen, and into the everyday lives of previous Eastern Shore residents.

Canoeists can put into the Corsica River at Centreville for a pleasant paddle in either direction.

For more information: Town Hall of Centreville, 101 Lawyers Row, Centreville, MD 21617. Phone (410) 758-1180. Queen Anne's Museum of Eastern Shore Life, PO Box 188, Centreville, MD 21617. Phone (410) 758-0166 or (410) 758-0349.

KENT ISLAND

[Fig. 18] This Chesapeake Bay island off the west coast of Queen Anne's County is a mere 4 miles east of Annapolis and the western shore by way of the William Preston Lane Jr. Memorial Bridge (known as the Bay Bridge). Seafood lovers, boaters, and anglers from Annapolis, Baltimore, Washington, DC, and surrounding areas flock to the island's many harbors and marinas, and to the excellent seafood restaurants with their nautical atmosphere.

The island was created by surging tides that gradually cut a channel through Kent Narrows, separating Kent Island from the mainland. This largest Chesapeake Bay island was once the home of Matapeake Ozinie Indians and later a trading post for the first permanent English settlement in Maryland. Trader William Claiborne established the colony in 1631. The only English settlements to predate it were at Jamestown (Virginia) and Plymouth Rock (Massachusetts). Later, Kent Narrows became a busy seafood processing area, with as many as 12 packing houses operating at once as watermen brought their heavily laden boats to the docks.

The town of Stevensville—the largest town on Kent Island—is located near the eastern end of the Bay Bridge. Coming across the Bay Bridge to Kent Island, many motorists zip past Stevensville, exiting from US 50/301 when they see the rustic docks and weathered seafood houses of Kent Narrows on the eastern side of the island.

But those who take the time to explore the island town will find, on Cockey's Lane, the colorful restored **Stevensville Train Depot** (circa 1902) and the **Cray House** (circa 1839), with its gambrel roof. The Cray House is listed on the National Register of Historic Places. At 117 East Main Street, is **Christ Church**, built about 1880. The congregation that worships here is the oldest in the state, begun in 1631 when the island was settled. A county visitor center is located at 102 Main Street.

For more information: Queen Anne's County Office of Tourism, 107 North Liberty Street, Centreville, MD 21617. Phone (410) 604-2100 or (888) 758-2126. Web site www.qac.org.

TERRAPIN BEACH NATURE PARK

[Fig. 18(9)] Just north of the Bay Bridge on Kent Island is a small natural gem called Terrapin Beach Nature Park. A new 1-mile nature trail, a pond, and two observation blinds are popular with those who enjoy the outdoors. Birds of prey, migratory birds, and breeding waterfowl draw bird watchers and photographers. A boardwalk leads to the Chesapeake Bay. The park is wheelchair accessible.

Directions: Heading east onto Kent Island on US 50/301, take the first exit (Exit 37) and go north on MD 18. Take the first left into Chesapeake Bay Business Park and continue to natural area.

Activities: Nature walk, bird-watching.

Facilities: Boardwalk, nature trail.

Dates: Sunrise to sunset, year-round.

Fees: None.

Closest town: The park is just west of Stevensville.

For more information: Terrapin Beach Nature Park, phone (410) 827-7577 or (410) 643-8170.

MATAPEAKE STATE PARK

[Fig. 18(10)] Matapeake State Park is located on the Chesapeake Bay on the western shore of Kent Island. From the park, there are panoramic views of the Bay Bridge to the north. This 3-acre park is basically a shady parking lot on the bay with two boat ramps, a picnic area, and a 900-foot fishing pier. The sturdy pier is on the site of the former ferry terminus in use before the construction of the Bay Bridge. Tall pines and oaks shade the picnic area. In the woods next to the picnic area are large American holly trees that have beautiful red berries in winter.

Anglers can also fish from a sandy path along the bulwarks that separate the waters of the bay from the park. Children should be watched carefully, as there is no railing to keep them from falling off the edge into deep water.

Directions: From US 50 on Kent Island, go 3 miles south on MD 8 to the park entrance on the right.

Activities: Fishing, boating, picnicking.

Facilities: 900-foot fishing pier, boat ramp, shaded picnic area with a Bay Bridge view, restrooms.

Dates: Open 24 hours a day, year-round.

Fees: There is a small parking fee.

Closest town: Stevensville is 3 miles north.

For more information: Matapeake State Park, phone (410) 974-2149.

BLOODY POINT BAR LIGHTHOUSE

[Fig. 18(11)] The Chesapeake Bay has its own leaning tower—the Bloody Point Bar Lighthouse. This 56-foot high tower on a caisson foundation stands in shallow water off the southern tip of Kent Island. It began to tilt shortly after it was constructed in 1882. A dredging operation under one side partially corrected the tilt, but a sharp observer can tell the tower is still a bit off plumb.

A fire in 1960 temporarily put the lighthouse out of commission and ended the manning operation. Today, the automated flashing white light still assists ship captains in the bay. The lighthouse is visible from Kent Point but is not open to the public.

KENT NARROWS

[Fig. 18(12)] An attractive mix of picturesque seafood restaurants, marinas, boat rentals, and factory outlets line both sides of picturesque Kent Narrows, which separates Kent Island from the mainland of Queen Anne's County. Also located on the waterfront here is an inviting new welcome center, the **Chesapeake Exploration Center**, where visitors can obtain pamphlets and view displays. The welcome center houses the Queen Anne's County Office of Tourism.

The Kent Narrows with its numerous seafood restaurants and dock bars, is the original seafood center of Queen Anne's County. The Narrows is famous for its nautical scenery. A public boat landing here has easy access from Piney Narrows Road. Footpaths and rental boats offer additional ways to become acquainted with this part of the Eastern Shore.

Directions: The Kent Narrows is located three miles east of the Chesapeake Bay Bridge in Queen Anne's County. Take Exit 41, Kent Narrows West, or Exit 42, Kent Narrows East, from US 50/301. The public boat landing, welcome center, factory stores, and Piney Narrows Marina are along Piney Narrows Road, which is on the north side of

US 50/301 off Exit 41, Kent Narrow West.

For more information: Queen Anne's County Office of Tourism, phone (410) 604-2100 or (888) 400-RSVP.

⬚ THE WILDFOWL TRUST OF NORTH AMERICA AT HORSEHEAD WETLANDS CENTER

[Fig. 18(13)] This 500-acre sanctuary east of Kent Island is a haven for bird watchers, photographers, decoy carvers, wildfowl artists—and anyone else who enjoys watching wildlife and wildfowl, including children. Visitors can take paths skirting six waterfowl ponds, each representing a different wetland habitat. At the visitor center, a large window overlooks a pond with a variety of native North American waterfowl such as northern shovelers, redheads, wood ducks, and tundra swans. A powerful scope is set up by the window for a close view.

Children are fascinated with clever hands-on displays in the center. Each of several boxes has a hole with objects inside for children to identify by feel, such as a feather, a snakeskin, or a pine cone. Youngsters may also examine the shells of an Eastern painted turtle, a tiny mud turtle, and a horseshoe crab. Those who have been unable to spot the endangered Delmarva fox squirrel can see a mounted one, in addition to a mounted oldsquaw and a muskrat. Natural history books, bird books, T-shirts, praying mantis puppets, and bat puppets are for sale. An aquarium contains fish and other life characteristic of the shallow waters of the Chesapeake Bay.

In addition to the visitor center pond, five more ponds exhibit wildfowl characteristic of woodlands, prairie potholes, the Atlantic and Pacific flyways, and even birds from overseas countries. In every instance, you are close to the ducks and geese, and in some cases you can walk among them. Wild ducks and geese often join the captive birds on the ponds.

Ponds at the center are modified and renovated from time to time. The Dusky Canada Geese Pond contains a rare subspecies of Canada goose. The Woodland Pond, which has no captive ducks, represents a typical wood duck habitat. The pond attracts, in addition to wood ducks, such wildfowl and critters as canvasbacks, black ducks, American wigeons, herons, and turtles. Some of these same ducks, in addition to lesser and greater scaups, green-winged and blue-winged teal, and cinnamon teal can be found on the Prairie Pothole Pond, a habitat similar to that formed by glacial action in the Central and Mississippi flyways. Several ponds have observation blinds, enabling visitors to view wild ducks and songbirds from close range.

The casual atmosphere of the center is wonderful. Several wild turkeys roam among the visitors, nearly as tame as pets. Benches invite people to relax and become attuned to the leisurely pace of life at the center.

No matter the time of year, there's always something to discover at Horsehead Wetlands Center. From November to February, wintering waterfowl and winter songbirds are abundant. White-tailed deer and red foxes are easier to spot than in summer, when

Ruby-throated Hummingbird

The ruby-throated hummingbird (*Archilochus colubris*) is the only hummingbird that breeds east of the Mississippi River. These bundles of energy must feed almost constantly to replace the calories their rapid metabolism burns. A dominant bird will vigorously guard a food source, dive-bombing other hummingbirds that try to feed. This activity is especially prevalent as fall migration approaches, possibly providing the added bonus of improving fitness. The long journey south often entails an incredible nonstop flight across the Gulf of Mexico.

foliage gives them cover. Bald eagles soar overhead, searching for a meal.

From March to May, spring wildflowers prompt identification questions by visitors. Osprey, songbirds, and waterfowl are busy building their nests. Late spring and early summer are the times to see baby ducks, geese, bluebirds, fawns, foxes, raccoons, and many other animals. Hummingbirds and butterflies are drawn like magnets to a garden of native plant species designed especially for them. Turtles sun themselves on fallen limbs.

Ducks are in full plumage in late summer and fall. The marsh is full of feeding herons, egrets, and shorebirds. Some 80 species of songbird migrants such as warblers, sparrows, flycatchers, orioles, and thrushes, on their way to warmer climes, pass through the wetlands center on their migration routes between August and October. Monarch butterflies also meander through on their own fall migration to Mexico.

In addition to the exhibits, the center engages in waterfowl research and in education. Hawks, owls, and waterfowl that have imprinted on people or have received injuries that prevent their release into the wild are kept in large outdoor aviaries or smaller pens. Volunteers and staff work with such birds as Cooper's hawks, red-shouldered hawks, red-tailed hawks, barred owls, great horned owls, and kestrels, training them to become natural ambassadors for their species. The birds travel to schools, meetings of various organizations, and festivals where their handlers teach people how the birds live in the wild, what habitat they need to survive, and what to do when injured birds are discovered.

Some 200 acres of recently acquired land at Horsehead Wetlands Center offer visitors several new habitats to discover. A pine plantation, a small hardwood forest, and some freshwater wetlands have a great variety of plants, flowers, and wildlife not found in the tidal wetlands.

Contact the center for a colorful map, a bird checklist, and a calendar of events. A popular Wetlands Festival is held the last weekend in September. Members may borrow the center's canoes to explore a canoe trail on Marshy Creek.

The Wildfowl Trust of North America is a private, nonprofit conservation organization patterned after the Wildfowl and Wetlands Trust of the United Kingdom. Sir Peter Scott founded the original organization for two purposes: to provide habitat for waterfowl and to demonstrate the importance of wetlands to people observing the waterfowl.

Directions: From MD 18 at Grasonville (just east of Kent Island), go south on Perry Corner Road 0.5 mile to the entrance, on the right. MD 18 runs parallel with US 301/50; the junction with Perry Corner Road is between Exits 43 and 45.

Activities: Wildfowl watching and photography, nature walks. Pets are not permitted.

Facilities: Visitor center, restrooms, trails leading to the outdoor wildfowl exhibits (some with blinds), aviaries, boardwalk and observation tower, screened pavilion. Canoes are available for members.

RUBY-THROATED HUMMINGBIRD
(Archilochus colubris)

Dates: Open 9 to 5 daily, year-round, except Thanksgiving, Christmas Eve, Christmas Day, and New Year's Day.

Fees: There is an admission fee and a membership program. Benefits for members include the use of the center's canoes and free admission to over 100 other wetlands and nature centers across the United States.

Closest town: Grasonville is 0.5 mile north.

For more information: Wildfowl Trust of North America at Horsehead Wetlands Center, 600 Discovery Lane, PO Box 519, Grasonville, MD 21638-0519. Phone (410) 827-6694. E-mail WTNA@shore.internet.com.

TRAILS OF HORSEHEAD WETLANDS CENTER

[Fig. 18(14)] In addition to the path winding through the exhibit ponds in the area of the visitor center, two more trails lead into the surrounding marsh, bay edge, meadows, and woodlands.

BOARDWALK TRAIL. A 0.66-mile Boardwalk Trail crosses a salt meadow and marsh, passing a berm planted with perennial flowers and native plants, and an observation blind at Lake Knapp where egrets, osprey, bald eagles, and herons make regular appearances. The walk leads to a beach on the Chesapeake Bay and a 15-foot observation tower. The sweeping view may reveal tundra swans, lesser scaups, buffleheads, wading birds, terns, and maybe even loons.

Trail: 0.66-mile easy walk from parking lot, including boardwalk to salt meadow and marsh.

MARSHY CREEK TRAIL. A variety of songbirds, varying according to season, use the woodlands along the 0.33-mile Marshy Creek Trail. Listen for various warbler calls, especially in spring and fall. Rufous-sided towhees, white-throated sparrows, flycatchers, orioles, thrushes, and cardinals are other possibilities. Another blind on Lake Knapp, this one on the east side, is on this trail. A 15-foot observation tower overlooks Marshy Creek,

False Indigo

Gardeners prize this native plant grown at Adkins Arboretum for its indigo-blue flowers in spring, its attractive silver-green foliage in summer, and its interesting dark seedpods in fall and winter. False indigo (*Baptisia australis*), also called blue indigo and wild indigo, puts down deep roots that give it a formidable toughness and tolerance to drought.

where a launch area is available for canoeists. The Marshy Creek Trail is especially interesting for its display boards, which are updated from time to time. These boards challenge hikers to be observant. A recent topic was identification of the surrounding plant life, with illustrations of both summer and winter forms.

Along the trail are wet meadow edge plants, plants of disturbed woodlands, and meadow plants. Vegetation in the wet meadow habitat includes the persimmon tree (*Diospyros virginiana*). The persimmon produces a mouth-puckering green fruit that has a memorable astringency if eaten before ripe. A rule of thumb is to wait until the first frost to eat them—that is, if raccoons and opossums don't get them first. Swamp rose mallow (*Hibiscus palustris*) is a showy plant with large, deep-pink flowers. Note the musky smell. The day lily, sweetgum, and Eastern redcedar also are found here.

Plants of the disturbed woodland habitat include vegetation that takes hold where soil has been altered, usually by man-made disturbances such as cultivation. Look for velvetleaf (*Abutilon theoprasti*), also called pie-maker, with its heart-shaped, toothed, velvety leaves and small yellow flowers tight in the leaf axils. Tiny deptford pink (*Dianthus armeria*) grows 8 to 20 inches tall, with white-spotted, pink flowers that are only 0.5 inch wide. Poison ivy, greenbriar, Queen Anne's lace, pokeweed, wax myrtle, American holly, shadbush, and willow oak are other common plants and trees in the understory and at the edges of the loblolly pine forest.

The meadows in summer are dotted with yarrow, oxeye daisy, black-eyed Susan, butterfly weed, and wild bergamot. Monarch butterflies seek out the common milkweed (*Asclepias incarnata*). They are totally dependent on the foliage of this plant, which contains a chemical that renders both the adult monarchs and their larvae toxic to would-be predators.

Trail: 0.33-mile easy path along meadow and through woodlands.

PINTAIL POINT RESORT

[Fig. 18(15)] This 1,000-acre private resort in Queenstown, just east of Kent Island, offers outdoor getaways for hunters, fishermen, sporting clay enthusiasts, or those who simply want to escape for a few hours in a horse-drawn carriage or charter boat. Reservations are required.

The sporting clays course—which is similar to a golf course for shooters—is positioned along the scenic banks of the Wye River. Fishing opportunities include the river, the Chesapeake Bay, and a stocked pond. Hunters may try for released pheasant, quail, chukar, Hungarian partridge, or mallard. Hunting for wild game includes deer and dove hunting in the resort's fields and forests, and duck hunting from blinds. Guides and expertly trained bird dogs are available, or visitors may bring their own bird dogs. Even combinations of activities can be arranged, such as chartering a boat to hunt sea ducks on a fall morning and casting for striped bass (rockfish) in the afternoon.

Pintail Point also offers fly-fishing lessons.

Directions: From the east end of William Preston Lane Jr. Memorial Bridge (Bay Bridge), go east on US 50/301, and follow US 50 when the highway splits. Watch for a sign, *Aspen/Wye Institute Next Right*, and turn right on Carmichael Road. Drive 1.5 miles to the resort, on the right.

Activities: Fishing (including fly-fishing), sporting clays, hunting, boating, carriage rides.

Facilities: Rental charter boats, sporting clays course, hunting lands, private kennel and dog training facility, duck blinds, rental guns, rental bikes, rental horse and carriage, limited lodging.

Dates: Open year-round.

Fees: All activities have fees.

Closest town: Queenstown is about 4.5 miles north.

For more information: Pintail Point Resort, 511 Pintail Point Lane, Queenstown, MD 21658. Phone (410) 827-7029

FALSE INDIGO
(Baptisia australis)

TUCKAHOE STATE PARK AND ADKINS ARBORETUM
[Fig. 18(16)] The 3,498 acres of Tuckahoe State Park spread along both sides of Tuckahoe Creek about 6 miles north of Hillsboro in both Queen Anne's and Caroline counties. Roads along the boundary and in the park provide access on both side of the river.

Hikers can keep cool as they pass through the park's dense woodlands on several miles of marked trails. A 2-mile fitness trail offers a great place to work out in a scenic environment. Tuckahoe Creek, bordered for most of its length by wooded marshlands, passes through the park, pausing at a dam that forms 60-acre Crouse Mill Pond. Boating (no gasoline motors) and fishing are permitted on the lake and in the surrounding flooded woodlands.

The lake and the creek waters above the lake have fresh water. Below the lake, the water is influenced by tides, but salinity is so low that anglers are able to capture such freshwater species as bass, pickerel, and bluegill all the way down to Hillsboro and beyond. The park is a fine hub for bikers, who can camp and explore the tranquil 10-mile loop of back roads that border the park. Hunters come seasonally for dove, quail, wild turkey, woodcock, rabbit, squirrel, and deer. Leashed pets are allowed on the park and arboretum trails.

Trees and shrubs native to the Mid-Atlantic Coastal Plain are grown at the 400-acre

Adkins Arboretum in the park. Three miles of surfaced walkways, some that are wheel-chair-accessible, lead beside streams and through dry upland woods, bottomland forests, and upland meadows. Trees and shrubs are tagged for easy identification. The arboretum is a cooperative project of the Maryland Department of Natural Resources and the nonprofit Friends of Adkins Arboretum, Ltd.

Directions: The park is located on both sides of Tuckahoe Creek in southeastern Queen Anne's County and western Caroline County. For the office and arboretum, from US 50, take MD 404 east across Tuckahoe Creek and go left on MD 480. Take an immediate left on Eveland Road and drive 2 miles to the office, on the left.

Activities: Hiking, horseback riding, fitness training, picnicking, camping, fishing, boating (no gasoline motors), canoeing, biking, seasonal hunting.

Facilities: Arboretum visitor center, hiking trails, fitness trail, picnic tables, campground with hookups, central bathhouse, boat ramp, canoeing/fishing waters, rental canoes from May to Oct., playground, restrooms, dump station.

Dates: The park is open daily, year-round. The campgrounds are open generally from late Mar. to Nov. The grounds of the arboretum are open 9 to 5 daily, year-round. The arboretum visitor center is open 9 to 5, Monday through Saturday, except on holidays.

Fees: There is a camping fee, boat rental fee, and pavilion rental fee in the park. None for arboretum.

Closest town: Denton is about 8 miles southeast of the park.

For more information: Tuckahoe State Park, 13070 Crouse Mill Road, Queen Anne, MD 21657. Phone (410) 820-1668. Adkins Arboretum, PO Box 100, Eveland Road, Ridgely, MD 21660. Phone (410) 634-2847.

WYE ISLAND NATURAL RESOURCE MANAGEMENT AREA

[Fig. 18(17)] Wye Island is a crooked 8 miles long. It is located south of Queenstown and east of Kent Island in the southwestern corner of Queen Anne County. The island is formed by the Eastern Bay to the west, the Wye River to the northwest, the Wye East River to the south, and Wye Narrows on the north and northeast.

Most of the island—2,515 of 2,800 acres—is managed by the Maryland Department of Natural Resources Forest and Park Service. A 30-acre area called School House Woods contains giant hardwoods that began life some two and one-half centuries ago when the nation was still young. This stand of mature oaks, hickory, and black gum is a rare sight on the Eastern Shore. The remainder of the management area is mostly comprised of corn and soybean fields separated by hedgerows—a great combination of food and cover for wildlife.

Six miles of trails invite hikers, bikers, and horseback riders to explore. Some 30 miles of shoreline are perfect for poking about in small boats. Rewards for patient observers include the sight and sound of a tremendous variety of ducks, geese, herons, egrets, and nesting osprey. White-tailed deer, raccoons, foxes, muskrats, rabbits, and even the endangered Delmarva fox squirrel make occasional appearances. The early morning and evening hours are most productive for bird and wildlife observation. In spring, summer, and fall, the borders of fields and roadsides are dotted with wildflowers including tickseed sunflowers, (*Bidens aristosa*), smooth aster, (*Aster laevis*), and multiflora rose (*Rosa multiflora*). The tall spikes of the dramatic cardinal flower (*Lobelia cardinalis*) grow in wet areas.

Participants in managed hunts in late fall and winter must obtain a permit or be chosen by lottery. The hunts include archery and muzzleloading for deer and limited fox chasing and coon hunting. Nonhunters should wear blaze orange during hunting season for safety. From the island's banks, anglers catch rockfish, white perch, yellow perch, catfish, and other species that inhabit the brackish water. A Maryland tidewater fishing license is required.

Pets must be on leash. A small lodge is available for conferences. Visitors can obtain information at the hunter check-in station located on the right just after crossing the entrance bridge and from the bulletin board at Granary Creek Picnic Area, which is 1.2 miles past the entrance bridge.

Currently there are no boat launching facilities at Wye Island NRMA, but county facilities are nearby. Boaters should use extreme care in coming ashore on the island to avoid damage to the shoreline embankments. The best places to come ashore are the Granary Creek Picnic Area, at the group campsite on Dividing Creek, at Ferry Point Landing at Drum Point, and at Grapevine Avenue in Grapevine Cove. Only boats that can meet the 10-foot clearance limit at the Wye Island Bridge in Wye Narrows can circumnavigate the island.

Directions: From Queenstown and the junction of US 50 and US 301, go southeast on US 50 about 3 miles. Turn right on Carmichael Road and drive about 5 miles across a bridge to the management area.

Activities: Hiking, biking, horseback riding, wildlife and waterfowl viewing, fishing, camping for organized youth groups. Trails may be closed to horseback riders and bicyclists, depending on conditions. Also, managed hunts include archery and muzzle-loading deer seasons (permits required), and fox chasing and coon hunting (permits required).

Facilities: 6 miles of hiking trails, small rental lodge for meetings, youth-group camping area.

Dates: Open sunrise to sunset daily, year-round. Managed hunts are conducted in late fall and winter.

Fees: There is a service charge for youth-group camping and for rental of the lodge.

Closest town: Queenstown is 8 miles north.

For more information: Wye Island Natural Resource Management Area, 632 Wye Island Road, Queenstown, MD 21658. Phone (410) 827-7577. Department of Natural Resources Web site www.dnr.state.md.us. For information on launching boats in the vicinity of Wye Island NRMA, contact the Queen Anne County Department of Parks and Recreation at (410) 758-0835 or Talbot County Department of Parks and Recreation at (410) 822-2955.

▒ BEACHES IN QUEEN ANNE'S COUNTY

Queen Anne's one public beach is on the Chester River.

Conquest Beach. This beach on the lovely Chester River north of Centreville has two picnic areas with grills, bathhouses, wheelchair-accessible restrooms, a ball field, horseshoe pits, and a volleyball court. Reservations required. Phone (410) 758-0835 or (410) 778-4430.

▒ RESTAURANTS IN QUEEN ANNE'S COUNTY

Most of Queen Anne's most sought-after restaurants are on Kent Island and at Kent Narrows on the east side of the Bay Bridge. Oysters, crabs, clams, rockfish, and other seafood is prepared expertly and the views are spectacular.

ANGLERS RESTAURANT. 3015 Kent Narrows Way South, Grasonville. This waterfront, casual restaurant features home-cooking. *Inexpensive to moderate. Phone (410) 827-6717.*

ANNIE'S PARAMOUNT STEAK AND SEAFOOD HOUSE. 500 Kent Narrows Way North, Grasonville. Award-winning restaurant, serving prime rib, steaks, and seafood. Take Exit 42 from US 50/301. *Moderate. Phone (410) 827-7103.*

HARRIS CRAB HOUSE. 433 Kent Narrows Way North, Grasonville. Located off US 50/301, Exit 42, on the east side of Kent Narrows. Dining is casual, in the open air or inside, with a view of the boating activity at Kent Narrows. Sample the she-crab soup, crabcakes, shrimp, and other Chesapeake Bay seafood purchased straight from watermen who come to the dock. Access available by water. *Moderate. Phone (410) 827-9500.*

FISHERMAN'S INN. Kent Narrows, Grasonville. Dine on fresh seafood or prime rib at this landmark restaurant of Kent Narrows since 1930. Award-winning crabcakes. Waterfront view. Open for lunch and dinner year-round. *Moderate. Phone (410) 827-8807.*

HEMINGWAY'S RESTAURANT. Bay Bridge Marina, Stevensville. This restaurant with an outside deck claims the best view of the Chesapeake Bay. Seafood, steaks, and pasta are on the menu. A downstairs crabhouse is open seasonally. *Inexpensive to moderate. Phone (410) 643-2722.*

▒ LODGING IN QUEEN ANNE'S COUNTY

Most inns and motels are located on or near Kent Island. However, for those who wish to stay in the countryside, there are other options.

COLE HOUSE BED AND BREAKFAST. Dudley Corners Road (MD 290), Crumpton. A restored Victorian home (circa 1860) with three charming bedrooms. Located on the Chester River, 8 miles east of Chestertown. *Moderate to expensive. Phone (410) 928-5514.*

HILLSIDE HOTEL. 2630 Centreville Road, Centreville. This modern hotel is located in the heart of historic Centreville and surrounded by excellent hunting opportunities. *Moderate. Phone (410) 758-2270.*

CHESAPEAKE MOTEL. 107 Hissey Road, Grasonville. Easy access to US 50/301 at

Exit 44A, 5 minutes east of Bay Bridge. *Inexpensive to moderate. Phone (410) 827-7272.*

COMFORT INN-KENT NARROWS. 3101 Main Street, Grasonville. Four-story waterfront hotel off US 50/301 east of Bay Bridge, Exit 42. Voted best hotel in county by Mid-Shore Reader's Choice Business Awards. Walking distance from seafood restaurants, docks. Charters pick up at hotel. *Moderate to expensive. Phone (800) 828-3361.*

KENT MANOR INN. 500 Kent Manor Drive, Stevensville. Victorian furnishings, wide verandas, groomed flower gardens, and outstanding water vistas at this historic country inn. Tennis, bicycling, pier fishing, crabbing, boat launch, fine restaurant. *Expensive. Phone (800) 820-4511.*

Caroline County

Caroline County claims no border on the Chesapeake Bay, but it is bordered and dissected by important bay tributaries in both the Choptank River watershed and the Nanticoke River watershed. The Choptank River enters the county on the northeast border from Kent County, Delaware, runs through the heart of the county and by the county seat of Denton, and then forms the county's southwestern border. Tuckahoe Creek, a Choptank tributary, provides the rest of the meandering county line on the western side. Marshyhope Creek, in the southeastern corner of the county, is in the Nanticoke watershed.

Two state parks—Tuckahoe and Martinak—and Idylwild Wildlife Management Area take advantage of the woodlands and wetlands along these waterways. Caroline's parks tend to be less crowed than many parks.

Tuckahoe State Park is on both sides of Tuckahoe Creek, which separates Caroline and Queen Anne's County. (*See* Queen Anne's County, page 225.) Martinak State Park is on the junction of the Choptank River and Watts Creek. Idylwild Wildlife Management Area is in the Nanticoke River watershed on Marshyhope Creek, in the southern part of Caroline County. After leaving Caroline, Marshyhope empties into the Nanticoke River, a Chesapeake Bay tributary in southern Dorchester County.

Private campgrounds in the county include Holiday Park (410-482-6797) and Lake Connie (410-482-8479).

For more information: Caroline County Economic Development, 218 Market Street, Denton, MD 21629. Phone (410) 479-0600.

MARTINAK STATE PARK

[Fig. 19(1)] This small park, named for George Martinak who donated the land to the state, packs a great deal of opportunity in its 107 acres. Most of the park is developed, but rental canoes and a boat ramp provide access to the Choptank River and Watts Creek where bass, perch, and sunfish challenge the skill of anglers. A state Chesapeake Bay sport-fishing license is required. Canoeists paddle the tidal flat water of both river and

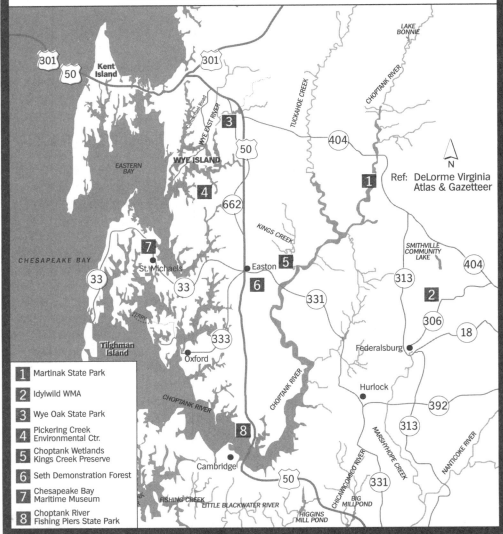

Caroline and Talbot Counties

Caroline and Talbot counties are bordered and dissected by important bay tributaries in both the Choptank River and the Nanticoke River.

LAKE BONNIE

301

50

Kent Island

301

Carmichael Road

WYE EAST RIVER

3

TUCKAHOE CREEK

CHOPTANK RIVER

50

404

EASTERN BAY

WYE ISLAND

1

Ref: DeLorme Virginia Atlas & Gazetteer

N

4

662

KINGS CREEK

7

SMITHVILLE COMMUNITY LAKE

CHESAPEAKE BAY

St. Michaels

33

33

Easton

5

6

313

404

2

331

306

18

FERRY

333

Federalsburg

Tilghman Island

Oxford

Hurlock

313

392

CHOPTANK RIVER

CHOPTANK RIVER

8

MARSHYHOPE CREEK

NANTICOKE RIVER

Cambridge

50

CHICAMICOMICO RIVER

331

BIG MILLPOND

FISHING CREEK

LITTLE BLACKWATER RIVER

HIGGINS MILL POND

1   Martinak State Park

2   Idylwild WMA

3   Wye Oak State Park

4   Pickering Creek Environmental Ctr.

5   Choptank Wetlands Kings Creek Preserve

6   Seth Demonstration Forest

7   Chesapeake Bay Maritime Museum

8   Choptank River Fishing Piers State Park

creek, enjoying the forest of Virginia and loblolly pines that was once the site of a Chop-tank Indian village.

Camping is available spring through fall. Some sites have electric hookups. Park rangers conduct evening fireside programs on summer Saturdays. Four rental cabins are available seasonally, with one of them available year-round, providing a means to hear in the dead of winter the mysterious night sounds of a barred owl in a faraway tree or a flock of Canada geese overhead.

Families can bring fried chicken and potato salad for a Sunday afternoon picnic, followed by a nap in the sun or a prowl for flowers and frogs on the banks of Watts Creek.

Directions: From MD 404, about 1 mile south of Denton in central Caroline County, turn right on Deep Shore Road and drive about 0.5 mile to the park.

Activities: Hiking, biking, picnicking, camping, flat-water canoeing, boating, fishing.

Facilities: Hiking and biking trail, picnic tables with grills, pavilions, boat ramp, canoe rental, campground (some with hookups, one handicapped-accessible loop), handicapped-accessible bathhouse, rental cabins, playground, restrooms, dump station.

Dates: The park is open daily, year-round, except Christmas and Thanksgiving. The campground and cabins are open Apr. through Oct. (1 cabin available all year).

Fees: There is a fee for camping and a rental fee for pavilions, cabins, and canoes.

Closest town: Denton is about 1 mile north.

For more information: Martinak State Park, 137 Deep Shore Road, Denton, MD 21629. Phone (410) 479-1619.

🦡 IDYLWILD WILDLIFE MANAGEMENT AREA

[Fig. 19(2)] The lovely freshwater marshes of Marshyhope Creek form the western boundary of this state wildlife management area located in the southeastern corner of Caroline County. The marshes of Idylwild combine with forested wetlands, dry forests, and agricultural fields to provide 3,000 acres of habitat for a large variety of plants and animals. An abandoned sand and gravel quarry left deep ponds that have become home to bass and pickerel.

Trails, though unmarked, are wide and well maintained. Fields are cultivated specifi-cally to provide food and cover for white-tailed deer, wild turkey, rabbits, and other wildlife. The conical, chiseled stumps left by beaver are evident around the marsh. The playful river otter makes occasional appearances. Old rotting trees in the forests of Virginia pines, loblolly pines, and oaks provide nesting cavities for bluebirds. Scarlet tanagers, identified by bright red plumage and black wings, catch the sun as they fly high in the oaks and pines. Woodcocks probe the muddy creek banks for earthworms. Gray foxes prowl the woods for small rodents at night. An occasional bald eagle steals a fish from an osprey.

In short, Idylwild is a great place to spot wildlife, especially in the early morning and at dusk. No one has to tell hunters of the opportunities here. Seasons are provided for waterfowl, deer, squirrel, turkey, rabbit, and woodcock. But wildlife watchers, bird watchers, and nature photographers can also have good luck at places like this where the lack of amenities also means a lack of disturbance by crowds of people.

The stretch of Marshyhope Creek between the wildlife management area and Federalsburg and the creek below Federalsburg are among the few places canoeists can access any of the beautiful Nanticoke River tributaries. The Nanticoke itself has too much large-boat traffic to be safe for canoeing or kayaking.

Directions: From Federalsburg, in southern Caroline County, take Central Avenue east across Marshyhope Creek. This road becomes Houston Branch Road (MD 306). Look for the road into the management area after about 0.75 mile, on the left.

Activities: Hiking, mountain biking, flat-water canoeing, horseback riding, fishing, swimming (in unguarded ponds), and seasonal hunting, trapping, and fox chasing.

Facilities: Hiking roads and trails, with access for the disabled.

Dates: Open year-round. Call for hunting seasons, which may vary annually.

Fees: None.

Closest town: Federalsburg is about 1 mile west.

For more information: LeCompte Work Center, phone (410) 376-3236 or (410) 820-7098.

Talbot County

Talbot County marks the midpoint of Maryland's Eastern Shore, with Queen Anne's County and the Wye East River to the north and Dorchester County and the Choptank River to the south and east.

The entire western side of the county is laced with peninsulas, coves, and inlets that are called creeks and rivers, but are really tidal estuaries where salt and fresh water mix. This topography is responsible for shaping Talbot County's history. The protected waters of the county's 602 miles of shoreline make fine harbors, allowing boats to penetrate far inland. Wintering waterfowl seek refuge from the weather in the same waters. Blue crabs, oysters, and clams inhabit the estuary around Talbot's islands and peninsulas. The Choptank River is a favored spawning area for rockfish (striped bass).

The rich bounty of fish, shellfish, and waterfowl attracts anglers, hunters, and nature lovers to Talbot County. Historic villages whose residents have subsisted by harvesting and processing seafood for centuries have their own stories to tell. Ports like the ones at St. Michaels, Tilghman Island, and Oxford are synonymous with Chesapeake Bay watermen.

The acclaimed Waterfowl Festival at Easton and other bay-related celebrations also have their roots in the area's culture. Museums such as the Chesapeake Bay Maritime Museum at St. Michaels help visitors comprehend the intimate ties between the people of the Eastern Shore and the bay. The adventurous can learn about Talbot by renting kayaks or canoes to investigate marshes that are home to herons, egrets, muskrats, beaver, and raccoons. The outdoors lovers can drop a crab line from a pier or rent a bicycle to pedal the quiet back roads.

Outfitters and guide services are ubiquitous and are available for sight-seeing, fishing, crabbing, hunting upland game or waterfowl, sailing, boating, canoeing, kayaking, and bicycling. A map of popular bicycle routes is available from the county chamber of commerce. Charter captains and cruise boats offer bay and river excursions. Several golf courses, including the plush **Easton Club Golf Course** on the Tred Avon River, provide another form of recreation.

The inviting aroma of Chesapeake Bay seafood drifts from harbor-side restaurants where tired wanderers relax over a glass of wine while awaiting a platter of steamed crab or grilled catfish. At the end of the day, after a satisfying meal, visitors can lay weary heads on a pillow in the Tidewater Inn at Easton, or at any of the other historic inns, waterfront inns, bed and breakfasts, and country hotels and motels of Talbot County.

For more information: Talbot Chamber of Commerce, Tred Avon Square, Easton, MD 21601. Phone (410) 822-4606 or (888) BAYSTAY; Web site www.talbotchamber.org.

🌿 WYE OAK STATE PARK

[Fig. 19(3)] Wye Oak State Park exists to protect the largest oak tree in the United States. The Wye Oak is a white oak (*Quercus alba*) that is thought to be more than 450 years old. It is located on MD 662 in the community of Wye Mills, just south of the Queen Anne's County line.

No one knows exactly what year the acorn that produced this amazing tree fell to the ground, but an educated guess is the year 1540. The tree has lived through the colonization of the Eastern Shore, the Industrial Revolution, the Civil War, and two world wars. It has weathered an untold number of thunderstorms, windstorms, and icings.

During that time, the Wye Oak grew 96 feet, its branches gradually reaching 119 feet across. A person standing beside this giant survivor is dwarfed. The massive, gnarled trunk is 31 feet and 4 inches in circumference. Some 3,500 feet of cables stretch from branch to branch for stabilization. An access hole in the trunk allows the tree's caretakers to keep tabs on the innards, where a fungus and termites once hollowed out the tree to a height of 10 feet.

Huge growths or knees at the base of the tree have an unknown origin. Speculation includes the theory that horses were tethered under the tree while their owners visited a nearby tavern or country store. The severe bruising from the horses' hooves may have caused the tree to produce the burls for protection.

Next to the ancient oak is a little one-room schoolhouse constructed of now faded brick. It is thought to be the oldest school in Talbot County, dating back to colonial times. Inside are a schoolmaster's desk and a long table made of pine. A dunce stool stands in the corner, where recalcitrant students were made to sit. Many students came and went, perhaps eating their lunch in the shade of the Wye Oak, while the tree grew imperceptibly but steadfastly to its enormous size.

On the other side of the tree is the **Wye Church**, built in 1721, one of the oldest Episcopal churches in Talbot County. Beneath the church are the remains of an even older structure thought to have been built in the late 1600s. The building's exterior is original. The interior has been restored to its original condition, featuring high box pews and a hanging side pulpit. The community of Wye Mills takes its name from **Old Wye Mill**, which has been in operation since 1664. Old grindstones still turn on weekends, making flour from grain. The same grindstones produced flour for the Continental Army during the Revolutionary War.

Directions: Wye Oak State Park is on the west side of MD 662 in Talbot County, just south of the Wye East River and the Queen Anne's County line.

Activities: Viewing old tree and schoolhouse, picnicking.

Facilities: Wye oak, a few picnic tables, old schoolhouse.

Dates: Open daily, year-round.

Fees: None.

Closest town: Queenstown is 6 miles west and Centreville is 7 miles north.

For more information: Wye Oak State Park, c/o Tuckahoe State Park, 13070 Crouse Mill Road, Queen Anne, MD 21657. Phone (410) 820-1668.

PICKERING CREEK ENVIRONMENTAL CENTER

[Fig. 19(4)] The 400 acres of hardwood forests, wildlife plantings, nontidal wetlands, and nature preserve at Pickering Creek Environmental Center are a sanctuary of the Chesapeake Audubon Society. A mature forest on the property was possibly once the site of a seasonal Matapeake Indian village, although evidence is sketchy.

Pickering Creek, which flows through the environmental center, is home to northern river otters. The otters are nocturnal and not often seen by hikers or canoeists. They feed primarily on fish in addition to crayfish, crabs, frogs, and other stream life. New at the center is a list to help people identify some of the 130 species of birds that have been sighted here.

A deep-water pier attracts anglers to try for striped bass, perch, and shad. The welcome center has a reference library and educational displays. Every Talbot County child in first through sixth grades learns about protecting the environment by visiting the center or from educators at the center who visit the schools.

Visitors may hike the trails of the sanctuary. Because of high insurance costs, canoes are no longer available for rent, but may be used free of charge by members of the center who wish to explore Pickering Creek. Leashed pets are allowed on farm trails, but not on nature trails.

Directions: From the northern border of Talbot County, go south about 5 miles on US 50. At mile marker 58, turn right on MD 662 (Longwoods Road). (Don't be confused by other places that MD 662 crosses US 50). After about 1.5 miles, go right onto Sharp Road. Go another 1.5 miles and turn right (still on Sharp Road). Go 1.25 miles and look for the Pickering Creek Environmental Center on the right. Turn right and follow the gravel driveway to the first turn. The welcome center is on the left.

Activities: Nature walks, canoeing, fishing.

Facilities: Welcome center, educational displays, reference library, nature trails, organic garden, rental canoes, bird observation blinds.

Dates: The grounds are open daily, year-round. The welcome center is open 8:30 to 5, Monday through Friday, and 10 to 4 on Saturday, year-round.

Fees: There is no entry fee. The annual membership fee is $25 for individuals and $35 for families. Members may use canoes at no charge.

Closest town: The center is about 9 miles northwest of Easton.

For more information: Pickering Creek Environmental Center, 11450 Audubon Lane, Easton, MD 21601. Phone (410) 822-4903. Web site www.pickeringcreek.org.

▒ EASTON

[Fig. 19] The tree-lined streets, old-fashioned lampposts, gift and antique shops, and historic buildings of Easton combine to give this town a charm that attracts many people to the heart of Talbot County.

The town's interesting mix of architecture tells a story of devastating fires (1810, 1855, and 1878), wars, and the rise and fall of the railroad. The oldest religious building still in use in the United States is the **Third Haven Friends Meeting House** at 405 South Washington Street. Quakers constructed it in 1682 next to an old Indian trail on land that was soon to become a town. The town was first called Talbot Court House, then changed to Easton in 1788 when it became the county seat.

The amenities of the town, surrounded as it is by picturesque countryside, make it an ideal base for bicyclists. Tilghman Island and the nearby towns of St. Michaels and Oxford are perfect destinations for scenic day trips. A circuit that includes Oxford, Easton, and scenic rides on Talbot County peninsulas makes use of the **Oxford-Bellevue Ferry** for one leg of the trip. A certain amount of backtracking through equally beautiful countryside is required to cycle to St. Michaels and Tilghman Island from Easton and back. Bikes may be rented in Easton, Oxford, or St. Michaels.

Maps for historical walking tours of the town are available through the **Historical Society of Talbot County**. The three-story Federal-style brick town house at 25 South Washington Street in which the society is housed is a landmark in its own right, constructed by a Quaker in 1810. In a neighboring building in the society's museum complex is a Talbot County history exhibit. On the grounds are Federal-style gardens, lovingly nurtured by the Talbot County Garden Club to achieve national recognition.

Another of the town's popular attractions is the **Academy of the Arts** (410-822-0455), housed in a restored 1820 schoolhouse at 106 South Street. Visitors may view the works of some of America's most famous nineteenth and twentieth century artists here.

The **Avalon Theatre** (410-822-0345) at 40 East Dover Street is located in a 1920 building that was once a movie and vaudeville house. The renovated Art-Deco building now boasts state-of-the-art sound and lighting, adding to Easton's eclectic mix of past and present. Today's theater-goers are treated to movies, plays, concerts, and other events. A small visitor center is also located here.

Least Bittern

The least bittern (*Ixobrychus exilis*) is a small, long-legged bird that frequents the marshes of the Choptank Wetlands. This secretive wader can disappear among the reeds quickly; a watcher is lucky to catch even a glimpse. The soft "coo-coo-coo" of the bittern is equally hard to detect.

Even more famous than the town itself is the world-renowned Waterfowl Festival (410-822-4567), an event that raises funds for waterfowl conservation. On the second full weekend of November, some 20,000 people from across the country flood the little town of Easton about the same time hoards of ducks and geese splash down on local ponds, marshes, and rivers. The waterfowl come to spend the winter. The people come to spend three days viewing exquisite waterfowl art, to watch the world's best decoy carvers work their magic, to hear goose- and duck-calling competitions, to marvel at the world's best working retrievers, and to collect some of the art and decoys for their homes. Millions of dollars taken in during the festival over three decades have been put to use protecting and providing habitat for waterfowl.

No description of Easton would be complete without a mention of the elegant and gracious **Tidewater Inn**. Called "the pride of the Eastern Shore," the Tidewater Inn is known for its fine service, its large open fireplaces, and its eighteenth century reproduction furniture. The inn caters to fishermen and duck hunters with early morning breakfasts, guide services, and dog kenneling. It is located in the heart of town at the intersection of Harrison and Dover streets.

Holiday lighting and the month-long Dickens-of-a-Christmas Festival (410-820-9616) make Easton a magical place to celebrate December. The festival is family-oriented, complete with carriage rides and a parade.

Night life is available at several spots in town. Both the **Eagle Spirits Restaurant at the Easton Club** (410-820-4100) on 28449 Clubhouse Drive and the **Columbia Restaurant** at 28 South Washington Street are upscale eateries that offer evening entertainment. Reservations are suggested. At 42 East Dover Street is the **Legal Spirits Restaurant** (410-820-0033), with a lively pub near the front and a small and quieter dining area in the back. Pricing is moderate.

Casual dining is also available daily at the **Washington Street Pub** (410-822-9011), located across from the courthouse at 20 North Washington Street. The pub has a raw bar and 19 beers on tap. **The Rustic Inn Restaurant and Tavern** (410-820-8212) in a corner of TalbotTown Shopping Center has an authentic historic interior and offers fine dining. Pricing is moderate to expensive.

Directions: Easton is off US 50 in the center of Talbot County.

For more information: Talbot Chamber of Commerce, Tred Avon Square, Easton, MD 21601. Phone (410) 822-4606 or (888) BAYSTAY. Talbot County Community Center, 10028 Ocean Gateway, Easton, MD 21601. Phone (410) 770-8050. The Historical Society of Talbot County, 25 South Washington Street, Easton, MD 21601. Phone (410) 822-

0773. The Tidewater Inn, 101 East Dover Street, Easton, MD 21601. Phone (410) 822-1300 or (800) 237-8775. E-mail www.tidewaterinn.com. Easton Cycle & Sport, 723 Goldsboro Street, Easton MD 21601. Phone (410) 822-7433.

CHOPTANK WETLANDS KINGS CREEK PRESERVE

[Fig. 19(5)] Canoeists and kayakers who would like to combine a pretty stretch of river with a side trip into a pristine tidal marsh will want to check out Kings Creek Preserve, located off the Choptank River east of Easton. This 250-acre marsh is part of the 656-acre Choptank Wetlands, a joint venture of The Nature Conservancy and the Waterfowl Festival, Inc., for the protection of wintering and nesting waterfowl and spawning fish. Such wetlands also provide an extraordinary benefit to the Chesapeake Bay watershed by assisting in sediment control and by filtering out excess nutrients from upstream pollution. In a survey, the Smithsonian Institution found the Choptank Wetlands to be one of the most important natural areas of the Chesapeake Bay.

The remaining 406 acres of the Choptank Wetlands is the Hog Island Preserve on the Caroline County side of the Choptank, a bit farther downriver. Hog Island is not open to the public.

Kings Creek Preserve is accessible by a 0.5-mile boat trip. Access by land is occasionally permitted by prior arrangement. Those who enjoy watching birds and studying plant life from the preserve boardwalk will also enjoy paddling the undisturbed area of the Choptank and Kings Creek to get to the preserve. Blue-winged teal (*Anas discors*) feeding on the wild rice (*Zizania aquatica*), tidemarsh waterhemp (*Amaranthus cannabinus*), and dotted smartweed (*Polygonum punctatum*) in the marshy edges may take to the air ahead of canoeists. At the preserve, a 2,000-foot boardwalk leads over the brackish wetland where red-winged blackbirds flash their red epaulets from a stand of phragmites and osprey build rough nests of sticks in tall pines.

In addition to the expanses of phragmites (*Phragmites australis*), dominating plant species include arrow arum (*Peltandra virginica*), switchgrass (*Panicum virgatum*), and cattails (*Typha latifolia*). Spring and summer are good times to see flowers. Signs along the boardwalk interpret the extremely rich mix of plants and animals in this ecosystem. An elevated platform gets you above the marsh for a better view. The brochure and bird checklist available at the entrance are also a help in understanding the marsh and in identifying such species as the northern harrier (*Circus cyaneus*), wood duck (*Aix sponsa*),

LEAST BITTERN
(*Ixobrychus exilis*)

245

and common snipe (*Capella gallinago*). The snipe is ordinarily a solitary bird, but it migrates in a flock, usually at night. It is a popular game bird.

Directions: Use a boat to access the preserve via the Choptank River. To get to the boat landing, from Easton and US 50, drive east on MD 331 (Dover Road) for 2.1 miles toward Preston. Turn left on Black Dog Alley Road and immediately right on Kingston Road. Go 3.7 miles and turn right again at the T intersection on Kingston Landing Road. Continue 0.7 mile to Kingston Landing on the Choptank River. Once on the water, go downriver (southwest) to the first tributary stream (Kings Creek), entering the Choptank from the northwest. Turn up this creek and look for the boat dock on the left. The preserve boardwalk is just a short walk from the dock. Access to the preserve by land is limited. Call for permission.

Activities: Bird-watching, nature walks.

Facilities: Boardwalk, elevated viewing platform, boat dock (no ramp).

Dates: Open daily, year-round.

Fees: None.

Closest town: Easton is 6 miles west.

For more information: Choptank Wetlands Kings Creek Preserve, The Nature Conservancy, Maryland/DC Chapter, 2 Wisconsin Circle, Suite 300, Chevy Chase, MD 20815. Phone (301) 656-8673.

SETH DEMONSTRATION FOREST

[Fig. 19(6)] Southeast of Easton on Dover Neck Road is Seth Demonstration Forest, a 125-acre forest of loblolly pine and hardwood trees where visitors can observe wildlife, hike, and hunt. The demonstration forests of the state's Department of Natural Resources are set aside to help private landowners learn about wise forest management practices.

Directions: From US 50 at Easton, go about 1.7 miles east on MD 331 (Dover Road). Turn right on Dover Neck Road and go 1.5 miles. The area is on the right for the next 0.7 mile.

Activities: Hiking, hunting (permit required).

Facilities: None.

Dates: Open sunrise to sunset daily, year-round.

Fees: None.

Closest town: Easton is 3 miles west.

For more information: Seth Demonstration Forest, c/o Martinak Forest Service, 105 Deep Shore Road, Denton, MD 21629. Phone (410) 479-1623.

ST. MICHAELS

[Fig. 19] This Talbot County town on MD 33 west of Easton is a destination point for many travelers because of its interesting blend of history, its small-town flavor, and its many gift shops, fine restaurants, and lodging facilities. The streets of town are lined with homes and shops from the eighteenth and nineteenth centuries, built in Colonial, Federal, and Victorian styles.

Also, **St. Mary's Square Museum** is housed in a building that was constructed in about 1800 as part of a steam and gristmill. This museum is located between Mulberry Street and East Chestnut Street on the original village green in the center of town. Brochures for the **St. Michaels Walking Tour**, which takes in the historic streets and the harbor, are available at the museum. Carriage rides, a tour and shuttle service, and river cruises provide additional ways to become acquainted with St. Michaels.

Newcomers to St. Michaels often ask townspeople to tell the story about how the little town fooled the British during the War of 1812. Because the important shipyards here produced privateers, blockade runners, and naval barges, the town became a target. Residents, forewarned that an attack was imminent in the early morning darkness of August 13, 1813, hoisted lanterns to the tops of trees and ship masts, causing the British to aim too high and overshoot the town. Only one house was hit, earning the name Cannonball House. The cannonball broke through the ceiling and rolled across the attic and down the stairs. A mother and her baby daughter were unhurt.

The cannon on St. Mary's Square were used in the Revolutionary War and transported here from Sewell's Point in Virginia. The smaller one was probably used in the defense of St. Michaels against the British in that 1813 bombardment. The bell on St. Mary's Square is known as the **Mechanics Bell**, once heard daily at 7 a.m., noon, and 5 p.m., marking the passage of the day for the workers in the nearby shipyards.

In addition to its shipbuilding past, St. Michaels is known for the tough watermen whose history is told at local museums. One local business distributed a million pounds of crabmeat a year and 16,000 gallons of oysters a week to Baltimore and Philadelphia. James Michener, who lived here while writing his novel, *Chesapeake*, delved into the history and culture of those watermen.

St. Michaels fine inns and restaurants are legendary. Look for several of them on Green, Chestnut, Cherry, North Harbor, and North Talbot streets. One of the popular places to find night life is the piano bar at **Jon and Mike's on the Miles**, located behind the St. Michaels Town Dock Marina at 125 Mulberry Street.

Directions: St. Michaels is located on MD 33 about 9 miles west of Easton in Talbot County.

For more information: St. Michaels Business Association, PO Box 1221, St. Michaels, MD 21663. Phone (800) 736-6965. For bicycle rental: St. Michaels Town Dock Marina, 305 Mulberry Street, St. Michaels, MD 21663. Phone (410) 745-2400 or (800) 678-8980.

CHESAPEAKE BAY MARITIME MUSEUM

[Fig. 19(7)] Many museums consist of a collection of artifacts inside a building. The Chesapeake Bay Maritime Museum at St. Michaels certainly has its share of artifacts demonstrating the close ties between the Eastern Shore and the Chesapeake Bay. The nearly 10,000 objects relate to commerce and trade, navigation, fisheries, and waterfowling. Items include working decoys by famous regional makers including Sam Barnes, Ben Dye, Daddy Holly, Ira Hudson, and the Ward brothers. There are tools used by oystermen, and relics from the War of 1812.

But this museum is more than the things inside. The structures—there are nine of them on a 16-acre site—*are* the museum. A bandstand on the grounds is the site for summer concerts of bluegrass, country, jazz, brass bands, and folk music. The Point Lookout fog bell tower, constructed at the mouth of the Potomac River in about 1888, is also on exhibit. The 1,000-pound bell, sounded automatically by a weight-driven machine, once helped guide boats in the bay's notorious fog.

One of the museum's most popular attractions is the old Hooper Strait Lighthouse, a cottage-style, screwpile lighthouse built in 1879 that has been fully restored, complete with flashing light. The lighthouse was moved to the museum site from its original location at Hooper Strait about 39 miles south of St. Michaels. Screwpile lighthouses were positioned in the water on iron pilings that were screwed into the bottom of the bay in an attempt to protect the house from damaging ice. Other historic buildings at the museum include the Eagle House, circa 1890, home of a steamboat captain, and a 1933 cannery warehouse.

The thousands of visitors who flock to the maritime museum are fascinated with the 85-vessel collection of wooden, sail, power, and row boats—the largest and most important collection of its kind in the world. The floating fleet of Chesapeake Bay workboats includes a Chesapeake Bay skipjack, a crab dredger, a river tug, a draketail, a dory boat, and a log-built bugeye. The bugeye, the *Edna E. Lockwood*, is a National Historic Landmark. Boats such as this one were the workhorses of the oyster industry in the late nineteenth and early twentieth century, designed with shallow draft and thick log bottoms to protect the boat from sharp oyster shells.

A small shed at the museum contains many more boats, including a dugout canoe such as those used by local Indians. Majestic tall ships, including *The Pride of Baltimore II*, a replica of a Baltimore clipper, regularly sail into the museum harbor.

Exhibits in the museum's Waterfowling Building describe the sporting traditions that

The Skipjack and Log Canoes

Oysters were becoming depleted in the Chesapeake Bay as far back as 1820, when Maryland passed a law restricting oyster dredging to sail-powered boats. The graceful skipjack was designed to meet the requirement. Traditional flat-bottomed crabbing skiffs were modified with a V-shaped hull, enlarged, and given a sail. They were inexpensive and easy to build, so that house carpenters and even watermen could make them.

Log canoes, a boat made with a bottom from hand-hewn logs fastened together, were originally used by oyster tongers. Just as cowboys develop competitions from their everyday work, so did Chesapeake Bay watermen develop contests to compare their skills. The log canoe evolved to become a racing craft, modified with springboards and wide spreads of canvas the boater could climb out on to keep the boat from capsizing in the wind. Visitors to the Chesapeake Bay Maritime Museum are sometimes treated to log canoe races.

have built up over the years around the annual visitation of thousands of migrating ducks, geese, and swans on the Atlantic Flyway. Outside the museum is a statue of Canton, ancestor of today's Chesapeake Bay retriever, a strong-swimming bird dog with webbed feet specifically bred for retrieving downed waterfowl.

The museum sponsors some of the Eastern Shore's most popular festivals and shows between May and December, including such events as the Antique and Classic Boat Festival in June, Crab Days in August, the Mid-Atlantic Small Craft Festival in October, and OysterFest in November.

Nearly 100,000 people from all over the world visit the Chesapeake Bay Maritime Museum annually, helping to support this private, not-for-profit facility with entry fees and donations.

Directions: The museum is located off MD 33 in St. Michaels at the end of Mill Street, on the harbor.

Facilities: The museum's 18 attractions include a lighthouse, a fleet of workboats, a small boat shed, a bell tower, and more. There are also restrooms and a gift shop.

Dates: The museum and museum store open at 9 a.m. daily, mid-Mar. to Jan., and weekends and holidays from Jan. to mid-Mar. Closing hours vary seasonally. Closed Thanksgiving, Christmas, and New Year's Day.

Fees: There is an entry fee.

For more information: Chesapeake Bay Maritime Museum, Mill Street, PO Box 636, St. Michaels, MD 21663. Phone (410) 745-2916.

TILGHMAN ISLAND

[Fig. 19] Tilghman Island, barely over 3 miles long, is at the southern tip of a long finger of land that reaches westward into the Chesapeake Bay from Talbot County. MD 33 and a drawbridge connect it to the mainland across Knapps Narrows on the northern end. The Choptank River meets the bay at the southern end of the island.

The shape of the long peninsula that is punctuated with Tilghman Island at the end is similar to the shape of Kent Island on the western side of Queen Anne's County to the north. A major difference in topography, however, has resulted in a great difference in traffic. Kent Island was much closer to the western shore—close enough to be connected by a bridge. The northern part of Kent Island became a thoroughfare between the two sides of the Chesapeake Bay. A motorist has to go out of the way, however, to follow MD 33 for 11 miles past St. Michaels to Tilghman Island.

People do go out of the way to find Tilghman, nevertheless. The island is a quiet refuge, known for its fine seafood restaurants, its bed and breakfast inns, its genteel hospitality, its sail charter opportunities, and its marshes teeming with waterfowl. Boaters love the island for its many harbors and marinas and the sport-fishing and crabbing opportunities. Tilghman Island is a fine place to become acquainted with the bay. There are narrated cruises, kayaks to rent, and sail-powered skipjacks and yachts to charter. In fact, the island is home to the largest commercial sailing fleet in the world.

From Tilghman Island's southern tip and the end of MD 33, **Sharps Island Lighthouse** is visible above the water 4 miles to the southwest. This round lighthouse on a caisson foundation is not open to the public.

Charter captains across the Chesapeake Bay bring parties to the island specifically to sample the delicious seafood and prime rib served family style at **Harrison's Chesapeake House** (410-886-2121). A 14-boat charter fleet, two cruise boats, and a country inn are all part of Harrison's, which is located on Dogwood Harbor on the island's eastern shore. Fantastic fishing makes Harrison's and other charter operations profitable. Rockfish (striped bass), Spanish mackerel, black drum, Norfolk spot, sea trout, and croaker reward anglers for their efforts.

Night life on the waterfront is available at Harrison's and at **Tilghman Island Inn** (800-866-2141 or 410-886-2141) at 21384 Coopertown Road.

Directions: Tilghman Island is at the end of US 33, 11 miles west of St. Michaels in Talbot County.

For more information: Talbot Chamber of Commerce, Tred Avon Square, Easton, MD 21601. Phone (410) 822-4606 or (888) BAYSTAY.

OXFORD

[Fig. 19] Oxford, officially founded in 1694, is one of Maryland's oldest towns. Its location near the mouth of the Tred Avon River was important to its future as a seaport. Beginning in 1694, the province of Maryland permitted only two ports of entry to operate on the Chesapeake Bay—Annapolis (which was then called Anne Arundel) on the west coast and Oxford on the Eastern Shore. Many tobacco growers established their plantations close to Oxford. British ships engaged in a brisk trade, bringing supplies from the old country and exporting tobacco and other products.

The American Revolution, however, brought the end of British shipping and the end of Oxford's affluence. Plantations changed their operations from tobacco to wheat. Businesses went bankrupt and grass grew in the city streets. It would take nearly a century and the coming of the railroad in 1871 for the people of Oxford to find a new wealth, which lay in the oyster beds at the bottom of the Chesapeake Bay. Until the oyster beds became seriously depleted in the early 1900s, the little town flourished again.

Following the decline of the oyster beds, and the consequent loss of the railroad and of steamship trade, Oxford once again became a quiet, out-of-the-way place, inhabited by a few inveterate watermen.

The very somnolence of the town on the Tred Avon River is what people who live in the metropolitan areas of Baltimore and Washington, DC, are seeking. In recent years, several businesses have sprung up to provide services to tourists. There are bed and breakfast inns, restaurants, gift shops, marinas, and boat and yacht repair yards.

Yachts and sailboats are available for charter or rent at several places. Bicycles can also be rented (**The Oxford Mews**, 410-820-8222) to tour the streets of town and the beautiful countryside. For those who still have energy at the end of the day, night life is available. **Pope's**

Tavern (410-226-5220) is downstairs at the **Oxford Inn** at 504 South Morris Street. **Latitude 38´ Bistro and Spirits** (410-226-5303) is at 26342 Oxford Road. The bistro is decorated with hand-painted murals. **Le Zinc** (410-226-5776) at 101 Mill Street, featuring a down-home French country cuisine, offers jazz piano music in its popular bar.

At the west end of North Morris Street is the terminus for the **Oxford-Bellevue Ferry** (410-745-9023), which is believed to be the nation's oldest privately operated ferry. It began its run in 1683, paused its operation from the American Revolution until 1836, and has been carrying people across the Tred Avon River to Bellevue since then. Note the **Oxford Custom House** here, an exact replica of an earlier customs house at the ferry terminal. The building is open on weekends from April through late fall. There is a small fee for the 10-minute ferry ride.

Relics and memorabilia from this waterfront town's protean past are on display at the **Oxford Museum** at Morris and Market streets. The museum is open afternoons, Friday through Sunday, spring through fall.

Directions: Oxford is on MD 333, 8 miles southwest of Easton in southern Talbot County.

For more information: Oxford Business Association, PO Box 544, Oxford, MD 21654. Phone (410) 226-5730. Talbot Chamber of Commerce, Tred Avon Square, Easton, MD 21601. Phone (410) 822-4606 or (888) BAYSTAY. Oxford Mews Bike Boutique, 105 South Morris Street, Oxford, MD 21654. Phone (410) 820-8222.

CHOPTANK RIVER FISHING PIERS STATE PARK

[Fig. 19(8)] The Choptank River Fishing Piers State Park on the Choptank River is the innovative result of searching for a new way to use an old bridge. When the Frederick C. Malkus Bridge was constructed, the adjacent Choptank River Bridge was abandoned by automobiles and the middle of the bridge was removed. The two bridge ends were turned into piers that became the domain of fishermen, crabbers, bird watchers, and runners.

The lighted piers—one extending 0.75 mile into the Choptank River from the Talbot County side, one extending 0.5 mile from the Dorchester County side—are popular places when striped bass (rockfish), yellow perch, hardheads, sea trout, and catfish are biting. Maryland blue crabs are also available in the brackish waters of the Choptank.

The pier on the Talbot County side adjoins 25 acres of land that extend upriver. A path leads along the Choptank River and Bolingbroke Creek, where a walker can see spring, summer, and fall wildflowers. Rabbits, groundhogs, opossums, raccoons, and other wildlife of overgrown fields are in the area. The piers provide an excellent observation deck for watching Canada geese, osprey, and ducks.

Directions: The two piers are located on opposite sides of the Choptank River adjacent to the Frederick C. Malkus Bridge at Cambridge.

Activities: Fishing, crabbing, bicycling, walking, running, picnicking, sunbathing.

Facilities: Two lighted handicapped-accessible piers. Picnic tables and a walking path are on the Talbot County side.

Dates: The piers are open 24 hours a day, year-round.

Fees: There is a small user fee.

Closest town: The pier on the south side of the river is at Cambridge. The other pier across the river is about 1.5 miles from Cambridge.

For more information: Choptank River Fishing Piers State Park, 29761 Bolingbroke Point Drive, Trappe, MD 21673. Phone (410) 476-3795. Also, Tuckahoe State Park, phone (410) 820-1668.

RESTAURANTS IN TALBOT COUNTY

It's no surprise that a county with more than 600 miles of shoreline would have wonderful seafood restaurants. Here is a sampling of Talbot County's finest:

208 TALBOT. 208 North Talbot Street, St. Michaels. Lunch and dinner are served Wednesday through Sunday at this exquisite restaurant that has been named a Distinguished Restaurant of North America. Reservations are recommended. *Moderate to expensive. Phone (410) 745-3838.*

CRAB CLAW RESTAURANT. Navy Point, St. Michaels. Sample Maryland's blue crabs and other Chesapeake Bay seafood while watching boats in the harbor. Open daily Mar. through mid-Dec. *Inexpensive to moderate. Phone (410) 745-2900.*

THE TILGHMAN ISLAND INN. 21384 Coopertown Road, Tilghman. Expansive views of the Chesapeake Bay enhance the fresh seafood and American cuisine at this upscale resort inn overlooking Knapps Narrows and a waterfowl sanctuary. Winner of the Wine Spectator Award of Excellence. Live piano music is featured on weekends. *Moderate to expensive. Phone (800) 866-2141 or (410) 886-2141.*

PIER STREET RESTAURANT. West Pier Street, Oxford. Dine inside or out on the waterfront at the junction of the Tred Avon and Choptank rivers at this restaurant, which is open seasonally. The menu includes fresh local seafood, steamed crabs, clams, and nonseafood items. *Moderate. Phone (410) 226-5171.*

SCHOONER'S LANDING. 318 Tilghman Street, Oxford. Sample fresh seafood, steamed crabs, and Sunday brunch at this casual waterfront restaurant and bar. An outdoor deck overlooks Town Creek. *Moderate. Phone (410) 226-0160.*

LODGING IN TALBOT COUNTY

Despite the remote locations of its historic villages, Talbot County is loaded with bed and breakfasts and historic inns. Here are a few of them:

ASHBY 1663 B&B. 27448 Ashby Drive, Easton. This elegant bed and breakfast has lovely waterfront views. *Expensive. Phone (410) 822-4235 or (800) 458-3622.*

THE INN AT PERRY CABIN. 308 Watkins Lane, St. Michaels. This inn features British hospitality and has been rated the fifth Best Resort Hotel in the USA. *Expensive. Phone (410) 745-2200.*

ST. MICHAELS HARBOUR INN AND MARINA. 101 North Harbor Road, St. Michaels. This harbor-front hotel has 45 luxury rooms and waterfront suites, 60 boat slips, a harbor-side pool and bar, a Jacuzzi, and a marina. Steak and seafood are on the menu at Windows, the waterfront restaurant. Pedal boats and bikes are available for rent. *Expensive. Phone (800) 955-9001 or (410) 745-9001.*

WADES POINT INN ON THE BAY. Wades Point Road, St. Michaels. This historic waterfront inn has a one-mile nature trail on a 120-acre farm. All rooms have a view of the water. *Expensive. Phone (410-745-2500).*

BLACK WALNUT POINT INN. Black Walnut Road, Tilghman Island. This inn is located on a 57-acre state-owned wildlife sanctuary at the southern tip of Tilghman Island. Enjoy the views from the pool, a nature trail, the tennis courts, and from rocking chairs and bay-side hammocks. *Expensive. Phone (410) 886-2452.*

CHESAPEAKE WOOD DUCK INN. Gibsontown Road at Dogwood Harbor, Tilghman Island. Called "luxurious, immaculate, and well-appointed" by the *New York Times*, this 1890 inn has period antiques, a sunroom, and a wide lawn that stretches to water's edge. *Expensive. Phone (800) 956-2070 or (410) 886-2070.*

THE MOORINGS B&B. 7857 Tilghman Island Road, Sherwood. This comfortable inn is known for its great breakfasts and proximity to Tilghman Island. *Moderate. Phone (800-316-6396 or 410-745-6396).*

THE OXFORD INN. 504 South Morris Street, Oxford. Located in Oxford's historic district, this three-story B&B has traditional Eastern Shore ambiance. It has quaint, beautifully decorated rooms and a historic restaurant, Pope's Tavern. *Moderate to expensive. Phone (410) 226-5220.*

Dorchester County

[Fig. 20] Dorchester County is nearly as much a part of the Chesapeake Bay as it is a part of the Eastern Shore. The bay and its tributaries permeate the county deeply and form a good part of its boundaries.

On its 70-mile journey to the bay, the Choptank River, the largest of some 20 rivers on the Eastern Shore, flows along the northern border of the county. Marshyhope Creek, a Nanticoke River tributary, meanders through the eastern part of the county near the Delaware line and the Nanticoke itself forms the county's southeastern border with Wicomico County. The Chesapeake Bay is on the west and south. Inland are the open waters and marshes of Fishing Bay, the sprawling Blackwater River, and innumerable other rivers and creeks.

In fact, where water ends and land begins is a mapmaker's nightmare, as much of the land area is comprised of wetlands, marshes, inlets, coves, and bays. Every storm that sweeps across the bay from the west or swirls in from the northeast does its job at resculpting the boundaries.

Both the human and natural history of Dorchester are inexorably linked to the watery surroundings. Fishing villages with workboats tied to docks and crab pots piled high are a common find for those who explore the back roads. Anglers can hire half- and full-day

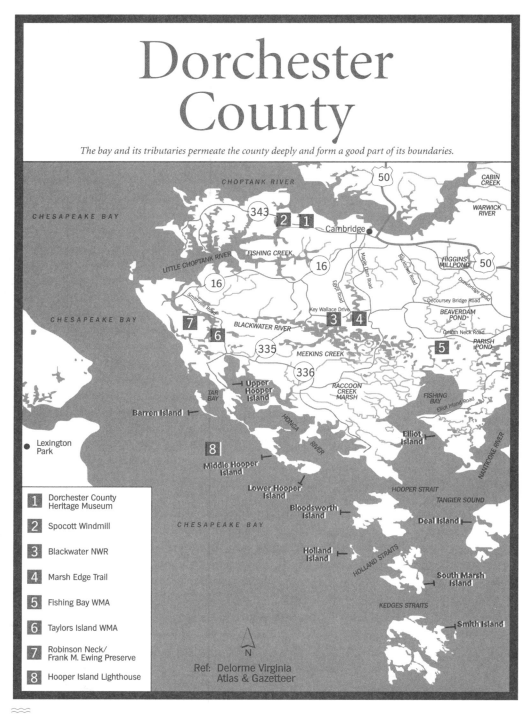

Dorchester County

The bay and its tributaries permeate the county deeply and form a good part of its boundaries.

1 Dorchester County Heritage Museum

2 Spocott Windmill

3 Blackwater NWR

4 Marsh Edge Trail

5 Fishing Bay WMA

6 Taylors Island WMA

7 Robinson Neck/ Frank M. Ewing Preserve

8 Hooper Island Lighthouse

Ref: Delorme Virginia Atlas & Gazetteer

charters in summer for flounder, sea trout, spot, and drum. Ravenous striped bass, known locally as rockfish, tear into bait during special seasons in spring and fall. The bay's tributary rivers hold white perch, catfish, and largemouth bass.

Six museums display the county's maritime and agricultural heritage and depict the life of the waterman and farmer. Wildfowl blinds invite hunters and photographers to the edges of ponds and marshes where the air is often filled with the chatter of geese and ducks.

The **Dorothy-Megan of the Choptank** (410-943-4775) is an authentic paddle wheel riverboat docked at 6304 Suicide Bridge Road west of Hurlock. Dinner cruises and sight-seeing cruises offer a peaceful way to enjoy the meanders of the Choptank River. The **Hooper's Island Crab Mania Tour** (800-648-7067) is a self-guided tour of the seaside watermen's villages on what is actually a string of three islands—Upper Hooper, Middle Hooper, and Lower Hooper—connected by MD 335 in the southwestern corner of the county. Remnants of the county's earliest settlements, all listed on the National Register of Historic Places, are on picturesque Taylors Island. These include the first **Dorchester Schoolhouse** (circa 1785), **Bethlehem M. E. Church** (1787), and the **Chapel of Ease** (1707). The old-fashioned Island General Store on the island is a pleasant place to stop for a soda, sandwich, and an ice cream sandwich. The **Taylor's Island Museum** (410-397-3338 or 410-397-3262) is housed in The Old School (circa 1916), where local memorabilia and regional antiques are displayed. The museum is open by appointment.

The **Underground Railroad Tour** (410-228-0401) includes the **Brodess Plantation,** birthplace of Harriett Tubman. Called the Moses of her people, Tubman was a runaway slave who came back many times to the Delmarva peninsula to help some 300 slaves escape along the Underground Railroad during the Civil War. A highway marker on Greenbrier Road off US 50 south of Cambridge honors the brave woman.

A partial list of annual events is further evidence of Dorchester's close ties to the bay. There's the Nanticoke River Canoe/Kayak Classic, the Nanticoke River Shad Festival, the Bay Country Festival, the Cambridge Sail Regatta, the Cambridge Classic Powerboat Regatta, the Seafood Feast-I-Val, the Chesapeake Bay Log Canoe Races, the Warwick Riverfest, and the Grand National Waterfowl Hunt.

Weekends in Dorchester County bring karaoke and other types of music at **Joyce's and Mike's Tavern** (410-943-1207) on Main Street in East New Market and at the **Suicide Bridge Restaurant** at Secretary (410) 943-4689. Billiards and arcade games are available at **Cambridge Arcade** at 403 Race Street (410-228-9683) in Cambridge.

Visitors can easily get caught up in the county's past and present. Many seafood restaurants and lodging facilities have waterfront views. There's a skipjack to sail, a riverboat to ride, seafood to sample, rivers to canoe, and sanctuaries where river otters play.

For more information: Dorchester County Department of Tourism, Sailwinds Park Visitor Center, 2 Rose Hill Place, Cambridge, MD 21613. Phone (800) 522-TOUR. Web site www.shorenet.net/tourism. E-mail dtourism@shorenet.net.

🌊 THE CAMBRIDGE AREA

Settled in 1864, Cambridge is the county seat and among the oldest towns in Maryland. For centuries, the town has served as a port for watermen harvesting the Chesapeake Bay's crabs and oysters. Processing plants became an important industry here, both for seafood and for crops produced by area farms. The industry spawned other work, such as barrel-making, a tradition that a local cooper carries on. Likewise, other handmade crafts of the community show the influence of the past.

In its early history, before the days of processing plants, the town served as a market for tobacco, then as the site for lumber and flour mills. A shipbuilding industry, supplied by oak and pine from the lumber mills, grew along the banks of Cambridge Creek. Skipjacks, bugeyes, and log canoes were among the vessels fashioned by local craftsmen.

In February, the town is home to an annual Outdoor Show with the National Muskrat Skinning Championship, an unusual event that grew out of a once-brisk fur trade here. A modern development called **Sailwinds Park** (410-522-TOUR or 410-228-SAIL) on the Choptank River is the site of many more festivals such as the Bay Country Festival in early July, the Seafood Feast-I-Val in August, and the Native American Festival in September. Speedboat, sailboat, and log canoe races are held here. A nonprofit corporation with a goal of revitalizing the community and the county is developing the multimillion-dollar, 35-acre waterfront park. The newest attraction is a state-of-the-art visitor center with two floors of information and exhibits on Chesapeake Bay heritage. The park also includes a boardwalk, a sandy beach with nettle nets, and a popular 14,000-square-foot festival hall. The visitor center at 2 Rose Hill Place off US 50 houses the Dorchester Department of Tourism and is open daily, year-round.

For the flavor of bygone days, take a self-guided **historic walking tour** along the tree-lined and historic streets of town, where homes date back to the eighteenth and nineteenth centuries. The tour begins on brick-lined High Street, which is located about a dozen blocks west of US 50 and stretches from Washington Street (MD 343) north to the Choptank River. The **Richardson Maritime Museum** (410-221-1871) at 401 High Street pays tribute to the wooden boat-building heritage of the Chesapeake Bay.

Feel the power as wind fills the sails during a river cruise aboard the **Nathan of Dorchester** (410-228-7141). This authentic skipjack is berthed at Long Wharf at the northern end of High Street on the Choptank River. For narrated boat tours aboard **Cambridge Lady,** call (410) 221-0776.

The **Brannock Maritime Museum** at 210 Talbot Avenue contains artifacts from the Chesapeake Bay and displays on the shipbuilding industry and what was called the Oyster Navy. The Oyster Navy consisted of a fleet of 40 boats that enforced fishing regulations in the 1800s and the first part of the 1900s. Those were violent times for Maryland and Virginia watermen, who fought sometimes bloody fights over fishing rights during what was called the Oyster Wars. The museum is open Fridays through Sundays or by appointment.

At 902 LaGrange Avenue is the **Meredith House and Nield Museum** (410-228-7953), a 1760 Georgian that is headquarters for the Dorchester Historical Society. Artifacts from six Maryland governors who were born in the county are on display in the Meredith House. The museum contains relics from the area's cultural, agricultural, maritime, and industrial past. Doors are open from 10 to 4, Thursday through Saturday, year-round, except major holidays.

Good fishing is available from a pier jutting into the Choptank River on the east side of the US 50 bridge. The pier, which is actually the remains of an earlier bridge, is part of **Choptank River Fishing Piers State Park** (*see* page 251).

At 1716 Taylors Island Road (MD 16) west of town is **Old Trinity Church** (410-228-2940), the oldest Episcopal Church in continuous use in the United States. In the old cemetery are the remains of a Maryland governor and one of Abraham Lincoln's aides. The simple brick building, built about 1675, stands among tall trees and boxwoods on the banks of Church Creek about 7 miles southeast of Cambridge.

For more information: Dorchester County Department of Tourism, Visitor Center at Sailwinds Park, 2 Rose Hill Place, Cambridge, MD 21613. Phone (800) 522-TOUR.

DORCHESTER HERITAGE MUSEUM

[Fig. 20(1)] The Dorchester Heritage Museum, located on a former duPont estate on Horn Point Road west of Cambridge, focuses on the county's colorful past, which is closely tied to the Chesapeake Bay. The four main areas of the museum are the Heritage Displays, the Waterman Room, the Archeology Room, and Aviation Hall. There are also exhibits designed especially for children. In May, antique and classic airplanes from across the country land here to be judged in the Antique Airplane Fly-in.

Also on the 850-acre former estate, along the shores of the Choptank River, is **Horn Point Environmental Laboratories** (410-228-9250), which is part of the University of

Submerged Aquatic Vegetation

Submerged aquatic vegetation, or SAV for short, is a fancy term for the underwater grass beds of the Chesapeake Bay. The underwater grasses help scientists monitor the bay's health. Not only do grasses indicate improved water quality, but they also provide both food and shelter for waterfowl, fish, clams, oysters, crabs, and smaller crustaceans.

However, the beds have been assaulted from various fronts such as siltation, pollution, and the scarring effects of clam dredging. Water clouded by excessive nutrients, such as from agricultural runoff, blocks the sunlight necessary for the growth of the underwater plants. The drastic decline of underwater grasses over the past few decades has paralleled an overall decline in the health of the estuary. Environmental changes, coupled with favorable amounts of freshwater flow into the bay during recent droughts, promote a tantalizing resurgence of grasses some years, except in the very important area of Tangier Sound. The disappearance of those grasses in other years is disappointing and frustrating. The problem continues to tax the ingenuity of scientists to come up with solutions and the willingness of the public to take necessary steps to keep the bay healthy.

Great Blue Heron

Even children watching this great bird with its slow wing beat, neck folded on its back, and long legs streaming behind, think they've seen an amazing sight—and indeed they have. The great blue heron (*Ardea herodias*), sometimes called a crane, can measure 4 or 5 feet from head to tail, with a nearly 6-foot wingspan. This fairly common slate-blue wading bird with the black crest patiently stalks its prey in the wetlands of Holland Island, standing motionless for many moments before striking with lightning speed to spear a fish with its long beak. The fish is then swallowed head first. A big fish on the banks with holes poked in its side may be a sign that the heron literally bit off more than it could swallow.

Maryland's Center for Environmental and Estuarine Studies. Both global environmental issues and local Chesapeake Bay resources are subjects of interest. Bay studies focus on aquaculture of striped bass and oysters, seafood science, and the role of wetlands and submerged aquatic vegetation in the health of the estuary. Several nature trails lead along the shores of the Choptank River. Tours of the center and of the aquaculture hatchery are available by appointment.

Directions: Go 2 miles west of Cambridge on MD 343. Bear right onto Horn Point Road. Go 1.5 miles to museum entrance, on the right.

Dates: Open from 1 to 4:30 on weekends from Apr. 15 through Oct. 30, or by appointment.

Fees: None.

Closest town: Cambridge is 3.5 miles east.

For more information: Dorchester Heritage Museum, 1904 Horn Point Road, Cambridge, MD 21613. Phone (410) 228-1899.

SPOCOTT WINDMILL

[Fig. 20(2)] Six miles west of Cambridge on MD 343 at Lloyds is the Spocott Windmill, the only grist post windmill still used for grinding grain in Maryland. Buildings that were once part of a small community are now open to the public as a museum. Included are a Colonial tenant house, a Victorian schoolhouse, and Lloyds Country Store Museum, which has World War II antiques on display. Twice annually (May and October), Spocott Windmill Day is held to celebrate the operation of this historic structure.

Directions: From Cambridge, go west on MD 343 approximately 6 miles and look for entrance, on the left.

Dates: Open daily, year-round, for self-guided tours. Guided tours are available by appointment.

Fees: Free. Donations are welcome.

For more information: Phone (410) 228-7090.

BLACKWATER NATIONAL WILDLIFE REFUGE

[Fig. 20(3)] When people think of refuges, they normally think of quiet places. At Blackwater National Wildlife Refuge there are certainly no honking horns, wailing sirens, or semis changing gears. But quiet is not necessarily the word you'd choose to describe this refuge that was established in 1933 for migratory birds.

In fall, the 23,000 acres of Blackwater come alive as thousands upon thousands of migratory ducks, geese, and tundra swans come cackling, squawking, and honking to a splashdown in the rich tidal marshes, freshwater ponds, and managed pools here. The various species come through in fairly predictable waves on their way south along the Atlantic Flyway. The beautiful blue-winged teal (*Anas discors*), for example, pass through in September.

Mornings and evenings most any time of year are full of the song of restless waterfowl, of warblers feeding among the bayberry, or of songbirds staking out territory. Even when visitors have gone home and the cold of a December night ices the bulrush fronds, the stillness may be broken by the wild, haunting yodeling of loons (*Gavis immer*) that head south to escape the frigid winters of northern Canada.

Noisy though it may be at times, the refuge is an exciting place, full of wonder. A place where schoolchildren laugh at the inelegant squawk of that graceful flyer, the great blue heron (*Ardea herodias*), or a photographer films a common merganser (*Mergus merganser*) as it runs across the water surface to become airborne like an airplane on a runway.

More than 250 species of birds including 20 species of ducks have been documented here. Two of them—the brown-headed nuthatch (*Sitta pusilla*) and chuck-will's-widow (*Caprimulgus carolinensis*)—are at the northern extent of their range at Blackwater. The nocturnal chuck-will's-widow, named for the sound of its evening and morning call, is a bit larger than its woodland cousin, the whip-poor-will.

When warming temperatures in late winter cause the ice in the ponds and marshes to break up, pied-bill grebes and great-crested cormorants arrive. During the nesting season, both expert and novice bird watchers enjoy observing or listening to the osprey, black-crowned night heron, great blue heron, glossy ibis, and willet.

If the very vocal willet (*Catoptrophorus semipalmatus*) is not noisily crying "will-will-willet," this large sandpiper gives away its identity when it spreads its flashy black-and-white banded wings. The willet resembles the greater yellowlegs (*Tringa melanoleuca*) in size and shape, but the greater yellowlegs normally nests farther north. Several species of flycatchers, vireos, and orioles also nest at the refuge

Marsh vegetation in the Chesapeake Bay suffers for many reasons—rising sea levels, siltation, and destruction by exotic

GREAT BLUE HERON
(*Ardea herodias*)

animals, to mention a few. The impoundments at Blackwater allow control of such factors as water level, salinity, and siltation. The pools are drawn down in spring to stimulate the growth of vegetation important to waterfowl. The draw-downs attract shorebirds such as dowitchers, dunlins, semi-palmated plovers, killdeer, and least sandpipers. Bird watchers are even rewarded with occasional glimpses of such rare migrants as the ruff (*Philomachus pugnax*), a sandpiper noted for its courtship dance that takes place in leks, or dancing grounds, established by the males.

The refuge is best known to travelers for its **Wildlife Drive**, a 3.5-mile auto tour along the dikes between pools and open marshland. The road is open to automobiles, pedestrians, and bicyclists. Allow extra time for getting out of the car with binoculars or spotting scope, but watch your step. Goose and duck droppings are everywhere. The trailheads for two short walking paths are also on the drive.

The National Wildlife Federation conducts an annual survey to count bald eagles at the refuge. In January of 1996, 129 were counted—the highest number since the survey began in 1976. The concentration of nesting bald eagles at Blackwater is one of the largest on the Atlantic Coast. Dead trees have even been installed at several locations by a power company as eagle perches.

Generally speaking, the larger and more cumbersome the bird, the shyer it is of humans. The hummingbird and the chickadee can be taught with relative ease to perch on a person's finger. The bald eagle, on the other hand, may not tolerate the intrusion of humans within 100 yards of a nesting site. The wide expanses of wetlands seem to be just what the eagles are looking for. For many people, the amazing sight of a soaring bald eagle over the refuge marshes forms a memory to last a lifetime.

Blackwater Refuge also has one of the largest concentrations of endangered Delmarva fox squirrels (*Sciurus niger cinereus*) in existence. Raccoons, rabbits, otters, opossums, white-tailed deer, red foxes, and muskrats are other inhabitants of the refuge and its environs. Non-native species such as the diminutive sika deer and the nutria must be controlled by hunting and trapping to keep them from overpopulating and destroying the wetlands. The nutria (*Myocastor coypus*) is a large rodent similar in appearance to the smaller and more valuable muskrat, but the voracious nutria destroys a wide variety of plants, roots and all, undermining the foundation of the wetlands. A list of other resident mammals, birds, reptiles, and amphibians is available at the visitor center.

Bicyclists can also obtain a map of two suggested bike loops. A 20-mile trail uses Key Wallace Drive, Maple Dam Road, MD 16, and MD 335 to form a loop between the refuge and Cambridge. A 25-mile southern loop connects Key Wallace Drive with MD 335, MD 336, Andrews Road, and Shorters Wharf Road. The terrain is flat and automobile traffic is usually light, especially on the southern loop.

Crabbing and fishing are permitted from April through September from boats, which must be launched outside the refuge or from Little Blackwater Bridge on Key Wallace Drive. Fishing is fair at best, with catches limited to white and yellow perch, sunfish, catfish, and an occasional largemouth bass.

The Spring Fling in May and an open house in December attract hundreds of people to demonstrations, exhibits, and discounted books and gifts at the refuge visitor center. Bird walks, eagle prowls, youth deer hunts, children's activities, and other events are scheduled throughout the year.

Directions: From US 50, just east of Cambridge in northwestern Dorchester County, go south on MD 16 (Church Creek Road) about 6 miles. Turn left on MD 335 (Church Creek-Golden Hill Road) and drive about 4 miles. Turn left at the refuge sign on Key Wallace Drive. Go 1 mile to the visitor center, on the right, or 2.5 miles for the entrance to Wildlife Drive, also on the right.

Activities: Bird-watching, walking, car touring, biking, fishing, crabbing, boating (no boat launching on refuge property), and seasonal hunting for white-tailed and Asian sika deer.

Facilities: Walking, driving, and bicycle trails. Visitor center with restrooms and gift shop.

Dates: The Wildlife Drive and outdoor facilities are open from dawn to dusk daily, year-round, except Thanksgiving and Christmas. The visitor center is open 8 to 4 Monday through Friday and 9 to 5 Saturday and Sunday. Fishing and crabbing are permitted from Apr. through Sept.

Fees: There are daily permit fees for vehicles, bicyclists, pedestrians, and commercial vans and buses on the Wildlife Drive.

Closest town: Cambridge is 12 miles to the north.

For more information. Blackwater National Wildlife Refuge, 2145 Key Wallace Drive, Cambridge, MD 21613. Phone (410) 228-2677. E-mail RSRW_BWNWR@fws.gov.

HIKING AT BLACKWATER NATIONAL WILDLIFE REFUGE

The 0.33-mile Marsh Edge Trail and the 0.5-mile Woods Trail are both connected to the Wildlife Drive. The Woods Trail, which loops through pines and mixed hardwoods, offers perhaps the best opportunity to spot the Delmarva fox squirrel. The trail is located on the Wildlife Drive about 1 mile from the entrance, on the right. Pets are not permitted on either trail.

MARSH EDGE TRAIL. [Fig. 20(4)] Allow 30 minutes for a leisurely walk along this self-guided nature trail that begins in a mature loblolly pine forest. The loblolly is at the northern end of its range on the Eastern Shore. The endangered Delmarva fox squirrel eats the tree's seeds, while bald eagles find its branches suitable for nests. The long, yellow-green needles of the loblolly grow in bundles of three.

The path emerges from the pines and leads along the edge of a typical Eastern Shore marsh on the Little Blackwater River. In the transition area between forest and marsh are shrubby plants such as groundsel-tree (*Baccharis halimifolia*) and northern bayberry (*Myrica pensylvanica*). These shrubs have adapted to the semi-saturated soils on the higher part of the marsh at the edge of the forest.

The bayberry is a wax myrtle with shiny evergreen leaves that have an aromatic smell when crushed. Cooks are familiar with the value of bay leaves in seasoning. Ingenious early settlers, who called it the candleberry bush, discovered that boiling would remove the waxy covering on the bayberry's fruits, leaves, and twigs. With the wax, they made candles, tallow, and soap.

An 80-foot boardwalk extends into the lower, wetter areas of the marsh. Look for plants tolerant of brackish wetlands such as cattails (*Typha augustifolia*) and three-square sedges such as saltmarsh bulrush (*Scirpus robustus*) and Olney three-square (*Scirpus americanus*). The three-squares have triangular stems. Their flowers are encased in overlapping scales, looking like little bunches of buds on the plant stem. The pink, five-petaled blossoms of the marsh mallow (*Althaea officinalis*) reward visitors from July through September. This showy hibiscus grows about 3 feet tall.

Avoid the three-leaved poison ivy, which is common here. Pack repellent to ward off biting insects from April to October.

Directions: After entering the Wildlife Drive, go about 0.3 mile. Go left and drive about 0.2 mile to trailhead parking.

Trail: Easy 0.33-mile wheelchair-accessible nature loop through pine forest and marsh.

✿ DORCHESTER COUNTY'S WILDLIFE MANAGEMENT

Four wildlife management areas totaling nearly 27,000 acres provide ample places for wildlife observation, hunting, boating, fishing, and crabbing in Dorchester County.

LeCompte Wildlife Management Area is a 485-acre tract of large oaks and loblolly pines that was set aside specifically to provide habitat for the Delmarva fox squirrel, which has been on the federal Endangered Species List since 1967. The area is located in the eastern part of the county about 5 miles southwest of Vienna. The habitat is so successful here that biologists have been able to trap and relocate squirrels from here to other promising locations in Maryland, Delaware, and Virginia.

Wild turkeys trapped in western Maryland were released at LeCompte to resupply the Eastern Shore's turkey population, which was once decimated by non-regulated hunting. Other wildlife that might be spotted along the numerous trails includes cottontail rabbits, bobwhite quail, woodcock, white-tailed deer, and sika deer.

Deer hunters come for muzzleloading, rifle, shotgun, and bow seasons. There are small-game seasons for rabbit, quail, and woodcock. Gray squirrels may not be hunted in order to protect fox squirrels, which can be hard to distinguish at a distance.

About 7 miles east of Cambridge is 313-acre **Linkwood Wildlife Management Area**, comprised of a mix of oaks, maple, black gum, and loblolly pine. Despite its small size, the dense forest provides an important nesting area for songbirds such as the scarlet tanager (*Piranga olivacea*). Tanagers and many other birds suffer from forest fragmentation in North American and from degradation of their winter range in the rain forests of South and Central America.

Bow, muzzleloading, and shotgun seasons draw deer hunters to Linkwood in the fall. Gray squirrels may also be hunted, but hunters must be able to distinguish between the gray squirrels and the endangered Delmarva fox squirrels, which are here in smaller numbers than at the LeCompte area. Hunters, hikers, and bird watchers should put boots in their car in case the ground is soggy.

Fishing Bay and Taylors Island wildlife management areas, which are more closely linked to the Chesapeake Bay, are described next. During warmer months at all these areas, bring inspect repellent and watch for poison ivy.

Directions: For LeCompte, from Vienna, in eastern Dorchester County, go south on Elliots Island Road about 1 mile. Turn right at a fork on Steele Neck Road and go about 4 miles to LeCompte, on left. For Linkwood, from the town of Linkwood, go 0.5 mile south on US 50 and turn left into entrance. Look for the sign marking the entrance, which looks like a private driveway of a house.

Activities: Hiking, seasonal hunting.

Facilities: Numerous unmarked trails and roads.

Dates (for all areas): Open dawn to dusk, year-round. Call for hunting seasons, which may vary from year to year.

Fees (for all areas): None.

Closest town: Vienna is about 5 miles northeast of LeCompte. Cambridge is about 7 miles west of Linkwood.

For more information (for all areas): LeCompte Work Center, 4220 Steele Neck Road, Vienna, MD 21869. Phone (410) 376-3236.

FISHING BAY WILDLIFE MANAGEMENT AREA

[Fig. 20(5)] Fishing Bay is the state's largest wildlife management area. With 25,000 acres of tidal wetlands broken only by little islands of loblolly pine, it's a good place to bring a boat. In addition to excellent opportunities for saltwater fishing and crabbing, the area is prime territory for observing nesting and wintering waterfowl.

The huge area complements the adjacent Blackwater National Wildlife Refuge (*see* page 258) by providing bay and river habitat and inland ponds for mallards, black ducks, teal, gadwall, pintails, scaup, and Canada geese. Sandpipers, plovers, and even the shy black rail (*Laterallus jamaicensis*) make use of the tidal flats. Even birders count this sparrow-sized rail a treasured find. Though it may be common in some areas, it is extremely wary as it pokes about under dead marsh grasses.

In Fishing Bay are Guinea and Chance islands, the ancestral home of the Nause-Waiwash Indian tribe. Descendants of the islanders still make annual visits.

Hunting is open seasonally for white-tailed and sika deer that live along the wooded marsh edges and for ducks and geese. Yearly leases may be obtained for fur trapping.

Directions: From Cambridge, go east on US 50 for about 1.5 miles. Turn right (south) on Bucktown Road and go about 7.5 miles. Turn left on Bestpitch Ferry Road and go about 4.5 miles, crossing the Transquaking River, where there is a boat landing. The entrance is on the right, past the boat landing. Other sections of the area and several more boat landings are accessible along Elliott Island Road on the eastern side and along Maple Dam Road on the western side.

Activities: Boating, fishing, crabbing, bird-watching, seasonal hunting, trapping (by yearly lease).

Facilities: Boat ramps, unmarked trails and roads.

Closest town: Cambridge is about 14 miles north and Vienna is about 14 miles east.

TAYLORS ISLAND WILDLIFE MANAGEMENT AREA

[Fig. 20(6)] The state wildlife management area on Taylors Island is a good place to experience a tidal marsh that is relatively untouched by human encroachment. Only a small part of the 1,100 acres of wetlands is accessible to those without boats. A state boat landing on Beaverdam Creek offers an entry to fishermen, crabbers, and nature enthusiasts.

Raccoons, muskrats, and river otters are some of the mammals that inhabit the marshlands. Small stands of loblolly pine and cedar forests support the Delmarva fox squirrel, white-tailed deer, and Asian sika deer, which is actually a species of elk. Because they are more strictly nocturnal, sika deer are less apt to be seen than white-tailed deer. Exposed mud flats at low tide are endlessly probed by plovers and sandpipers such as the dunlin (*Calidris alpina*), which breeds in the Arctic but migrates south during the winter. Look for the slight downward droop at the tip of the long bill to distinguish this very approachable sandpiper from others.

Out on more open water, osprey and eagles search for fish at the surface. Diving ducks such as scaup, canvasbacks, goldeneyes, and buffleheads disappear and reappear as they feed underwater. The small buffleheads (*Bucephala albeola*), also known as butterballs or spirit ducks, feeds on insects, crustaceans, and weeds. Males are predominantly white, with black markings.

For those who would like to camp nearby, **Taylors Island Family Campground** (410-397-3275) is located on Bay Shore Road. **Tideland Park** (800-673-9052 or 410-397-3473) is at 525 Taylors Island Road.

Directions: From US 50, just east of Cambridge in northwestern Dorchester County, go about 16 miles west on MD 16 (4 miles past the town of Madison) and turn left on Smithville Road. Drive about 3 miles (watch for signs) to parking lot or about 4 miles to county boat landing. This boat landing is at the western edge of Blackwater National Wildlife Refuge (*see* page 258).

Activities: Boating, fishing, crabbing, seasonal hunting, trapping (by yearly lease),

Facilities: Boat ramp.

Closest town: Cambridge is 20 miles to the northeast.

ROBINSON NECK/FRANK M. EWING PRESERVE

[Fig. 20(7)] In 1974, the Smithsonian Institution surveyed Chesapeake Bay natural areas and designated a portion of Taylors Island as a significant wetland. The undisturbed tidal marshlands make ideal waterfowl habitat, while the forested uplands provide sanctuary for the endangered Delmarva fox squirrel (*Sciurus niger cinereus*) and nesting space for the bald eagle (*Haliaeetus leucocephalus*). Frank M. Ewing donated the land to The Nature Conservancy in 1977. The 920 acres of pines and marshlands of the Robinson Neck/Frank M. Ewing Preserve represent one of the Conservancy's largest holdings in the state of Maryland. The preserve, which consists of half pine forest, half brackish tidal marsh, is open year-round for bird-watching and nature walks.

In the forest understory are wax myrtle (*Myrica cerifera*), American holly (*Ilex opaca*), and a profusion of poison ivy (*Toxicodendron radicans*). If catbirds and cedar waxwings don't get them first, beautiful red berries adorn the female hollies through the winter. Together, the berries and prickly leaves have inspired much Christmas card art. In the marsh, look for the typical wetland plants such as Olney three-square (*Scirpus americanus*), narrow-leaved cattail (*Typha augustifolia*), black needlerush (*Juncus roemerianus*), big cordgrass (*Spartina cynosuroides*) and saltmarsh cordgrass (*Spartina alterniflora*).

The preserve's nature trail begins at an old logging road and passes through the loblolly pine forest and marsh as it leads eastward to Slaughter Creek. To the north, this tidal creek joins the Chesapeake Bay at the mouth of the Little Choptank River. Look for deer tracks along the trail and the prints of muskrats and wading birds along the marsh edge, and be alert for possible sightings of the northern harrier, bald eagle, and osprey or fish hawk. Many migratory birds make use of the preserve in fall. Ducks and geese seek winter refuge. As in all preserves, stay on the trail to keep from damaging sensitive plants and habitat.

Several varieties of ferns thrive in the damp habitat along the trail. In waterlogged soil, royal fern (*Osmunda regalis*) can grow as tall as a man can. Cinnamon fern (*Osmunda regalis*) and netted chain fern (*Woodwardia areolata*) add their lacy accent to the understory.

Boaters may put into Slaughter Creek at Taylors Island Marina on the east side of the Taylors Island bridge and head southeast. After a 1.5 mile down the creek, the preserve is along the southwestern shore. Wildlife and waterfowl that are hard to approach on foot may be easier to study from a boat.

The preserve is adjacent to Taylors Island Wildlife Management Area. Wear bright clothing during hunting seasons. Prepare to deal with biting insects and poison ivy seasonally.

Directions: From MD 50, about 1 mile east of Cambridge, go south on MD 16 (Church Creek Road) for 16 miles to Taylor's Island bridge, which is just past a boat landing and Taylors Island Marina. Cross the bridge and go left (south) on Robinson Neck Road. Go 2.7 miles to a grassy road on the left that is blocked by a gate. Park on the left shoulder of the road. For the nature trail, walk 0.75 mile down the grassy road to the registration box and another 200 yards to the trailhead. The nature trail is a 1-mile round trip to the marsh and back.

Activities: Bird-watching and nature walks.

Facilities: Hiking trails, nature trail.

Dates: Open year-round.

Fees: None.

Closest town: Cambridge is 19 miles northeast.

For more information: Robinson Neck/Frank M. Ewing Preserve, The Nature Conservancy, Maryland/DC Chapter, 2 Wisconsin Circle, Suite 300, Chevy Chase, MD 20815. Phone (301) 656-8673.

HOOPER ISLAND LIGHTHOUSE

[Fig. 20(8)] This round tower on a caisson foundation was built in 1901 and began operating the next year. It is located exactly halfway up the Chesapeake Bay in Dorchester County, about 3.5 miles west of Hooper Island. The 63-foot-high lighthouse stands in 18 feet of water and is accessible only by boat. For two years, a white light flashed, magnified by a Fresnel lens. Then the light was changed to a steady white light with a flash every 15 seconds. The original fog bell was upgraded to a foghorn. Finally, the lighthouse became automated. It is not open to the public.

HOLLAND ISLAND

[Fig. 20] At the southernmost tip of Dorchester County is little 80-acre Holland Island. Just 1.5 miles long and vulnerable to the storms that sweep across the wide-open Chesapeake Bay from the west, the island and its trees serves as a buffer and a windbreak for the shallow waters and wetlands of Holland Straits to the east. Over the years, the island has been reduced by half from its original 160-acre size.

Bird watchers have identified hundreds of shorebirds, waterfowl, and migrating songbirds. The trees and isolation of Holland Island are perfect for the nesting bald eagles and the rookery of great blue herons. Oystercatchers and curlews poke about the shoreline. Geese, egrets, swans, ducks, gulls, and terns nest here. Osprey cruise the shoreline, looking for a fish swimming too close to the surface. Brown pelicans soar by in formation, sometimes gliding so close to the water they disappear from sight briefly behind the small waves. Diamondback terrapins and even occasional white-tailed deer that swim to the island to feed have been spotted.

The island was not always so undisturbed by humans, however. In the late 1800s and early 1900s, about 360 people maintained a general store, a church, a grade school, a post office, and a fleet of schooners and skipjacks that prowled the bay. Erosion gradually wore away the island's west side until residents were forced to leave. Three graveyards were left to the vagaries of the sea. Two remain, but one has slipped beneath the waves.

Recently, a nonprofit organization has surfaced to save what is now called the Holland Island Preserve by shoring up the western side. With luck, the work will keep shellfish beds from being silted over, protect wildlife and wildfowl habitat, save valuable underwater grasses, and preserve the remaining two cemeteries.

For more information: The Holland Island Preservation Foundation, 317 Beaglin Park Drive, Salisbury, MD 21804. Phone (410) 742-0737 or (410) 546-0155.

RESTAURANTS OF DORCHESTER COUNTY

Cambridge, the only large town in Dorchester County, is the obvious place to find good seafood restaurants. But several more are tucked into out of the way places. Here are a few selections:

PORTSIDE SEAFOOD RESTAURANT. Cambridge Creek, Cambridge. Casual dining overlooking Cambridge Creek. Sample the local seafood, which includes steamed crabs, soft crabs, and oysters. *Inexpensive. Phone (410) 228-9007.*

SNAPPER'S WATERFRONT CAFE. 112 Commerce Street, Cambridge. Enjoy fresh seafood in a casual waterfront atmosphere on Cambridge Creek. The huge variety of menu items also includes southwestern fare, Jamaican items, steaks, and ribs. *Inexpensive to moderate. Phone (410) 228-0112.*

SPICERS SEAFOOD. Woods Road, Cambridge. Casual dining, featuring fresh salads and seafood. Closed Tuesdays. *Inexpensive to moderate. Phone (410) 221-0222.*

OLD SALTY'S RESTAURANT. Hooper's Island Road, Fishing Creek. This casual restaurant sometimes offers family dining. Creative menu and excellent food. *Inexpensive. Phone (410) 397-3752.*

TAYLORS ISLAND GENERAL STORE. Route 16, Taylors Island. Where there's a glut of local parked cars at lunchtime, the food is sure to be good. Try the crab or lima bean soup, oyster chowder, or crab cakes. Soup and sandwich menu. *Inexpensive. Phone (410) 221-2911.*

SUICIDE BRIDGE RESTAURANT. 6304 Suicide Bridge Road, Secretary. Fresh seafood and steaks are on the menu at this waterfront restaurant next to the paddlewheel boat, *Dorothy Megan. Inexpensive. Phone (410) 943-4689.*

LODGING IN DORCHESTER COUNTY

There are several bed and breakfast inns in Dorchester County, in addition to a couple of motels and a retreat.

NORTHFORK BED AND BREAKFAST. 6505 Palmers Mill, Hurlock. Accommodations are in a main house and guest house in a pastoral waterfront setting. Open year-round. *Moderate. Phone (410) 943-4706 or (800) NFORK-BB.*

CAMBRIDGE INN. Route 50 East, Ocean Gateway, Cambridge. Motel with 96 rooms is just east of Cambridge. *Moderate. Phone (410) 221-0800.*

GLASGOW INN. 1500 Hambrooks Boulevard, Cambridge. Colonial riverside plantation bed and breakfast, circa 1760, in a small park. National Register of Historic Places. *Moderate to expensive. Phone (410) 228-0575.*

LODGECLIFF ON THE CHOPTANK. 103 Choptank Terrace, Cambridge. Country bed and breakfast with an outstanding view overlooking the Choptank River. *Moderate. Phone (410) 228-1760.*

BECKY PHIPPS INN. Taylors Island Road, Taylors Island. Bed and breakfast with four rooms on Slaughter Creek near the Choptank River. Convenient to several areas that offer birding, boating, hunting, fishing, and bicycling. *Moderate. Phone (410) 221-2911.*

TWIN WILLOWS FARM. Meekins Neck Road, Golden Hill. This 1200-acre retreat is adjacent to Blackwater National Wildlife Refuge and Taylors Island Wildlife Management Area, catering to sportsmen and naturalists. Two spacious homes for up to 20 guests. *Expensive. Phone (888) 726-7863.*

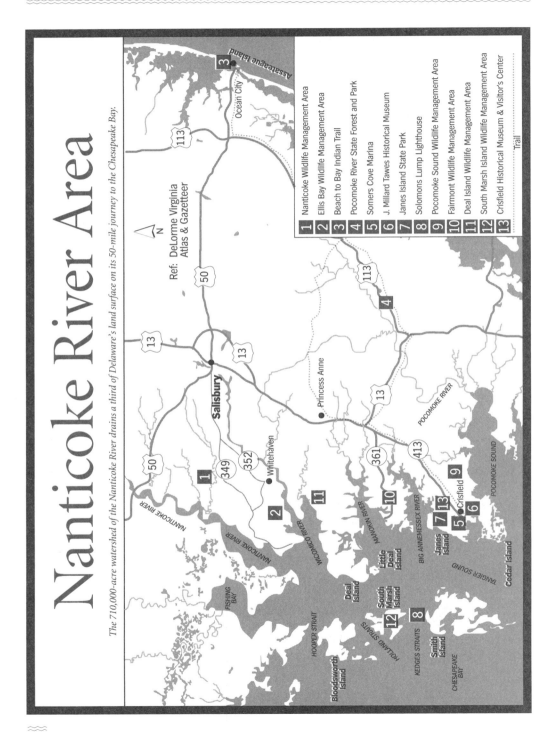

Nanticoke River Area

The 710,000-acre watershed of the Nanticoke River drains a third of Delaware's land surface on its 50-mile journey to the Chesapeake Bay.

Ref: DeLorme Virginia Atlas & Gazetteer

1. Nanticoke Wildlife Management Area
2. Ellis Bay Wildlife Management Area
3. Beach to Bay Indian Trail
4. Pocomoke River State Forest and Park
5. Somers Cove Marina
6. J. Millard Tawes Historical Museum
7. Janes Island State Park
8. Solomons Lump Lighthouse
9. Pocomoke Sound Wildlife Management Area
10. Fairmont Wildlife Management Area
11. Deal Island Wildlife Management Area
12. South Marsh Island Wildlife Management Area
13. Crisfield Historical Museum & Visitor's Center

---- Trail

Nanticoke River

[Fig. 21] Traditionally, public attention and funding is directed toward cleaning up heavily polluted waterways rather than protecting those that are still fairly pristine. However, that approach results in neglect and even abuse of those lakes, rivers, and streams that have relatively good water quality.

Of the many Chesapeake Bay tributaries, only four have been singled out as "best-chance waterways" by the Maryland/District of Columbia chapter of The Nature Conservancy. These four—the Nanticoke River, Sideling Hill Creek, Nassawango Creek, and Nanjemoy Creek—have the best chance by far of sustaining a rich natural diversity and exceptional water quality.

The streams are very different from one another. Nanjemoy Creek, which supports a fascinating and often noisy blue heron rookery, empties into the Potomac River below Washington, DC, in Charles County. Sideling Hill Creek is a trout stream in the western Maryland mountains. Nassawango Creek, location of the beautiful Nassawango Creek Cypress Swamp Preserve (*see* page 278), empties into the Pocomoke River in Worcester County in the southeastern corner of the Eastern Shore of Maryland. The Nanticoke flows southwestward from its headwaters in Delaware to Tangier Sound and the Chesapeake Bay, providing a natural boundary between the counties of Dorchester and Wicomico.

The 710,000-acre watershed of the Nanticoke drains a third of Delaware's land surface, then a huge chunk of the lower Eastern Shore of Maryland on its 50-mile journey to the Chesapeake Bay. The black duck, the canvasback, and the blue-winged teal that sail in for landings, then stretch their wings or dive for food are doing much as ducks have done for centuries on the river. In addition to the ducks and other wildfowl that find refuge or nesting territory here, the river has also sheltered wildlife such as the muskrat, beaver, red fox, white-tailed deer, and raccoon for thousands of years.

Humans have also benefited from the riches of the Nanticoke over the millennia. Anthropologists have discovered artifacts indicating that humans were in the area in ancient times, beginning in the Middle Archaic period around 5,500 B.C. Careful excavation of archeological sites is ongoing. The river takes its name from the Nanticoke Indians, who fished its water and hunted its banks. This tribe was large, even feared, at the time Captain John Smith came up the Chesapeake Bay.

Among some 50 tributaries of the Chesapeake Bay, the Nanticoke is one of the most pristine. Some 38 percent of the watershed is forested, including the largest unbroken pine forest on the Delmarva peninsula. Woods of loblolly pine, sweetgum, red maple, red cedar, and a variety of oaks stretch for miles, harboring birds such as vireos and thrushes that need unfragmented forests to survive. Huge, gnarled baldcypress trees (*Taxodium distichum*) emerging from the water make up one of the northernmost stands of its kind on the East Coast.

In addition to the extensive forests, the Nanticoke watershed includes thousands of

Reversed Bladderwort

Most bladderworts are carnivorous herbs of bogs and marshes with a marvelous adaptation for survival in the form of tiny bladders attached to the roots. Larvae, fry, crustaceans, and other minute life forms in the water are sucked in when they touch the trigger-like flagella at the edge of the bladder, causing the bladder to suddenly expand, creating a vacuum. Once inside, the plant secretes enzymes that digest the prey. Above ground, the two-lipped flowers resemble snapdragon blossoms. The reversed bladderwort (*Utricularia resupinata*) of the Nanticoke watershed has purplish flowers. Other varieties sport blossoms of yellow, blue, pink, or red.

acres of freshwater wetlands along the streams and salt marshes, and then becomes a brackish estuary influenced by tides between Dorchester and Wicomico counties. In fact, the Nanticoke contains nearly a third of Maryland's tidal wetlands.

The variety and size of habitat, the lack of development, and the temperate climate translate into diversity of species. The river supports healthy populations of striped bass (rockfish), which come far upriver in May to spawn, in addition to sea trout, largemouth bass, yellow perch, pickerel, and catfish.

The wetlands are wintering grounds for a large percentage of the various species of migratory waterfowl that use the Atlantic Flyway such as redhead ducks and green-winged teal. Spring nesters include a vast array of ducks such as the gadwall, wood duck, and mallard, as well as many other waterfowl and songbirds of marshes and woodlands.

The Nanticoke watershed also protects 120 rare and threatened species of plants and animals. Among this astounding number of imperiled life forms are plants with descriptive, even amusing names, such as box huckleberry (*Gaylussacia brachycera*), seaside alder (*Alnus maritima*), spreading pogonia orchid (*Cleistes divaricata*), Parker's pipewort (*Eriocaulon parkeri*), and reversed bladderwort (*Utricularia resupinata*).

Delmarva fox squirrels (*Sciurus niger cinereus*), peregrine falcons (*Falco perigrinus*), black rails (*Laterallus jamaicensis*), and bald eagles (*Haliaeetus leucophalus*) are important species that find refuge in the Nanticoke's upland forests and wetlands.

Maryland's portion of the Nanticoke River is too wide to be good for canoeing or kayaking. However, several tributaries offer fine waters for quiet, shady paddles. See Idylwild Wildlife Management Area, page 239 for information on Marshyhope Creek, which flows through parts of western Caroline and Dorchester counties on its way to the Nanticoke. In Wicomico County, Plum Creek enters the Nanticoke about 3 miles west of the Delaware line. About 1 mile downriver from Sharptown, Chicone Creek enters just above where US 50 crosses the river at Vienna. In addition to these creeks, four others on the Wicomico County side of the river are recommended to paddlers. The creeks are, from north to south, Barren Creek, Rewastico Creek, Quantico Creek, and Wetipquin Creek.

Boat landings are on Barren Creek at Mardela Springs and on Wetipquin Creek at Tyaskin. Accessing the other creeks can be difficult. Many stretches of the tributaries have segmented public and private holdings. Contact the county tourism offices, the state Department of Natural Resources, or the Maryland/DC Chapter of The Nature Conservancy for more information.

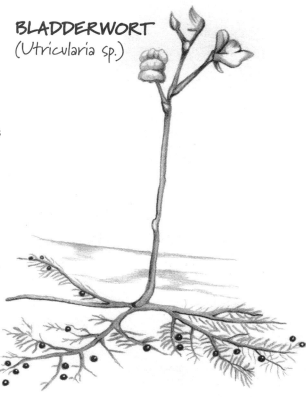

BLADDERWORT
(*Utricularia* sp.)

To a boater, the lovely meanders of the Nanticoke River may appear much as they did when Christopher Columbus explored them in 1608. However, important changes have occurred, just as they have throughout the Chesapeake. In the last 50 years, half of the marshes at the mouth of the river have been lost to rising sea levels and sedimentation, which have also done their share to wipe out most oyster reefs. Crabbing, clamming, and striped bass fishing have taken a hit from pollution and disease.

The nontidal wetlands of the upper river are also hurting because of poor agricultural practices and bulldozers operating in the streambeds. Several conservation-minded organizations, including the Nanticoke Watershed Alliance at Tyaskin, work with private citizens, industry, government, and educators to protect the river. The health of the Nanticoke watershed is a priority in a program of The Nature Conservancy called Campaign for the Chesapeake Rivers.

Despite its problems, the river and the land it empties remain a haven to creatures of wing, fin, and fur. The river's rich history is fodder for campfire stories of Indians, pirates, tall ships, steamboats, slave runners and the underground railroad. Its deep woods and dark waters are a focal point for students of the environment; lure to hunter, boater, canoeist, and angler; and solace for those who simply need to get away.

For more information: Dorchester County Department of Tourism, 203 Sunburst Highway, Cambridge, MD 21613. Phone (800) 522-TOUR. Wicomico County Convention and Visitors Bureau, 8480 Ocean Highway, PO Box 2333, Salisbury, MD 21802-2333. Phone (410) 548-4914 or (800) 332-8687. Maryland Department of Natural Resources, 580 Taylor Avenue, Tawes State Office Building, Annapolis, MD 21401. Phone (410) 260-8000. Nanticoke Watershed Alliance, PO Box 79, Tyaskin, MD 21865. The Nature Conservancy, Maryland/DC Chapter, 2 Wisconsin Circle, Suite 300, Chevy Chase, MD 20815. Phone (301) 656-8673.

NANTICOKE WILDLIFE MANAGEMENT AREA

[Fig. 21(1)] This 1,700-acre marshy area spreads along the tidal Nanticoke River and Quantico Creek. A picturesque trail leads from the parking lot onto a peninsula where nature photographers and wildlife observers can find osprey, herons, ducks, geese, and songbirds, and can perhaps catch a glimpse of a pair of bald eagles that nest near Quantico Creek. March through June is the best time to catch sight of them as they carry fish in their talons to their nestlings.

Biologists have released wild turkeys back into the Nanticoke Wildlife Management Area. This popular game bird, which was once native here before unregulated hunting took its toll, is regaining a foothold. Hikers, fishermen, and hunters may also spot large nest boxes placed over the marsh in an attempt to lure barn owls. These flat-faced raptors suffer from loss of habitat and from the gradual decline in the number of barns, their favorite nesting site.

Check the information board at the entrance for hunting and fishing seasons and regulations. The area is managed for mourning dove, cottontail rabbit, bobwhite quail, white-tailed deer, wild turkey, woodcock, and waterfowl. Hikers should wear bright clothing during these hunting seasons. Largemouth bass, striped bass (rockfish), catfish, and perch may be caught from the bank or from boats. Trappers may apply for yearly leases. Biting insects make repellent necessary spring through fall.

Directions: From US 50, just east of Hebron in Wicomico County, drive about 5.5 miles southwest on MD 347 through Hebron to Quantico. Turn right on Cherry Walk Road and go just under 2 miles. Turn left on Nutters Neck Road and go about 2.5 miles to the parking lot and trailhead in the wildlife management area.

Activities: Hiking, seasonal hunting, fishing, and trapping (by yearly lease).

Facilities: Hiking trail.

Dates: Open daily, year-round.

Closest town: Hebron is about 9 miles east.

For more information: Nanticoke WMA, Wellington Work Center, 32733 Dublin Road, Princess Anne, MD 21853. Phone (410) 543-8223.

Wicomico County

Those who are looking not for plush resorts or big-city excitement but for outdoor sports and natural beauty have come to the right place in Wicomico County. The many waterfowl that winter here are depicted in paintings by the famous and the not-so-famous. They've been photographed by professionals and amateurs. They've been sought by hunters and their well-trained retrievers. And their images have been exquisitely carved into wood decoys by some of the world's best.

There are thousands of acres of woods and wetlands where people may hike, fish, crab, hunt, or launch a canoe or motorboat. Two state wildlife management areas (Ellis

Bay and Nanticoke) and the Wicomico State Demonstration Forest provide habitat for wildlife and trails for those who would like to observe or hunt wildlife or to study nature. An outing can be as simple and inexpensive as buying a couple of chicken necks and some string at a food market and stopping at a county bridge to catch some crabs for dinner.

The county and the river and creek that flow through the heart of it and along the southeastern border take their name from a local Indian tribe. Although Wicomico County does not touch the Chesapeake Bay, it does sneak a western toe into Tangier Sound. The Nanticoke River—an important bay tributary—comprises the county's entire western border.

The 1,207 heavily wooded acres of the **Wicomico State Demonstration Forest** (410-543-1950) are located between US 50 and MD 353, 10 miles east of Salisbury. The area is intersected by Sixty Foot Road, which runs between those two highways. The headquarters is located on this road about 1.8 miles south of MD 353, on the left. A network of unmarked trails and roads provide access for hiking and seasonal hunting.

Wicomico County is rich in city and municipal parks. Several of the 50 parks have small beaches, access to rivers and creeks, fishing, picnicking, and nature walks. A brochure is available. Camping is available at **Roaring Point Campground** (410-873-2553) off MD 349 at Nanticoke, just a couple of miles before the highway ends at Wicomico County's southern tip at Waterview. A small beach and a boat landing are nearby.

Shopping, antiquing, lodging, and gourmet restaurants are available at Salisbury, the county seat. But those who explore the back roads will find quiet harbors where watermen pile crab pots high, old boats creak in the afternoon sun, and dragonflies flit among the grasses. Here, the traveler can discover little mom-and-pop seafood restaurants, or a riverbank where the waters hold tasty catfish and a forked stick will support a cane pole for catching them. Sometimes, all it takes to find something interesting is just getting off the main drag. On MD 54, about 3 miles east of US 50 at Mardela Springs, is the **Mason-Dixon Marker**, the first stone boundary marker placed in 1768 that later came to delineate the line between the North and the South before the Civil War. The Mason-Dixon Line takes its name from its surveyors, Charles Mason and Jeremiah Dixon. The old, barely readable marker is under a shelter at the southwestern corner of Delaware.

Two of Wicomico's little towns—Whitehaven and Quantico—are on the National Register of Historic Places. Whitehaven is described on page 275. Quantico is located on MD 347, about 5.5 miles west of its connection with US 50 near Hebron Springs.

A **Tourist Information Center** (410-548-4914) is located at Leonard's Mill Park on US 13, 4 miles north of downtown Salisbury and 2 miles south of the Delaware border. The center is open daily, year-round, excluding major holidays. Near the tourist center, you can take MD 675 north off US 13 to Delmar, a town that sits in both Maryland and Delaware. State Street, which goes east/west through the center of town, runs straight as an arrow along an old railroad bed. One lane of traffic on State Street is in Delaware, the other in Maryland.

For more information: Wicomico County Convention and Visitors Bureau, 8480 Ocean Highway, PO Box 2333, Salisbury, MD 21802-2333. Phone (410) 548-4914.

SALISBURY

[Fig. 21] At the junction of two major Eastern Shore highways—US 13 and US 50—in central Wicomico County is Salisbury, the county seat and the largest town on the Eastern Shore. The Salisbury-Ocean City Regional Airport is just east of town.

The Wicomico River flows through the western side of town on its way to Tangier Sound and the Chesapeake Bay. Boats of many descriptions moor at the busy Port of Salisbury.

The Ward Museum of Wildfowl Art (410-742-4988), housed in a modernistic building at 909 South Schumaker Drive, has on display the most comprehensive collection of wildfowl carvings in the world. The museum is named for Lem and Steve Ward of Crisfield, known among decoy carvers and collectors for raising their craft of making working decoys to a fine art. In the museum shop, visitors can buy original art, decoys, and wonderful books on natural history, butterflies, Eastern Shore art, and so on.

The short **Marsh Walk** off the museum parking lot provides views of a small freshwater lake with ducks and geese. Markers identify such wetland plants as arrow arum (*Peltandra virginica*) and wild rice (*Zizania aquatica*). You could hide a basketball team in the wild rice, which sends its grasslike fronds from the deep mud of the shallows up to 9 feet in the air. Call for the current calendar of events. The museum is open daily, year-round, except major holidays.

The **Salisbury Zoo** (office 410-548-3188, tours 410-546-3440) at 755 South Park Drive is one of North America's best small zoos. It has received the U.S. Humane Society's top rating for its natural habitats that house some 500 specimens of wildlife indigenous to North, Central, and South America. A numbered map leads visitors past an herb garden and tropical birds to Morgan Visitor's Center. Past the visitor's center are exhibits that contain macaws, sloths, tamarins, bobcats, coatis, and ocelots. An extensive collection of waterfowl, ducks of North and South America, and birds of prey are also along the walking path. Children love to watch exuberant river otters and athletic spider monkeys. The entrance on Memorial Drive is recommended for first-time visitors so they can follow the map in sequence. The zoo is free and opens at 8 a.m. daily, year-round, except Christmas and Thanksgiving.

Poplar Hill Mansion (410-749-1776) at 117 Elizabeth Street is centrally located in the **Newtown Historic District** of Salisbury and is listed on the National Register of Historic Places. Work began on the mansion in 1799. Built in the Federal style, the frame building has three stories and a steeply pitched roof. The mansion is a survivor. It made it through raging fires that destroyed most of the old buildings around it in 1860 and again in 1886 to become what is perhaps the oldest building in town. The mansion is open some Sundays, by appointment, and for special events such as a Christmas open house. The other spacious homes of the Newtown district are mostly Victorian, constructed after the fires and lovingly restored in the 1970s.

Pemberton Historical Park (410-548-4870) on Pemberton Drive in western Salisbury is the location of **Pemberton Hall**, a plantation home built in 1741. On Sunday afternoons from May through September, visitors can tour the restored building, see meat curing and woodworking demonstrations, watch a blacksmith at work, and examine vegetable and herb gardens typical of Colonial times. The 234-acre park also offers environmental education, nature study, and special events. Six loops of quiet hiking paths totaling 4.5 miles crisscross tidal and freshwater wetlands, upland pine forests, hardwood forests, and meadows, with views of the Wicomico River. A trail guide is available at the contact station beside the parking lot.

Also part of the park tour is the **Heritage Centre Museum** (410-860-0447). Both county history and Eastern Shore history are depicted in exhibits by the Wicomico Historical Society. Even the museum building—which resembles an eighteenth century tobacco barn—is part of the show.

Night life is available in Salisbury some weekends at the **Shorebird Lounge** (410-546-4400) in the Ramada Inn at South Salisbury Boulevard. Big-name entertainers, all-star wrestling, rodeos, and even the Harlem Globetrotters attract crowds from miles around to events at the **Wicomico Youth and Civic Center** (410-548-4900) on Civic Avenue in Salisbury. Tickets might be easier to come by here than they would for the same act in a larger city or resort area.

Salisbury has its own Class A minor league baseball team, the Delmarva Shorebirds, an affiliate of the Baltimore Orioles. Call (410) 219-3112 for a schedule of home games at **Purdue Stadium** just east of town. If there's no baseball, youngsters will find plenty to occupy them in the video arcade at the **Centre at Salisbury** on US 13 north of downtown. On Wednesdays, join local crowds and the Backfin Banjo Band for sing-a-longs at the **Red Roost** (451-546-5443 or 800-953-5443) in Whitehaven, where no one takes their musical talent—or lack of it—too seriously.

WHITEHAVEN

[Fig. 21] The history of Whitehaven on the lower Wicomico River is representative of many waterside towns of Maryland's Eastern Shore. Established in the eighteenth century, the town was one of the Chesapeake Bay's original tobacco ports. In the nineteenth century, shipbuilding and canning brought prosperity. But with the dwindling bay resources and the use of rails instead of ships to haul goods, Whitehaven went into decline. Also, the river was dredged to allow ships to pass by it and reach Salisbury, and Whitehaven was all but forgotten by the midtwentieth century.

Today, however, tourism and an interest in preserving history are bringing the little town back to life. Of the 22 buildings in town, only two were constructed in the twentieth century. Restoration has begun on the old structures and the entire village has been placed on the National Register of Historic Places.

A small ferry where ferries have operated for some 300 years still takes people, bicycles, and cars for free across the Wicomico River between the village of Whitehaven and Somerset County.

Directions: Whitehaven is located on the north banks of the Wicomico River about 1 mile south of the southernmost tip of MD 352 in southwestern Wicomico County.

ELLIS BAY WILDLIFE MANAGEMENT AREA

[Fig. 21(2)] Those with a kayak or canoe strapped to the top of their car are well equipped for Ellis Bay Wildlife Management Area. These crafts provide the perfect means for prowling the numerous waterways unobtrusively and getting close to ducks, geese, egrets, herons, osprey, and even bald eagles without alarming them. The 3,000 acres of these Chesapeake Bay marshes and forested wetlands that were brought under state protections in 1957 also provide habitat for white-tailed deer, squirrels, woodcock, and cottontail rabbits.

One small boat landing in the area and several others nearby make access easy for those who want to catch white perch, rockfish, and crabs. Trappers may apply for yearly leases. Biting insects make repellent necessary spring through fall.

Directions: From MD 352, on the north side of Whitehaven in southwestern Wicomico County, go 2 miles west on Mezick Road, which becomes Muddy Hole Road after crossing Clara Road. Less than 1 mile after crossing Clara Road (before the junction with Trinity Church Road), turn left (south) into the area. Go about 1 mile to the boat landing on Muddy Hole Creek.

Activities: Hiking, fishing, crabbing, boating, seasonal hunting, trapping by yearly lease.

Facilities: Small boat landing.

Dates: Open from sunrise to sunset daily, year-round.

Fees: None.

Closest town: Whitehaven is about 2 miles east.

For more information: Ellis Bay WMA, Wellington Work Center, 32733 Dublin Road, Princess Anne, MD 21853. Phone (410) 543-8223.

RESTAURANTS OF WICOMICO COUNTY

Most of Wicomico's restaurants are in the Salisbury area. Here are a few places that are popular with local people.

CRAB WORLD. 507 West Salisbury Parkway (US 50), Salisbury. Crack crab claws on tables covered in brown paper in this casual seafood restaurant. Menu items include top neck and cherrystone clams, steamed oysters, steamed crabs, soft crabs, crab cakes, baked lobster, fried scallops, and more. *Inexpensive to moderate. Phone (410) 742-2028.*

DAYTON'S. 909 Snow Hill Road. Specials include traditional Eastern Shore cuisine. Known for superb food and service. *Inexpensive. Phone (410) 548-2272.*

FRATELLI'S. 1306 South Salisbury Boulevard, Salisbury. Daily specials in addition to Italian fare. Pasta made fresh daily. *Inexpensive to moderate. Phone (410) 341-0807.*

LEGEND'S. 213 West Main Street, City Center, Salisbury. Specialties include seafood, lamb, and steaks. Voted best dining on the Eastern Shore. *Moderate. Phone (410) 749-7717.*

THE RED ROOST. Clara Road, Whitehaven. The informal dining room in an expanded, refurbished chicken house gives this restaurant a reputation as one of the most unique eating establishments on the Eastern Shore. In addition to regular menu items, steamed crabs, barbecue ribs, steamed shrimp, and snow crab are on the all-you-can-eat menu. *Inexpensive to moderate. Phone (451) 546-5443 or (800) 953-5443.*

WATERMAN'S COVE. 925 Snow Hill Road, Salisbury. Seafood specialties served daily. A favorite among locals. *Moderate. Phone (410) 546-1400.*

▓ LODGING IN WICOMICO COUNTY

Most Wicomico County lodging facilities are in the Salisbury area. Here is a sampling of places to stay. Many more hotels and motels lie east of Salisbury in Ocean City (Worcester County), on the Atlantic seaboard.

BEST WESTERN SALISBURY PLAZA. 1735 North Salisbury Boulevard, Salisbury. Hospitality suite, swimming pool. *Moderate. Phone (410) 546-1300 or (800) 636-7554.*

HOWARD JOHNSON. 2625 North Salisbury Boulevard, Salisbury. Swimming pool, conference facilities, restaurant. *Moderate. Phone (410) 742-7194 or (800) 446-4656.*

SLEEP INN. US 50 east at Autumn Grove Road, Salisbury. Restaurant, swimming pool. *Moderate. Phone (410) 572-5516 or (800) 627-5337.*

WHITEHAVEN BED & BREAKFAST. 23844-48 River Street, Whitehaven. Five Victorian rooms on two historic properties, the Charles Leatherbury House (circa 1886) and the Otis Lloyd House (1850s). All rooms have views of the Wicomico River and marsh. Tour the river in a classic Chesapeake Bay workboat. *Moderate. Phone (410) 873-3294 or (888) 205-5921. E-mail whavnbb@dmv.com.*

Beach to Bay Indian Trail

[Fig. 21(3)] Even the name of the trail has appeal—Beach to Bay Indian Trail. This National Recreation Trail is a driving or biking tour (with a boat trip across Tangier Sound) that ties the barrier islands on the Atlantic seashore to Smith Island in the Chesapeake Bay. It runs along highways and byways through Worcester and Somerset counties, roughly following routes once used by tribes of the Algonquin nation such as Animuses, Acquinticas, Manokins, Assateagues, and Pocomokes.

The names are magical. But the trail has more than Indian lore. Someone who drives or bikes it from beginning to end, even missing a site or two, will put together a history that moves through time, from the days when the Algonquin tribes fished the Nassawango to today. Along the way are 10 museums and historic sites and several nature trails. The museums and historic sites highlight the cultures of Indians and European immigrants.

A round trip on the Beach to Bay Indian Trail, beginning at Ocean City on the Atlantic, going some 74 miles to the Chesapeake Bay along the more northerly route, and leading back to Assateague Island on the Atlantic via a 67-mile southern route, totals about 141 miles. Some of the return trip will traverse the same highways as the first half. The trail makes use of all or parts of US 50, MD 611, MD 376, MD 113, MD 12, MD 388, MD 13, MD 413, and MD 667.

Let's say you were to begin driving the trail at the **Ocean City Life Saving Station Museum** (410-289-4991) on the Ocean City Boardwalk (*see* page 279) on the Atlantic coast. Go west on US 50 for 1 mile, then south on MD 611. After about 4.5 miles, turn left on MD 376 at Lewis Corner and go 4.5 miles to Berlin. Here, you could visit the **Calvin B. Taylor Museum** (410-641-1019), a meticulously restored nineteenth century house at North Main Street and Baker Street in Berlin's Historic District.

From Berlin, go south to Snow Hill via MD 113 (15.1 miles). On Market Street at Snow Hill is the **Julia A. Purnell Museum** (410-632-0515). This museum, which has artifacts depicting Eastern Shore life from Colonial times to the present, is one of those little discoveries that makes prowling the back roads and villages an adventure.

At Snow Hill, the Beach to Bay Indian Trail heads northwest on MD 12. Canoeists who would like to explore The Nature Conservancy's **Nassawango Creek Cypress Swamp Preserve** (410-632-2032) should turn left (west) after 2.7 miles onto Red House Road, then go 1 mile and park in the designated area. Rental canoes are available in Snow Hill. For a leisurely day trip, launch next to the sign and head south on the 2-mile section of the tidal Nassawango between Red House Road and Nassawango Road. After canoeing for about 1 mile, look for yellow signs indicating the **Francis M. Uhler Nature Trail**, an easy 0.25-mile loop on the western side of the creek.

River otters, gray foxes, white-tailed deer, and painted turtles are just some of the wildlife that inhabit the cypress swamp. The woods are also home to ovenbirds, flickers, pileated woodpeckers, and more than 14 species of warblers, including the prothonotary, Swainson's, worm-eating, Kentucky, and yellowthroat.

To access the preserve's **Paul Leifer Nature Trail**, follow MD 12 north for 5.3 miles from Snow Hill (past the turn on Red House Road) and turn left (westward) on MD 388 (Old Furnace Road). After about 1 mile, turn into the parking area of the **Furnace Town Historic Site** (410-632-2032). The historic site encompasses the nineteenth century Nassawango Iron Furnace and a village of artisan shops that includes a broomhouse, blacksmith shop, printshop, and weaving area. The bog-ore furnace is a National Historic Mechanical Engineering Landmark.

Walk (or drive if the gate is open) through the historic site to the trailhead for the easy 1-mile loop along the Paul Leifer trail. The trail follows Nassawango Creek across boardwalks into the mysterious Nassawango Creek Cypress Swamp Preserve and along the towpath of the Furnace Town Canal. Pink lady's slipper (*Cypripedium acaule*), mayapple (*Podophyllum peltatum*), and jack-in-the-pulpit (*Arisaema triphyllum*) are among the spring bloomers on the trail. Cardinal flower (*Lobelia cardinalis*) and spotted jewelweed

(*Impatiens capensis*) are moisture-loving plants that spread red and gold color through the marsh in summer.

About 4 miles west of this site on MD 388 is the parking area for the **Pusey Branch Nature Trail** (410-632-2032 or 410-632-2566), an easy 0.5-mile loop along Pusey Branch, which lies in a northern corner of **Pocomoke River State Forest**. Illustrated signs on the trail depict the state forest in the four seasons.

The Beach to Bay Indian Trail follows MD 388 for 14.3 miles from MD 12 to Princess Anne (*see* page 285). From Princess Anne, go south on MD 13 about 4.5 miles and southwest on MD 413 about 15 miles to Crisfield (*see* page 286).

A 9.5-mile boat trip across Tangier Sound will take you to fascinating Smith Island (*see* page 289), the trail's most westward point. Backtrack across Tangier Sound and travel about 6 miles northeast along MD 413. A right turn on MD 667 leads 9.5 miles east through lovely rural countryside to MD 13, just west of Pocomoke City. A 4-mile drive south along MD 13 leads through Pocomoke City to MD 113.

At Pocomoke City, the Beach to Bay Indian Trail takes in the **Pocomoke City Nature and Exercise Trail** (410-957-1334) at Cypress Park. This 1-mile self-guided path passes under large white cedars and cypresses, encircling an 8-acre fishing pond.

Then the trail leads northeastward on MD 113 for 29 miles to Berlin, taking in Pocomoke River State Forest and Park (*see* page 283) and Snow Hill along the way. At Berlin, go east on MD 376 (4.5 miles) to MD 611 and go right on MD 611 for 4.5 miles to Assateague Island National Seashore (*see* page 300) and Assateague State Park (*see* page 282), finishing the trip at the **Barrier Island Visitor Center** (410-641-1441).

A brochure detailing the tour is available from the **Tourism Information Center** for Somerset County on US 13 on the south side of Princess Anne or the **Tourism Information Center** for Worcester County on US 13 on the south side of Pocomoke City. Or call ahead to Somerset County Tourism (800-521-9189) at Princess Anne or Worcester County Tourism at Snow Hill (800-852-0335). Dates and hours of operation of the various museums are included in the brochure.

Many of the stops along the Beach to Bay Indian Trail that are in Worcester County are also on a 100-mile circular bicycle tour of the county called **Viewtrail 100**. The scenic trail makes use of small country roads through farmlands and forest, passing through the historic towns of Snow Hill, Berlin, and Pocomoke City and along the scenic Pocomoke River. A brochure with a tour map is also available from the county tourism office.

For more information: Somerset County Tourism, PO Box 243, Princess Anne, MD 21853. Phone (410) 651-2968 or (800) 521-9189. E-mail somtour@dmv.com. Worcester County Tourism, 105 Pearl Street, PO Box 208, Snow Hill, MD 21863. Phone (410) 632-3110 or (800) 852-0335. E-mail econ@ezy.net.

OCEAN CITY

[Fig. 21] Ocean City is on Fenwick Island—a long, narrow barrier island at the eastern end of US 50 in Worcester County. The glitz and glamour of this ocean resort are in striking contrast to the old seaports, quiet back roads, and bucolic countryside of the less populated areas of the Eastern Shore.

A wide, 3-mile boardwalk as well as glistening beaches of white sand and crashing surf invite strollers, sunbathers, beachcombers, and swimmers to enjoy the Atlantic Ocean. In addition to long rows of high-rise hotels and motels that will pamper the guest, posh restaurants that serve seafood fresh off the boat, and 10 area golf courses, there are water slides, miniature golf, arcade games, T-shirt shops, countless gift shops, and fast food restaurants. The **Ocean City Convention and Visitors Bureau** (800-OC-OCEAN or 410-289-8181) is located on the bayside of the island at 4001 Coastal Highway, between 41st Street and Convention Center Drive.

Despite the development of the island, nature is at the doorstep. At the rock jetties at Ocean City inlet at the southern tip of the island, bird watchers have recorded the southernmost winter sightings of species such as the king eider (*Somateria mollissima*), harlequin duck (*Histrionicus histrionicus*), and purple sandpiper (*Calidris maritima*). The king eider has been known to dive as deep as 150 feet in search of food.

Offshore Nature Cruises (410-213-0926 or 800-457-6650) offers dolphin, bird-, and whale-watching tours aboard the cruising yacht, *Ocean City Princess*. The tour boat **Bay Queen** (410-213-0926) hosts trips on the inland waterways to view the wild ponies of Assateague Island and to search the wild bird sanctuaries for osprey, piping plovers, pelicans, cormorants, and a variety of seagulls.

Fishing boats may be rented or chartered from April through October at the **Ocean City Fishing Center** (410-213-1121 or 800-322-3065) at US 50 and Shantytown Road for exciting offshore trips for white and blue marlin, tuna, mako shark, bluefish, and mackerel. The **Shantytown Lighthouse Pier** is located at the center. Another pier, the **Ocean City Fishing and Sightseeing Pier** (410-213-2504), is near the southern end of the island at Wicomico Street and Philadelphia Avenue (about five blocks south of US 50).

At night, live bands have long been an attraction at **Seacrets on the Bay** (410-524-4900) at 49th Street on the bay, a restaurant and lounge with a Jamaican atmosphere, and at **Fager's Island** (410-524-5500) at 60th Street on the bay, where Tchaikovsky's *1812 Overture* is performed as the sun sets over the bay. There are two shows nightly at the **Princess Royale Comedy Club** (410-723-HAHA) at 9100 Coastal Highway. Music lovers can reserve a seat in the rustic theater of **The Ocean City Jamboree** (410-213-7581) at MD 611 and 12600 Marjan Lane, where country, pop, '50s rock and roll and gospel music are all rolled into one live show.

Special events are held at Ocean City throughout the year, including the Ward World Championship Wildfowl Carving Competition, which has been called the world's most prestigious wildfowl carving competition. The Ward Museum of Wildfowl Art in Salisbury (410-742-4988, extension 106) sponsors it. Also, the White Marlin Open (410-289-9229), the city's premiere fishing event held in August, is the world's largest billfish tournament in terms of the number of boats and anglers. Awards are given for the largest white marlin, blue marlin, tuna, wahoo, dolphin, and shark. The lucky angler who reels in the largest billfish overall receives thousands of dollars in prize money.

Directions: From US 13 east of Salisbury, follow US 50 (or the more scenic MD 343 that runs parallel for part of the way) some 25 miles east to Ocean City.

For more information: Maryland Department of Tourism, 4001 Coastal Highway, Ocean City, MD 21842. Phone (800) OC-OCEAN. Web sites www.ocean-city.com, www.ococean.com.

RESTAURANTS IN OCEAN CITY

Seafood restaurants are abundant in Ocean City, but hungry visitors can also find steaks, pastas, fast food, Mexican, and Italian food.

MO'S SEAFOOD FACTORY. 82nd Street Bayside, Ocean City. The large and varied menu includes steamed crabs, 23 varieties of fish, and early bird specials. *Inexpensive to moderate. Phone (410) 723-2500.*

THE WHARF RESTAURANT. 128th Street, Ocean City. Enjoy fresh seafood daily from a menu that includes fish, stuffed lobster, pasta/seafood combinations, and award-winning crab cakes. *Inexpensive to moderate. Phone (410) 250-1001.*

JORDAN'S ROOFTOP RESTAURANT. 138th Street and Coastal Highway, Ocean City. Enjoy the spectacular view of the Atlantic Ocean from this eighth-story restaurant atop the Fenwick Inn. Sunday brunch, casual dining, children's menu, nightly entertainment. *Inexpensive to moderate. Phone (410) 250-1867.*

HARRISON'S HARBOR WATCH RESTAURANT. Boardwalk South, Ocean City. Known for the beautiful view overlooking the ocean, bay, and Assateague Island. Fresh seafood is prepared daily. Homemade pasta specialties, breads, steaks, and chicken. *Moderate. Phone (410) 289-5121.*

LODGING IN OCEAN CITY

This resort strip has a wide variety of accommodations, ranging from economy motels to plush hotels. Rates for lodging are considerably higher during the summer tourist season. Camping is available at nearby state and national parks and at private campgrounds such as **Ocean City Travel Park** (410-524-7601) at 105 70th Street and **Bali-Hi RV Park** (410-352-5477) on St. Martins Neck Road off MD 90, just west of Fenwick Island and Ocean City. Here's a sampling of the motels and hotels:

CASTLE IN THE SAND HOTEL. 3701 Atlantic Avenue, Ocean City. This beachfront hotel has a coffee shop, restaurant, nightclub/lounge, outdoor Olympic pool, and spring and fall packages. *Moderate. Phone (410) 289-6846 or (800) 552-SAND.*

THE DUNES MANOR HOTEL. 2800 Baltimore Avenue, Ocean City. Have afternoon tea in the lobby of this Victorian-style hotel or rock on the oceanfront porch. Located one block from the boardwalk. Restaurant, lounge. *Moderate to expensive. Phone (800) 523-2888 or (410) 289-1100.*

ECONO LODGE OCEANFRONT. 45th Street, Ocean City. Oceanfront efficiencies and suites have private balconies. Nightclub/lounge, outdoor pool, spring/fall packages.

Inexpensive to moderate. Phone (410) 289-6424 or (800) 638-3244.

THE LIGHTHOUSE CLUB HOTEL. 201 60th Street, Ocean City. Located on the Isle of Wight Bay, this white frame octagonal hotel is a replica of the Chesapeake Bay's Thomas Point Lighthouse at Annapolis. Pie-shaped suites have marble bathrooms, private decks, and upscale service. *Expensive. Phone (888) 371-5400 or (410) 524-5400.*

ASSATEAGUE ISLAND

[Fig. 21] In startling contrast to the highly developed Fenwick Island to the north, where Ocean City plays host to multitudes of vacationers, Assateague Island is a narrow windswept barrier island separating and protecting the mainland of the Eastern Shore from the Atlantic Ocean. The island runs some 37 miles from just south of Ocean City and Fenwick Island into Virginia. About 23 miles of the island is in Maryland, and 14 miles are in Virginia.

Assateague Island National Seashore [Fig. 23(1)] encompasses most of the island and the waters around it. Visitor centers are at both the Maryland end and the Virginia end (*see* page 299 for a description of the Virginia portion of the island). Three nature trails, a guarded swimming beach (summer season), picnicking, bicycling, camping, clamming, surf fishing, and crabbing are available on the north end. After about 1 mile, the paved road gives way to sand, where only off-road vehicles are allowed, by permit. Wild ponies that roam the island are a major tourist attraction. The Barrier Island Visitor Center at the island's northern end has an aquarium, exhibits on natural history of barrier islands, maps and publications, and an interesting driving tour of the island on audio cassette tapes.

Two miles of guarded swimming beaches (in the summer season), as well as camping, fishing, picnicking, bicycling, and bayside canoeing are available at **Assateague State Park** on the Maryland end of Assateague Island. The park was selected by *National Geographic Traveler* as one of the 50 best parks in the United States. There is a boat ramp on the west side of the bridge to the island.

The island is not a good place to bring pets. They are not allowed anywhere in the state park or on any nature trails in the national seashore, and they must be on short leashes elsewhere.

Directions: For the Maryland end of the island, from US 50, about 1 mile west of Ocean City, go south on MD 611 for 9 miles to the Barrier Island Visitor Center (on the right, before crossing the bridge to the park entrance). Or from US 113 on the east side of Berlin, go east on MD 376 for 4 miles. Turn right (south) on MD 611 and go about 3 miles to the visitor center. The state park begins on the east side of the bridge to the island. Travel about 2 miles south through the state park to the beaches and nature trails of the national seashore.

Activities: National seashore: Swimming (ocean), beachcombing, picnicking, bicycling, camping, clamming, surf fishing, crabbing, flatwater canoeing, off-road driving (permit required). State park: Swimming, camping, fishing, picnicking, hiking, biking, flatwater canoeing, surf fishing, surf boarding.

Facilities: National seashore: Guarded swimming beach, bathhouses, picnic tables, primitive campgrounds (no hookups) with drinking water and rinse-off showers, nature trails, visitor center. State park: Swimming beach, campground (electric hookups in 32 sites), picnic tables and shelters, bathhouses, bait and tackle shop, small restaurant. Most facilities are handicap-accessible.

Dates: The state park is open from Apr. 1 through Oct. 31. The national seashore is open daily, year-round. The life-guarded swimming beaches, camp store, and restaurant are open in summer only.

Fees: There are entrance fees, a fee for boat rentals, and a nominal fee for a backcountry camping permit.

Closest town: Berlin is 8 miles west.

For more information: Assateague State Park, 7307 Stephen Decatur Highway, Berlin, MD 21811. Phone (410) 641-2120. Assateague Island National Seashore, 6206 National Seashore Lane, Berlin, MD 21811. Phone (410) 641-1441 or (410) 641-3030. Summer reservations for the national seashore campground can be made by calling (800)-365 CAMP and for the state park campground by calling (888) 432-CAMP.

THE POCOMOKE RIVER

The dark tannin-stained waters of the Pocomoke River are characteristic of cypress swamps. The Pocomoke's tannin leaches out of the Great Cypress Swamp at its headwaters on the Maryland/Delaware border. Beginning just a few miles west of the salty Atlantic, the tidal river runs southwestward through Worcester County, carves the marshy border between Worcester and Somerset counties, then empties into Pocomoke Sound on the Maryland/Virginia line on its way to the Chesapeake Bay.

Anglers tackle yellow and white perch, pickerel, catfish, crappie, bluegill, herring, spot, croaker, bluefish, and largemouth bass. No Chesapeake Bay sport-fishing license is required when fishing from the banks at several designated free fishing areas. A list of these places is available wherever licenses are sold. Fishing from a boat requires a license.

The river, where 172 species of birds have been identified, is a favorite of ornithologists. Canoeists may see nesting wood ducks (*Aix sponsa*), or hear prothonotary warblers (*Protonotaria citrea*) in the forest. A shadow across the water could prove to be that of a soaring bald eagle (*Haliaeetus leucophalus*).

POCOMOKE RIVER STATE FOREST AND PARK

[Fig. 21(4)] Pocomoke River State Park is divided into two sections in Pocomoke River State Forest—the seasonally open Milburn Landing Area northwest of Snow Hill and the Shad Landing Area southwest of Snow Hill. The Shad Landing Area is the larger of the two, with camping facilities, a marina, boat rentals, and a large swimming pool. The park provides access to the Pocomoke River along with facilities to make river or riverside outings more enjoyable.

The Trail of Change at the Shad Landing Area of the park is a 0.75-mile self-guided trail over hard-packed sand on what was once the Shad Landing Road where fishermen would bring in their catches of shad and other fish from the Pocomoke River. The trail leads through uplands of loblolly pine and drops down into cypress swamps where boardwalks and raised berms allow the hiker to view life in the wetlands.

American holly, black gum, red maple, sassafras, wax myrtle, mountain laurel, and highbush blueberry are samples of trees and shrubbery found in the undergrowth. Common polypody ferns and Christmas ferns provide a delicate carpet of green in summer. There is also a self-guided canoe trail around an island in the Pocomoke River. Carry insect repellent during warm weather. If there are no trail brochures at the beginning, ask for one at the park office.

Directions: For the Shad Landing Area of the state park (where the swimming pool, boat rental, and campgrounds are), from US 133 at Snow Hill in Worcester County, go 4 miles southwest to the park entrance, on the right. For the Milburn Landing Area, from MD 12 at Snow Hill, go about 8 miles northwest to the park entrance, on the left.

Activities: Hiking, biking, picnicking, camping, swimming, boating, flatwater canoeing, fishing.

Facilities: Picnic tables and shelters, large swimming pool, campground with hookups, camp store, hiking trails, multi-use trails, boat ramp, rowboat and canoe rentals, playground, visitor center, dumping station.

Dates: The Shad Landing Area and the state forest are open daily, year-round. The campgrounds are open May 1 through Sept. 30. The Milburn Landing Area is open mid-Apr. through mid-Dec.

Fees: There is no entrance fee. There are fees for camping, swimming, and boat rental.

Closest town: Snow Hill is 4 miles northeast of the Shad Landing Area and 8 miles southeast of the Milburn Landing Area.

For more information: Pocomoke River State Park, 3461 Worcester Highway, Snow Hill, MD 21863. Phone (410) 632-2566.

Somerset County

Somerset is Maryland's southernmost county, touching the northwestern corner of Accomack County on Virginia's Eastern Shore. The actual boundaries of Somerset also reach westward, past Smith Island, extending far across the waters of Tangier Sound and the Chesapeake Bay to Smith Point on Virginia's Northern Neck. These western borders of the county out in the Chesapeake Bay are composed of straight lines and sharp angles, defined by the whims of humans, and are important when it comes to which state controls fishing regulations and environmental policy. But the borders of the Somerset County mainland, where land actually meets water, are anything but straight. Instead, they are defined by the meanderings of tidal or freshwater rivers—rivers that take their names from local Indian tribes, including the tranquil Pocomoke River, a State Scenic

River, on the southeastern side. Other rivers, from north to south, that define the mainland include the Wicomico, the Manokin, and the Big Annemessex.

There are no large towns to take away from the ambiance of the little fishing villages, the historic sites, or the huge expanses of salt marshes where the melodious voice of the willet (*Catotrophorus semipalmatus*) rings across the cordgrass. US 13 runs north/south through the county, carrying travelers up and down the Eastern Shore. Those who have the good fortune to get off the through highway, whether by chance or by design, will discover the historic county seat of Princess Anne, charming Crisfield in the southwestern corner, or perhaps the cruise boat across Tangier Sound to Smith Island. Six wildlife management areas offer thousands of acres for canoeing, kayaking, hiking, hunting, fishing, crabbing, and observing wildlife. And the remote sandy beaches of Janes Island State Park are right in keeping with the gentle side of Somerset County.

A daffodil show, skipjack race, hard crab derby, clam bake, oyster roast, and fish fry are more reasons people come by car, boat, and bicycle to share the Chesapeake Bay culture of Somerset County.

For more information: Somerset County Tourism, PO Box 243, Princess Anne, MD 21853. Phone (410) 651-2968 or (800) 521-9189. E-mail somtour@dmv.com.

PRINCESS ANNE

[Fig. 21] Named for the 24-year-old daughter of King George II of England, Princess Anne is interesting for its many Federal-style buildings in addition to Victorian homes from the 1800s. Many of these structures are included on a self-guided walking tour of this historic county seat off US 13 in northern Somerset County.

The oldest building is the **William Geddes House** (circa 1755) at 11790 Church Street. At 11736 Mansion Street is the **Teackle Mansion** (410-651-2238), begun about 1802. This impressive example of Federal-style architecture is listed on the National Register of Historic Places. The town's heritage is celebrated in October during Olde Princess Anne Days. A brochure and map of the walking tour and other county information is available at the Somerset Information Center (410-651-2968 or 800-521-9189) on US 13 west of town.

For more information: Somerset County Tourism, phone (800) 521-9189 or (410) 651-2968.

DEAL ISLAND

[Fig. 21] To follow MD 363 west from Princess Anne to its end on Deal Island is almost to drive from today into yesterday. Everyday pressures slip away. The driver lets up on the gas, rolls down the windows, and lets the Deal Island version of the Eastern Shore work its wonders. A bridge from the mainland leads across an inlet to harbors where island visitors can check out an oyster hatchery, walk out on the dock as fishermen bring in the day's catch from Tangier Sound, or witness the amazing dexterity of crab pickers.

The hatchery, crab pickers, and one of the island's two public boat landings are at

Deal Island Harbor on the northern tip of the island. A public beach and the skipjack, *Ida May*, are also located here. Soft crabs processed at the villages of Deal Island and Wenona are shipped all over the world.

On Labor Day weekend, crowds gather to share in the fun of an island festival and to cheer on teams in the annual skipjack races. Skipjacks are workboats normally used to harvest oysters, but for the past 40 years, captains have taken time off for this weekend of fun. Outdoor lovers are also drawn to Deal Island Wildlife Management Area [Fig. 23(8)] (*see* page 292), where extensive wetlands support healthy populations of wildlife and wildfowl.

Directions: From US 13 at Princess Anne, go west on MD 363 for 11 miles and cross the bridge to the island. A right turn at the foot of the bridge leads to Deal Island Harbor on Tangier Sound, an oyster hatchery, the skipjack *Ida May*, a public beach, and a boat landing. Or follow MD 363 for 3 more miles, through Wenona, to the southern end of the island to another boat landing.

For more information: Somerset County Tourism, phone (800) 521-9189 or (410) 651-2968.

CRISFIELD

[Fig. 21] MD 413 in southern Somerset County is shaped like a 14-mile-long fairway that makes a dogleg right between US 13 south of Salisbury and the mouth of the Little Annemessex River at Tangier Sound. Just before the highway would empty its travelers into the Annemesex, the activity at the city dock in the picturesque town of Crisfield and the aroma of fresh seafood from numerous waterfront restaurants lure motorists to the side of the road.

Crisfield takes its name from John W. Crisfield who was instrumental in bringing the railroad in 1867 to a relatively unknown little fishing village that was then called Somers Cove. The railroad provided a means to transport the riches of Tangier Sound to people hungering for seafood in faraway places. The incredible oyster harvest turned the community into a boom town.

Recognizing the man, John Crisfield, who helped the town earn its nickname, seafood capital of the world, the townspeople renamed the town Crisfield. Although the blue crab has replaced the depleted oyster as the mainstay of the local economy, the bed of crushed oyster shells beneath downtown buildings is an ever-present reminder of the debt the town owes to the American oyster (*Crassostrea virginica*).

The decline of the oyster can be attributed to several factors, including overharvesting and deterioration of the underwater grassbeds that help maintain the water quality and protect fish and crustaceans in Tangier Sound. The primary grasses here are eelgrass and wigeon grass, which have begun to make a comeback in many other parts of the Chesapeake Bay, but they are still in rapid decline here. Although the oyster is now scarce, the grasses are still needed to serve as a nursery for the blue crab and sea trout.

Cruises to nearby Smith Island, Maryland (*see* page 289), and Tangier Island in Virginia (*see* page 294) leave the City Dock daily.

Directions: From US 13, about 20 miles south of Salisbury, go south on MD 413 and drive 14 miles to Crisfield.

For more information: Crisfield Chamber of Commerce, PO Box 292, Crisfield, MD 21817. Phone (410) 968-2500 or (800) 282-3913.

SOMERS COVE MARINA

[Fig. 21(5)] Somers Cove Marina, one of the largest marinas on the East Coast, is in a large protected harbor in the center of downtown Crisfield. Before the marina was built, the decline of the local economy in conjunction with the deteriorating oyster industry was all too evident in the harbor. The rusting, rotting hulls of abandoned boats sank gradually into the mud flats, and silt collected around them. Crab-shedding shanties sagged and were reclaimed by the tides. But the citizens found their footing, developed alternatives to the oyster industry, and regrouped. Now the modern, full-service marina stands as testament to the indomitable spirit of the town.

Open year-round, this fishing center has 450 slips for sailboats, motorboats, yachts, and boats for fishing parties. Anglers can charter boats with knowledgeable guides to take them into the surrounding creeks and marshes or into the waters of Tangier Sound, Pocomoke Sound, and the Chesapeake Bay to fish for striped bass, flounder, sea trout, and perch. Headboats, which charge by the person (by the head), are another option.

Many popular festivals and celebrations draw crowds from across the bay to the Lower Shore, as the southernmost counties on Maryland's Eastern Shore are called. Some of the best known events are held at or near Somers Cove Marina. These include the Soft Shell Spring Fair (last Sunday in May), the Tawes Crab and Clam Bake (third Wednesday in July), the National Hard Crab Derby (Labor Day weekend), and the Oyster and Bull Roast (third Saturday in October).

The center has two launch ramps, fish-cleaning facilities, a shuttle service, a pool, picnic tables, six restrooms and shower facilities spread through the area, dump stations, and even golf packages for nearby Great Hope Golf Course. The marina is operated by the Forest and Park Service of the Maryland Department of Natural Resources.

Directions: The marina is located at 715 Broadway in downtown Crisfield.

For more information: Somers Cove Marina, PO Box 67, Crisfield, MD 21817. Phone (410) 968-0925 of (800) 967-FISH.

CRISFIELD HISTORICAL MUSEUM AND VISITOR'S CENTER

[Fig. 21(13)] On the waterfront at Somers Cove Marina in Crisfield is the Crisfield Historical Museum and Visitor's Center, where exhibits trace the history of the Chesapeake Bay, with special emphasis on the Lower Shore and the Crisfield area. The museum's name is taken from a former governor of Maryland.

One exhibit depicts the importance of Native Americans to the survival of early colonists. Friendly Indians showed the new arrivals how to build log canoes and eel pots, and how to make oyster tongs. Other subject matter includes seafood harvesting and processing, decoy carving and painting, and Chesapeake Bay boats.

The Port of Crisfield Escorted Walking Tour begins at the museum and includes a fascinating visit to a crab- and oyster-processing plant where skilled hands pick crabs and shuck oysters almost faster than the eye can see. Workers sometimes sing hymns to help pass the time during the monotonous work.

Directions: The museum is located on 9th Street at Somers Cove Marina.

Dates: Open 9 to 4:30 weekdays, year-round, and 10 to 3 on weekends from Memorial Day through mid-Oct.

Fees: There is an admission fee.

For more information: Crisfield Historical Museum and Visitor's Center, phone (410) 968-2501.

JANES ISLAND STATE PARK

[Fig. 21(7)] It would be possible to enjoy the way the breeze plays with the tall stalks of the phragmites and cordgrass near the nature trail, or to sit outside a tent under the loblolly pines in the campground, listening to soft birdsong in the evening, and never realize there's a huge chunk of the park that's hidden from view.

But a canoe, john boat, or motorboat will open up the other half of the park. Just beyond the Daugherty Creek Canal west of the parking lot and campground is 5-mile-long Janes Island, accessible only to fish, birds, wildlife—and those people with a boat. To the north and south lie the Big and Little Annemessex rivers, named for the Indians who once relied on these waters and marshes for food. To the west of the island are Tangier Sound and the Chesapeake Bay. Flat Cap Beach on the Tangier Sound side of the island offers 8 miles of sandy beach and gentle waves, where people may swim, picnic, jog, or comb the beach for shells.

Fortunately, for those who don't bring their own boat, the park rents canoes, kayaks, john boats, and motorboats. Boaters can go crabbing or they can fish for rockfish, bluefish, spot, flounder, croaker, white perch, and sea trout. Or they can simply paddle around the inlets and creeks of the tidal marshes of Janes Island. A camp store can supply the necessary lures, crabbing supplies, sandwiches, sodas, and bug repellent. A nature center and the 16-bed Daugherty Creek Conference Center are also on the park grounds.

Winter is an excellent time to come to Janes Island. Biting insects are not a problem and there's an abundance of wildfowl such as the black duck (*Anas rubripes*) that depend on the grains, grasses, and submerged aquatic vegetation of the marsh for food. Wintering black ducks were once estimated at 200,000 in the bay. Loss of habitat and other stresses have brought that number down to just a fourth of its former size. The duck seems to be rebounding, partly due to areas such as Janes Island that have been set aside for wildlife.

Directions: From MD 413 at Crisfield, go north on Jacksonville Road about 1 mile to the park entrance (Alfred Lawson Drive), on left.

Activities: Hiking, camping, picnicking, softball, volleyball, swimming (on island), boating, fishing, crabbing, seasonal hunting.

Facilities: Hiking trails, 30 miles of water trails, swimming beaches, picnic area, rental pavilion, softball field, volleyball courts, observation tower, campsites with hookups and fire ring, four full-size log cabins and five smaller camper cabins (reservations required), nature center, fish cleaning table, dock, rental john boats and motors, rental canoes and kayaks, boat slips, conference center, dump station, restrooms. All facilities are accessible to the handicapped.

Dates: The park is open and rental log cabins are available daily, year-round. Camping is available Mar. through Nov. Camper cabins are available from Apr. through Oct.

Fees: There are fees for daily use, for camping, and for rental of the pavilion, boats, canoes, and boat slips.

Closest town: Crisfield is about 1 mile south.

For more information: Janes Island State Park, 26280 Alfred Lawson Drive, Crisfield, MD 21817. Phone (410) 968-1565.

SOLOMONS LUMP LIGHTHOUSE

[Fig. 21(8)] This lighthouse on a caisson foundation stands in 7 feet of water in Kedges Strait about 1 mile north of Smith Island and Martin National Wildlife Refuge. The original screwpile lighthouse built here in 1875, like many Chesapeake Bay light-houses, was destroyed by heavy ice in 1893. The keepers escaped to Smith Island when the tower toppled over and washed away.

Work on the present lighthouse with an octagonal brick tower started the following year and was completed in 1895. Keepers became unnecessary when the light was auto-mated in 1950. A white light now flashes every 6 seconds. The structure is accessible by boat only and is not open to the public.

SMITH ISLAND

[Fig. 21] Smith Island, Maryland's only inhabited island that is accessible only by boat, is actually made up of several small islands separated by creeks, shallows, tidal guts, and thoroughfares. It is located between the Chesapeake Bay and Tangier Sound, 12 miles west of Crisfield. Three close-knit communities—Ewell, Rhodes Point, and Tylerton—are of considerable interest to the outside world. The communities on Smith Island have no mayors and the residents pay no local taxes. Citizens come together to make decisions, and they share in the cost of maintaining community property. The Methodist Church is the only organized religion on the island. Church leaders are well respected. Ewell is the best known community because cruise boats and ferries dock here. Rhodes Point is a derivation of the original Rogues Point, so named for the pirates that once prowled the area. Tylerton is separated by water from Ewell and Rhodes Point.

A few miles to the south in Virginia waters is Tangier Island (*see* page 294) which, like Smith Island, is inhabited by less than 1,000 people. Because of the isolation, nearly all the inhabitants on Smith and Tangier islands are descended from the first settlers, who arrived in the early 1700s. Customs, traditions, even the Elizabethan/Cornwall dialect are unique.

Seafaring has long been a way of life on Smith Island, but as Chesapeake Bay waters have become less productive over the years, islanders have made some accommodations for the tourist trade. However, the island is remarkably free of the usual trappings of tourism such as convenience stores and fast food restaurants. Visitors who stroll the narrow streets or prowl the inlets and coves by boat are treated to views of life in a seafaring community with no pretensions. Watermen care for their boats and repair their nets while women tend to their homes and families just as Smith Island folk have done for centuries. Cruise boats to the island are available seasonally from Crisfield on Maryland's Eastern Shore, from Point Lookout State Park in St. Mary's County on Maryland's western shore, and from Reedville on Virginia's Northern Neck (*see* page 89). A mail boat and a freight boat that also carry passengers depart from and return to Crisfield twice daily. Cars and pets must be left on the mainland, so a little planning ahead for a place to board the family pet is a good idea. Paddlewheel Motel at Crisfield offers an overnight package for two including the cruise and a tour of Smith Island, lunch at Smith Island's famous **Bayside Inn** (410-425-2771), and a stay at the motel. Somerset County Tourism offers a brochure detailing a walking tour of the island.

Boats dock near the new handicap-accessible **Smith Island Center** at Ewell where visitors may tour the center's museum, rest on the wide, breezy porches, or take the 200-foot boardwalk above marshlands that are habitat for Virginia rails (*Rallus limicola*), great egrets (*Casmerodius albus*), osprey (*Pandeon haliaetus*), and great blue herons (*Ardea herodias*). Mink, muskrats, otters, red foxes, and abundant domestic cats have also adapted to life in the wetlands. The habitat along the boardwalk is representative of the 4,400 acres of undeveloped marshlands of the **Martin National Wildlife Refuge** on Smith Island. Because of the fragile ecosystem, the refuge is best viewed from cruise boats on the way to and from the island.

The tranquil pace of life on the island has a calming effect that makes visitors want to stay. The clock ticks at a slower pace, perhaps with the rhythm of a rocking chair on a creaky porch. The friendly residents make travelers feel immediately at home, answering questions about their flat-bottomed skiffs and wooden workboats, and about the fishing shanties that rise on stilts above the water. Visitors who bring bicycles to the island can pedal the easy 5 miles from Ewell to Rhodes Point and back, with the melodic song of the yellowthroat (*Geothlypis trichas*) for company. The afternoon sun on the weathered hulls of abandoned fishing boats, gradually decaying and being claimed by the tides, makes them subject matter for photographer and artist.

Tidal islands—islands that flood easily, change shape over time, and sometimes disappear completely beneath the waves—are often poor choices for permanent settlements. The residents of Smith Island must constantly battle the loss of shoreline to erosion. In recent years, proposals to spend millions of government dollars to shore up the disappearing coastline have put Smith Island in the news. The expensive fill would give the island 10 to 20 years at most, say some engineers. With no assistance, the end to a centuries-old way of life may come much sooner.

Directions: For Crisfield departures to Smith Island on the cruise boats *Captain Tyler* or the *Chelsea Lane Tyler*, take MD 413 into Crisfield. Turn left just past the fire department onto 7th Street and stop at the Paddlewheel Motel to purchase tickets. For trips aboard the mail boat, *Island Belle II*, or the freight boat, *Captain Jason*, follow MD 413 to its terminus at the City Dock in Crisfield. At Point Lookout State Park on the western side of the bay, the boat dock is next to the camp store (*see* page 104). For the ferry from Reedville (*see* page 89) on Virginia's Northern Neck, follow US 360 to its eastern end. The ferry departs from the KOA Campground.

Activities: Cruises and tours of islands, marshes, and museum. Cruises and ferries are for passengers only, not for cars.

Facilities: Cruise boats, visitor center with museum and gift shop, restaurants, general store.

Dates: Smith Island Center is open 12 to 4, daily, Apr. through Oct. From mid-May through Oct., ferries (including cruises and the mail and freight boats) leave Crisfield daily at 12:30 p.m. and return at 5 p.m. (4:30 in winter). The mail boat and freight boat also leave the City Dock at Crisfield at 5:30 p.m. (earlier in winter) and return around 8 the next morning. The trip between Crisfield and Smith Island takes an hour.

On the western shore of Maryland, the cruise ship leaves Point Lookout State Park at 10 and returns at 4. This trip from Point Lookout to the island takes an hour and 40 minutes. A 90-minute narrated ferry ride from Reedville on Virginia's Northern Neck also begins at 10 daily during the summer season and returns at 4.

Fees: There is a fee for entering the Smith Island Center and for cruises.

Closest town: Crisfield is 12 miles east.

For more information: Smith Island Center, phone (410) 425-3351 and Somerset County Tourism, phone (800) 521-9189 or (410) 651-2968. To book a trip from Crisfield on the Eastern Shore or from Point Lookout State Park in St. Mary's County on the western side of the Chesapeake Bay on the 65-foot cruise ship *Captain Tyler* or the 65-foot catamaran, *Chelsea Lane Tyler*, contact Captain Alan Tyler, PO Box 41, Rhodes Point, MD 21824. Phone (410) 425-2771. For the mail boat, *Island Belle II*, call Captain Otis Ray Tyler, (410) 968-1118. For the ferryboat, *Captain Jason*, from Crisfield, phone Captains Terry and Larry Laird at (410) 425-5931 or (410) 425-4471. For reservations on the ferryboat, *Spirit of Chesapeake*, from Reedville on Virginia's Northern Neck, call Captain Gordon Evans, phone (410) 453-3430. For Paddlewheel Motel reservations at Crisfield, phone (410) 968-2220 or (410) 425-2771.

WILDLIFE MANAGEMENT AREAS OF SOMERSET COUNTY

Somerset County has six of the state's 37 wildlife management areas—more than any other county. Five of these—South Marsh Island, Deal Island, Fairmount, Cedar Island, and Pocomoke Sound—are primarily tidal marshlands on the various peninsulas and islands on the western side of the county. Black ducks, mallards, scaup, widgeons, pintails, gadwalls, green and blue-winged teal, shovelers, and other ducks attract hunters to the marshes. Saltwater fishing and crabbing are also popular.

The sixth—**Wellington Wildlife Management Area**—is comprised of 400 acres of forestland in the eastern part of the county on Dublin Road at Wellington. [Fig. 23(6)] Habitat at this one is managed for game including the white-tailed deer, turkey, gray squirrel, woodcock, bobwhite, and cottontail rabbit. By managing the habitat for game, many other animals benefit including songbirds, butterflies, mink, turtles, hairy and downy woodpeckers, and warblers. Frog species around the ponds include spring peepers, green treefrogs, and wood frogs.

South Marsh Island Wildlife Management Area [Fig. 21(12)] is a 3,000-acre marshy island in the Chesapeake Bay north of Smith Island. Peregrine falcons, American oyster-catchers, black skimmers, black rails, and nesting barn owls hang out where pirates used to hide after plundering American ships during the Revolutionary War.

Deal Island Wildlife Management Area [Fig. 21(11)] is huge. Its 13,000 acres are mostly tidal marsh broken by expanses of open water, in addition to some forested wetlands and a 2,800-acre man-made impoundment. Hikers use a trail around the pond. Overnighters can use a primitive camping area.

Fairmount Wildlife Management Area [Fig. 21(10)] is comprised of 4,000 acres of marshland between the Manokin and Annemessex rivers at the western end of MD 361. Two man-made impoundments are managed to feed a wide variety of ducks. Trails lead around the impoundments, providing close access to the area's wildlife and wildfowl enabling hikers, hunters, and photographers.

Cedar Island Wildlife Management Area [Fig. 23(11)] is a 3,000-acre island in Tangier Sound, about 3 miles southeast of Crisfield. **Pocomoke Sound Wildlife Management Area** [Fig. 21(9)] has 900 acres on a marshy peninsula about 3 miles east of Cedar Island. Both these areas attract hoards of ducks, wading birds, and other marsh wildlife similar to that of the other areas. Anglers enjoy crabbing and fishing for sea trout, flounder, croaker, rockfish, spot, and white perch. Neither area is good for hiking because of the soggy soil.

Directions: South Marsh Island WMA—The southern tip of South Marsh Island is about 2 miles north of the northern tip of Smith Island between Tangier Sound and the Chesapeake Bay. It is accessible only by boat. Deal Island WMA—From US 13 at Princess Anne, go west on MD 363 about 11 miles to Deal Island. In addition to the island, much of the wildlife management area is on the mainland on both sides of the highway before you get to the island. Fairmount—From US 13 near Westover, go south on MD 413 about 1 mile. Go west on MD 361 about 7 miles to the area. Cedar Island—The island is located about 3 miles southwest of Crisfield and is accessible only by boat. Pocomoke Sound— The boat ramp at Crisfield is often used to access this area, which is about 3 miles southeast of Crisfield and 3 miles northeast of Cedar Island.

Activities: Hunting, saltwater fishing, crabbing, boating, and wildlife observation.

Facilities: Waterfowl impoundments surrounded by trails.

Dates: Open sunrise to sunset, year-round.

For more information: Maryland Department of Natural Resources, Wellington Work Center, phone (410) 543-8223.

RESTAURANTS OF SOMERSET COUNTY

ARBY'S AND DEB'S SEA-RATIONS. 9968 Deal Island Road, Deal Island. The menu of this island eatery features fresh seafood. Open for breakfast, lunch, and dinner Monday through Saturday, and for breakfast and lunch on Sunday. *Inexpensive. Phone (410) 784-2313 or (410) 784-2749.*

PEAKY'S RESTAURANT. 30361 Mt. Vernon Road, Princess Anne. A large variety of seafood sandwiches and entrées plus nonseafood are on the menu. Specialties include steak Chesapeake (filet mignon topped with crabmeat) and shrimp-and-crab thermidor. Casual. *Inexpensive to moderate. Phone (410) 651-1950.*

CAPTAIN'S GALLEY. 1021 West Main Street, Crisfield. Located at the western end of MD 413, this seafood restaurant is known for its crab cakes. *Inexpensive to moderate. Phone (410) 968-3313.*

BAYSIDE INN RESTAURANT. Smith Island Road, Ewell. Fresh seafood is a natural at this restaurant located on Ewell's City Dock. *Inexpensive to moderate. Phone (410) 425-2771.*

LODGING IN SOMERSET COUNTY

Most lodging facilities are located in the county's two largest towns—Princess Anne on US 13 and Crisfield in the southwestern corner. In addition, there are campsites at Janes Island State Park (*see* page 288), and two private campgrounds are located in the Princess Anne area—**Lake Somerset Family Campground** (410-957-1866 or 410-957-9897) and **Princess Anne Campground** (410-651-1520).

THE HAYMAN HOUSE. 30491 Prince William Street, Princess Anne. Located in the heart of historic Princess Anne, this Georgian-style bed and breakfast was built in 1898. Victorian parlor, richly decorated guest rooms. *Moderate. Phone (410) 651-2753. E-mail haymanbnb@aol.com.*

WATERLOO COUNTRY INN. 28822 Mount Vernon Road, Princess Anne. Pre-Revolutionary waterfront estate from the 1750s, restored and listed on the National Register of Historic Places. Restaurant, nature trails, outdoor pool, canoes, and bicycles for use by guests. *Expensive. Phone (410) 651-0883. E-mail innkeeper@waterloocountryinn.com.*

SOMERS COVE MOTEL. Somers Cove, Crisfield. Located on the water at Somers Cove Marina, this motel has an outdoor pool, picnic tables, and a nearby boat ramp. *Moderate. Phone (800) 827-6637 or (410) 968-1900.*

SMITH ISLAND MOTEL. 4025 Smith Island Road, Ewell. This 7-room motel is open seasonally. Reservations are recommended. *Moderate. Phone (410) 425-3321.*

INN OF SILENT MUSIC. 2955 Tylerton Road, Tylerton. Excellent food (full hot breakfast included, seafood dinner available) and views of the Chesapeake Bay are offered at this waterfront bed and breakfast inn. Ask about birding, canoeing, and charters. *Moderate. Phone (410) 425-3541. E-mail silentmu@shore.intercom.net.*

FIG. 22: EASTERN SHORE OF VIRGINIA

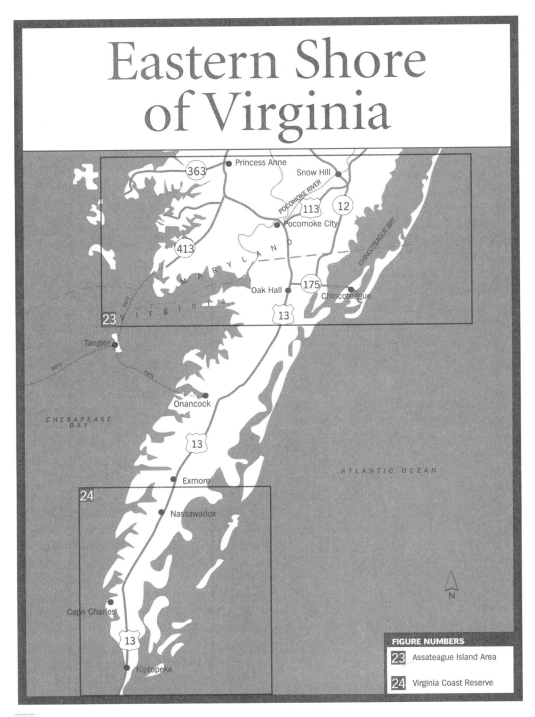

Eastern Shore of Virginia

FIGURE NUMBERS

23 Assateague Island Area

24 Virginia Coast Reserve

The Eastern Shore: Virginia

A h, the Eastern Shore of Virginia—the third part of the word Delmarva, which refers to the peninsula that contains all of Delaware, as well as the Eastern Shore of Maryland and Virginia. As the Delmarva Peninsula heads southward into Virginia, it narrows into a fingerlike projection that separates the lower Chesapeake Bay from the Atlantic Ocean.

The peninsula dwindles in size but expands, at least in some minds, in wild and remote beauty. For the Eastern Shore of Virginia is a holdout, a last outpost for a culture and a way of life barely known if known at all by many fellow Virginians across the bay. As the waters along the bayside tidal marshes grow saltier near the mouth of the Chesapeake, the people of southern Delmarva grow even hardier. From Chincoteague to Onancock to Wachapreague to Oyster to Cape Charles, the tough, seafaring watermen, the farmers, and their hard-working families have for many generations sustained

[*Above:* Wild horses on Chincoteague]

themselves on the waters of the bay and ocean and the riches of the Eastern Shore soil.

Less than four decades have passed since mainland Virginians gained access to the peninsula via the 17.6-mile Chesapeake Bay Bridge-Tunnel (*see page 312*) at the southern end. Even since then, the distance from the mainland and the high toll (currently $10 for a one-way trip) necessary to pay for the engineering marvel has hindered any explosion in local traffic.

Marylanders on the western side of the bay gained access to the upper Eastern Shore in 1952 by way of the 4-mile Bay Bridge from Annapolis, but that access is some 110 miles away from the lower Eastern Shore. The lack of access has served as a barrier to commercialism and development, leaving this part of the Eastern Shore much less affected by the rapid changes that occurred when the upper shore was joined at the hip to Annapolis, Maryland.

It is possible to drive the 70 miles of US 13 from the bridge-tunnel up to the Maryland border in 1.25 hours. To appreciate the Eastern Shore of Virginia, however, the traveler should plan for a few hours, days, or longer to poke about the back roads. Rewards can be lasting for the person who sets aside a little time to explore Chincoteague and the Eastern Shore of Virginia national wildlife refuges, where red-backed sandpipers (*Calidris alpina*) probe the mud flats, or Assateague Island National Seashore, where wild ponies run free.

There's a state park (Kiptopeke) that has a modern boat ramp and a fall birding festival. Two wildlife management areas (Saxis and Mockhorn Island) have huge flocks of snow geese (*Chen caerulescens*) and tundra swans (*Cygnus columbianus*) that fill the air with their winter chatter and willowy saltmarsh cordgrass that undulates in a summer breeze.

A good place to start if you're coming to Virginia from the north is the state's **New Church Welcome Center** at 3420 Langford Highway (US 13) at the Maryland border north of New Church.

The **NASA/Wallops Visitor Center** [Fig. 7(14)] (757-824-1344) is on VA 175 between US 13 and Chincoteague Island. The center has exhibits on the United States space flight program and (by advance reservation) tours of the spacecraft launch sites. Tourists at Chincoteague are thrilled when a launch happens to go with a roar and trail of fire while they're watching.

At Oak Hall, on US 13, four miles south of the Maryland border, is **The Decoy Factory** (757-824-5621), the world's largest of its kind. Artisans carve and paint wooden ducks, geese, and other waterfowl native to the Eastern Shore as visitors watch. Decoys and other gifts are available for purchase.

Several picturesque waterfront towns are off US 13 on one side or the other. Onancock, in Accomack County on the bayside of US 13, was founded in 1680 as Port Scarburgh. Travelers can stop here for groceries, dry goods, and locally made crafts at **Hopkins and Brothers Store**, one of the oldest general stores on the East Coast. Owned and maintained by the Association for the Preservation of Virginia Antiquities, the store has been named both a Virginia and U.S. historic landmark.

Onancock also has a newly renovated wharf beside its deep-water harbor. Cruises to Tangier Island (*see* page 294) in the Chesapeake Bay begin and end on Onancock Creek. The Eastern Shore of Virginia Historical Society (757-787-8012) is housed at Onancock in the **Kerr Place**, an impressive Federal-style manor house built in 1799. The structure is a Virginia Historic Landmark and is on the National Register of Historic Places.

Known for the outstanding flounder fishery in the nearby creek mouths and tidal guts, Wachapreague is a popular fishing port on the ocean side of the peninsula. It is located at the eastern end of VA 180 off US 13, about 6 miles north of the Accomack County border.

Many charter boat captains here and out of seaside harbors at Chincoteague, Quinby, and Oyster specialize in offshore deep-sea fishing for marlin and tuna, and fishing over sunken wrecks for tautog and sea bass. Spot, croaker, bluefish, rockfish, speckled trout, cobia, and big red and black drum can be caught closer to shore or from piers or surf on both sides of the peninsula. See appendix A, page 315, on Outfitters, Guides and Suppliers for charter and headboat information.

In fact, the peninsula is brimming with marinas, boat landings, charter boats, and bait shops to supply the angler with everything he needs. Despite its lack of commercialism, the Eastern Shore of Virginia also has a surprising number of motels, affordable bed and breakfast inns, campgrounds, and outstanding seafood restaurants. Cooks from little towns like Cheriton and Temperanceville have been preparing fritters, crab cakes, softshell crabs, and fried oysters since they were big enough to flip a fillet.

The entire town of Cape Charles is on the National Register of Historic Places because of its Historic District. Cape Charles has what is probably the largest concentration of late-Victorian and turn-of-the-century buildings on the East Coast. The town is located at the western end of VA 184 near the southern end of the Eastern Shore.

Charter boat operators of this bayside port city are busy spring through fall taking anglers to such popular fishing spots as The Cell and the rock islands of the Chesapeake Bay Bridge-Tunnel. The **Cape Charles Museum and Welcome Center** (757-331-1008) is also here, in addition to several restaurants and shops. The annual Between-the-Waters Bicycle Tour is run out of Cape Charles in October.

Campgrounds are at Chincoteague, Quinby, and Cheriton. **Inlet View Waterfront Campground** (757-336-5126) at Chincoteague has a restaurant, camp store, boat ramp, fishing pier, go-cart track, and pony rides. **Maddox Family Campground** (757-336-3111 or 757-336-6648) at Chincoteague has a playground and gift shop. **Virginia Landing** (757-336-5126) at Quinby has a camp store, boat ramp, fishing pier, marina, and ball fields. **Cherrystone Family Camping Resort** (757-331-3063) at Cheriton is open year-round. It has a restaurant, boat rentals, fishing piers, boat ramp, bait shop, and mini-golf.

For more information: Virginia's Eastern Shore Tourism Commission, PO Box 460, US 13 South, Melfa, VA 23410. Phone (757) 787-2460. E-mail esvatourism@esva.net. Web site www.esva.net/-esvatourism. New Church Welcome Center, PO Box 215, 3420

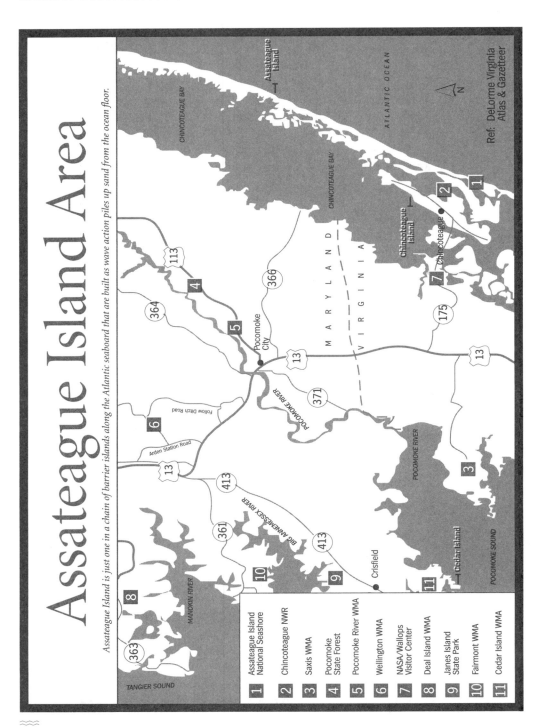

Assateague Island Area

Assateague Island is just one in a chain of barrier islands along the Atlantic seaboard that are built as wave action piles up sand from the ocean floor.

Ref: DeLorme Virginia Atlas & Gazetteer

1. Assateague Island National Seashore
2. Chincoteague NWR
3. Saxis WMA
4. Pocomoke State Forest
5. Pocomoke River WMA
6. Wellington WMA
7. NASA/Wallops Visitor Center
8. Deal Island WMA
9. Janes Island State Park
10. Fairmont WMA
11. Cedar Island WMA

Langford Highway, New Church, VA 23415. Phone (757) 824-5000. Virginia's Eastern Shore Bed and Breakfast Association, 645 Tazewell Avenue, Cape Charles, VA 23310. Phone (757) 331-4960. Web-site bbonline.com/va/easternshore. Tangier-Onancock Cruises, PO Box 27, Tangier Island, VA 23440. Phone (757) 891-2240.

Assateague Island

[Fig. 23] When relentless gales of a northeaster pound the coast for days on end, people who live on Virginia's upper Eastern Shore are glad that 37-mile-long Assateague Island lies off the coast to protect them from the fierce Atlantic. Assateague is just one in a chain of barrier islands along the Atlantic seaboard that are built as wave action piles up sand from the ocean floor.

What is not apparent is that islands such as Assateague are not stationary, but dynamic. Just as waves and water build the island, so they also are constantly moving it around. In addition to daily tidal movements, there are seasonal movements as well. Gentle summer waves bring sand from offshore sandbars, forming wide beaches. In winter, waves pack more energy and the pounding on the beaches makes them more narrow as sand is carried back out and deposited on the sandbars. Major storms can bring in heavier grains of black sand made up of minerals that make the beach look dirty. Time is required to restore the smaller and lighter grains of white sand that vacationers desire.

The natural movement of barrier islands poses no problem until humans decide to put hotels, swimming pools, and highways on them. Then, somewhere down the road, it becomes necessary to build sea walls, to shore up dunes in front of buildings by pumping in sand from offshore, or to build rock jetties to keep the island from continuing to transport itself somewhere else. What engineers have found, though, is that for every mechanical thing done to make the island stay put, there is a reaction somewhere else. For instance, the rock jetties built on the southern end of the next barrier island to the north—the one that holds Ocean City—have caused wide beaches to pile up there. But, in turn, the adjacent northern end of Assateague is eroding severely and migrating toward the mainland at a much faster speed than it once did.

What is best? Should moving beaches be bent to the will of man or should they be left to time and nature? The problem is a sticky one, and there are no easy solutions. Heated discussions occur at every level of government over what should be done and who should pay for it.

At Assateague, the erosion has allowed storms to overwash the dunes. Consequently, the modern Toms Cove Visitor Center has already had to be moved three times and the parking lot redesigned. On other more developed islands, damage can be far more costly as high-rise hotels built too close to the surf are threatened and beach cottages collapse one by one into the sea with each passing storm.

ASSATEAGUE ISLAND NATIONAL SEASHORE

[Fig. 23(1)] Most of this long barrier island that extends from just south of Ocean City, Maryland, to Virginia's upper Eastern Shore near Chincoteague is part of the 18,000-acre Assateague Island National Seashore, managed by the National Park Service and the U. S. Fish and Wildlife Service. The island is accessible from the mainland from both the Maryland end and the Virginia end (*see* page 298 for the Maryland end), but there are no roads on the island that connect the north and south ends. A fence on the state line keeps even the wild ponies that roam the island from mixing.

Toms Cove Visitor Center on the Virginia part of the island is located just west of the oceanfront dunes on the eastern side of Chincoteague National Wildlife Refuge. In addition to exhibits, maps, and publications, children will enjoy learning about maritime life and viewing aquariums. The 0.25-mile Toms Cove Nature Trail loop is near the visitor center. Toms Cove Hook on the southern end of the island is closed during the nesting season of the endangered piping plover between March 15 and August 31. Beachcombing is always fun, but only occasionally turns up large shells that have not been pounded into pieces by the Atlantic. Surf fishing, crabbing, and clamming are other popular activities.

Directions: From US 13 on the northern end of Virginia's Eastern Shore, go east on VA 175 for 9 miles to the town of Chincoteague. Go left on Main Street about seven blocks, then turn right on Maddox Boulevard. Go 2 miles, crossing the causeway, to Assateague Island National Seashore and Chincoteague National Wildlife Refuge. Continue through the refuge another 3 miles to Toms Cove Visitor Center.

Activities: Lifeguarded swimming (ocean), picnicking, beachcombing, surf fishing, clamming, crabbing, hiking, wildlife bus tour, off-road driving (permit required). Pets must be on short leashes.

Facilities: Visitor center, nature trail, off-road vehicle area. Campgrounds are on the Maryland end of the island.

Dates: Open daily, year-round. Toms Cove Visitor Center is open 9 to 5 daily, year-round. Beaches are guarded only in summer.

Fees: There is a user fee.

For more information: Assateague Island National Seashore, 6206 National Seashore Lane, Berlin, MD 21811. Phone (410) 641-1441 or (410) 641-3030. Camping reservations, phone (800) 365-CAMP.

CHINCOTEAGUE NATIONAL WILDLIFE REFUGE

[Fig. 23(2)] Anyone who has wondered what is done with revenue from the sale of duck stamps would enjoy a visit to Chincoteague National Wildlife Refuge. Before the 1900s, the flocks of ducks, geese, and other waterfowl migrating along the Atlantic Flyway seemed too endless ever to become imperiled. But in the early part of the century, their numbers took a startling dive. Conservationists became alarmed as more and more wetlands were drained for farming or developments. Feathers and plumes were used to decorate ladies' hats, and game management was in its infancy. In short, wildfowl needed a hand.

In 1943, funds collected from the sale of duck stamps bought a magnificent refuge where the migrating birds could feed and rest. Although the birds and animals come first, people who enjoy watching and learning about them also benefit.

Chincoteague refuge is located on the southern end of 37-mile-long Assateague Island, within the boundaries of Assateague Island National Seashore, just east of the island and village of Chincoteague. Among the thousands of birds that come here, the snow geese (*Chen caerulescens*), with their beautiful white plumage and black primary wing feathers, are among the favorites.

Hikers have 15 miles of trails to explore, and half of those are paved for bicycling and wheelchairs. The 3.2-mile, paved Wildlife Loop gives hikers and bikers access to Snow Goose Pool and Swan Cove. Vehicles are permitted on the loop between 3 p.m. and dusk. The waterways and ponds beside the road always hold a snowy egret, or the elegant great blue heron, or perhaps a flock of Canada geese. Photographers who have not experienced the bonanza of subject matter may find themselves dashing back to the car for more film.

Bird watchers armed with scopes can identify sea ducks such as as oldsquaws and scoters, or puddle ducks such as widgeons, pintails, and mallards. In spring, where a knot of onlookers has gathered, there are sure to be a couple of baby foxes playing, or maybe a group of tiny raccoons peeking through the grass fronds.

In addition to the Wildlife Loop, other hiking opportunities include the 1.6-mile Woodland Trail loop (walking and bicy-

Crabbing and Clamming

Part of the appeal of crabbing and clamming is the simplicity. How many activities are there where nothing but a piece of baited string or a rake, along with a net and bucket, will obtain something akin to the food of the gods for dinner? Assateague Island has many places to find crabs and clams, but Toms Cove at the southern end of the island is good place to begin.

To catch the delicious blue crab (*Callinectus sapidus*), tie a chicken neck or other bait available at bait shops onto a string, toss the bait a few feet away in shallow water, and keep the string taut until something latches on. When crabs are around, it doesn't take long for them to locate the bait. Pull the bait and crab slowly to you across the bottom, then up off the bottom enough to slowly slip the net beneath. If the crab lets go as you pull, simply wait a few seconds and it will probably return.

Crabs may also be caught in shallow water from boats, docks, and piers. In Maryland, crabs must measure 5 inches across, from point to point, to be legally kept—a good rule of thumb for conservation reasons in Virginia and other states, also.

Clammers generally use a rake in shallow water to dislodge hard clams (*Mercenaria mercenaria*) from just beneath the muck on the bottom. It's also possible to find the clams with your toes, then reach down to dig them out.

Surf Fishing

Many fishermen who are familiar with stream or lake fishing discover a whole new sport in surf fishing. Surf anglers wade out into the Atlantic, waves washing against their legs. They use the leverage of the long surf rod to cast a weighted piece of squid bait far out into the green waters. It comes naturally in just a few tries. The action is much easier than casting a spinning rod.

Tasty spot, croaker, and flounder make great eating after a day on the beach. Latching onto a warrior like a bluefish or a behemoth like a 70-pound red drum can provide a memorable challenge. Surf rods, much longer and heftier than standard rods, are available for rent at tackle shops. Demonstrations on surf fishing by naturalists are part of the summer program at the national seashore. Check at Toms Cove Visitor Center for current fishing information and regulations or to request an after-hours fishing permit. No saltwater license is required along the Virginia or Maryland coast.

cling allowed) and the 0.25-mile (one-way) Lighthouse Trail to the photogenic **Assateague Lighthouse**, emerging from the wax myrtles. Built in the 1860s, this tower lighthouse with its alternating red and white rings still operates with a flashing light. The pine forests of the refuge hold white-tailed deer and the much smaller Sika deer. Sikas, which are actually an Oriental species of elk, were released on a Chesapeake Bay island in the early 1900s. They were released on what became Assateague Island in the 1920s. Wild ponies also roam the island and are a common sight as they graze the salt marshes. Sometimes, like restless children just let out of school, they may take a notion to gallop wildly along the water's edge of Chincoteague Channel, ears laid back in mock rage, splashing and nipping one another. Interpretive programs that explain the barrier island natural and cultural history are held outdoors and in the refuge auditorium. Pets are prohibited in the refuge, even in vehicles.

Directions: From US 13 on the northern end of Virginia's Eastern Shore, go east on VA 175 for 9 miles to the town of Chincoteague. Go left on Main Street about seven blocks, then turn right on Maddox Boulevard. Go 2 miles (Maddox Boulevard becomes Beach Road), crossing the causeway, to the island.

Activities: Hiking, biking, picnicking (at beach), driving (vehicles are allowed on the Wildlife Loop from 3 p.m. to dusk only).

Facilities: Paved Wildlife Loop, nature trails, visitor center, picnic tables, auditorium, off-road vehicle area.

Dates: The refuge is open daily, year-round. Hours vary according to season, but they are roughly pre-dawn to just after nightfall.

Fees: There is an entry fee.

Closest town: Chincoteague is on the west side, across a causeway.

For more information: Chincoteague National Wildlife Refuge, PO Box 62, Chincoteague, VA 23336. Phone (757) 336-6122. E-mail R5RW_CHNWR@fws.gov.

Chincoteague

[Fig. 23] Visitors to Chincoteague National Wildlife Refuge must pass through the colorful village of Chincoteague on Chincoteague Island. The name Chincoteague comes from *Gingoteague*—a word early white settlers heard local Indians use, which translated to "beautiful land across the water."

Many gift shops and boutiques offer antique wildfowl carvings, art and photography of local artists, and books about the area. It's easy to find restaurants that serve today's catch. There are also a wide variety of places to stay, including economically priced motels, private cottages and efficiencies, and bed and breakfast inns. Dancing is available nightly at Chattie's Lounge in Don's Seafood Restaurant (757-336-5715) at 4113 Main Street.

Several private campgrounds offer a place to stay for those who relish the idea of dreams punctuated with the sound of wild geese. Toms Cove Campground (757-336-6498) has shaded campsites under pine trees, a boat ramp and marina, piers for fishing and crabbing, and a bait and tackle shop. Maddox Family Campground (757-336-3111) and Inlet View Waterfront Family Campground (757-336-5126) are also located at Chincoteague.

In addition to the popular Volunteer Firemen's Carnival with the annual pony round-up and swim each July, there is a popular Easter Decoy Festival in spring, the Oyster Festival in October, and a Waterfowl Open House during the week of Thanksgiving, corresponding with Waterfowl Week in the wildlife refuge. The **Oyster and Maritime Museum** (757-336-6117) at

The Wild Ponies of Chincoteague

The wild ponies in the Chincoteague National Wildlife Refuge have been made famous by Marguerite Henry's book, *Misty of Chincoteague*. They are actually small, sturdy horses that have adapted to the harsh environment of the tidal marshlands.

The National Park Service position on the origin of the ponies is that though they are now wild, they are descendants of domestic horses owned by seventeenth and eighteenth century Eastern Shore planters, who brought them to the island to graze to avoid building fences and paying mainland taxes. Various legends about their past, however, also include a story about a Spanish galleon that wrecked off the coast, releasing its cargo of mustangs, some of which made it to shore.

The ponies on the Virginia end of Assateague Island are owned by the Chincoteague Volunteer Fire Company, which protects the homes on Chincoteague Island across Assateague Channel from the refuge. A popular pony swim and summer carnival draws huge crowds to the island annually. On the last Wednesday and Thursday of July, volunteer firemen on horseback come to the refuge and herd the ponies into the water for a swim across Assateague Channel. On Chincoteague Island, the ponies are corralled for Pony Penning Day and many of the foals are sold to the highest bidder.

the refuge entrance tells the island history and the importance of oystering and the seafood business to the local economy in the early days.

Directions: From US 13 on the northern end of Virginia's Eastern Shore, go east on VA 175 for 9 miles, crossing Chincoteague Bay.

For more information: Chincoteague Chamber of Commerce, 6733 Maddox Boulevard, PO Box 258, Chincoteague, VA 23336. Phone (757) 336-6161.

Public Lands

SAXIS WILDLIFE MANAGEMENT AREA

[Fig. 23(3)] Like so much of the land on both sides of Virginia's Eastern Shore, most of the 5,574 acres of Saxis Wildlife Management Area are comprised of tidal marshes. There was a day when such marshes were considered useless areas of muck and mud full of strange amphibians and reptiles, not to mention the hoards of biting insects.

Today, however, with public appreciation growing for the value of wetlands, the Virginia Department of Game and Inland Fisheries oversees the use of the Saxis area for both recreation (hunting, fishing, and bird-watching) and the protection of the habitat. The marsh is divided into two portions that take up most of two peninsulas on the bay side of Virginia's upper Eastern Shore.

Michael Marsh is the southernmost tract, and is closed to hunting. The Saxis area on the northernmost peninsula is located about 1 mile south of the Maryland border and is a prime breeding and wintering ground for the black duck (*Anas rubripes*). Mallards, blue-winged teal, green-winged teal, and pintails are some of the puddle ducks that are found on the lakes and creeks. The open water attracts mergansers, redheads, goldeneyes, and canvasbacks. Grebes, loons, and a multitude of shorebirds and songbirds make Saxis an excellent place to add another bird or two to a life list.

Hunters come to Saxis not only for the excellent waterfowl hunting but also for white-tailed deer that slip through the forests on the higher ground. In addition to the usual raccoons, muskrats, opossums, and rabbits of the Eastern Shore habitat, Saxis contains red and gray foxes and river otters. At dusk, car lights may even pick up the yellowish-green glow of two mink eyes.

The mink (*Mustela vison*) has everything it needs here. Fish are a favorite food, as are birds and their eggs. Soft mud banks above the high tide, or even a muskrat hole will do fine for a den. And if disturbed, the mink has a little-known weapon. It can emit a foul odor—perhaps not so strong as a skunk's, but disagreeable enough to do the job.

Striped bass (rockfish), flounder, gray trout, speckled trout, croaker, and bluefish benefit from the nutrients and prey that are in rich supply around such undisturbed marshes. Anglers, in turn, cast to the grasses and the points, or come up into Messongo Creek and Pocomoke Sound to find the fish. Boats may be launched at Saxis, Messongo

Creek, and Marsh Market. Contact the fish and game department for a detailed map.

Directions: From US 13 at Temperanceville on the upper Eastern Shore of Virginia, go west on VA 695 for about 8 miles to the area. Several parking areas are on the roadside, but there are no trails.

Activities: Fishing, seasonal hunting, bird-watching, boating, primitive camping.

Facilities: None.

Dates: Open from sunrise to sunset daily, year-round. Primitive camping is also allowed.

Fees: None.

Closest town: Temperanceville is 8 miles east.

For more information: Saxis Wildlife Management Area, Virginia Department of Game and Inland Fisheries, Region 1 Office, 5806 Mooretown Road, Williamsburg, VA 23118. Phone (757) 253-7072.

MOCKHORN ISLAND WILDLIFE MANAGEMENT AREA

[Fig. 24(1)] The 7,000 acres of tidal marshes that make up Mockhorn Island are perfect habitat for the clapper rail (*Rallus longirostris*), known more for its loud clattering call across the saltmarsh cordgrass than for its mottled brown appearance. The best time to catch a glimpse of the secretive bird is at high tide, when rising water may force it into the open. The wildlife management area itself, on the other hand, nearly disappears: Just 5 percent of it remains above the water at high tide.

The island, managed by the Virginia Department of Game and Inland Fisheries, attracts rail and waterfowl hunters from the nearby boat ramp at Oyster. Black ducks spend the winter at Mockhorn. Occasional bird watchers study ducks such as buffleheads, goldeneyes, and Atlantic brant. Sea ducks such as oldsquaws and scoters bob on the open water around the island.

Anglers know the area for saltwater species such as flounder, croaker, and gray trout. Monstrous red drum (channel bass) and black drum will tire even the strongest fisherman when they start hitting bait in early summer.

On the hummocks of marshland, muskrat chew on grasses and raccoons open crustaceans, leaving little piles of shells beside their tiny handlike paw prints in the mud. River otters may emerge from the water onto shore, only to make a C turn and torpedo back into the water.

In addition to the cordgrass of the marshes, a coastal forest of loblolly pine, red cedar, and wax myrtle covers the higher ground. Herons and egrets, looking gangly in their nests of sticks in the low shrubs, are transformed into pure artistry in flight.

A second, much smaller portion of the area is the 356-acre GATR Tract on the mainland adjacent to the island's southern tip. Besides the fishing here, the game department offers an archery season for deer in the fall. A small trail system begins at the gated road at the parking lot. The game and fish department can supply a map showing both tracts in detail.

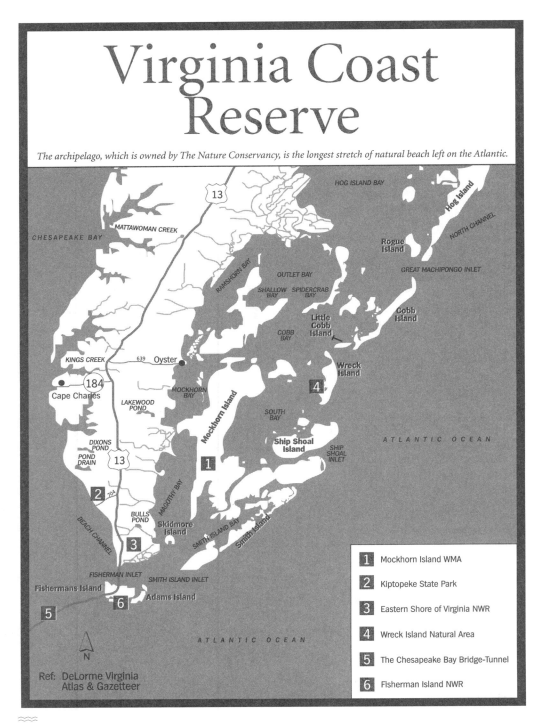

Virginia Coast Reserve

The archipelago, which is owned by The Nature Conservancy, is the longest stretch of natural beach left on the Atlantic.

HOG ISLAND BAY

Hog Island

13

MATTAWOMAN CREEK

CHESAPEAKE BAY

NORTH CHANNEL

Rogue Island

GREAT MACHIPONGO INLET

RAMSHORN BAY

OUTLET BAY

SHALLOW BAY

SPIDERCRAB BAY

Cobb Island

Little Cobb Island

COBB BAY

KINGS CREEK

639 Oyster

Wreck Island

184

MOCKHORN BAY

4

Cape Charles

LAKEWOOD POND

Mockhorn Island

SOUTH BAY

ATLANTIC OCEAN

DIXONS POND

POND DRAIN

13

Ship Shoal Island

SHIP SHOAL INLET

1

704

MAGOTHY BAY

2

BULLS POND

Skidmore Island

SMITH ISLAND BAY

Smith Island

BEACH CHANNEL

3

FISHERMAN INLET

SMITH ISLAND INLET

Fishermans Island

Adams Island

6

5

N

Ref: DeLorme Virginia Atlas & Gazetteer

ATLANTIC OCEAN

1	Mockhorn Island WMA
2	Kiptopeke State Park
3	Eastern Shore of Virginia NWR
4	Wreck Island Natural Area
5	The Chesapeake Bay Bridge-Tunnel
6	Fisherman Island NWR

Directions: To access the island from the boat ramp at Oyster, go east on VA 639 about 3 miles from Business US 13 at Cheriton in lower Northampton County, and follow signs to ramp. The northern end of the island is about 2 miles east across Mockhorn Bay. For the GATR Tract, from the VA 600 Byway at the town of Kiptopeke in lower Northampton County, go north on VA 600 for just under 2 miles. Go east on Jones Cove Road about 0.7 mile to the entrance.

Activities: Boating, bird-watching, seasonal hunting and fishing.

Facilities: Boat ramp (at Oyster).

Dates: Open sunrise to sunset daily, year-round.

Fees: None.

Closest town: Oyster is 2 miles across the water to the west from Mockhorn Island.

For more information: Mockhorn Island Wildlife Management Area, Virginia Department of Game and Inland Fisheries, Region 1 Office, 5806 Mooretown Road, Williamsburg, VA 23118. Phone (757) 253-7072.

VIRGINIA COAST RESERVE

[Fig. 24] When some developers look at what seems to be marshy, vacant coastal islands, they may envision gleaming resort cities, with rows of hotels, swimming pools, and parking garages. Sometimes, though, there are people with other ideas—people who not only see the value and beauty of tidal marshes, but also people with the financial and legal clout to step in and offer protection.

Were it not for the second kind of visionaries, Virginians—and all Americans—might have lost a natural treasure on the Eastern Shore. All or part of 14 barrier islands encompassing 45,000 acres between the Virginia/Maryland border of the Eastern Shore and the mouth of the Chesapeake Bay make up the Virginia Coast Reserve. Some of the larger islands (from north to south) are Metomkin, Cedar, Parramore, Hog, Cobb, and Smith. The archipelago, which is owned by The Nature Conservancy, is the longest stretch of natural beach left on the Atlantic Coast. According to the Conservancy, it represents the best example of the barrier island community in the country. Combined with Assateague Island National Seashore and Chincoteague National Wildlife Refuge on the northern end and Eastern Shore of Virginia and Fisherman Island national wildlife refuges on the southern end, in addition to holdings of the Virginia Department of Natural Resources, the stretch of islands forms an impressive refuge for plants and animals.

Even here, along this segmented expanse of now-deserted windswept islands, there were once resorts and sportsmen's hotels (Cobb Island), and a village of 250 people (Hog Island). Pirates have hidden in the sloughs, musket fire of Revolutionary War battles has startled clamoring geese and ducks into the air, ships have wrecked on offshore reefs, and colonists have turned hogs and cattle loose to graze.

As The Nature Conservancy has bought the islands, silence has once again settled like evening mist over the grasslands. Over the years, biologists have come to realize the importance of the saltmarsh cordgrass (*Spartina alterniflora*) marshes on the backside of

Assateague Island lighthouse.

the islands to the health of the Chesapeake Bay. An incredible 90 percent of the shellfish—the crabs, clams, oysters, and such—that are harvested in the bay are dependent on the marshes for at least some of their lives. Nutrients filter through the marsh soil and grasses and are released slowly into the water.

In addition, many plants and animals depend on the islands. Upland pine and hardwood forests spread across the larger islands. The inland reaches of these larger islands supports brackish and even fresh-water marshes.

Perhaps the best known resident of the reserve is the rare piping plover (*Charadrius melodus*). Because the plover nests in a depression on the sand, it is very vulnerable to predators. Its numbers have gone into serious decline in recent years due to loss of habitat to development, a fact that has gotten this little bird a great deal of news coverage in recent years as naturalists scramble to arrange for its protection. Of course, anything that benefits the plover also benefits other birds. Besides thousands of nesting birds, a vast number of migratory shorebirds and wintering waterfowl use the wide expanses of marshes and mud flats.

Because of its pristine nature, the United Nations has designated the Virginia Coast Reserve a World Biosphere Reserve and the U.S. Department of the Interior has listed it as a National Natural Landmark.

The old U.S. Coast Guard Station on Parramore Island was in the process of being renovated to serve as a center for educational programs until it was destroyed by fire in 1999. The Nature Conservancy is planning a new structure to take its place. Boaters may visit the islands for low impact day use such as bird-watching and beachcombing. However, with tidal marshes on the western or shore sides of the islands, ocean waves on the eastern sides, and dangerous currents in the inlets, access may be tricky at times. Perhaps the best way to see the islands is to contact headquarters to find when educational tours are scheduled. No fires, no overnight camping, and no pets are allowed on the islands. Boaters should not come ashore where there are nesting colonies of birds.

Directions: The reserve is made up of 13 barrier islands along the eastern side of the Eastern Shore of Virginia. To reach the headquarters at Nassawadox in upper Northampton County, from the traffic light on US 13 at Nassawadox, go east on VA 606 about 0.1

mile. Turn left onto VA 600 and drive another 0.1 mile. Turn right onto VA 608 (Browns-ville Road) and go about 0.5 mile to the office.

Activities: Wildlife observation, occasional educational tours.

Facilities: None.

Dates: The islands are open to the public for low-impact day use. Some areas are posted seasonally to protect nesting bird colonies.

Fees: None.

Closest town: The headquarter is less than 1 mile east of Nassawadox. The islands are spread along the entire Virginia portion of the Eastern Shore oceanfront.

For more information: Virginia Coast Reserve, Brownsville Road, Nassawadox, VA 23413. Phone (757) 442-3049.

KIPTOPEKE STATE PARK

[Fig. 24(2)] The name Kiptopeke—pronounced KIP-toe-peek—is an Indian name meaning "big water" and has an interesting origin. When Captain John Smith left Jamestown to explore the Chesapeake Bay in 1608, he met the king of the Accawmack Indians and his friendly younger brother, Kiptopeke. The site of the former ferry termi-nus at the park was named Kiptopeke Beach in honor of this friendly Indian.

Kiptopeke State Park is called a work in progress. Each year, repeat visitors find new facilities—hookups for the campgrounds, improved bathhouses, a new boat ramp, new landscaping, and so on. But one of the best things people find if they happen to arrive in fall is one of the premier bird-banding operations of its kind on the East Coast.

Since 1963, the Kiptopeke area has been the hub of activity for the Virginia Society of Ornithology, a group of enthusiasts who keep tabs on bird populations. Volunteers have banded over a quarter of a million birds. Together with the Hawk Migration Society, they have also recorded more than 400,000 hawks and other birds of prey since 1977.

The site is a natural for the study. The Eastern Shore peninsula narrows from north to south like a huge finger, literally pointing the way for birds on their southward migration. Birds instinctively stay over land as long as possible, so the peninsula's configuration funnels them in huge numbers to the small southern tip.

Visitors at the park are treated to demonstrations of the banding process during the Eastern Shore Birding Festival (757-787-2460). Warblers, titmice, sparrows, and other birds are plucked gently from mist nets that snag them as they flit through the understo-ry. They are then processed, which includes weighing them, determining their fat content visually by blowing gently to part their breast feathers, placing a lightweight band on one leg, and releasing them to continue their flight.

The festival is held every weekend following the first Wednesday in October. In addition, on Saturday mornings from September 15 to November 15, park interpreters lead tours of the bird-banding station and visits to the hawk observatory. Canoe tours to nearby conservation areas and walks at Fisherman Island National Wildlife Refuge are also part of the fall interpretive program.

Another interesting feature of Kiptopeke State Park is the row of nine sunken concrete ships from World War II that forms a breakwater and artificial fishing reef about 1,500 feet offshore. In 1998 the park system opened a new boat ramp that can handle two cars at a time. The extremely popular landing gives boaters access not only to the concrete ships but also to the productive rock islands of the Chesapeake Bay Bridge-Tunnel, Fisherman Island, the seaside barrier islands, and the Atlantic Ocean.

Anglers fishing from the park shore reel in nice-sized speckled trout. Specks, as they're called for short, along with striped bass (rockfish), perch, spot, gray trout, flounder, tautog, and crappie also hit bait cast from the 1,000-foot-long lighted fishing pier, which has been converted for use from the old ferry terminal.

Lifeguards are stationed at the approximately 0.5-mile northern beach from Memorial Day through Labor Day. The beach is connected to the picnic area by a boardwalk across the dunes. The full-service wooded campgrounds have sites with or without hookups, in addition to restrooms and warm showers.

Hikers can cool off in the shade of a hardwood forest along the 1.5-mile Baywoods Trail, where white-tailed deer, red and gray foxes, and raccoons live. Bicycling is restricted to park roads only. Leashed pets are allowed.

Directions: From US 13 at the northern end of the Chesapeake Bay Bridge-Tunnel, go 3 miles north. Turn west on VA 704 and go 0.5 mile to the entrance.

Activities: Swimming in bay, picnicking, saltwater fishing, crabbing, boating, flatwater canoeing, camping, hiking, biking (only on park roads), bird-banding demonstrations, hawk watching.

Facilities: Picnic tables and grills, 0.5-mile swimming beach, modern beach house, modern boat ramp, concrete ships (fish attractant), full-service campground with hookups and bathhouses, primitive campground, nature trail and five dune walks (three are handicap-accessible), 4,276-foot beach for surf fishing and beachcombing, bird-banding station, hawk observatory.

Dates: Open daily, year-round. Hawk observatory and bird-banding station programs in Sept. and Oct. Lifeguarded beach, Memorial Day through Labor Day.

Fees: There is a daily user fee, and fees for camping and launching a boat.

Closest town: Cape Charles is about 9 miles north.

For more information: Kiptopeke State Park, 3540 Kiptopeke Drive, Cape Charles, VA 23310. Phone (757) 331-2267. For camping reservations, call (800) 933-7275.

EASTERN SHORE OF VIRGINIA AND FISHERMAN ISLAND NATIONAL WILDLIFE REFUGES

[Fig. 24(3), 24(6)] Two adjacent national wildlife refuges—Eastern Shore of Virginia and Fisherman Island—are valuable especially for the large number of birds that funnel through here on their southward migration.

The Eastern Shore of Virginia refuge lies along both sides of US 13 at the southern tip of Northampton County. The refuge was established in 1984 to provide habitat for migratory and endangered species on the 725 acres of wildlife habitat. Consequently, visitors who walk the maritime forests, grasslands, and the thickets of wax myrtle (*Myrica cerifera*) and bayberry (*Myrica pensylvanica*) may be lucky enough to spot one of the bald eagles (*Haliaeetus leucocephalus*) or peregrine falcons (*Falco peregrinus*) the refuge is designed to protect.

More likely, they will catch glimpses of migrating warblers and songbirds in the undergrowth or see a northern harrier (*Circus cyaneus*) in flight over the marsh. Kestrels (*Falco sparverius*), also known as sparrow hawks, perch on power lines. Bobwhite quail (*Colinus virginianus*) call on spring evenings from the fields. Eastern bluebirds (*Sialia sialis*) flutter to the ground to pick up insects.

American Redstart

Many people have never seen this little wood warbler, though it's one of North America's most common birds. Like many warblers, the American redstart (*Setophaga ruticilla*) spends its time in second-growth shrubbery and does not come to feeders. It's a striking bird with a habit of flashing its colorful wing and tale patches as it flutters like a butterfly chasing insects. The male's patches are orange, the female's, yellow. A good time to see this and many other common and not-so-common warblers is during the fall bird banding at Kiptopeke State Park.

Ponds have been created to attract ducks and other waterfowl of freshwater wetlands, while the mud flats and salt marshes provide habitat for shorebirds and shallow waders such as the glossy ibis (*Plegadis falcinellus*), cattle egret (*Bubulcus ibis*), and willet (*Catoptrophorus semipalmatus*). The variety of habitats and birds that use them make the Eastern Shore of Virginia National Wildlife Refuge an important part of the bird banding and bird counts that take place at nearby Kiptopeke State Park (*see* page 309).

The visitor center is on VA 600, about 0.25 mile north of the bridge-tunnel tollgate. Down the road, a 0.5-mile interpretive trail loops through a stand of hardwoods, past an old graveyard, and up a mound to a World War II bunker where there is a sweeping view across the low marshes and barrier islands to the Atlantic.

The past military use of the area is understandable because of the strategic location of the refuge at the mouth of the Chesapeake Bay. Fort John Custis was built here at the beginning of World War II, with 16-inch guns mounted in the bunkers as protection for naval bases and shipyards at Virginia Beach and Norfolk.

If time allows, instead of driving on refuge roads to the interpretive trail and overlook, take the 0.5-mile Butterfly Trail that leads southeast from the center to the interpretive trail. In addition to many varieties of butterflies drawn to the flowering shrubs and wildflowers, hikers could startle a woodcock (*Philohela minor*) into sudden flight. Refuge naturalists say the site has a higher population of this woodland worm-eater than any other place in the United States.

Fishermans Island National Wildlife Refuge off the southern tip of the Eastern Shore is aptly named. Its waters are a popular place for anglers. Positioned at the mouth of the Chesapeake Bay, the wetlands around the island are frequented by many species of fish that migrate seasonally into and out of the estuary. In late spring and summer, the tidal marshes and inlets hold flounder, spot, croaker, gray trout, rockfish, and bluefish.

Also, the island is the last stop before the bay crossing for birds that migrate down the Eastern Shore peninsula on their way south. Bird banders keep meticulous records of both migrating birds and the diverse nesting colonies of terns, gulls, herons, and ibis. To take a guided 4-mile hike on the island, join a scheduled hike from the Eastern Shore of Virginia refuge. Access is by permission only and the island is closed during late spring and early summer while royal terns (*Thalasseus maximus*), ring-billed gulls (*Larus delawarensis*), and shorebirds nest on the beaches.

Directions: For Eastern Shore of Virginia refuge, from the northern end of the Chesapeake Bay Bridge-Tunnel, go north from the tollgate on US 13 about 0.25 mile. Turn right on VA 600. The visitor center is on the right. Fishermans Island, located beneath the bridge-tunnel, is accessible only by boat and by permission. To fish the waters around the island, use the Kiptopeke State Park boat ramp about 5 miles northwest of the island (*see* page 310).

Activities: Eastern Shore of Virginia: bird-watching, hiking. Fisherman Island: fishing, bird-watching.

Facilities: Visitor center, restrooms, photography blind, nature and interpretive trails.

Dates: Eastern Shore of Virginia: open sunrise to sunset daily, year-round. Fisherman Island: open Saturdays from Oct. through mid-Mar. for guided tours; closed during nesting season.

Fees: None.

Closest town: Cape Charles is 11 miles north of Eastern Shore of Virginia refuge. The Kiptopeke State Park boat ramp is 5 miles north of Fisherman Island.

For more information: Eastern Shore of Virginia National Wildlife Refuge (and Fisherman Island NWR), 5003 Hallett Circle, Cape Charles, VA 23310. Phone (757) 331-2760.

THE CHESAPEAKE BAY BRIDGE-TUNNEL

[Fig. 24(5)] The world's largest bridge-tunnel complex is the 17.6-mile span across the mouth of the Chesapeake Bay. The Chesapeake Bay Bridge-Tunnel opened to traffic in 1964, ending an old ferry service and dramatically upgrading the connection between residents of the Eastern Shore of Virginia with the mainland. On a drive from Virginia Beach to New York, the crossing on US 13 saves travelers 1.5 hours of driving time and cuts 95 miles off their trip.

The highway connects Virginia Beach and Norfolk on the south side with the southern tip of the Eastern Shore of Virginia to the north. Travelers drive to breathtaking heights on high trestles above the water. Twice they come down into mile-long tunnels, while military ships from the Norfolk Naval Base and giant ocean tankers from distant world ports pass overhead.

The bridge-tunnel is officially named the Lucius J. Kellam Jr. Bridge-Tunnel after the man who had the foresight and vision to make the dream a reality. In 1965, competing with more than 100 other major feats, the Chesapeake Bay Bridge-Tunnel was named one of the Seven Engineering Wonders of the Modern World.

In 1998, a new parallel span of bridge opened and the old one was closed for rehabilitation. In April 1999, the spruced-up old span reopened. Costing nearly $200 million, the construction of the new span and renovation of the old turned the two-lane highway into four. No longer does an entire line of motorists have to wait for a slow vehicle, or do motorists need to take unnecessary risks by passing on the bridge. New tunnels will be built later.

Fishermen bobbing in the water far below the highway see the bridge-tunnel not for its value to get from one place to another, but as the world's largest artificial reef. The rock islands and the pilings have proven to be fantastic fish attractants. Some of the Chesapeake Bay's best catches of bluefish, rockfish, flounder, gray trout, tautog, and cobia come from the bridge-tunnel complex. The 625-foot Seagull Pier is midway across the bridge on a rock island behind the Seagull Pier Restaurant. No fishing license is needed to fish from the pier.

Directions: The bridge-tunnel is the US 13 connection between Virginia Beach/Norfolk and the Eastern Shore of Virginia.

Activities: Pier fishing.

Facilities: Restaurant, fishing pier (bait available), fish weigh station, gift shop, emergency road service.

Dates: Open 24 hours a day, year-round.

Fees: There is a $10 toll for a one-way trip.

For more information: Chesapeake Bay Bridge and Tunnel District, Cape Charles, VA 23310. Phone (757) 331-2960. Web site www.cbbt.com.

RESTAURANTS ON THE EASTERN SHORE OF VIRGINIA

The Chincoteague area has the lion's share of restaurants on Virginia's Eastern Shore, but there are plenty of other choices sprinkled down the two counties.

AJ'S. Maddox Boulevard, Chincoteague. Seafood, pasta, aged beef, veal, and lamb are on the menu at this casual restaurant. *Moderate. Phone (757) 336-5888.*

CHINCOTEAGUE INN. Maddox Boulevard, Chincoteague. Enjoy seafood and pasta at a family restaurant. *Moderate. Phone (757) 336-5040.*

WRIGHT'S SEAFOOD RESTAURANT AND CRAB GALLEY. Watts Bay, Atlantic. Features all-you-can-eat dinners in a casual atmosphere. Situated near NASA, about 15 minutes from Chincoteague. Ask about the former poultry processing plant and button factory on the site. Overlooks the bay. *Moderate. Phone (757) 824-4012.*

ISLAND HOUSE RESTAURANT. 15 Atlantic Avenue, Wachapreague. A popular place for local people and boaters to find the catch of the day. *Moderate. Phone (757) 787-4242.*

THE TRAWLER RESTAURANT AND DINNER THEATER. US 13, Exmore. Eat fresh seafood or steaks, followed by a play. Located just south of the Northampton/Accomack county line. *Moderate. Phone (757) 442-2092.*

STING-RAY'S. 26507 Langford Highway, Cape Charles. Award-winning chili, fresh local seafood, charbroiled steaks. Located on US 13 about 6 miles north of the southern tip of Northampton County. *Inexpensive to moderate. Phone (757) 331-2505.*

LODGING ON THE EASTERN SHORE OF VIRGINIA

For a home away from home on the Eastern Shore of Virginia, choose anything from an inexpensive motel to a luxurious bed and breakfast inn.

1848 ISLAND MANOR HOUSE. 4160 Main Street, Chincoteague. Federal-style home is a historic island landmark, furnished with antiques. Rose garden, brick courtyard, fountain. *Moderate to expensive. Phone (757) 336-5436 or (800) 852-1505. E-mail imh@shore.intercom.net. Web site www.chincoteague.com/b-b/imh.html.*

REFUGE MOTOR INN. 7058 Maddox Boulevard, Chincoteague. This inn is within walking distance of Chincoteague National Wildlife Refuge and has spacious luxury suites, rental bikes, wooded picnic areas, an indoor/outdoor heated pool, and a playground. *Moderate to expensive. Phone (757) 336-5511 or (800) 544-3469, extension 2.*

SEA SHELL MOTEL. 3720 Willow Street, Chincoteague. Choose from motel rooms, apartments, and completely furnished cottages. Pool, shaded porches, and shaded play area with picnic tables and grills. *Inexpensive to moderate. Phone (757) 336-6589.*

Waterside Motor Inn. 3761 South Main Street, Chincoteague. Luxury accommodations, 220-foot private pier, waterfront pool, spa. *Moderate to expensive. Phone (757) 336-3434.*

Colonial Manor Inn. 84 Market Street, Onancock. Stroll the well-kept grounds or spend an evening in the candle-lit gazebo at this Victorian inn, circa 1882. Shops, restaurants, and theaters are within walking distance. Bikes available. *Moderate. Phone (757) 787-3521.*

Wachapreague Motel and Marina. 17 Atlantic Avenue, Wachapreague. New marina with boat slips, bait and tackle shop, charter boats, a boat ramp, and small boat rentals. *Moderate. Phone (757) 787-2105.*

Cape Charles House. 645 Tazewell Avenue, Cape Charles. This bed and breakfast is in a restored Colonial Revival home, furnished with antiques and collections. *Moderate to expensive. Phone (757) 331-4920. E-mail stay@capecharleshouse.com. Web site www.capecharleshouse.com.*

Sunset Beach Inn. US 13, Cape Charles. Located just north of the bay bridge-tunnel, this inn lays out the welcome mat for participants in the Eastern Shore Birding Festival in September and October. It has a bayside beach, pool, restaurant, lounge, boat ramp, and RV campground. *Moderate. Phone (800) 4-SUN or (757) 331-4786.*

Appendices

A. Outfitters, Guides, and Suppliers

▒ CHESAPEAKE BAY, GENERAL

Ken Penrod's Life Outdoors Unlimited Bass Fishing. Beltsville, MD. Bass and striper fishing in the upper Chesapeake Bay, the Potomac River, and other bay tributaries. Phone (301) 937-0010.

Marine Trades Association of Maryland. Annapolis, MD. Maintains list of charter boat and rental boat services, marinas, and boat access points around the Maryland portion of the Chesapeake Bay. Ask for the *Waterfront* Guide. Phone (410) 335-8722. Web site mtam.org.

Upper Bay Charter Captains Association. Annapolis, MD. Ask for a list of charter boat operators around the upper Chesapeake Bay. Phone (410) 974-0605. Web site www.baycaptains.com/index.htm.

Virginia Charter Boat Association. Gloucester, VA. As for a list of charter boat operators around the Virginia portion of the Chesapeake Bay. Phone (757) 229-2878.

▒ MOUTH OF BAY, VIRGINIA

Adventure Parasail. Virginia Beach. Go parasailing off Virginia Beach. Phone (757) 422-UFLY.

Lynnhaven Dive Center. Virginia Beach. Equip yourself or hire a guide to explore dozens of underwater shipwrecks off the Virginia Beach coast. Phone (757) 481-7949.

Mid-Atlantic Dive Center. Virginia Beach. Snorkeling and diving equipment for exploring the underwater world off Virginia Beach. Phone (757) 420-6179.

Ocean View Watersports. Norfolk. Rent surfboards, fishing boats, sailboats, paddle boats, personal watercraft, and other equipment. Phone (757) 583-8888.

Ocean Rentals, Inc. Virginia Beach. Rent kayaks and canoes to tour Back Bay National Wildlife Refuge. Bring fishing or crabbing gear for bass, catfish, bream, perch, and blue crabs. Located next to Sandbridge Realty. Phone (757) 721-6210.

Parasail Express. Virginia Beach. Go parasailing off Virginia Beach. Phone (757) 437-7700.

Rudee Inlet Jet Skis. Virginia Beach. Rent personal watercraft for exploring the Atlantic coast. Phone (757) 714-6634.

Tidewater Adventures. Norfolk. Kayak eco-tours in cities around Hampton Roads to Eastern Shore, Great Dismal Swamp, Back Bay National Wildlife Refuge, First Landing State Park, Plum Tree Island National Wildlife Refuge, and more. Dolphin tours are also available. Phone (757) 480-1999 or (888) 669-8368. Web site www.TidewaterAdventures.com.

▒ WESTERN BAY, VIRGINIA

Bay Trail Outfitters. Mathews. Rentals, sales, guided tours for kayak and canoe. Phone (804) 725-0626.

Captain's Billy's Charters. Wicomico Church. Daily fishing charters, sunset cruises to waterfront restaurant. Phone (804) 580-7292.

Capt. Rick DeVivi. Reedville. Fishing charter boat. Phone (804) 453-7644.

Capt. Steve Bernardo Fishing Charter. Deltaville. Fish the Rappahannock River and Chesapeake Bay aboard the *Lady Catherine II*. Phone (804) 730-1595.

Chesapeake Bay Sportfishing Adventures. Reedville. Charter a fishing trip aboard the *Red Osprey* with Capt. Ferrell McLain. Phone (703) 691-1758.

Capt. Chuck O'Bier. Lottsburg. Fishing charters. Phone (804) 529-6450.

Mattaponi Canoe and Kayak. Aylett. Rental canoes and kayaks and guided environmental excursions on the Pamunkey and Mattaponi rivers. Phone (800) 769-3545.

Pamunkey and Mattaponi River Excursions. King William. Narrated river cruises from the Pamunkey Indian Reservation. Phone (804) 769-0841.

The Red Osprey. Reedville/Smith Point. Charter a fishing trip with Capt. Ferrell McLain. Phone (703) 691-1758.

Roy Amburn Fishing Charter. Reedville. Fishing trips aboard the charter *Robin Sue*. Phone (804) 798-5183.

WESTERN BAY, MARYLAND

Fun Cruise Inc. Solomons Island. Special event parties, group rental. Phone (410) 326-3303.

Rod-N-Reel Charter Captains. Chesapeake Beach. Offering over 25 charter boats and the headboat, *Tom Hooker*. Phone (301) 855-8450.

Solomons Boat Rental. Solomons Island. Ski boats, power skiffs, motorboats. Phone (410) 326-4060 or (800) 535-BOAT. Pager (410) 495-0096.

Skipjack Tours, Inc. St. George Island. Group hands-on tours on St. Mary's and Potomac rivers, focusing on natural history. Phone (301) 994-2245.

Solomons Charter Captains Association. Solomons. Fish Apr. through Nov. with licensed charter captains for rockfish, blues, trout, flounder, mackerel, spot, drum, croaker, perch, sea bass. Phone (410) 326-2670.

Terra Mariae Tours. Leonardtown. Professional guides help plan itinerary on Maryland's western shore. Phone (301) 475-5441.

ANNAPOLIS/BALTIMORE AREA

Guided Tours of Annapolis. Whether you want to walk the historic area, take a water taxi, sail on a schooner, or charter a fishing boat, Annapolis has something to fit your needs. Here is a partial list:

Annapolis Walkabout. Phone (410) 263 8253.

Chesapeake Marine Tours & Charters, Inc. Phone (410) 268-7600

Discover Annapolis Tours. Phone (410) 626 6000.

Historic Annapolis Foundation Walking Tours. Phone (410) 268 5576

Maryland State House Tours. Phone (410) 974-3400.

Schooner Woodwind Tours. Phone (410) 263-7837.

Three Centuries Tours of Annapolis. Phone (410) 263 5401 or (410) 263 5357.

Chesapeake Charters. Pasadena. Chesapeake Bay three-sail bateau, the *Cindy Jean*, sails out of Rock Creek in the Patapsco River, just east of Baltimore's Inner Harbor. Overnight charters to the Eastern Shore are also available. Phone (410) 563-7346.

Clipper City Tall Ship Cruises. Baltimore. Cruise Baltimore's Inner Harbor in a legendary clipper ship. Operates from Apr. 1 through Oct. 31. Phone (410) 539-6277.

Harbor Cruises Ltd. Baltimore. Charter the *Bay Lady* or *Lady Baltimore* for a romantic harbor cruise. Food prepared on board. Phone (410) 727-3113 or (800) 695-BOAT.

T&D Bass Guide Service. Baldwin. Hire an experienced guide for bass fishing. Phone (410) 557-9055.

UPPER BAY, MARYLAND

Skipjack Martha Lewis. Havre de Grace. Two-sail bateau can take 32 passengers for cruises, environmental exploration, catered parties. Phone (800) 406-0766 or (302) 777-5488.

Lantern Queen. North East. Sunset and moonlight cruises on Mississippi paddleboat on the Susquehanna River. Phone (888) 937-3740.

Miss Clare Cruises. Chesapeake City. Boat tours of the upper Chesapeake Bay, Turkey Point Lighthouse, fall foliage. Phone (410) 885-5088.

Chesapeake Horse Country Tours. Chesapeake City. Motorcoach tour to historic Chesapeake City, county horse farms, C&D Canal Museum, old churches. No children. Phone (410) 885-1797 or (800) 874-4558.

UPPER EASTERN SHORE, MARYLAND

Chester River Cruises. Chestertown. View the historic waterfront of Chestertown. Phone (410) 778-0088.

Chester River Kayak Adventures. Rock Hall. Environmental tours of the Chesapeake Bay. Phone (410) 639-2001. Web site rockhallmd.com/crkayak.

Great River Yacht Charters. Rock Hall. Sail cruises at sunset, overnight, or by day. Phone (410) 639-2166.

Gratitude Yachting Center. Rock Hall. Sail cruises. Phone (410) 639-7111.

Haven Charters. Rock Hall. Sail cruises. Phone (410) 639-7140.

The Sailing Emporium. Rock Hall. Sail cruises. Phone (410) 778-1342.

Schrader's Hunting. Millington. Hunt or photograph waterfowl, snow geese, upland birds, dove, deer, small game, and released mallards on this shooting preserve. Fishing and archery also available. Phone (410) 778-1895.

Sea Dux Outfitters. Chestertown. Hire a waterfowl guide for sea ducks, oldsquaws, and scoters or charter a fishing boat. Phone (410) 778-4362. Web site www.marylandcharterfishing.com.

Chester River Marine Services, Ltd. Chestertown. Fish, crab, or cruise the Chester River in rental boats. Phone (410) 778-2240.

Capt. E. Meredith Charters. Grasonville. Fishing headboat leaves daily out of Kent Narrows. Phone (410) 827-7737 or (410) 827-8541.

C & C Charters Maryland. Grasonville. Sail and power yachts for bareboat and captained charters, boat rentals. Phone (410) 827-7888 or (800) 733-SAIL.

Island Boat Rentals. Stevensville. Phone (410) 827-4777.

J & P Hunting Lodge. Sudlersville. Guided upland bird and goose hunts, sporting clay range, lodge, pro shop. Phone (410) 438-3832.

Rob's Jet Ski and Outdoor Sports Rentals. Grasonville. Jet skis, bicycles, boats, fishing tackle, crabbing equipment. Open seasonally. Phone (410) 827-4436.

Little Boat Rentals at Easton Point. Easton. Rental crab skiffs, pontoon deck boats, sailboats, or canoes to explore the Tred Avon River and tributaries on the west side of Easton. Phone (410) 819-0881 or (800) 221-1523.

Oxford Sailing Charters. Oxford. Sail during the day, at sunset, or overnight on a Pearson 33-foot sailing sloop. Phone (410) 226-0038.

Rebecca T. Ruark. Tilghman. Sail the Choptank River near Tilghman Island aboard one of the oldest and fastest skipjacks. Oyster dredging included. Phone (410) 886-2176.

Patriot Cruises. St. Michael's. Cruise aboard the climate-controlled *Patriot* on the Miles River, while learning about the history of Talbot County. See historic homes, waterfowl, and the watermen. Phone (410) 745-3100.

Skylark Sailing Yachts. Oxford. Explore the Tred Avon River aboard a rental 16-foot sailboat. Phone (410) 822-4581.

LOWER EASTERN SHORE, MARYLAND

Loblolly Landings & Lodge, Inc. Church Creek. Hunting for sika and white-tailed deer. Accommodations available. Located a short distance from the Blackwater National Wildlife Refuge. Phone (800) 862-7452.

Sawyer Fishing Charters. Church Creek. Charter fishing, B&B packages with fishing, bay tours. Phone (410) 397-3743.

Tom Flemmings Sika Camp. Cambridge. Sika deer hunting. Phone (410) 228-7452.

Nature's Best Charters. Salisbury. Fishing parties, wildlife tours, photography, sightseeing. Phone (410) 546-5456.

Barbara Ann II & Barbara Ann III. Crisfield. Charter boat and headboat out of Somers Cover Marina. Phone (410) 957-2562.

Prime Time II Charter Boat Fishing. Crisfield. Enjoy fantastic bottom fishing aboard this 50-foot, fiberglass, custom-built charter boat. Phone (800) 791-1470. Web site <u>www.crisfield.com/prim.</u>

▒ LOWER EASTERN SHORE, VIRGINIA

Assateague Adventures. Chincoteague. Group lectures and tours on the ecology and traditions of the islands. Phone (800) 221-7490.

Assateague Island Tours. Chincoteague. Tour Chincoteague National Wildlife Refuge by boat or bus, Apr. through Sept. Phone (757) 336-6155, (757) 336-6698, or (757) 336-6122.

Barnacle Bill's. Chincoteague. Charter fishing inshore for croaker and flounder or offshore for bluefin and yellowfin tuna, dolphin, and wahoo. Phone (757) 336-5188.

Captain Barry's Back Bay Cruises. Chincoteague. Bird-watching, crabbing, clamming, romantic evening cruises. Phone (757) 336-6508.

Island Cruises Inc. of Chincoteague. Chincoteague. Guided boat tours, spring through fall. Phone (757) 336-5593 or (757) 336-5511.

Capt. Bob's Marina. Chincoteague. Fish the channels, inlets, and offshore waters for flounder, trout, croaker, tuna, and shark. Phone (757) 336-6654.

Kings Creek Marina. Cape Charles. Charter boats, headboat, tackle shop, boat ramp. Phone (757) 331-2058.

Wachapreague Seaside Marina. Wachapreague. Charter all-day and half-day boats for deep-sea fishing offshore. Phone (757) 787-4110.

End of Outfitters, Guides, and Suppliers.

B. Books And References

The Barrier Islands : A Photographic History of Life on Hog, Cobb, Smith, Cedar, Parramore, Metompkin and Assateague, by Curtis J. Badger and Rick Kellam, Stackpole Books, Harrisburg, PA 1989.

Bay Beacons: Lighthouses of the Chesapeake Bay, by Linda Turbyville, Eastwind Publisher, Trappe, MD 1996.

Bay Country, by Tom Horton, Johns Hopkins University Press, Baltimore, MD 1994.

Beautiful Swimmers: Watermen, Crabs and the Chesapeake Bay, by William W. Warner, Little Brown & Company, New York, NY 1994.

Birds and Marshes of Chesapeake Bay Country, by Brooke Meanley, Tidewater Publishers, Centreville, MD 1975.

Butterflies of Delmarva, by Elton N. Woodbury, Tidewater Publishers, Centreville, MD 1994.

Chesapeake, by James A. Michener, Fawcett Books, New York, NY 1990.

Chesapeake Almanac, by John Page Williams Jr., Tidewater Publishers, Centreville, MD 1993.

Chesapeake Bay Cruising Guide: Upper Bay: Susquehanna River to Patuxent River and Little Choptank River, by Tom Neale, Wescott Cove Publishing Company, Stamford, CN 1996.

Chesapeake Bay: Nature of the Estuary, A Field Guide, by Christopher P. White, Tidewater Publishers, Centreville, MD 1989.

A Cruising Guide to the Chesapeake, by William T. Stone, Fessenden S. Blanchard and Anne M. Hays, G. P. Putnam's Sons, New York, NY 1989. (Out of print.)

Cruising the Chesapeake, by William H. Shellenberger, International Marine Publishing Company, Camden, ME 1994.

Exploring Flatwater: Northeastern North Carolina, the Outer Banks, and Eastern Virginia, by Ed White (self-published, phone 757-631-8478 to order a copy), Flatwater, Inc., Virginia Beach, VA 1997.

Exploring the Chesapeake in Small Boats, by John Page Williams, Tidewater Publishers, Centreville, MD 1992.

A Field Guide to Coastal Wetland Plants of the Northeastern United States, by Ralph W. Tiner Jr., University of Massachusetts Press, Amherst, MA 1987.

An Island Out of Time: A Memoir of Smith Island in the Chesapeake, by Tom Horton, Vintage Books, Vancouver, WA 1997.

Life and Death of the Salt Marsh, by John and Mildred Teal, Ballantine Books, New York, NY 1991.

Life in the Chesapeake Bay, by Alice Jane Lippson and Robert L. Lippson, Johns Hopkins University Press, Baltimore, MD 1997.

The Lighthouses of the Chesapeake, by Robert D. Garst, Johns Hopkins University Press, Baltimore, MD 1973.

Lighting the Bay: Tales of Chesapeake Lighthouses, by Pat Vojtech, Tidewater Publishers, Centreville, MD 1997.

Maryland Department of Natural Resources Publications:

Wildlife Abounds: A Guide to Maryland's Wildlife Management Areas

Hunting and Trapping in Maryland (annual)

Maryland's Eastern Shore: A Journey in Time and Place, by John R. Wennersten, Tidewater Publishers, Centreville, MD 1992.

Naturalist on the Nanticoke, by Robert A. Hedeen, Tidewater Publishers, Centreville, MD1982.

Natural Wonders of Virginia: Parks, Preserves and Wild Places, by Garvey and Deane Winegar, NTC Publishing Group, Lincolnwood, IL 2000.

Preserving the Chesapeake Bay, by Gerald L. Baliles, EPM Publications, McLean, VA 1996.

Salt Tide: Cycles and Currents of Life Along the Mid-Atlantic Coast, by Curtis J. Badger, Stackpole Books, Harrisburg, PA 1999.

Smithsonian Guide to Seaside Plants of the Gulf and Atlantic Coasts, by Wilbur H. Duncan and Marion B. Duncan, Smithsonian Institution Press, Washington, DC 1988.

Virginia Department of Game and Inland Fisheries (phone 804-367-1000) selected publications:

Public Fishing Lakes

Virginia Freshwater Fishing Guide (annual)

Virginia Marine Angler's Guide, annual publication of the Virginia Marine Resources Commission (phone 757-247-2200).

Virginia Outdoors, annual publication of the Virginia Tourism Corporation, available at Virginia Welcome Centers or by calling (phone 804-371-8163).

Wanderer on My Native Shore, by George Reiger, The Lyons Press, New York, NY 1991.

Water's Way: Life Along the Chesapeake, by David W. Harp (photography), Tom Horton (essays), in association with the Chesapeake Bay Foundation, Elliott & Clark Publishing, Washington, DC 1992.

Wild Side of Maryland, An Outdoor Guide, by the *Baltimore Sun*, Baltimore, MA 1998.

C. Annual Events

GENERAL

Maryland Renaissance Festival, Crownsville, MD. Re-creation of a sixteenth century village draws thousands. Performers, combat jousting, craft shops, food. Weekends, Labor Day weekend through the end of Oct. Phone (800) 296-7304.

JANUARY

Heritage of the Bay Festival, St. Mary's County Fairgrounds, Leonardtown, MD. All you can eat oysters and clams. Phone (301) 769-4951.

▓▓ FEBRUARY

February Freeze, Cape Charles, VA. A plunge into the frigid winter waters of the Chesapeake Bay benefits the Shore Habitat for Humanity. Bonfire, pig roast, chili. Phone (757) 331-2304.

National Outdoor Show, Golden Hill, MD. A tribute to watermen, hunters, and trappers. Contests for muskrat skinning, trap setting, log sawing, duck and goose calling, crab picking, and oyster shucking. Food and exhibits. Phone (800) 522-TOUR.

▓▓ MARCH

Artists of the Chesapeake Annual Art Auction, Centreville, MD. Auction to benefit Queen Anne's County art organizations. Phone (410) 758-2520.

Decoy Waterfowl Show and Auction, Bel Air, MD. Decoy and waterfowl artists, benefits American Red Cross. Late Mar. Phone (410) 838-4568.

▓▓ APRIL

Chincoteague Island Easter Decoy and Art Festival, Chincoteague, VA. Carvers and artists compete for awards and sell their work. Easter weekend. Phone (757) 336-6161.

Easter Sunrise Service, Hampton, VA. Watch the day dawn on the Chesapeake Bay at Fort Monroe's Continental Park. Phone (747) 727-2611.

Easter Sunrise Service, Norfolk, VA. Ocean View Beach Park. Phone (757) 441-2345.

Maryland Hunt Cup Race, Tufton Avenue, Glyndon, MD (Baltimore County). Oldest and most difficult steeplechase race in the country. Phone (410) 833-4188.

Virginia Waterfront International Arts Festival, Newport News, VA. Held at various locations. Phone (757) 664-6492.

Oyster and Bull Roast, Upper Chesapeake Bay Skipjack Invitational Races, Earth Day Celebration, Havre de Grace, MD. Roast to welcome skipjack crews on eve of races. Benefits the skipjack ***Martha Lewis***. Free boat rides. Mid Apr. Phone (800) 406-0766.

My Lady's Manor Steeplechase Races & Champagne Reception, Monkton, MD. One of Maryland's best timber races. Fund raiser for Ladew Topiary Gardens. Phone (410) 557-9466.

Waterfront Festival, Inner Harbor, Baltimore, MD. Food, music, family entertainment. Late Apr. Phone (410) 837-4636.

Nanticoke River Shad Festival, Vienna, Dorchester County, MD. Traditional shad planking, music, food, canoe and kayak races, and activities for children to celebrate the restoration of the spring run of shad. Sponsored by the Chesapeake Bay Foundation. Phone (800) 522-TOUR.

Nanticoke River Canoe/Kayak Classic, Vienna, Dorchester County, MD. An 8-mile canoe and kayak race down Barren Creek. Phone (800) 522-TOUR.

Historic Garden Week on the Eastern Shore, Cape Charles, VA. Visit historic homes and landmarks on the Eastern Shore of Virginia on the garden tour. Phone (757) 331-2304.

Downtown Hampton Boat Expo, Hampton, VA. Watercraft displays, seminars, demonstrations, seafood. Phone (757) 727-6429.

Delmarva Birding Weekend, Snow Hill, MD. Worcester and Somerset counties celebrate the arrival of migrating shorebirds, waterfowl, and many nesting birds. Boat and canoe trips, guided tours. Last weekend in Apr. Phone (800) 852-0335 for Worcester County or (800) 521-9189 for Somerset County.

▓▓ MAY

Seafood Festival, Chincoteague, VA. Seafood-lovers' event on Assateague Island National Seashore. First Wednesday in May. Phone (757) 787-2460.

International Migratory Bird Celebration, Chincoteague, VA. Workshops, nature walks, birdwatching, drawing thousands to the wildlife refuge. Phone (757) 336-6122.

Decoy, Wildlife Art and Sportsman Festival, Havre de Grace, MD. Wildfowl carvers and artists, decoy carving competitions, live decoy auction. Sponsored by the Havre de Grace Decoy Museum. Phone (410) 939-3739.

Lock House Days, Havre de Grace, MD. Festival, entertainment, historical presentations, health screening, sponsored by the Susquehanna Museum. Late May. Phone (410) 939-5780.

Preakness Celebration, Baltimore, MD. Week of events leads up to the Preakness, one of Triple Crown's thoroughbred races, on the third Saturday of May. Phone (410) 837-3030 or (410) 542-9400.

Blackwater National Wildlife Refuge Spring Fling, Cambridge, MD. Nature walks and bird walks, turtle races, storytelling, carriage rides, children's activities, book signings. Refuge tours by bus, bike, or canoe. Phone (410) 228-2677.

Hampton Roads Regional Chili Cook-Off, Hampton, VA. Cooks from all over the country vie for the right to represent Hampton Roads on the national level. Live music. Phone (757) 72706429.

Chestertown Tea Party Festival, Chestertown, MD. Reenactment of the merchants' revolt against the British Tea Act, parade, arts and crafts, food booths, Chestertown Classic Long Distance Run. Saturday of Memorial Day weekend. Phone (410) 778-0416.

Bay Bridge Walk, Stevensville, MD. Sunday-morning walk in early May across the 4.3-mile Bay Bridge. Craft exhibits, food, music. Phone (410) 228-8405 or (410) 643-8530.

The Kent Island Day, Kent Island, MD. Costumed craftspeople commemorate the culture and heritage of Queen Anne's County. Historic buildings and homes tours. Coincides with the Spring Art Fair. Mid-May. Phone (410) 643-1690 or (410) 604-2100.

JUNE

National Trails Day, Susquehanna State Park, Jarrettsville, MD. Early June. Phone (410) 557-7994.

Scottish Festival, Steppingstone Museum, Havre de Grace, MD. Scottish clans, vendors, pipe band music, dancers, sheep herding, storytelling. Mid-June. Phone (410) 939-2299.

Rockfish Tournament, Rock Hall, MD. Rockfish anglers vie for large prizes. Phone (410) 778-0416.

Blackwater Eagleman Triathlon, Cambridge, MD. One of 14 qualifiers for the Iron Man Triathlon. Includes a 1.2-mile swim, a 13.1-mile run and a 56-mile bike ride. Phone (410) 964-1246 or (800) 522-TOUR.

Eastern Shore Chamber Music Festival, Easton, MD. Two-week event at Easton's Avalon Theatre. Phone (410) 819-0380.

Hampton Jazz Festival, Hampton, VA. Top blues, soul, pop, and jazz musicians perform at the Hampton Coliseum. Phone (757) 838-4203.

Waterman's Festival, Kent Narrows, MD. Celebrates the waterman and the Chesapeake Bay seafood industry. Competitions include docking, anchor throwing, preparing crab soup. Phone (410) 604-2100.

Tilghman Island Seafood Festival, Tilghman, MD. Seafood, live music, arts and crafts, crab race, crab-picking contest, firefighters' parade. Phone (410) 822-4653.

JULY

Heritage Fair, Dundalk, MD. Three-day fair, parade, and fireworks. Phone (410) 284-4022.

Fourth at the Fort, Hampton, VA. Celebrate Independence Day with food, music, and fireworks at Fort Monroe on the Chesapeake Bay. Live music includes the Continental Army Band. Phone (757) 727-2312.

Screwpile Lighthouse Challenge, Solomons, MD. One of many racing events sponsored by the Southern Maryland Sailing Association. Mid-July. Phone (410) 326-4364 or (301) 862-3100.

Unlimited Hydroplane Races, Norfolk, VA. Virginia Is For Lovers Cup held at Willoughby Bay at Norfolk Naval Air Station. Phone (800) 368-3097.

Yacht Club Sailing Regatta, Rock Hall, MD. Phone (410) 778-0416.

Bay Country July 4th Festival, Cambridge, MD. Four-day festival at Sailwinds Park on the Choptank River. Carnival, food, games, live outdoor entertainment, fireworks. Phone (800) 522-TOUR.

Down River Race, Chestertown, MD. This Chester River race begins at the Chester River Yacht and County Club. Phone (410) 810-0707 or (800) 380-8614.

AUGUST

Drums Along the Bay, Hampton, VA. Competition among internationally ranked drum and bugle corps. Phone (757) 728-3200.

Eastern Shore Music Festival and Chili Cook-off, Cape Charles, VA. Blues, rhythm and blues, country, and rock music with legendary performers. Phone (757) 442-5175.

Havre de Grace Seafood Festival, Havre de Grace, MD. Crabcake challenge, crab calling contest. Mid-Aug. Phone (410) 939-1525.

Hampton Cup Regatta Power Boat Race, Hampton, VA. The oldest continuously run powerboat race and the largest inboard hydroplane race in the country, between Mercury Boulevard Bridge and Fort Monroe. Free. Phone (800) 800-2202.

Governor's Cup Yacht Race, St. Mary's City, MD. Overnight sailboat race from Annapolis to St. Mary's College. Phone (301) 862-0380.

Calvert County Jousting Tournament, Port Republic, MD. Oldest tournament of Maryland's official state sport. Last Saturday in Aug. Phone (410) 586-0565.

Seafood Feast-I-Val, Cambridge, MD. All-you-can-eat seafood feast at Sailwinds Park. Boat tours, live entertainment. Phone (800) 522-TOUR.

Cambridge Classic Power Boat Regatta, Cambridge, MD. Races between power boats include classes of hydroplanes, jersey skiffs, and flatbottoms. Phone (800) 522-TOUR.

Party on the Bay, Rock Hall, MD. Visitors arrive by land and sea on the third Saturday of Aug. to celebrate the Eastern Shore's Chesapeake Bay heritage. Phone (410) 778-0416 or (410) 639-7611.

SEPTEMBER

Artsfest, Solomons, MD. Fine arts at Annmarie Garden. Mid-Sept. Phone (410) 326-4640.

IRHA President's Cup Nationals, Maryland International Raceway, Budds Creek, MD. Largest motorsports event in Maryland. Phone (703) 791-8445 or (301) 449-RACE.

Hampton Bay Days, Hampton, VA. Headline musical entertainment, seafood, exhibits, fireworks, juried art show, sporting and water events, carnival. Phone (757) 727-6122.

Duck Fair, Havre de Grace, MD. Exhibits by wildfowl carvers and artists, regional duck and goose calling championship, retriever demonstrations, children's decoy painting, live and silent auctions, whittling contests. Mid-Sept. Phone (410) 939-3739.

Mid-Atlantic Surf Fishing Tournament, Ocean City, MD. Teams fish the surf for prizes. Phone (410) 213-2042.

Neptune Festival, Virginia Beach, VA. Air shows, live entertainment, arts and crafts, sand sculpting competition. Phone (757) 498-0215.

Poquoson Seafood Festival, Poquoson, VA. Fresh seafood, arts and crafts, music, fireworks. Phone (75) 868-3580.

OCTOBER

Blessing of the Fleet, St. Clement's Island, MD. Boat tours provided by St. Clement's Island Potomac River Museum to the island. Family entertainment, food, exhibits, arts and crafts, fireworks. First full weekend of Oct. Phone (301) 769-2222.

Fall Festival, Newport News, VA. Long-running festival at Newport News Park. Phone (757) 926-8451.

Harvest Festival at Sunset Beach Inn, Kiptopeke, VA. Eastern Shore feast, arts and crafts, live music. Phone (757) 787-2460.

Willis Wharf Homecoming and Waterman's Festival, Willis Wharf, VA. Aquaculture exhibits, demonstrations of waterman skills, boat rides, hay ride tour of Hog Island homes, seafood. Phone (757) 442-9472.

Phoebus Days, Hampton, VA. A three-day block party includes music, a fish fry, a parade, sporting events, and more. Phone (757) 722-0625.

Chestertown Wildlife Exhibition and Sale, Chestertown, MD. Wildlife art, carvings, music, food, entertainment, carving demonstrations, retriever demonstrations, state and regional duck and goose-calling championship. Phone (410) 778-0416.

St. Mary's County Oyster Festival, Leonardtown, MD. Folk festival draws thousands for oysters and other seafood, National Oyster Cook-off, oyster shucking contest, music, pony rides, clowns, arts and crafts. Third weekend in Oct. Phone (301) 863-5015.

Annual Sailboat Show and Annual Powerboat Show, Annapolis, MD. Nation's oldest and largest sailboat show, followed by oldest and largest in-water powerboat show. Mid to late Oct. For more information, call (410) 268-8828.

Upper Shore Decoy Show, North East, MD. Expert carvers compete for best decoys. Educational exhibits. Phone (410) 287-2675.

Tilghman Island Day, Tilghman Island, MD. The entire island turns festive. Watermen exhibits, fresh seafood, auction, live music, boat-docking contests, and skipjack and workboat races. Phone (888) BAYSTAY.

Wetlands Fest, Horsehead Wetlands Center, Grasonville, MD. Guided bird walks, wildflower identification, children's activities, face paintings, environmental craft exhibits, food, music. Phone (410) 827-6694.

Woodland Indian Culture Days, St. Mary's City, MD. Storytelling, flintknapping, archery. Phone (301) 862-0990.

Chincoteague Oyster Festival, Chincoteague, VA. All the oysters you can eat. Phone (757) 336-6161.

The Great Chesapeake Bay Schooner Race, Norfolk, VA. Race of classic vessels ends at Town Point Park during the Virginia Wine Festival. Phone (757) 588-6022.

NOVEMBER

Waterfowl Festival, Easton, MD. Renowned event features some of the world's best decoy carvers and wildfowl artists. Phone (410) 822-4567.

Chili Night in November—A Chili Cook-Off, Hampton, VA. Cast your vote for the best chili. Live music. Phone (757) 727-6429.

Christmas Boat Parade, Kent Narrows, MD. Sailboats, work boats, and motorboats decked out for the season are judged as they parade through Kent Narrows. Phone (410) 827-8200 or (410) 827-4322.

Grand National Waterfowl Hunt, Cambridge, MD. Celebrity waterfowl hunt held throughout the county. Luncheon at Sailwinds Park in Cambridge. Phone (410) 228-0111.

Chesapeake Wildlife Showcase, Salisbury, MD. Ward Foundation exhibition at the Ward Museum with an auction of antique decoys and a buy-sell trade area. Phone (410) 742-4988.

Assateague Island Waterfowl Week, Chincoteague, VA. Open house at the National Wildlife Refuge. Phone (757) 336-6122.

Fantasy of Lights, Edgemere, MD. See more than 40,000 lights on stunning 1.5-mile drive through historic Fort Howard Park. Three weekends, beginning in late Nov. Phone (410) 887-3873.

DECEMBER

Candlelight Tour of Historic Havre de Grace, MD. Tours of private historic homes, shops, B&Bs. Sponsored by the Susquehanna Museum. Phone (410) 939-3947. Mid Dec.

Solomons Christmas Walk, Solomons, Calvert County, MD. Island-wide tree-lighting ceremony, boat light parade, breakfast with Santa, live nativity scene, island wagon rides, concerts. 2nd weekend in Dec. Phone (800) 953-3300 or (410) 326-3366.

Christmas on Cockrell's Creek, Reedville, VA. Victorian mansions are opened for candlelight tours. Phone (804) 453-6529. Mid Dec.

First Night in Norfolk, Norfolk, VA. Welcome the New Year with classical to avant-garde performances throughout the evening, ending with fireworks over the Elizabeth River. Phone (757) 441-2345.

D. Conservation & Outdoor Organizations

Academy of Natural Sciences' Estuarine Research Center. 10545 Mackall Road, St. Leonard, MD 20685. Phone (410) 586-9700. Web site www.anserc.org.

Alliance for the Chesapeake Bay. 6600 York Road, Suite 100, Baltimore, MD 21212. Phone (410) 377-6270 or (800) 662-CRIS. Web site www.acb-online.org.

Atlantic States Marine Fisheries Commission. 1444 Eye Street, NW 6th Floor Washington, DC 20005. Phone (202) 289-6400. Web site www.asmfc.org.

Chesapeake Bay Foundation. Headquarters, 162 Prince George Street, Annapolis, MD 21401. Phone (888) SAVEBAY or (410) 268-8816. Maryland office, 111 Annapolis Street, Annapolis, MD 21401. Phone (410) 268-8833. Virginia office, 1001 East Main Street, Richmond, VA 23219. Phone (804) 780-1392. Web site www.cbf.org.

Chesapeake Bay Program. 410 Severn Avenue, Suite 109, Annapolis, MD 21403. Phone (800) YOUR-BAY. Web site www.chesapeakebay.net.

The Chesapeake Bay Trust. 60 West Street, Suite 200A, Annapolis, MD. Phone (410) 974-2941. Web site www2.ari.net/home/cbt.

Chesapeake Chapter of the United States Lighthouse Society. PO Box 1270, Annandale, VA 22003-1270. Web site www.cheslights.org.

Coastal Conservation Association. 2100 Marina Shores Drive, Suite 108, Virginia Beach, VA 23451. Phone (757) 481-1226. Web site: www.virginiamag.com/cca.

The Maryland Department of Natural Resources (including Chesapeake Bay NERR). 580 Taylor Avenue, Tawes State Office Building, Annapolis, MD 21401. Phone (410) 260-8000. NERR, phone (410) 974-3382. Web site www.dnr.state.md.us.

The Nature Conservancy, Virginia Chapter. 1233A Cedars Court, Charlottesville, VA 22903-4800. Phone (804) 295-6106. Web site www.tnc.org/infield/State/Virginia.

The Nature Conservancy, Maryland/DC Chapter. 2 Wisconsin Circle, Suite 300, Chevy Chase, MD 20815. Phone (301) 656-8673. Web site www.tnc.org/infield/State/Maryland.

U.S. Fish and Wildlife Service, Northeast Region. (including Maryland and Virginia), 300 Westgate Center Drive, Hadley, MA 01035-9589. Phone (413) 253-8200. Web site www.fws.gov/r5fws.

The Virginia Department of Conservation and Recreation. 203 Governor Street, Suite 302, Richmond, VA 23219. Phone (804) 786-1712. Web site www.state.va.us/~dcr.

Virginia Department of Game and Inland Fisheries. PO Box 11104, Richmond, VA 23230. Phone (804) 367-1000. Web site www.dgif.state.va.us.

Virginia Institute of Marine Sciences. PO Box 1346, Gloucester Point, VA 23062-1346. Phone (804) 684-7000. Web site www.vims.edu.

Virginia Marine Resources Commission. PO Box 756, 2600 Washington Avenue, Newport News, VA 23607-0756. Phone (757) 247-2200. Web site www.state.va.us/mrc/homepage.

Virginia Natural Heritage Program. 217 Governor Street, Richmond, VA 23219. Phone (804) 786-7951. Web site www.state.va.us/~dcr/vaher.

E. Lighthouses of Chesapeake Bay

Who ever heard of Laban Gossigan?

The name would probably stump *Jeopardy*'s finest. But when Laban Gossigan climbed the spiral, stone staircase and lighted the lantern of the Cape Henry Lighthouse in 1792, he became the first keeper of the first lighthouse on the Chesapeake Bay, beginning a long tradition.

People are fascinated by lighthouses in a way that is hard to explain. These towers and houses of brick, stone, wood, iron, and steel attract people like few other man-made structures.

Many of them—especially those standing in or above the water—are obvious engineering achievements. Pick most any point or shoal on the Chesapeake Bay where the earliest of the 61 lighthouses stood, and you'll see a progression of changes and improvements as flaws were found in the old building systems. Take Smith Point Light off Virginia's Northern Neck, for instance. A tower was built at water's edge in 1802, then moved in 1807 away from the eroding shoreline. The second tower was supplemented by an offshore lightship in 1821. Lightships are simply ships moored into place with lights on top. The lightship was destroyed by Confederate raiders in 1861, and the second tower on land was replaced with a third tower in 1828, again because of erosion. In 1855, a fourth-order Fresnel lens replaced the original 15-lamp reflector system. Fresnel lenses, named for French physicist Augustin Fresnel who designed them in 1822, incorporated an ingenious prism-and-magnifier system that was state of the art for years to come. The seven orders referred to the sizes, the first order being the largest.

The Smith Point light tower was again replaced with a new lightship in 1859, and this lightship was replaced by the new screwpile-style lighthouse in 1868. Screwpile lighthouses are built on pilings literally screwed deep into the bedrock. This structure suffered the fate of many screwpile lighthouses on the bay when it was damaged by ice in 1893, repaired, then knocked completely off its pilings and carried away by ice floes in 1895. An ice-resilient caisson foundation was used in 1897 for the present lighthouse. Caissons are watertight enclosures, usually round, that enable construction to be carried on underground. The Smith Point Light was automated in 1970 and is known today not only by ship captains, who are guided by it, but by anglers, who regard it as one of the best fish attractants on the Chesapeake Bay.

The history of the Smith Point light also illustrates the shuffling acceptance rather than warm embracing of new lighthouse design. It took bureaucrats and politicians years to cough up the cash for the screwpile, then the caisson foundations, and decades to realize the value of the French-made Fresnel lenses.

The historic aspect of lighthouses is another obvious cause for their appeal. In today's cost-conscious market, when a functional light is needed to guide ships, the poles, buoys, and automated lights now installed do the job and are practically indestructible. Charming, however, they are not. So the old octagonal or round towers of faded brick and the attractive cottages with cupolas on top are like the red caboose, the little tugboat, the Model A. They remind us of days gone by, when even the uninitiated could appreciate the engineering that went into design, and it was okay to build something not only functional but pleasing to the eye as well.

The stories attached to the houses and lights have their own allure. The Thimble Shoals Light at Hampton Roads—rebuilt after being destroyed by fire in 1880—was subsequently hit three times by ships. The third hit was by a schooner that rammed the lighthouse with such force the keeper's stove turned over, causing a fire that again burned the lighthouse to the ground. The Sharps Island Lighthouse off Tilghman Island, Maryland, was carried off on its side by heavy ice floes, its keepers clinging to life for what must have seemed an interminable 16 hours before they were rescued. Many if not most lighthouses even have ghost tales associated with their sad and violent histories.

But there's something else—something intangible—which causes our hearts to skip a beat when we spy lighthouses. Perhaps it's what they represent. For those who hug their sailors goodbye and watch the ship grow smaller until it disappears at the curvature of the earth, the lighthouse stands for the hope that the ship will return, and loved ones will come home.

The attempt to build something bold enough to overcome the elements has universal understanding. The engineering is a tribute to the capacity of the mind. But the purpose comes from the heart. And the optimism, the fist raised to the angry storm, resides in the human spirit. The beacon sent out into the fog is everyone's candle in the window, the light on the front porch.

Lighthouses, simply put, are the yellow ribbons of the soul.

Here is a list of most of the lighthouses still standing on the Chesapeake Bay. Refer to the book chapters for more detail.

MOUTH OF THE CHESAPEAKE BAY

Cape Henry Lighthouses. The old and the new Cape Henry lighthouses stand near one another at Fort Story. (*See* page xx.)

Old Point Comfort Lighthouse. Completed in 1802, this lighthouse at Fort Monroe in Hampton is the second oldest on the Chesapeake Bay. (*See* page xx.)

New Point Comfort Lighthouse. This lighthouse sits on an island at the southern tip of Mathews County, and is visible from the New Point Comfort Preserve. (*See* page xx.)

Wolf Trap Light. The red brick of this 54-foot tower sets it apart from its near-twin, Smith Point Light. In 1894, Wolf Trap Light replaced a hexagonal screwpile structure built in 1870 that was destroyed by ice. This one, on a caisson foundation, can be seen by boat or from the Mathews County shore, northeast of Horn Harbor.

Smith Point Light. This lighthouse at the mouth of the Potomac River is a destination of fishermen heading out from Reedville and Smith Point. Many fish are thigmotropic and like to hang around artificial or natural structures. (See page xx.)

SOUTHERN MARYLAND

Point Lookout Lighthouse. On Point Lookout at the southern tip of St. Mary's County is this 1830 house with a lantern on top. (*See* page xx.)

Piney Point Lighthouse. The Piney Point Lighthouse is one of just four lighthouses still in existence on the Potomac River. (*See* page xx.)

Point No Point. This two-story, octagonal, brick lighthouse is 52 feet high. It was completed in 1905—one of only a handful of lighthouses built in the 1900s. The stocky-looking structure is on a caisson foundation in the Chesapeake Bay 2 miles off the coast of St. Mary's County and 4 miles north of Point Lookout.

Cedar Point Lighthouse. This abandoned house and tower still stand on an eroding spit east of the Patuxent Naval Air Station. Its lantern and cupola can be seen at the Patuxent River Naval Air Museum. (*See* page xx.)

Drum Point Lighthouse. The restored cottage-style Drum Point Lighthouse is part of the Calvert Marine Museum complex on Solomons Island. (*See* page xx.)

Cove Point Lighthouse. The brick tower of the Cove Point Lighthouse near Solomons is visible from a gate, but it is not open to the public. (*See* page xx.)

CENTRAL MARYLAND

Thomas Point Lighthouse. This screwpile lighthouse southeast of Annapolis is still used by the U.S. Coast Guard. (*See* page xx.)

Sandy Point Shoal Lighthouse. The U.S. Coast Guard still makes use of Sandy Point Shoal Lighthouse, which was built on a caisson foundation off Broad Neck in 1858. (*See* page xx.)

Baltimore Light. Located near the mouth of the Magothy River south of Baltimore, this lighthouse is on a caisson foundation and is accessible only by boat. (*See* page xx.)

Bodkin Island Lighthouse. The crumbling remains of the Bodkin Island Lighthouse are barely visible at Downs Park's North Overlook. (*See* page xx.)

LIGHTHOUSES OF BALTIMORE COUNTY

The importance of Baltimore as a major shipping port is obvious by the number of lighthouses built at the entrance to the Patapsco River and Baltimore Harbor. These six remain (*see* page xx). All are built over water except Sevenfoot Knoll, which has been moved to shore and is the only one open to the public.

Fort Carroll Lighthouse: a wooden frame tower on the Patapsco River.

Craighill Channel Upper Range—Rear: an iron pyramidal tower.

Craighill Channel Upper Range—Front: an octagonal brick tower.

Craighill Channel Range—Front: a round lighthouse on a caisson foundation.

Craighill Channel Range—Rear: at 105 feet, one of the highest towers on the Chesapeake Bay.

Sevenfoot Knoll: a round iron structure on screwpile foundation, moved to Pier 5 in Baltimore from its original location at the mouth of the Patapsco River.

HEAD OF THE CHESAPEAKE BAY

Pooles Island Lighthouse. This stone tower is on Pooles Island in the middle of the Chesapeake Bay off the southern tip of Harford County's Gunpowder Neck. (*See* page xx.)

Concord Point Lighthouse. From the 36-foot stone tower of this restored 1827 lighthouse, you can enjoy the view of Havre de Grace at the mouth of the Susquehanna River. (*See* page xx.)

Turkey Point Lighthouse. On a 100-foot bluff in Elk Neck State Park, high above the Chesapeake Bay, stands this 35-foot tower. It has been in operation since its construction in 1833. (*See* page xx.)

Bethel Bridge Lighthouse. A full-size replica of the Bethel Bridge Lighthouse stands near the C&D Canal Museum at Chesapeake City. A series of wooden lighthouses such as this one along the canal warned ships of locks and bridges. (*See* page xx.)

Bloody Point Bar Lighthouse. Visible from the southern tip of Kent Island is this 56-foot tower on a caisson foundation. The lighthouse is still in use, but it is not open to the public. (*See* page xx.)

MARYLAND'S EASTERN SHORE

Hooper Strait Lighthouse. The Chesapeake Bay Maritime Museum at St. Michaels is now the home of this cottage-style, screwpile lighthouse that used to guard Hooper Strait between Tangier Sound and the Chesapeake Bay. (*See* page xx.)

Sharps Island Lighthouse. This round lighthouse is the third to have been built on Sharps Island. The island has been swallowed up by the ever-rising sea, but the lighthouse is still visible standing in the water off the southern tip of Tilghman Island. (*See* page xx.)

Hooper Island Lighthouse. Exactly halfway up the Chesapeake Bay is Hooper Island Lighthouse, a 63-foot round tower on a caisson foundation. (*See* page xx.)

Solomons Lump Lighthouse. This octagonal brick tower was built on a caisson foundation in Kedges Strait to replace a screwpile lighthouse that was destroyed by a heavy icing in 1893. (*See* page xx.)

VIRGINIA'S EASTERN SHORE

Assateague Lighthouse. The red-and-white-ringed tower on Assateague Island has become, along with wild ponies, one of the symbols of Chincoteague National Wildlife Refuge. (*See* page xx.)

Cape Charles Lighthouse. This 191-foot steel tower was erected at the entrance to the Chesapeake Bay on Smith Island to replace the second of two brick towers that preceded it. The 1.2-million-candlepower airport beacon in the Cape Charles Lighthouse is visible for two dozen miles. It is far brighter than any other lighthouses in the Chesapeake Bay region. A replica of the lighthouse is on the mainland at nearby Cape Charles.

F. Glossary

Amphipod—A crustacean of the order Amphipoda, including the sand fleas and beach hoppers. There are 3,000 species of amphipods.

Anadromous—Moving from seawater into fresh water to spawn, as salmon or striped bass.

Arthropod—Invertebrate animals belonging to the phylum Arthropoda, with jointed legs, a segmented body, and an exoskeleton. Arthropods include insects, crustaceans, and arachnids.

Bivalve—Mollusks belonging to the class Bivalvia, with two-part hinged shells, including mussels and clams.

Benthos—Collectively, those plants and animals, usually invertebrates, living on or near the bottom of the bay or ocean (benthic, adj.).

Biomass—The quantity of living organisms in a particular area.

Bog—A wetland characterized by acidic peat soil formed from decaying mosses.

Brackish—Salty, but less so than seawater.

Bryozoan—Any member of the phylum Bryozoa, which consists of tiny moss-like water animals that live in colonies.

Crustaceans—Arthropods that live in the water and breathe by gills, such as lobsters, barnacles, crabs, and shrimps.

Copepod—A small, sometimes parasitic, crustacean belonging to the class Copepoda.

Detritus—Decomposed plant and animal matter that has been worked to sediment size through the action of water and sand.

Diatoms—One-celled algae with cell walls of silica. Diatoms make up the first links in the aquatic food chain.

Ecosystem—A biological community existing in a specific physical environment.

Emergent—A plant that grows directly in the water and stays erect to emerge from the water surface, regardless of the water level.

Estuary—A partially enclosed area where the fresh water of rivers mixes with tidal salt water.

Euryhaline—Able to live in waters with a wide variation in salinity.

Exoskeleton—An external skeleton, such as the shell of a mollusk or arthropod.

Habitat—Where an animal or plant lives; its natural home.

Hummock—A rise of fertile, densely wooded land that is higher than a surrounding marsh.

Inlet—An opening through which ocean waters enter and leave an enclosed body of water, such as a sound, bay, or marsh.

Intertidal zone—The zone along the shore between high and low tide marks.

Littoral—Pertaining to the seashore, especially the intertidal area.

Marsh—Low, wet land that is covered by water at least part of the time and supports grasses rather than trees.

Neap tide—Lowest range of the tide, occurring at the first and last quarter of the moon.

Pelagic—Pertaining to the open waters of the ocean, as distinguished from the benthic regions.

Phytoplankton—Plant plankton.

Plankton—Aquatic plant life that floats at the mercy of the currents or has limited swimming abilities.

SAV—The commonly used acronym for submerged aquatic vegetation.

Sessile—Attached permanently, immobile.

Spring tide—Tide of maximum range, occurring at the new and full moon.

Stenohaline—Able to live only in waters with little variation in salinity.

Substrate—The foundation that lies beneath and supports an organism.

Swamp—Spongy or boggy ground that is covered with water at least part of the time and supports the growth of shrubs and trees.

Thigmotropic—Pertaining to the orientation some living things have toward objects, such as the orientation many fish have toward rocks, reefs, sunken ships, and other structure.

Zooplankton—Animal plankton.

Index

un Follow

140 CHARACTERS

ROB WILLIAMS Writer

MIKE DOWLING
R.M. GUÉRA
Artists

QUINTON WINTER
GIULIA BRUSCO
Colorists

CLEM ROBINS
Letterer

MATT TAYLOR
Cover Art and Original Series Covers

Special thanks to **PAHEK**

UNFOLLOW created by **ROB WILLIAMS** and **MIKE DOWLING**

Ellie Pyle Editor – Original Series
Molly Mahan Assistant Editor – Original Series
Jeb Woodard Group Editor – Collected Editions
Scott Nybakken Editor – Collected Edition
Steve Cook Design Director – Books
Damian Ryland Publication Design

Shelly Bond VP & Executive Editor – Vertigo

Diane Nelson President
Dan DiDio and **Jim Lee** Co-Publishers
Geoff Johns Chief Creative Officer
Amit Desai Senior VP – Marketing & Global Franchise Management
Nairi Gardiner Senior VP – Finance
Sam Ades VP – Digital Marketing
Bobbie Chase VP – Talent Development
Mark Chiarello Senior VP – Art, Design & Collected Editions
John Cunningham VP – Content Strategy
Anne DePies VP – Strategy Planning & Reporting
Don Falletti VP – Manufacturing Operations
Lawrence Ganem VP – Editorial Administration & Talent Relations
Alison Gill Senior VP – Manufacturing & Operations
Hank Kanalz Senior VP – Editorial Strategy & Administration
Jay Kogan VP – Legal Affairs
Derek Maddalena Senior VP – Sales & Business Development
Jack Mahan VP – Business Affairs
Dan Miron VP – Sales Planning & Trade Development
Nick Napolitano VP – Manufacturing Administration
Carol Roeder VP – Marketing
Eddie Scannell VP – Mass Account & Digital Sales
Courtney Simmons Senior VP – Publicity & Communications
Jim (Ski) Sokolowski VP – Comic Book Specialty & Newsstand Sales
Sandy Yi Senior VP – Global Franchise Management

Logo design by **Tom Muller**

140

PART ONE

140

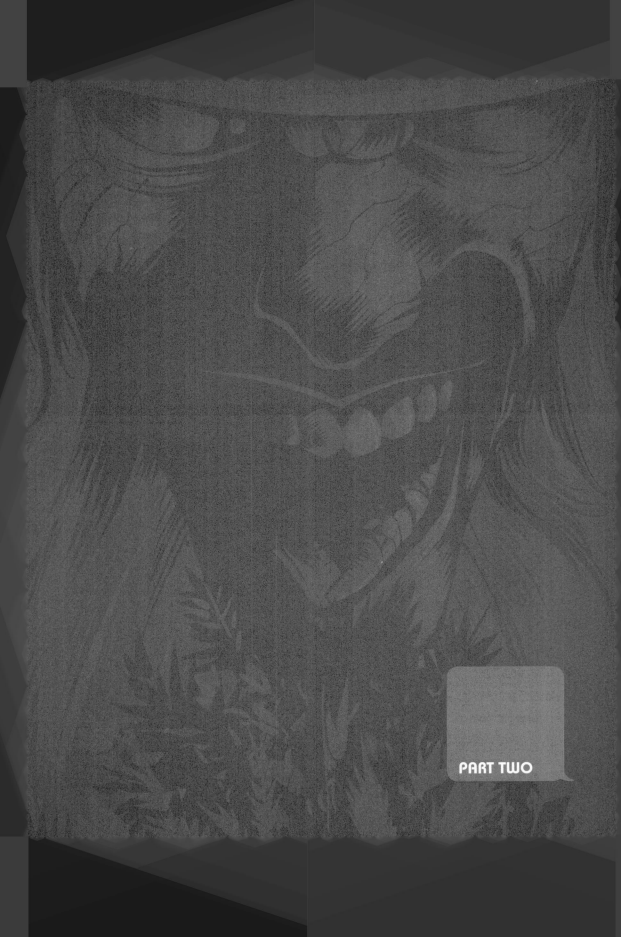

PART TWO

*TRANSLATED FROM JAPANESE.

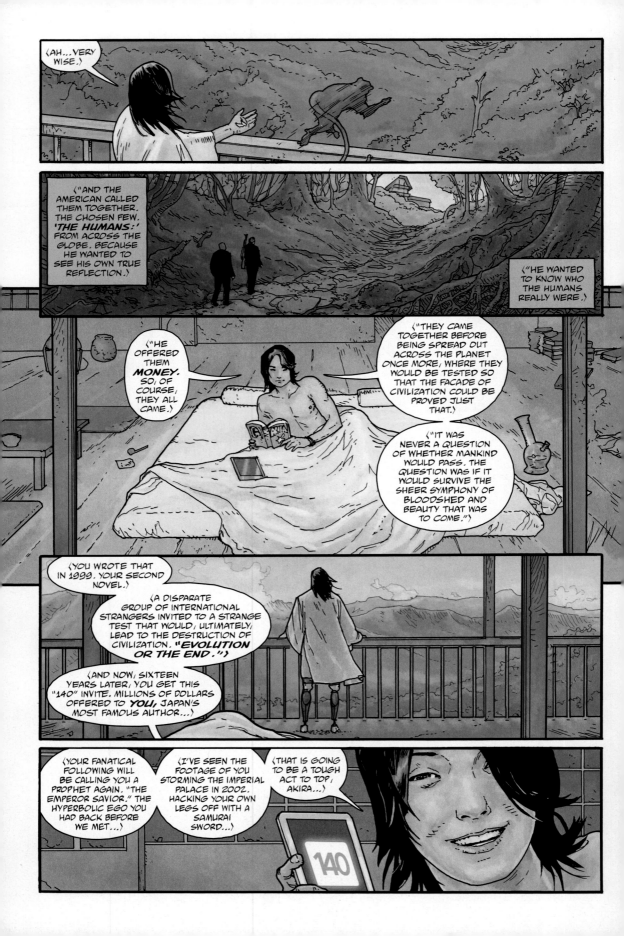

"IN SUCH A CIRCUMSTANCE, FALLING IN LOVE WAS THE MOST OBVIOUS THING IN THE WORLD.

"SO WAS GETTING MY HEART BROKEN BY AN OLDER MAN.

"A MAN WHO STOLE MY WORK, AND TOLD ME IN OUR PARTING ARGUMENT THAT I HAD NOTHING OF WORTH TO SHARE WITH THE WORLD.

"...'A UNIQUE MOMENT OF BEAUTY.'

"WHEN MY NEPHEW WAS BORN, IT WAS A RELIEF TO RETURN HOME TO TEHRAN. FATHER'S DEATH WAS SO RAW. MOTHER AND ADILEH NEEDED ME.

"I LIED TO MYSELF THAT I JUST NEEDED TIME TO HEAL, BUT THEN THE BBC'S TEHRAN CORRESPONDENT POSITION BECAME AVAILABLE.

"IT WAS THE SAFE OPTION TO STAY IN IRAN. THE COWARDLY OPTION.

"ADILEH TALKED ENDLESSLY ABOUT HOW HER BEAUTIFUL BOY HAD GIVEN HER *HOPE*. HOPE FOR MANKIND.

"THE *PURITY* OF THEIR LOVE. THE *INNOCENCE* OF FRESH LIFE."

"AS I WATCHED THE BOY OVER THE COMING WEEKS—PURE, UNFILTERED HUMAN LIFE—I NOTICED ONE THING ONLY.

"ALL HE HAD, *EVERYTHING* HE DID, HIS EVERY INSTINCT AND NEED..."

"IT WAS *ALL* SELFISH.

"WE ARE ANIMALS."

PRIVATE AIRFIELD. TEHRAN, IRAN.

〈SO YOU THINK THAT YOU CAN JUST LEAVE TO JOIN THIS SUPER-RICH "140" LIST? TO BECOME A DECADENT WESTERN MILLIONAIRE WHEN YOU HAVE NOT *EARNED* IT?〉*

〈THAT WE ARE JUST GOING TO LET THIS MR. FERRELL'S MEN TAKE YOU AWAY IN THEIR PRIVATE JET TO HIS ISLAND? NOW? WITHOUT GOING THROUGH THE PROPER CHANNELS?〉

〈NOW, NOW, MISS SALEHI. I HAVE TO ASK YOU...〉

〈WHERE WOULD SOCIETY *BE* WITHOUT THE PROPER CHANNELS?〉

*TRANSLATED FROM PERSIAN.

140

140

PART THREE

YOU KNOW WHAT I'VE BEEN THINKING OF LATELY, GIVEN WHAT'S HAPPENED TO ME WITH THIS WHOLE CRAZY HEADSPACE '140 LIST' THING?

HOW EVERYONE IN THE WORLD WAS *ONLINE* READING WHAT WAS HAPPENING RIGHT THERE IN THE LOU. LIKE THEY WERE *PART* OF IT.

WHEN THEY WEREN'T.

YOU KNOW THAT PEOPLE IN *PALESTINE* WERE USING THE HASHTAG "SOLIDARITYWITHFERGUSON" AND GIVING BROTHERS ADVICE ON HOW TO DEAL WITH *TEAR GAS*?

THEY'RE LIVING IN RUBBLE AND BOMBED-OUT BUILDINGS, MAN, AND THEY'RE TRYING TO HELP *US*?

WHO *ARE* WE ANYMORE?

C'MON, LET'S GO, SIS. THAT'S *TEAR GAS.* AND IT LOOKS PRETTY DAMN *WHITE.* AIN'T THAT STRANGE?

DON'T GET SUCKED INTO THE SURFACE LEVEL, DAVID. JUST ONE PEOPLE OUT HERE TONIGHT, ARGUING AMONG THEMSELVES.

YOU CRAZY.

YEAH? THEN TELL ME...

...HOW MANY *RICH* FOLK DO YOU SEE IN FERGUSON RIGHT NOW?

VISITORS BLISS CAY, THE BAHAMAS.

PRIVATELY OWNED BY LARRY FERRELL, INVENTOR OF HEADSPACE.

"THIS WORLD CONTAINS SO MUCH DISPARATE BEAUTY.

"HUMANS OF LANDS AND LANGUAGES, RELIGIONS AND RACES. THEY ARE APPROACHING. HERE. NOW. LINKED...

...CONNECTED.

@TheLarryFerrell   140 Verified
I have a surprise for you all.
(Followers: 829,596   Following: 156)

"WE SPEAK IN ONE *ELECTRONIC LANGUAGE* NOW. ALL OF US.

"I INVITE THE 140 HERE. A DIGITAL SUMMONS. A BUTTON, INTANGIBLE, MADE OF PIXELS ON A SCREEN IS 'PRESSED.'

SHOW THE WAY AKIRA

"AND THEN SEVERAL HUNDRED HYSTERICAL FANS CROWD BOTH OF TOKYO'S MAIN AIRPORTS IN THE HOPE OF GLIMPSING THEIR 'SAVIOR.'

"TWENTY-THREE HOURS AFTER I REVEALED THE '140' TO THE WORLD, A 54-YEAR-OLD JAPANESE FAN DIES FROM A HEART ATTACK IN THE CRUSH OUTSIDE AN AIRPORT.

"DID *I* KILL HIM?

"NO. I HAD NO INTENT. IT WAS MERELY...SOMETHING THAT HAPPENED.

"MEANWHILE, THE OBJECT OF HIS HYSTERIA, *AKIRA,* BOARDED ONE OF MY JETS ON A PRIVATE AIRFIELD 930 MILES AWAY.

"STRANGE THAT A MAN AS FAMOUS AND AS WEALTHY AS AKIRA SHOULD BE RANDOMLY CHOSEN BY THE COMPUTER TO JOIN THE 140.

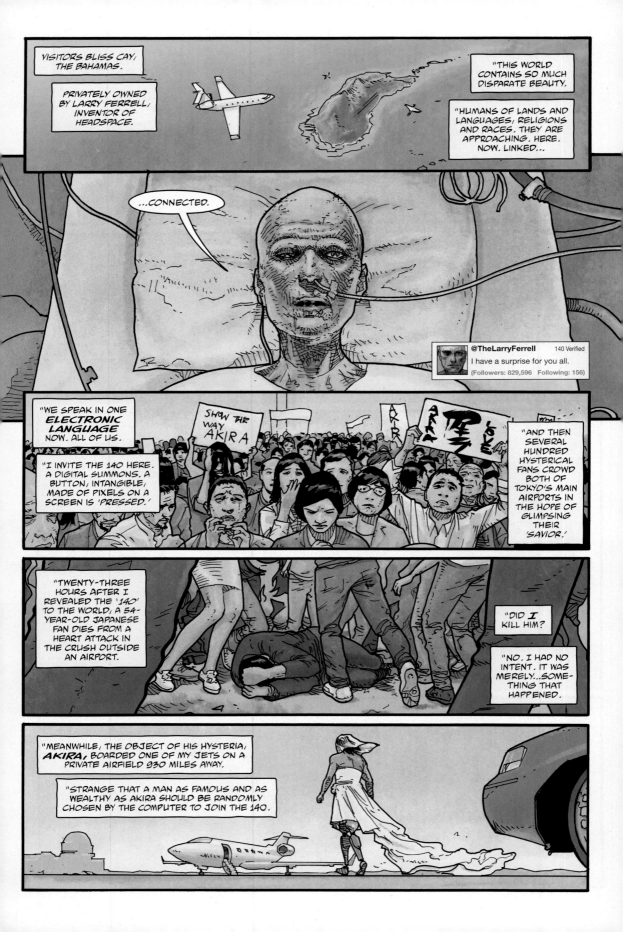

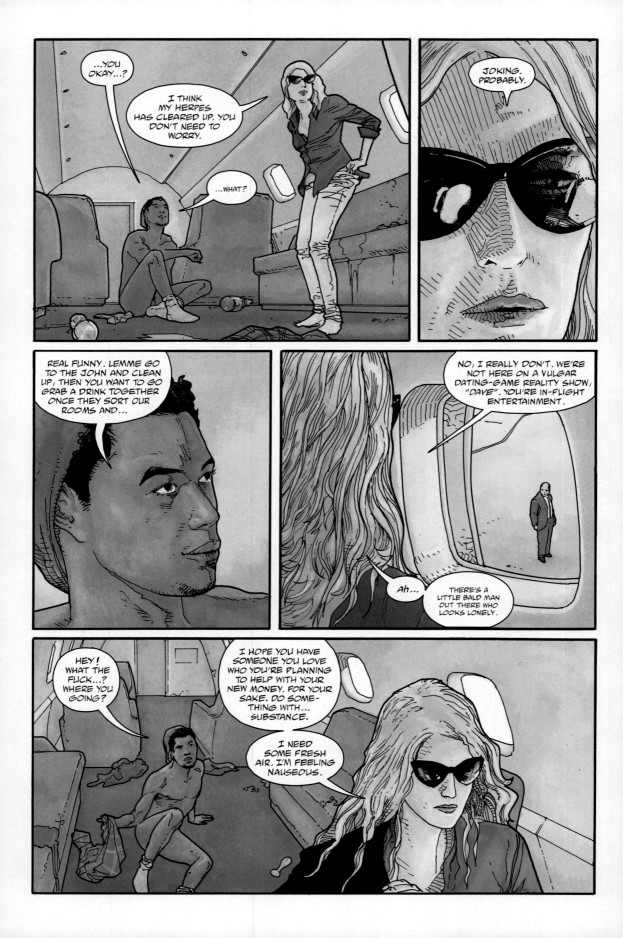

TURBULENCE 139

WRITER **ROB WILLIAMS**   ARTIST **MIKE DOWLING**

COLORIST **QUINTON WINTER**   LETTERS **CLEM ROBINS**   COVER ARTIST **MATT TAYLOR**   ASSISTANT EDITOR **MOLLY MAHAN**   EDITOR **ELLIE PYLE**   EXECUTIVE EDITOR **SHELLY BOND**   UNFOLLOW CREATED BY **WILLIAMS & DOWLING**

139

PART FOUR

WE'RE ALL
GOING TO DIE...

139

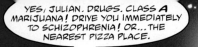

YES, JULIAN. DRUGS. CLASS *A* MARIJUANA! DRIVE YOU IMMEDIATELY TO SCHIZOPHRENIA! OR...THE NEAREST PIZZA PLACE.

DO YOU KNOW THAT I WAS *KIDNAPPED* TWO TIMES BEFORE I WAS FOURTEEN YEARS OLD, JULIAN? BY NASTY MEN WHO WANTED MY FATHER'S MONEY?

HATE TO BREAK IT TO YOU, JULIAN, BUT NONE OF US ARE SAFE.

EVER.

AND THAT INCLUDES YOU.

THE SKY'S VERY PRETTY HERE.

NOW YOU'RE GETTING IT.

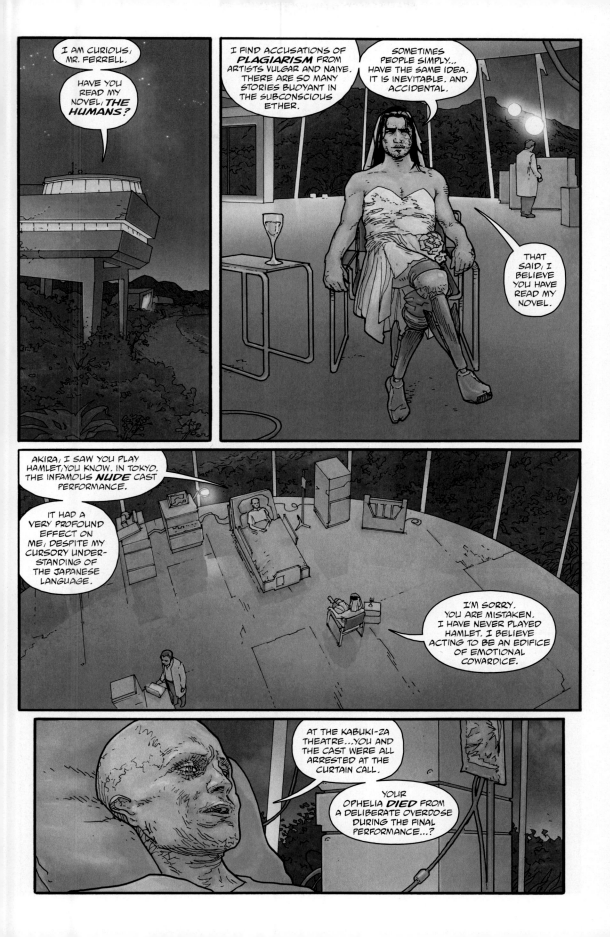

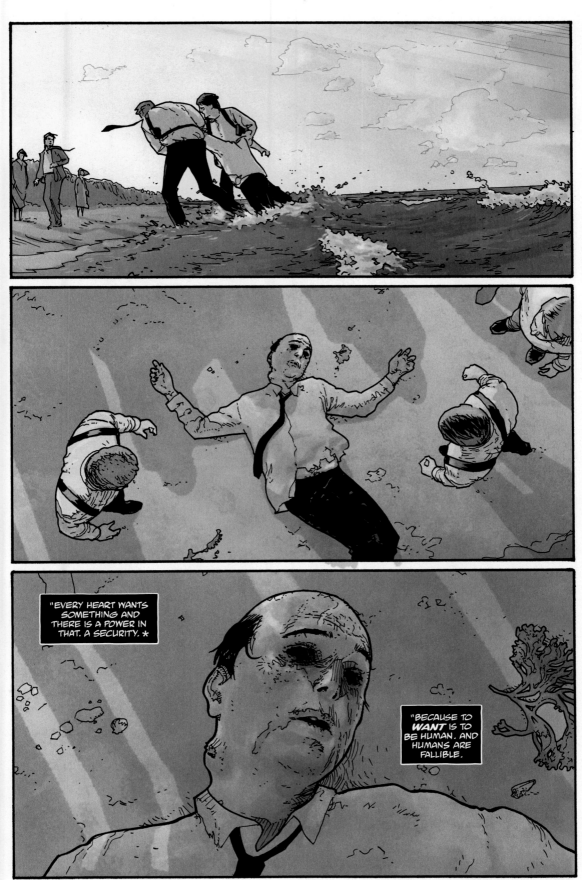

"EVERY HEART WANTS SOMETHING AND THERE IS A POWER IN THAT. A SECURITY. *

"BECAUSE TO *WANT* IS TO BE HUMAN. AND HUMANS ARE FALLIBLE.

* FROM *THE HUMANS* BY AKIRA.

"THE GREAT TERROR COMES FROM THE UNIVERSE'S ACTIONS THAT DO NOT HAVE A COGNIZANT MIND BEHIND THEM.

"WHAT IF ALL WE ARE IS SWEPT AWAY BY SOMETHING THAT WANTS NOTHING? THAT MEANS NOTHING?

"WHAT IF SOMETHING, OR SOMEONE, KILLS FOR *NO REASON?*

"WHAT CHANCE DO WE STAND BEFORE SUCH INDIFFERENCE?"

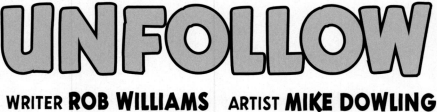

UNFOLLOW 138

WRITER **ROB WILLIAMS**   ARTIST **MIKE DOWLING**

COLORIST
QUINTON WINTER

LETTERS
CLEM ROBINS

COVER ARTIST
MATT TAYLOR

ASSISTANT EDITOR
MOLLY MAHAN

EDITOR
ELLIE PYLE

EXECUTIVE EDITOR
SHELLY BOND

UNFOLLOW CREATED BY
WILLIAMS & DOWLING

138

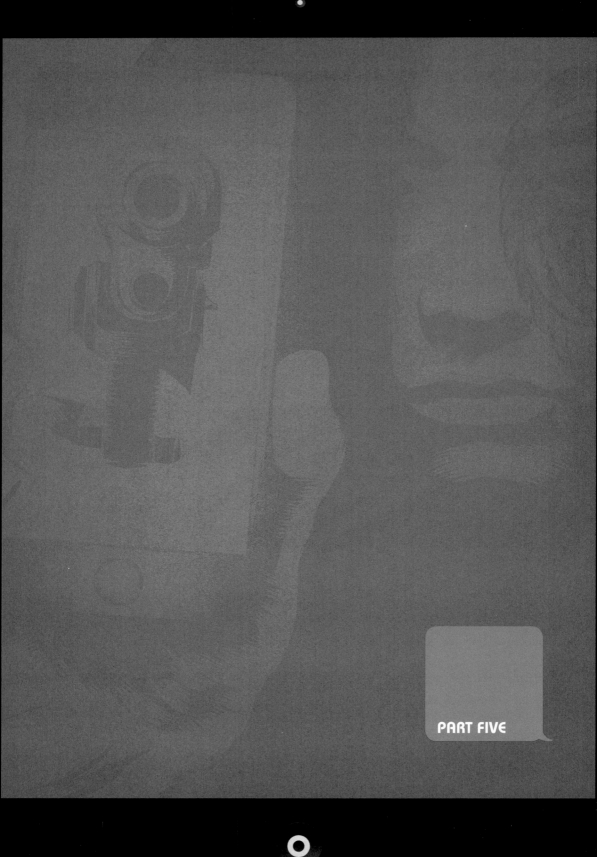

PART FIVE

BLOCKED 138

WRITER **ROB WILLIAMS** ARTIST **MIKE DOWLING**

COLORIST **QUINTON WINTER** · LETTERS **CLEM ROBINS** · COVER ARTIST **MATT TAYLOR** · ASSISTANT EDITOR **MOLLY MAHAN** · EDITOR **ELLIE PYLE** · EXECUTIVE EDITOR **SHELLY BOND** · UNFOLLOW CREATED BY **WILLIAMS & DOWLING**

DO YOU NEED SAVING
Contact @DeaconOfTheLord

NB Please do not contact
if in league with The Dragon

PART SIX

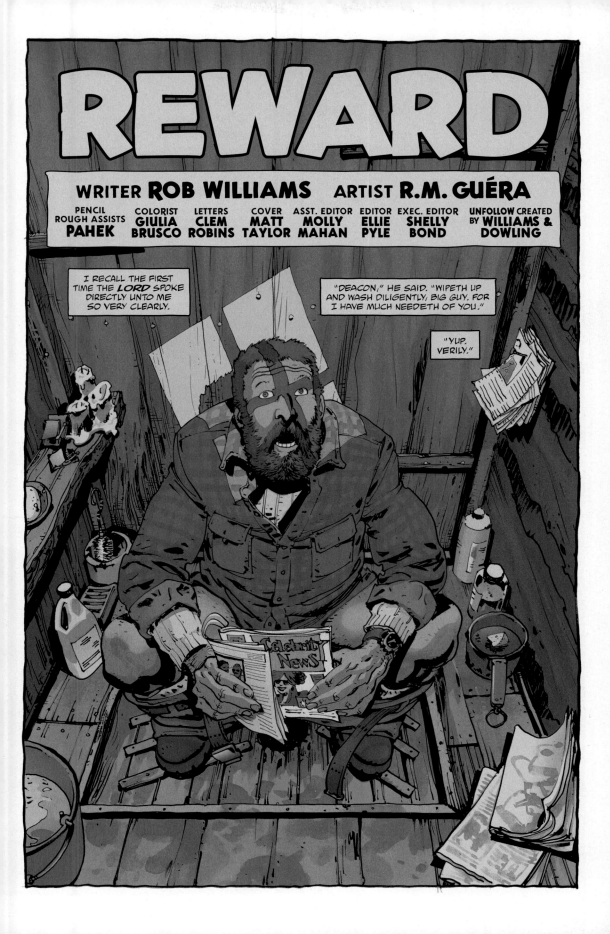

THE DRAGON...

I HAVE TO **SAVE** THEM.

BUT I AM SCARED, LORD.

AND THE LORD ANSWERED IN THIS MOMENT, CLEAR, RESONANT AND TRUE, WITH A DEFINITE AND TANGIBLE **SOLUTION** TO THIS PREDICAMENT.

"TAKE ALL YER CLOTHES OFF, PLEASE."

ALASKA.

THE PAST.

I WOKE. I WAS ALIVE. SOMEONE HAD TREATED MY WOUND WHILE I HAD BEEN UNCONSCIOUS.

SHOWN ME GRACE. BREATHED MERCY UPON ME.

BUT THE CABIN WAS EMPTY.

NO SIGN OF HUMAN HAND ANYWHERE NEAR.

138

I COULD ONLY ASCERTAIN THAT IT WAS A MIRACLE.

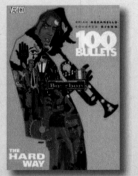